→ 112

→ 128

→ 148

→ 156

→ 182

→ 198

→ 222

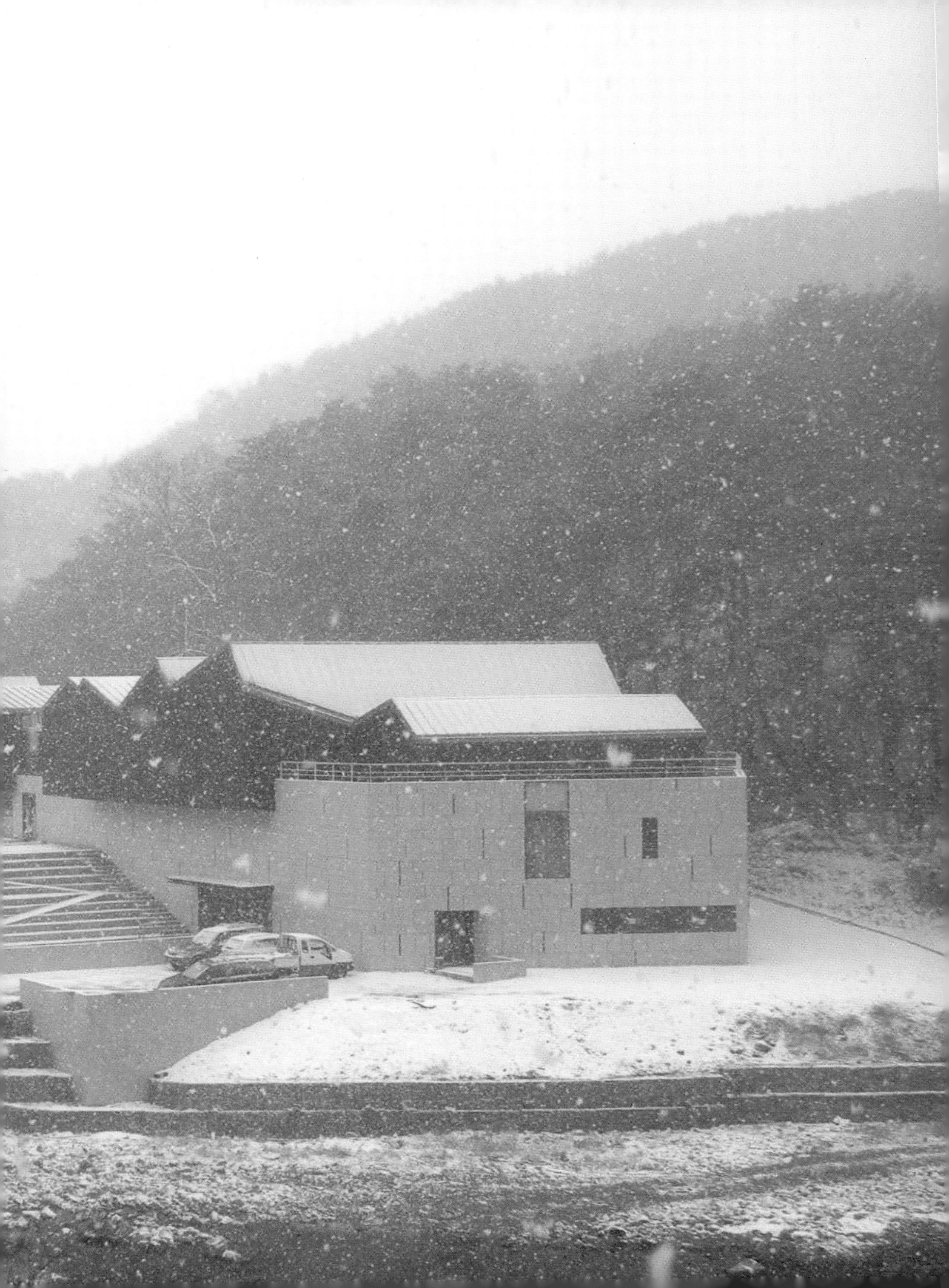

→ 232

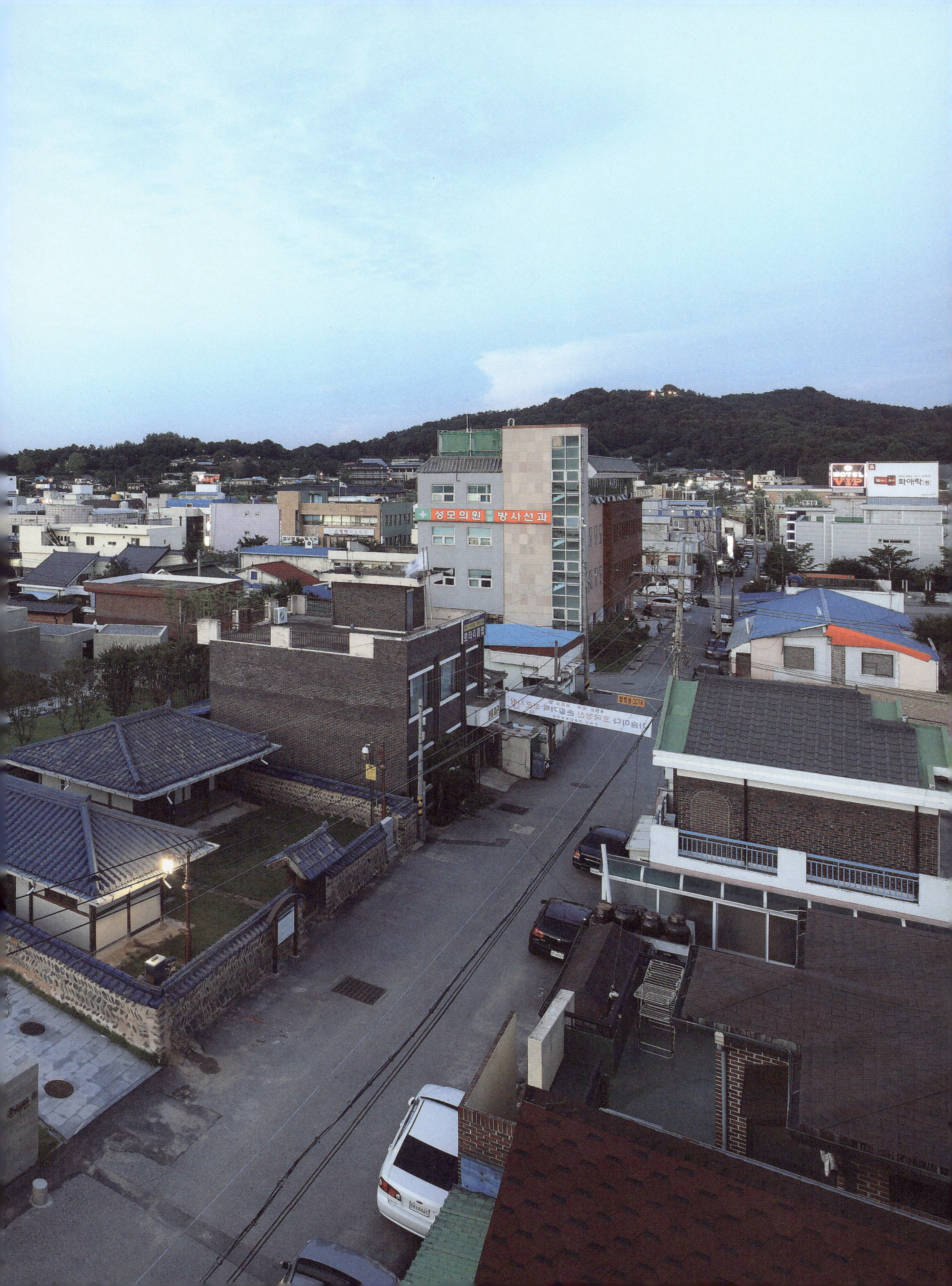

성모의원
방사선과
VIP
화애락

→ 240

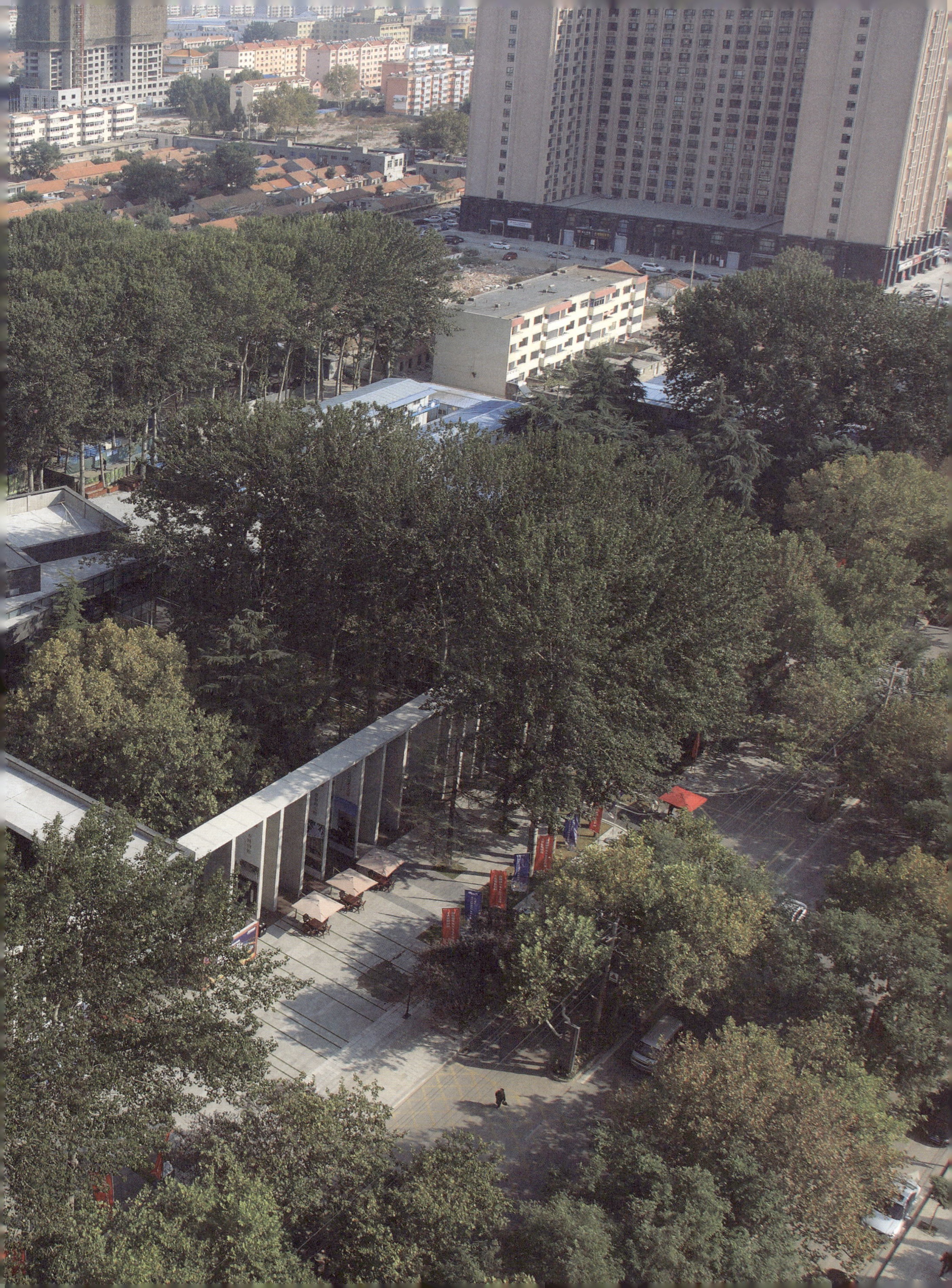

→ 248

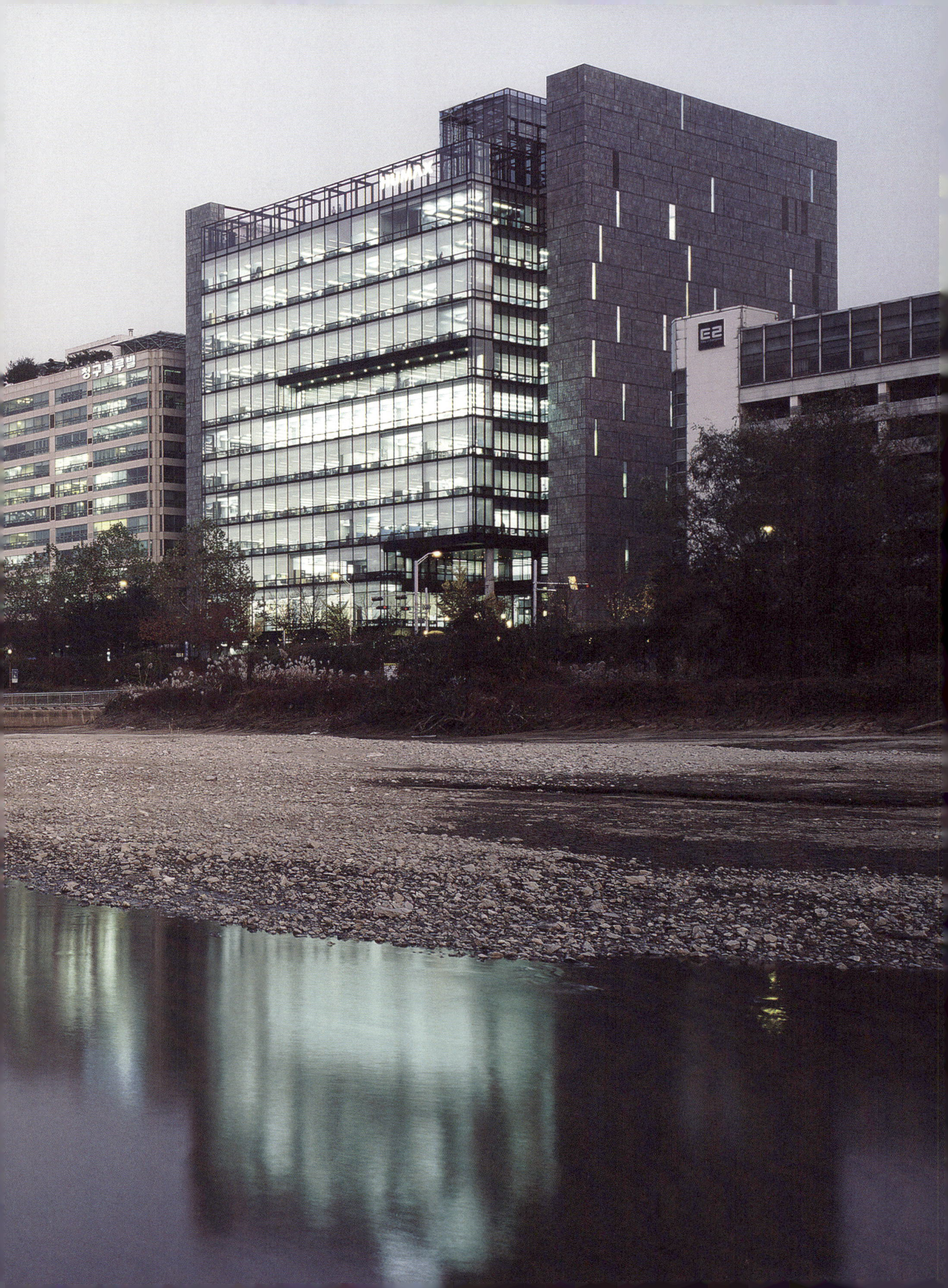
청구블루빌
HUMAX
E2

→ 256

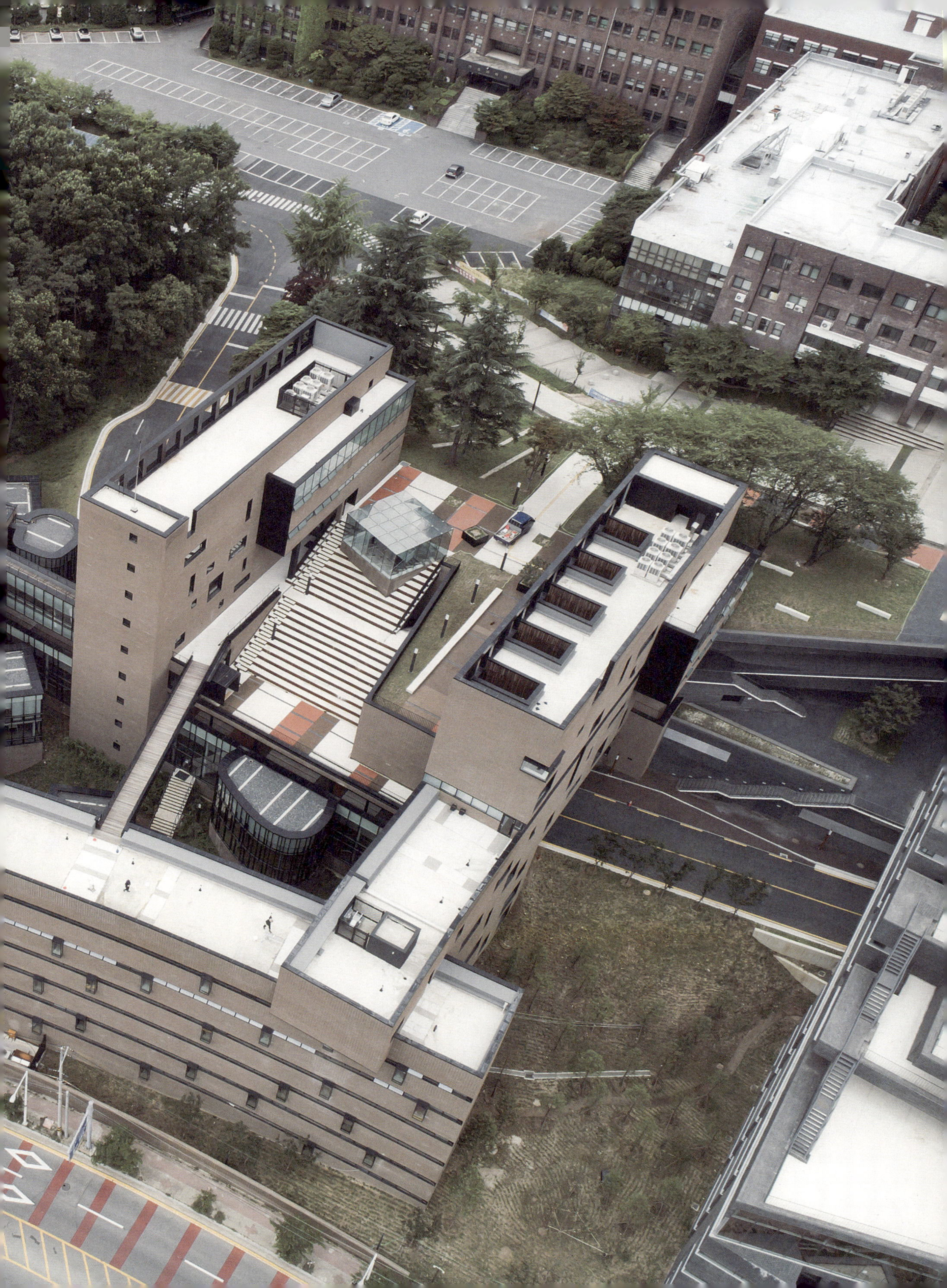

→ 264

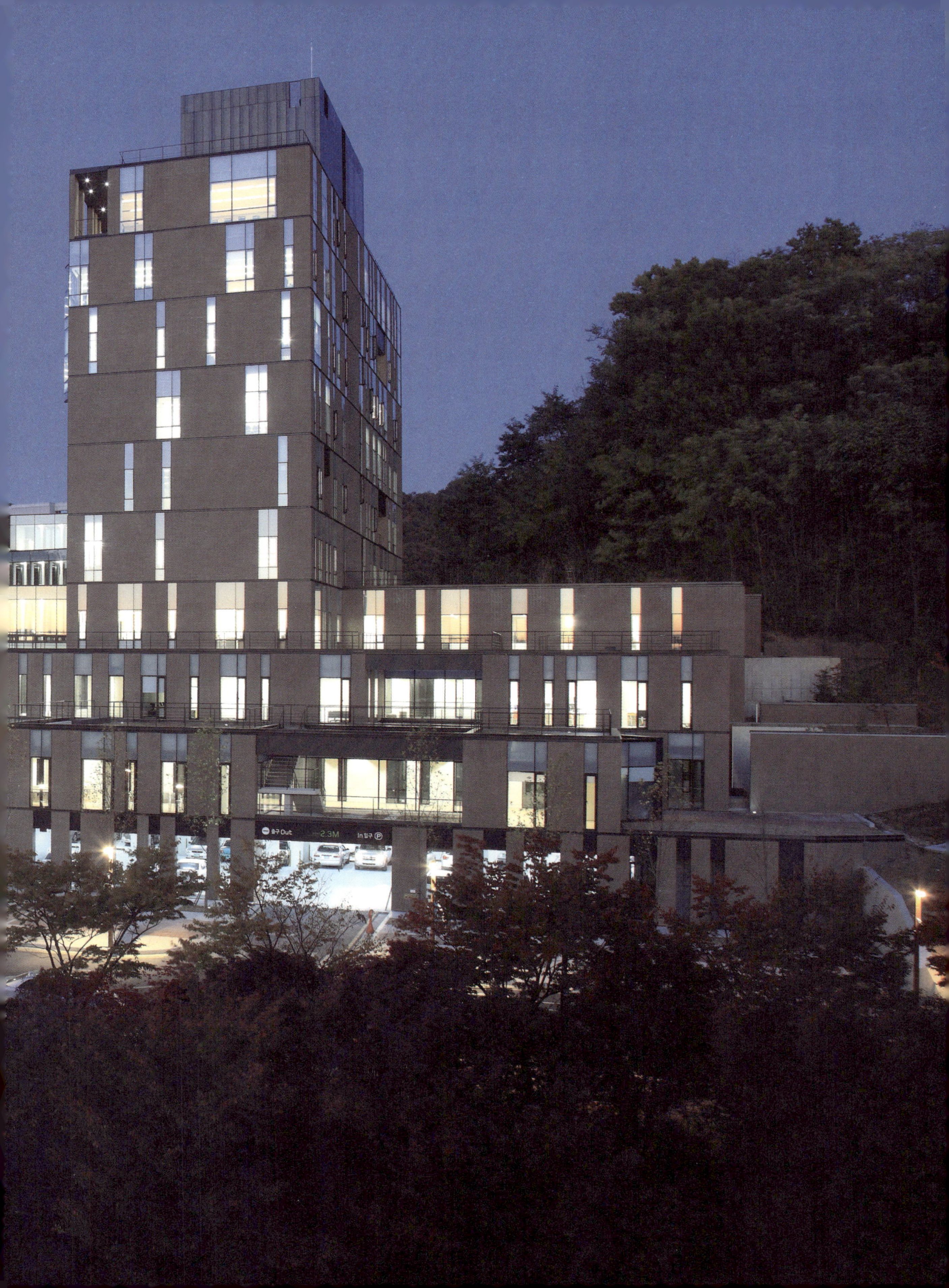
출구 Out
2.3M
In 입구

→ 272

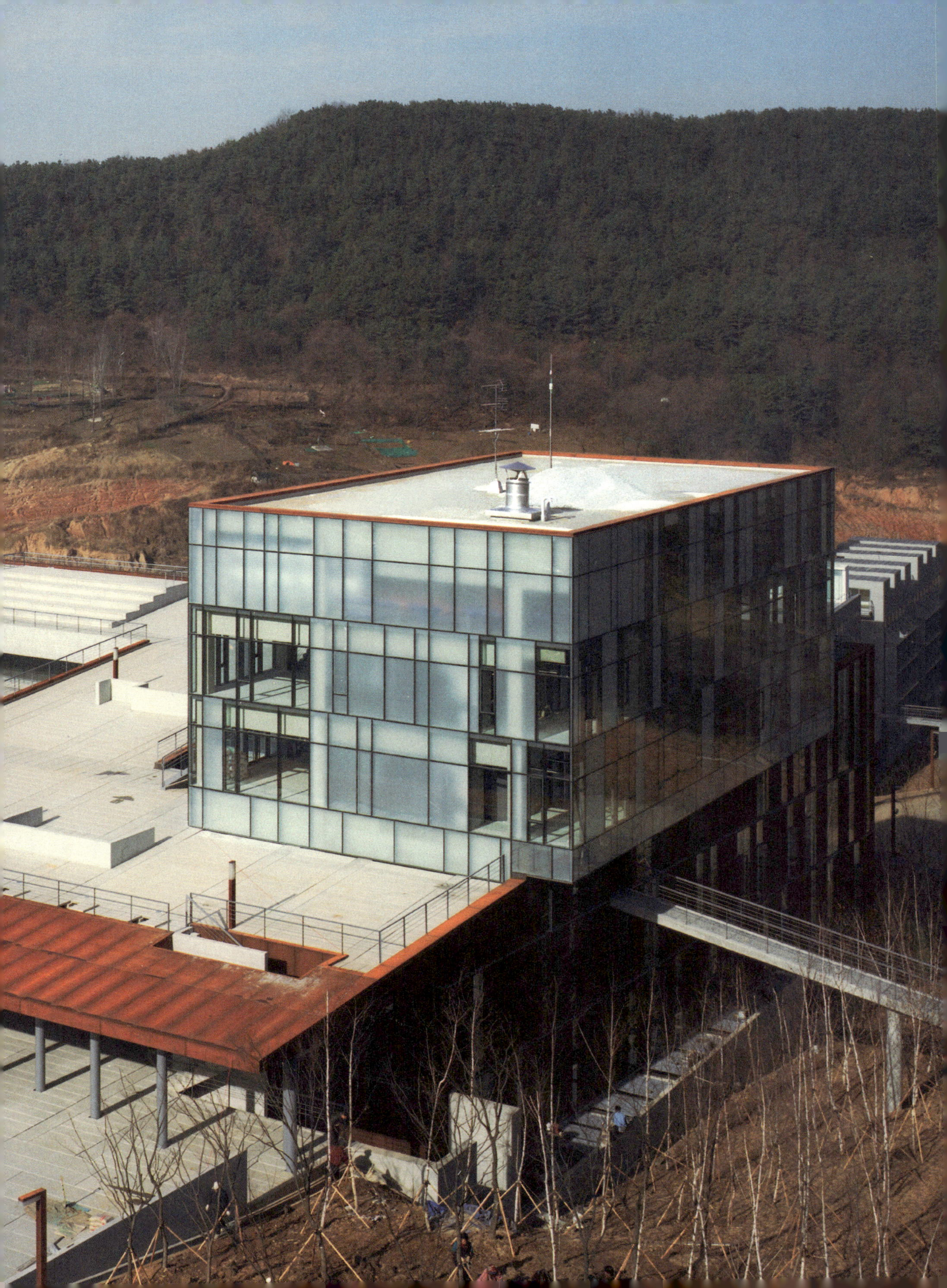

→ 280

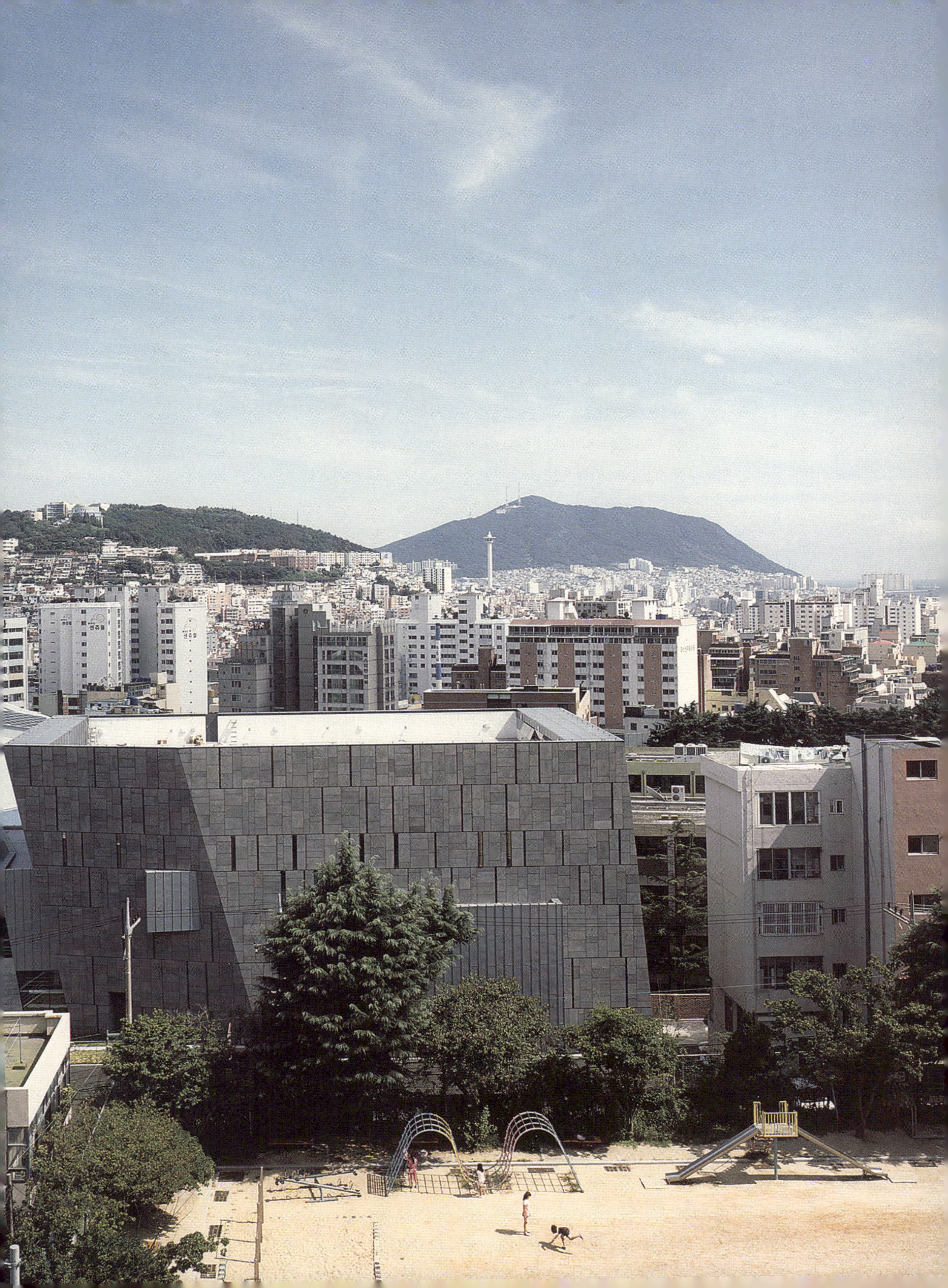

→ 288

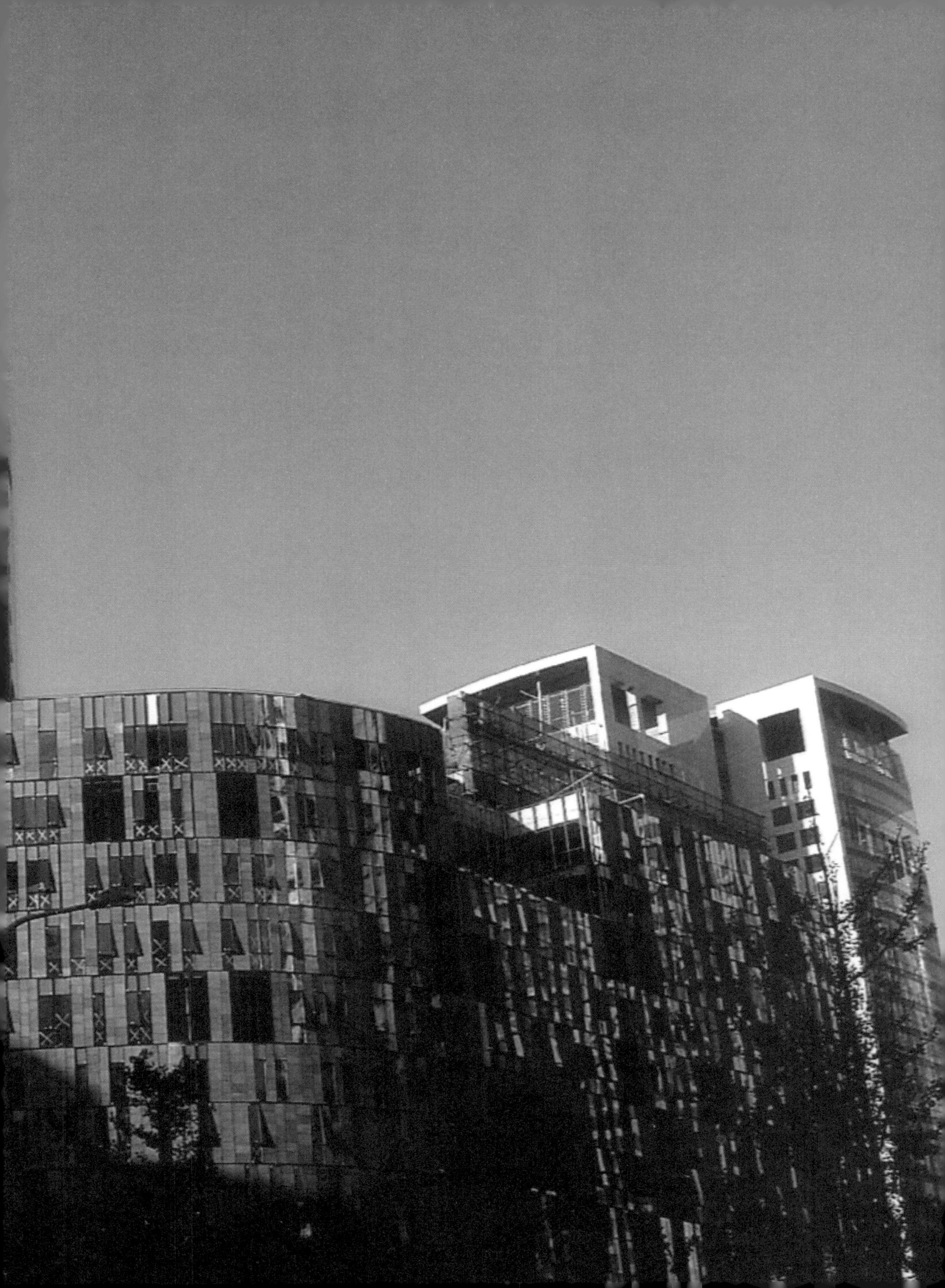

→ 296

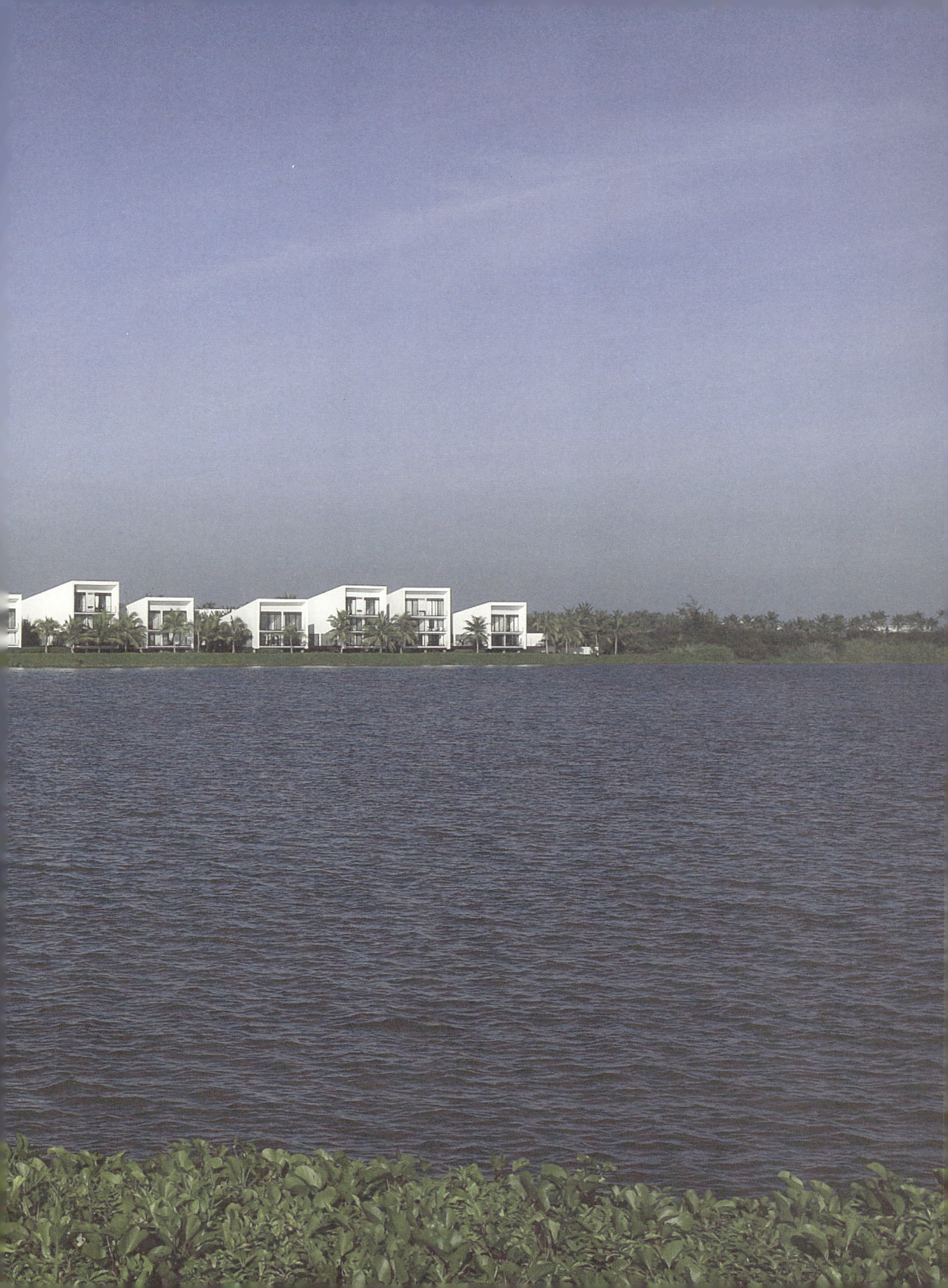

304

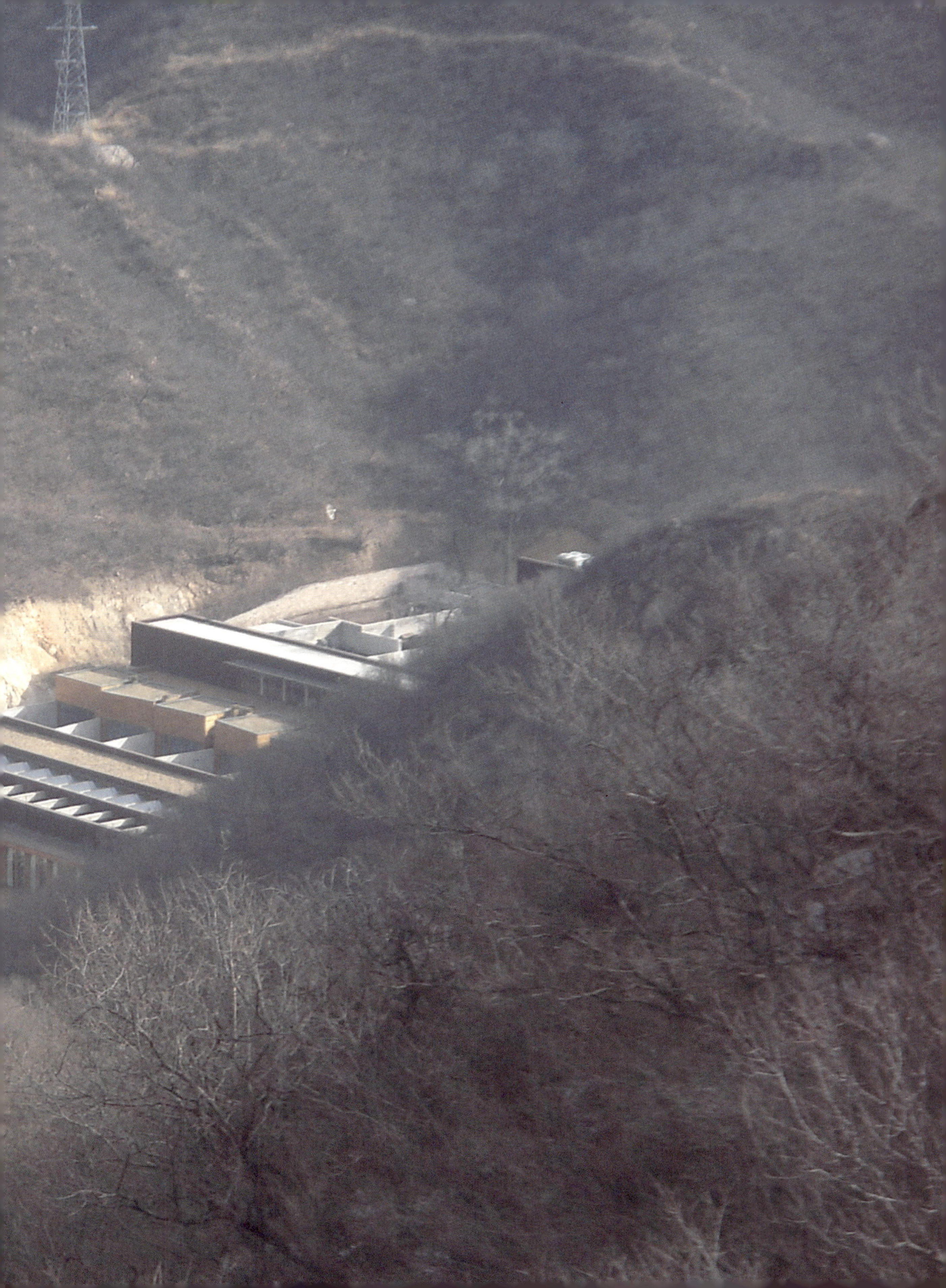

→ 312

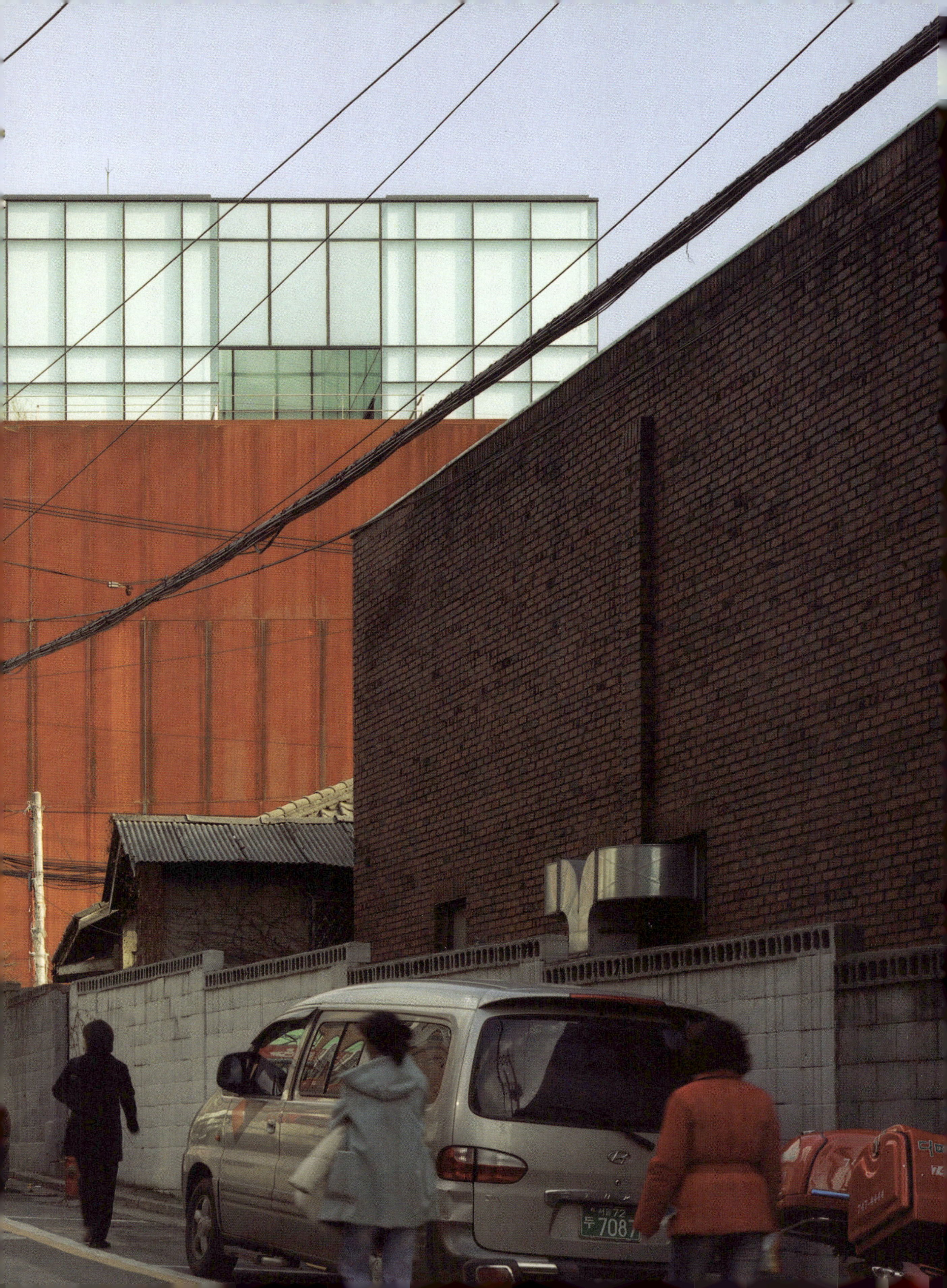

→ 320

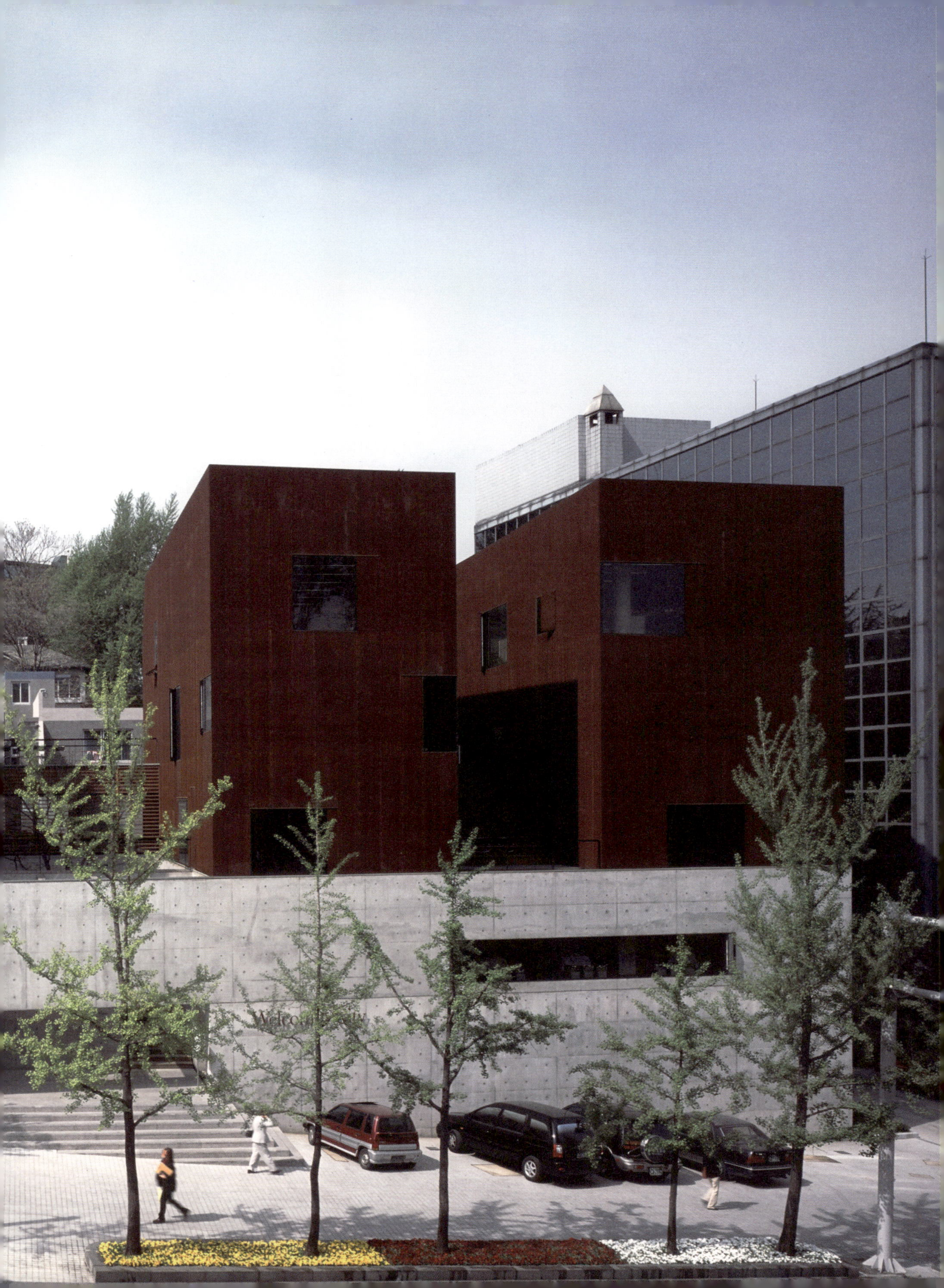

→ 328

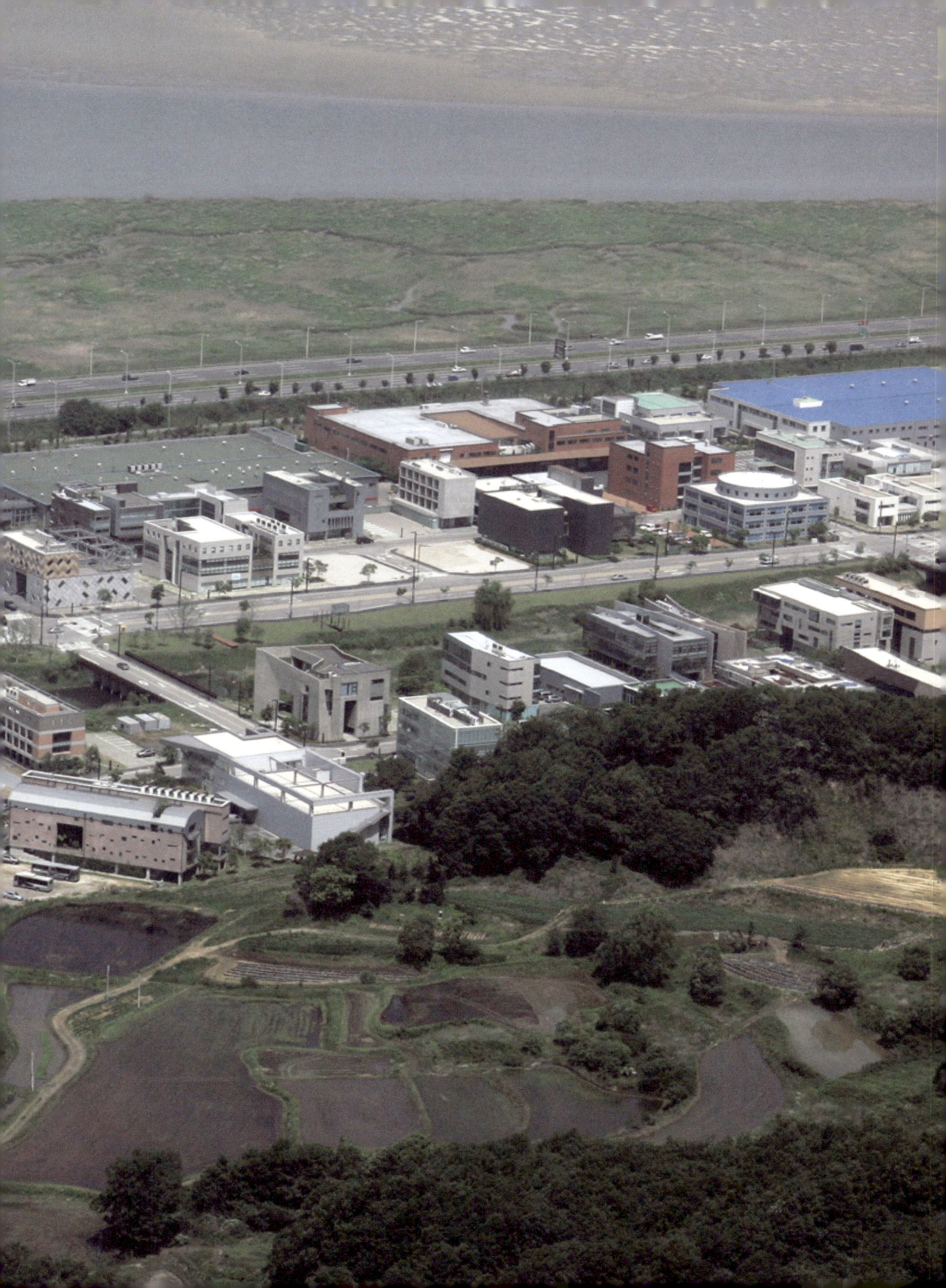

→ 336

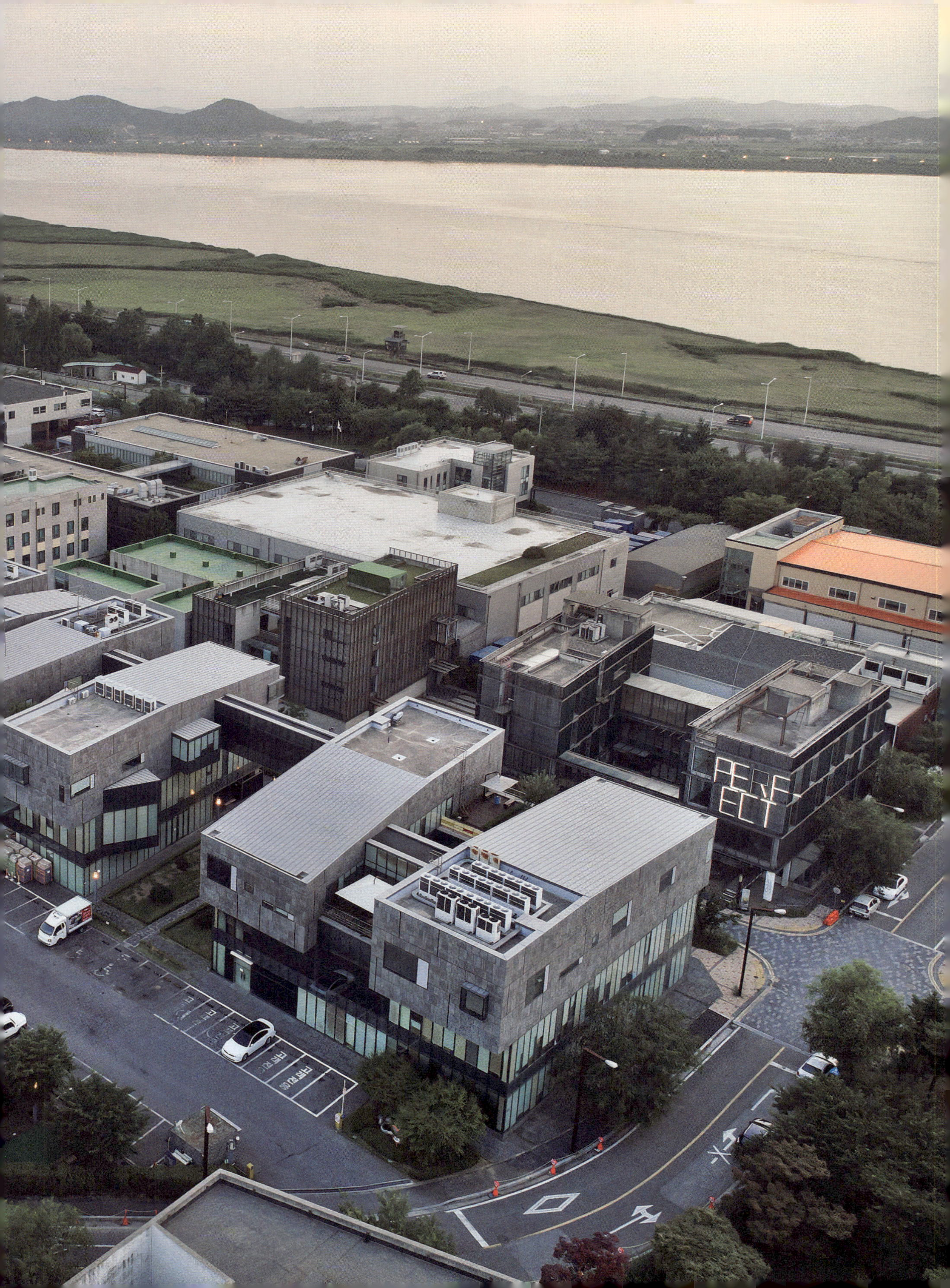
PERF
ECT

→ 344

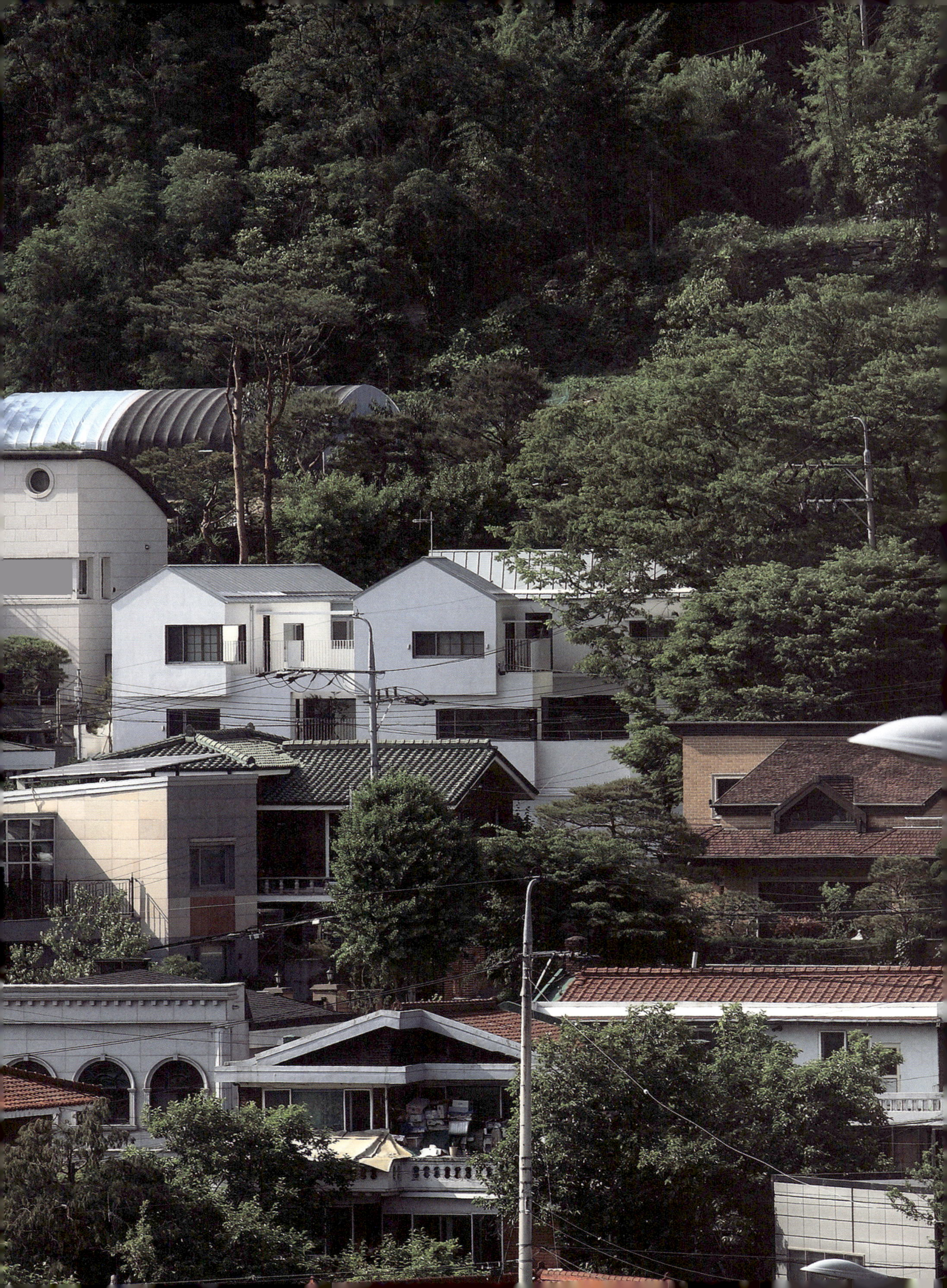

→ 352

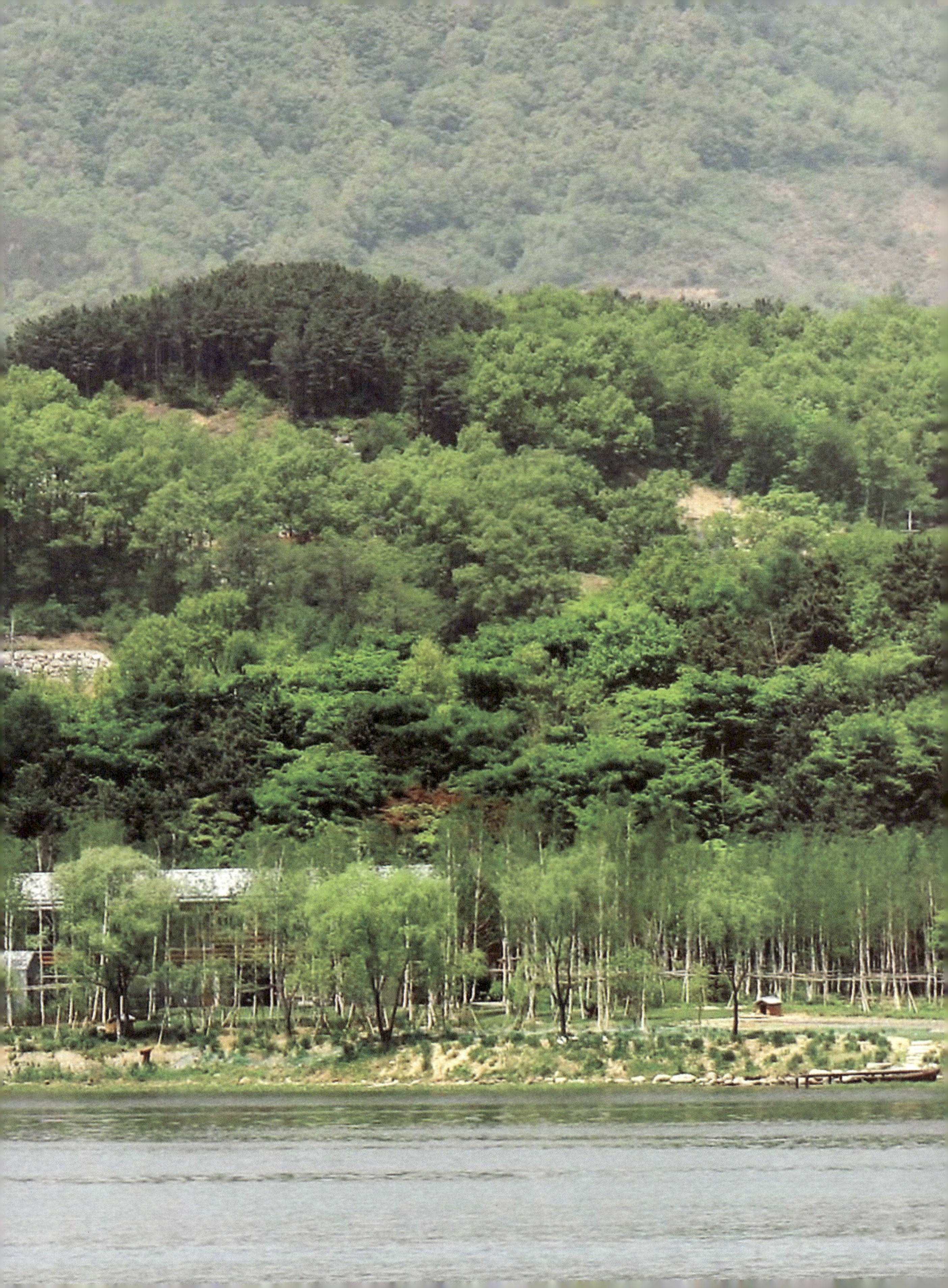

→ 360

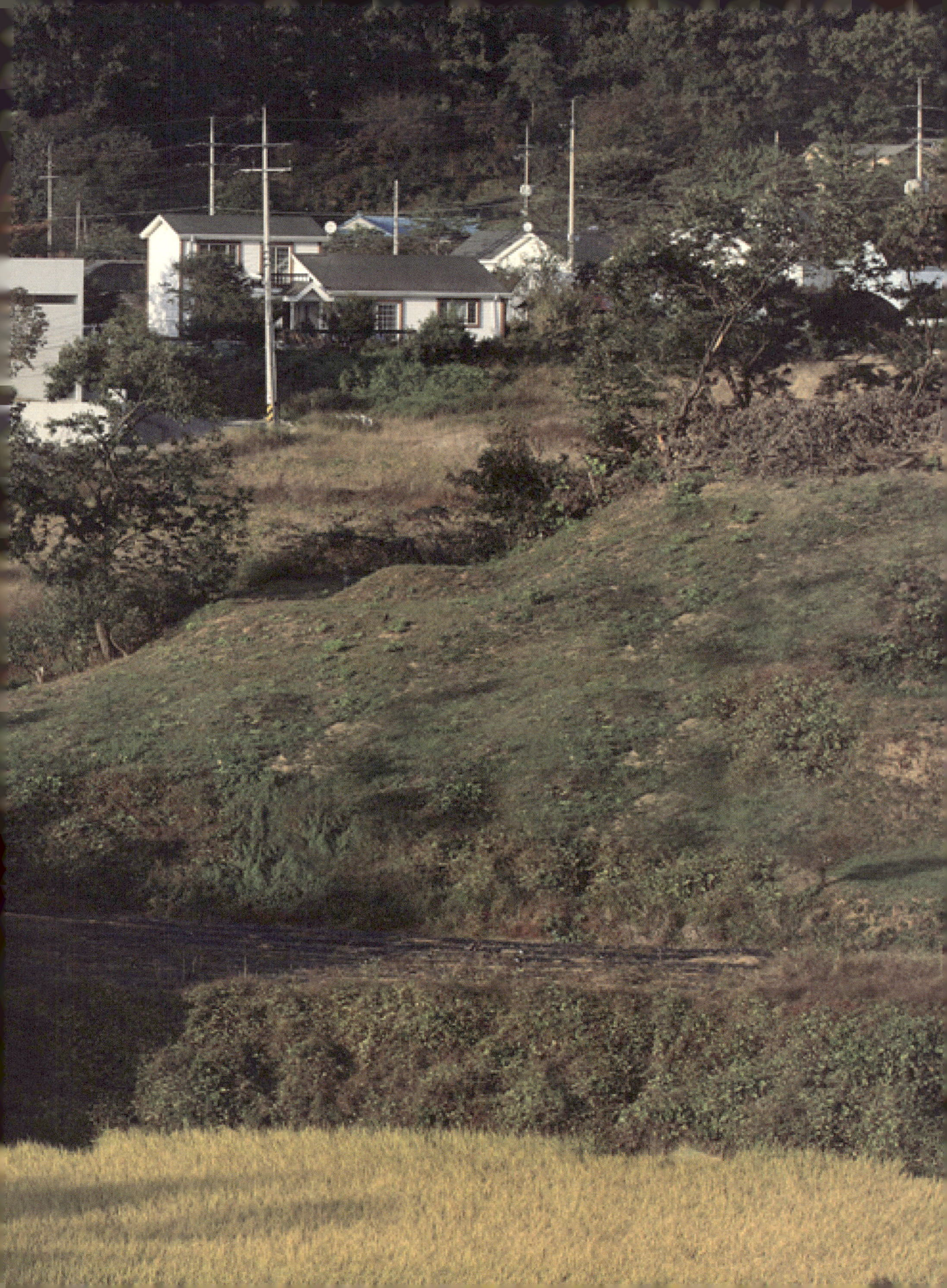

→ 368

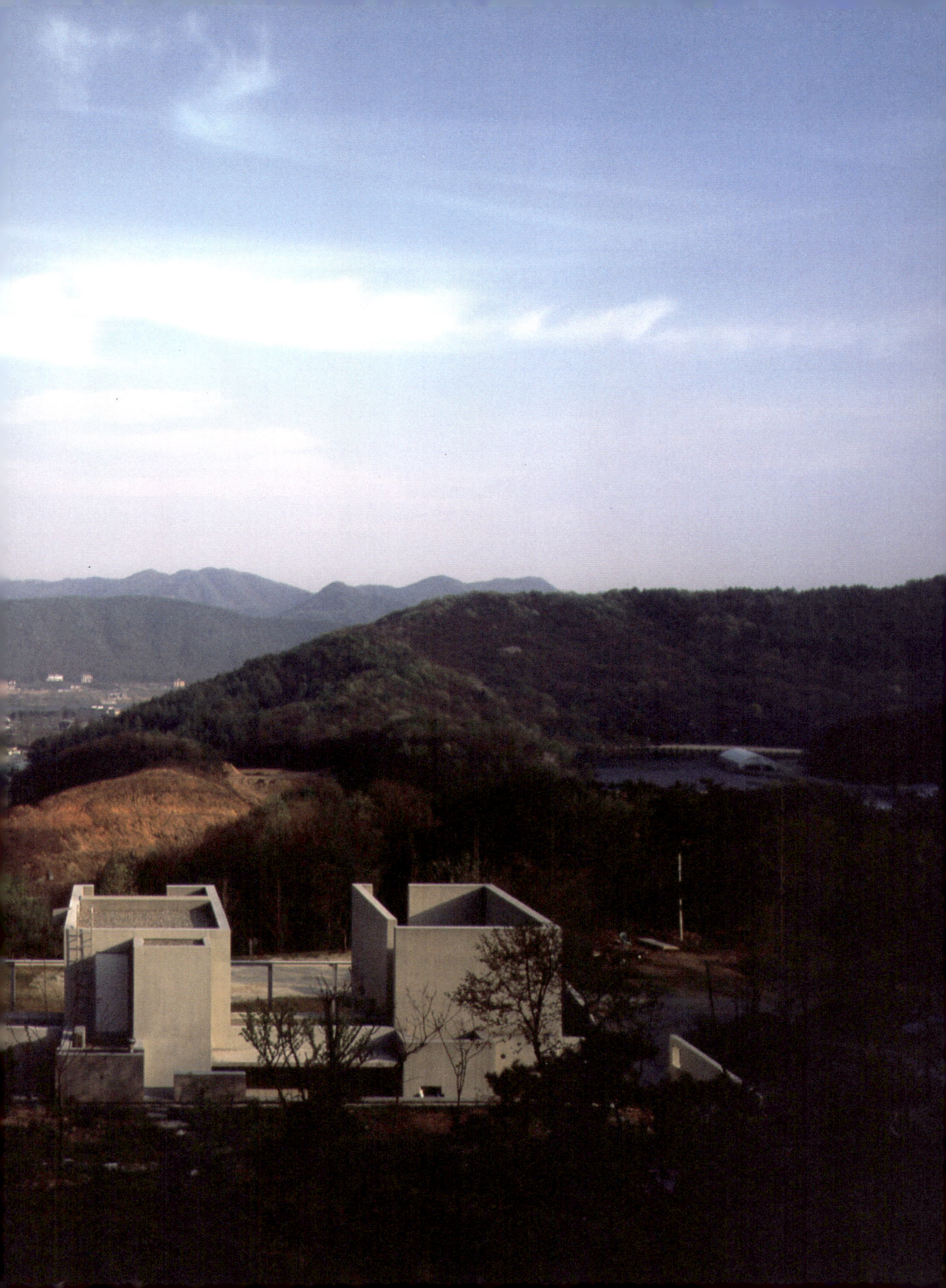

Sitting with Seung H-Sang, Around the Table of Architecture

Pai Hyungmin
University of Seoul

Humanitas is never acquired in solitude and never by giving one's work to the public. It can be achieved only by one who has thrown his life and his person into the "venture into the public realm."
Hannah Arendt, "Karl Jaspers: A Laudatio," 1958[1]

I begin with a quote from Hannah Arendt. It is a sentence from a celebratory address to her friend and former teacher, Karl Jaspers, on the occasion of his reception of the Peace Prize of the German Book Trade. In tune with the spirit of the Peace Prize, Arendt praised Jaspers for not only his work as a scholar but his simultaneous engagement in the public and political arena. It is an apt beginning to this essay because Seung H-Sang has in recent years used this quote to justify and explain his involvement in the public affairs of architecture and urbanism in Korea.[2] Between 2014 and 2016, Seung functioned as the first City Architect of the Seoul Metropolitan Government and is presently the Chair of the Presidential Commission on Architecture Policy (PCAP). Through these positions, and certainly beyond these official appointments, he has been the force behind the creation of new institutions and policies that are changing the way architecture is practiced in Korea. The City Architect and public architect system are now part of almost all the major cities of Korea. With the vision of a public design system that engages with everyday life, he is changing the way public projects are procured, convincing policy makers to move toward neighborhood-based regeneration. He has been the primary force in the creation of the Seoul Biennale of Architecture and Urbanism, for which I served as inaugural director; a new kind of biennale woven together with the realities of urban governance. Among his many major initiatives as Chair of the PCAP, he is pushing to abolish price bidding systems and subjective design reviews that impair the integrity and proper purpose of the architect's design. Working with mayors and governors, cabinet ministers, and the President himself, his fingerprint can be seen in an array of public projects and policy initiatives. What had largely been a symbolic organization since its establishment in 2008, the PCAP under Seung is now a hotbed of activity and controversy. His supporters and opponents will both agree that he is, without doubt, the most influential architect in Korea.

It must be noted that before his recent engagements in the public sector, Seung H-Sang was already the most prominent architect in Korea. He is a prolific writer who has published manifestoes and best-selling books. He is the first and still the only architect to receive recognition as Artist of the Year by the National Museum of Modern and Contemporary Art. He is of course a prolific architect; a designer of buildings with great presence. Seung is the youngest of a post-colonial and post-fascist generation of creative architects. Born after the independence of Korea in 1945, the architects of this generation began their own practices in the 1990s when Korea emerged as a democracy and a global economic force. I raise these points not merely to laud Seung as an individual architect but to point to the central question of this essay - the status of architecture in society as well as in the longer duration of human civilization.

1. Hannah Arendt, "Karl Jaspers: A Laudatio," in *Men in Dark Times* (New York: Harcourt Brace, 1968), pp. 73-74.

2. See for example, Seung H-Sang, "Stepping Down from the Role of the 1st City Architect of Seoul," *Seoul, Where Life Creates the Meta-City: White Paper on the 1st City Architect of Seoul* (Seoul Metropolitan Government, 2016), p. 7.

In considering Seung as an architect, there is, on the one hand, the work: the buildings that he has designed and realized as things in physical space. On the other hand, there is what Arendt has called "personality," that which must be thrown fully into the public realm. Following Arendt, the social theorist Kim Hyun Kyung provides the following definition of personality:

> Personality is neither something we were born with (and thus have to try not to lose) nor an essence that has to be attained by socialization. Rather, we regard personality as something we have, something we feint having, one that exists by believing in each other's play.[3]

In other words, personality is a social phenomenon without essence. We are all born human, but to be a *person*, one has to be acknowledged by others in the social body. Hence, the person is formed only through the performance and interaction of individuals that form society. Seung indeed engages with a wide range of clients, media, and colleagues, forming a personality that is at once consistent and multi-dimensional. How do we then understand the relation between his "work," the things that are given to the public, and "his life and his person" that has been so passionately thrown into the political arena?

With this question, we return to Hannah Arendt and the quote that launches this essay. We immediately see that the relation between work and life is in fact the central issue in Arendt's statement. It must also be pointed out that when Seung uses this quote, he curiously omits the part "and never by giving one's work to the public." Why this omission? Was it because he felt uncomfortable with the statement that "giving one's work to the public" would never be enough for the lofty achievement of humanity? But before this question, we must delve into what Arendt meant with this statement. Why did Arendt so specifically state that the work, the artifice created through man's activity – a key idea in her expansive thesis on "the human condition" – within the public realm could never achieve humanity? For the purposes of this essay, we must take the full measure of Arendt's statement. Though art and architecture were rarely her main topic of interest, Arendt was someone who understood the profound importance of work. As Seung has himself led us to Arendt, Arendt leads us to think about the relation between work and person. As the following pages will show, it is the question that provides the key to understanding the architecture of Seung H-Sang.

Here, with the boundaries of this essay, I will not be able to discuss the wide range of projects in Seung's oeuvre. I will focus on three examples – Pajubookcity, the Funerary Ground of Roh Moo-hyun, and Arboretum Sayoowon – that illustrate the different ways Seung, as the architect of a work and as a multi-dimensional person, engages in the architectural project. Among the many dimensions to Seung's work and personality, I focus on a key element of his architecture: the ground as an idea and a physical presence. In my 2007 book *Sensuous Plan: The Architecture of Seung H-Sang*, I had already stressed the platform, its expressiveness and its role in the organization of space. It is an aspect of his work that has been

---

3. Kim Hyun Kyung, *Person, Place, Hospitality* (Seoul: Munhak and Jisung, 2015), pp. 83-84.

consistent during the past 25 years. These three projects, divergent in program, scale, context, and client, show how Seung as an active person plays different roles. Each project, hence, has a different story to tell.

Pajubookcity as Cultural Landscape

Pajubookcity is an industrial cluster for the publishing sector located 30 km from the center of Seoul and just 10km from the DMZ. First conceived of in 1989 as a response to an industry in crisis, a group of small-medium sized publishers led by Yi Ki-Ung devised the ambitious idea of a "book city." The project went through several stages before a new direction was formulated in 1999 by the urban design team comprised of Seung H-Sang, Florian Beigel, Min Hyun Sik, Kim Jong Kyu, Kim Young Joon, and Philip Christou. The 1,600,000 m² area of Phase 1 contains Korea's largest distribution center, 130 publishing houses, 57 printers, and a hotel. With its successful completion in 2007, the second phase of Pajubookcity, in an area slightly smaller than Phase 1 and now including the film and media industries, is now fully in progress. Seung has several important built projects in Pajubookcity, (such as the Myung Films Complex, pages 190-197, Design Vita Paju Office, pages 198-205, and Kyobo Book, pages 336-343), but his role in this major initiative goes well beyond the traditional role of the architect-designer. His activity in moving Pajubookcity towards its present status as an innovative cluster involves an intense *vita activa*, the political and social engagement of the person.

Almost every day, for more than two months, Seung went to Paju for meetings with publishers, politicians, bureaucrats, and fellow architects. Seung planned architectural tours for the publishers, traveling together to change their sense of what architecture could do for their immense project. He set up seminars and workshops, curated exhibitions, all part of a process of convincing the publishers to implement a culture that moved away from existing conventions. The existing conditions of the site were in fact not conducive to new planning strategies. With its infrastructure already laid out by the Korea Land Corporation's conventional plan; as a neighborhood with just 160 units of housing; as a military zone prohibiting any structure over four stories; an industrial zone that disallows mixed-use, the architectural possibilities were limited.

However, as a result of all this activity, the publishers and architects agreed to a voluntary design guideline. Influenced by landscape urbanism but based on a series of architectural typologies, the guideline regulated open spaces, common views toward the Han River and the adjacent mountains, and the selection of building and landscape materials. Publishers were further obliged to choose their architects from a select pool, a system that we now see implemented in the public architect system of numerous municipalities in Korea. Despite lacking ample resources, Pajubookcity has provided two generations of architects with opportunities to build, becoming an exhibition ground for the top architects of Korea and the world. Even with the death of the book, something that the publishers would not have imagined in 1989, Pajubookcity has sustained its vision as an innovative city. With the changing relations between North and South Korea and the continuous expansion of the

Pajubookcity, book-shelf type, photo by Kim JongOh

surrounding commercial and residential areas, it is expected to become an urban corridor for new social, political, and economic configurations.

If what I have just described about the nature of Pajubookcity revolves around the personality of Seung, we must at the same time highlight the architectural mechanisms employed within this social process. In this matter, Florian Beigel was Seung's key partner, as it was the former's ideas and sketches that provided the key inspiration in formulating the design guidelines. Beigel was constantly conscious of the different horizons that extend throughout the site - the horizon of the Han River, the level of the wetlands, and the expansive eye-level horizon of the viewer. As Joseph Grima noted in an article on Florian Beigel's Korean work, the "programmatic allocation throughout the [Paju Book City] occurs not in plan but in section."[4] Certainly, before Seung's encounter with Beigel,

Florian Beigel, Sketch of bookshelf buildings, 1999

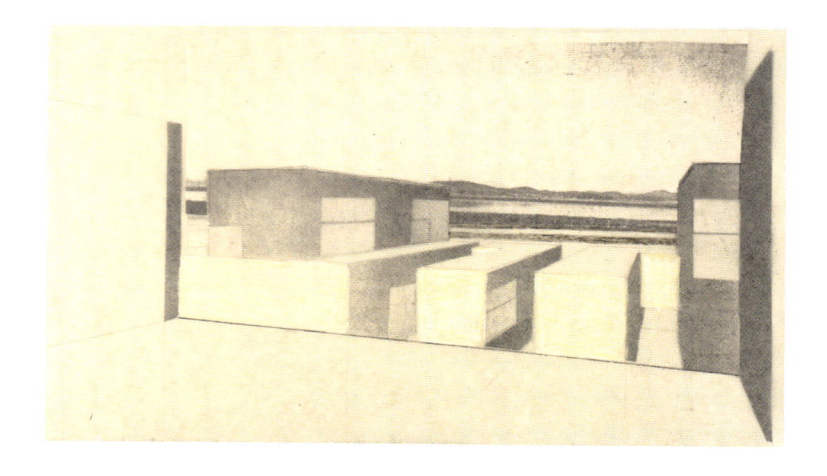

4. Joseph Grima, "The Art of Void," *Domus* 879, Mar. 2005. P. 43.

consideration of multiple topographic horizons was already a key aspect of the former's work. It is a key character of architecture in Korea where, with its hilly terrain, buildings must carefully maneuver the different sections of an uneven, sloping land. Seung accepted Beigel's scheme but his approach to these horizons was quite different. In contrast to Beigel's phenomenological inheritance of an integrated horizon inherent within both the viewer and the object, Seung approaches the horizons of Pajubookcity as historical and natural realities of the land. His horizons neither extend into infinity nor internalize in the subjective core of the viewer as in the singular perspectival tradition of the West. They should certainly be respected and followed, but as his invention of the term "culturescape" implies, they are by no means universal or inherent. In other words, horizons are part of culture and formed through locality. These multiple sections are again found in his vision of Seoul as a multi-level city that encompasses its mountains and grounds as well as the modern artifice of elevated decks and underground spaces. As he reminds us, it is a spatial organization and social sensibility rarely found in the Western urban tradition. For Seung, these sections and horizons are matters immediate to the site and immediately sensual. In this sense, he is not a fundamentalist.

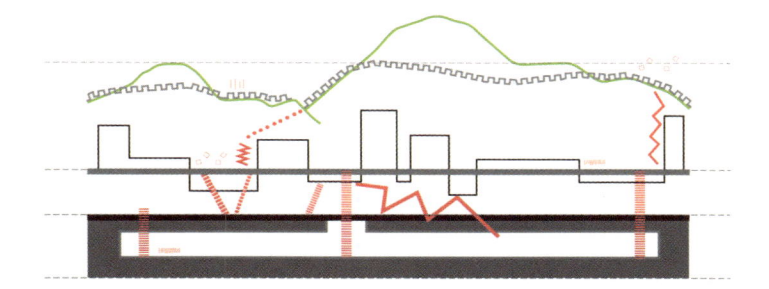

Seung H-Sang, Four levels of Seoul Walk, 2016

The Funerary Ground of Roh Moo-hyun and the Time of Things

As a single work, there is no other project that better tells the story of this entwinement of work and person than the burial ground of Korea's former president Roh Moo-hyun. Roh Moo-hyun was the ninth President of the Republic of Korea and a revered leader of its democratic movement. Unlike former Korean presidents who went into protective urban enclaves after leaving office, Roh returned to his home village of Bongha. With his return, the small struggling farm village became a public site of the former-president's humble ambitions. It became a lively public landscape comprised of not only the former-president's private residence, farmlands, and working farm houses but also tourist shops and a refurbished museum house where Roh was born. Soon after his return to his home village, his family and former aides became targets of investigations into corruption and influence peddling. Rather than face the humiliation of drawn-out legal procedures, rather than participate in the destruction of his legacy, Roh took his own life. In the early morning of May 23, 2009, he threw himself off Owl Rock, a steep hill next to his house in Bongha.

Great controversy surrounds his life and death, but many have surmised that Roh believed that his death would preserve the force of his ideas.

Following his own wishes, Roh is the first former-president of Korea whose remains are not enshrined at the National Cemetery. Immediately after his death, the Committee for a Small Burial Stone was formed to realize the last wishes of the former-president. This committee selected Seung H-Sang as the architect of the funerary ground. It would not be an exaggeration to say that it was a kind of miracle that, even within the chaotic swirl of political forces, such a bold and consistent design was realized. Again, it is a testament to not only Seung as a person but the shared commitment of all those who came together in the aftermath of one of the most tragic events of modern Korea. Following the participatory spirit of Roh's politics, his funerary ground was created through the collaboration of artists, writers, scholars, and most importantly, the tens of thousands of people who left their messages of grief and hope in the 15,000 pavement blocks that comprise its pathways. In the decade since its completion in the spring of 2010, more than ten million people have come to Bongha Village, making it a site of pilgrimage and tourism.

Like many of Seung's projects, the essential aesthetic of Roh Moo-hyun's Funerary Ground lies in the way it builds a new ground into the fabric of the landscape. Once again, true to his edict of the "landscript," the architect sought to extract elements and boundaries from the ground. Existing waterways, roads and pathways, the existing contours of the surrounding mountains, the pattern of the adjacent farmlands provide the physical and intellectual infra-structure of the new site. Even the long corten wall, marking the boundary between the mountains and the funerary platform, is less a vertical wall and more an element that emerges from the conditions of the ground. The only element that yields to the vertical is a thick flag pole carrying a spot-light for the funerary stone. From his first sketches, from the first conception of the project, Seung was dedicated to building the ground. The architectural task is to build a platform that is part of the ground and the landscape.

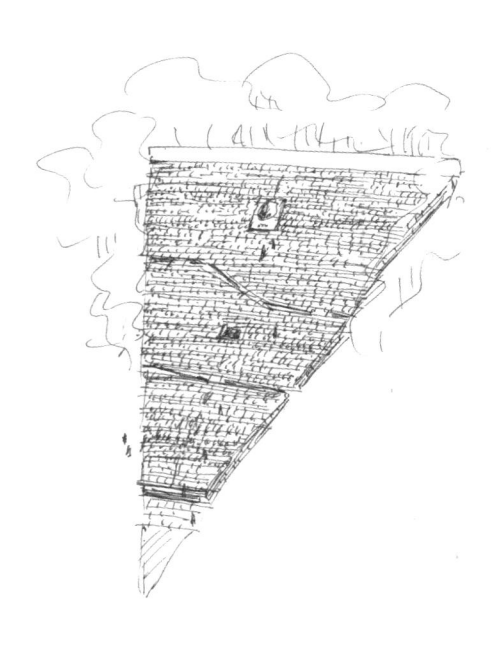

Seung H-Sang, Sketch for Funerary Ground of Roh Moo-hyun, 2009

The Funerary Ground's orientation toward the ground, its aversion to the grandiose and the triumphant, is akin to the character of the "counter-monument," a term coined in the early 1990s by James Young in his perceptive analysis of German Holocaust memorials. According to Young, the counter-monument is defined by the way it appropriates time: the way it understands that "Time mocks the rigidity of monuments, the presumptuous claim that in its materiality, a monument can be regarded as eternally true...It seeks to stimulate memory no less than the everlasting memorial, but by pointing explicitly at its own changing face, it re-marks also the inevitable - even essential - evolution of memory itself over time."[5] Indeed, Seung often mentions Jochen Gerz and Esther Shalev-Gerz's sinking black pillar, the Harburg Monument to Fascism, as an important project that reminds us of the mortality of architecture. Compared to the Harburg Monument, the funerary ground has a longer rhythm of waiting. It waits with hope as the footsteps that walk along the platform will eventually erase the words engraved onto its stone blocks. The more people come to Bongha, the less time it will take the words of mourning to disappear. Rather than an unchanging monument, it is the slow wear-and-tear of stone that manifests the "organized power of an awakened citizenry" - the words of Roh Moo-hyun etched onto the base of his funerary stone.

Jochen Gerz and Esther Shalev-Gerz, Harburg Monument to Fascism

Jongmyo Shrine, begun 1394
photo by Seung H-Sang

A Holocaust memorial is obviously very different from the burial ground of a former Korean president. Beyond their common critique of the everlasting monument, Seung's project brings a different approach to architectural forms. If the counter-monument works through a reversal of older traditions and a critique of context, Seung retrieves Korea's older traditions and reconciles his work with existing conditions of the landscape. Though the site may seem different and strange because of its departure from Korea's recent state-sponsored monuments, unlike the Holocaust monuments that sink and reverse, Seung's gesture is more of retrieval and rescue. Seung seeks inspiration from the low, horizontal platform of Jongmyo, the royal Confucian shrine of the Joseon Dynasty. Begun in 1394, this granite platform, 109m

5. James E. Young, "The Counter-Monument: Memory against Itself in Germany Today," *Critical Inquiry* 18, No. 2 (Winter, 1992), p. 294.

in width and 69m in depth, shows how the ground defines the human condition. Without building upward, it is one of the great monuments of human civilization. Seung's reverence to Korean tradition may further be read in the writing of the floor. In contrast to the Western tradition that equates civilization with the erect human figure distanced from the impurities of the ground, the Korean way of life sustains a variety of affinities with the floor. The words on the platform comprise less a critique of reading and more an affirmation of the Asian calligraphic tradition of horizontal writing. It is a project that relies, on the one hand, on a stable, conservative set of conventions. However, unlike Western traditions, it performs as architecture without the will to enclose and to build up.

Funerary Ground of President Roh Moo-hyun, photo by Kim JongOh

This accommodating attitude toward older traditions is also present in the way the project finds its place on the land. Like the flat cultivated paddy fields of Bongha Village, the triangular platform enters the landscape as part of the existing field conditions. Like Pajubookcity, it is a cultural landscape. The low, flatness of the site preserves and amplifies the surrounding mountains that are the larger, more permanent containers of memory. Its essential humility lies in the way it opens up the view to Owl Rock, to Bonghwa Mountain, and to the open vistas that extend our mind and sensibilities beyond this small village. It understands that its architecture functions to provide an array of positions. You walk on it, look down to read, and kneel to pay your respects. Toward the mountains and from the mountains, it is a place both to see and to be seen. Without didactic arrogance, the funerary ground comprises a landscape that asks as us where we are and where we want to go.

Sayuwon and Solitude

The third and last project that I shall discuss, Arboretum Sayuwon, brings these mechanisms of time and place into a totally different setting. An ongoing project, Sayoowon is a private park, a 1,000,000m^2 mountainous area in Gunwi, located in the southeast region of the Korean peninsula. First conceived in 2006 as a personal project, it is the dream child of Yoo Jae Sung, the President of the Tae Chang Steel Company. A self-made man, a patron of the arts, and a maverick, he has been quoted as saying that "Steel is one of the things I do, the garden is part of my life." Since the spring of 2012, Seung has designed several structures within the park: Hyeonam, a small viewing house, the first of his designs to be built; Sadam, a cafeteria and waterfront performance stage; Myeongjeong, a contemplative outdoor water courtyard; Wasa, a corten structure sitting over an artificial pond along the valley stream; Cheomdan, a small lookout tower renovated from a water tank; the parking lot; a series of outdoor toilets; and finally, a hotel, the largest facility in the park and the only structure of his design that has not been built. They are work that co-exist with the landscape designs of Jung Youngsun and Kawagishi Matsunobu; several structures designed by Álvaro Siza; the calligraphy of Wei Eerang; and the many interventions of Yoo Jae Sung himself. Despite the sublime nature of its landscape, Sayuwon is characterized by its open, undefined nature as a facility. It is an enormous park without a masterplan. The only possible master planner is Yoo Jae Sung, who moves with the consistent purpose of self-fulfillment. They are bold moves that often defy logic and calculation. What is Sayuwon? Is it private or public? It is a commercial venture or a personal dream? What will be the extent of its development? Will the buildings have use or are they part of that rare species of useless architecture? Sayuwon is a beautiful puzzle comprised of artistic work, the complex relation of different personalities, and an artificial nature. It is an irresistible, maddening project for those, including the client himself, who work in it.

Without going into the details of all of Seung's projects in Sayuwon, I state that the architect's most important capacity in this process is that of waiting, in all its different temporal scales. He waits both intently and with soft repose. Seung the person waits, in the everyday sense, for decisions to be made, for uncertainties and conflicts to clear itself. Seung's waiting also extends beyond the practical matters of everyday patience, a virtue that is required in almost all professional practice. At the furthest extent of human cognition, it encompasses his sense of the finitude of not only man but also of the things he produces. In this sense, his built work also waits.

Let us imagine the pavilions in Sayuwon as ruins. Imagine at some future point in time, perhaps in an era past the earth's sufferings of the Anthropocene, a group of explorers venturing into the hills of Gunwi. The clearings that were created will have returned to a primordial forest. Walking along the narrow valley, they will discover the mangled corten steel of what was once Wasa. Clearing the steel and bushes, they will uncover the concrete basin and guess that this spot was a man-made pond. Reaching one of the mountain tops, they will see the crumbled concrete walls of Myeongjeong and puzzle over what it was used for. They will know that there was an empty square space, a courtyard, in the middle but will not understand what its surrounding spaces were for. Was it a well or a place to worship the sky? We can imagine them oscillate between reading Myeongjeong as a practical space and a useless space. If they are adept at reading the land, without knowing that it was the meticulous work of an architect, they may sense how carefully these structures were placed. One thing that these future adventurers will not know is that these works, when they were first built, looked very much like ruins.

Myungjeong,
photo by Kim JongOh

Seung H-Sang, Hyeonam,
photo by Kim JongOh

As we have encountered with his appreciation of the Harburg Monument to Fascism, Seung approaches his work as a future ruin.

> As man cannot deny the fatality of death, architecture ultimately falls down and disappears. No matter how firmly it is built to celebrate the glory of its patron, there is no building that can finally resist the law of gravity. What remains is only the memory.[6]

I believe Seung to be an existentialist. He is someone who believes in the profound finiteness of humanity and the mortality of its artifice; finitude in the face of the unknowable but certain existence of God. While his buildings fully operate as part of the practical social world, his best work inevitably contains moments that confirm the solitude of man: the in-between sloped steps of Welcomm City, the empty stepped courtyard of Hyehwa Center, the peripatetic tunnel lying in the valley stream of Sayuwon. I argue that his best work centers not on congregational spaces but in spaces that are meant for single occupation. That is why the pavilions of Sayuwon are so exceptional. While most buildings necessarily contain some public function, the structures in Sayuwon (with perhaps the exception of Sadam) can assume a solitary presence. In this manner, they crystalize Seung's sense of the finitude of men and things. And that is why, unlike the everyday raison d'etre of most architecture, these pavilions also contain the possibility of hubris; of the arbitrariness of willful design.

Seung H-Sang, Welcomm City, photo by Osamu Murai

6. Seung H-Sang, "On the Ruin of Hwangryong Temple," *Good Thoughts*, May 21, 2006. http://www.iroje.com/index.php?mid=essay

We may certainly agree with Arendt and many others that "if the world is to contain a public space, it cannot be erected for one generation and planned for the living only; it must transcend the life-space of mortal men."[7] At the same time, as we have seen with the Harburg Monument, the Funerary Ground of Roh Moo--hyun, and the Sayuwon pavilions, man-made things take on different temporal rhythms. From dawn to sunset, there are the daily rhythms that bring forth different hues and angles of light. The seasonal changes of hot sun, snow, and wind accumulate to bring wear and tear to these things. Time thus affects the way architecture relates to the construction of public space. There is the time for *vita activa* and there is the longer time for man's work in public space. There is also a time beyond humanity.

At the Table of Things

To live together in the world means essentially that a world of things is between those who have it in common, as a table is located between those who sit around it: the world like every in-between, relates and separates men at the same time…The public realm, as the common world, gathers us together and yet prevents our falling over each other, so to speak. What makes mass society so difficult to bear is not the number of people involved, or at least not primarily, but the fact that the world between them has lost its power to gather them together, to relate and to separate them. The weirdness of this situation resembles a spiritualistic séance where a number of people gathered around a table might suddenly, through some magic trick, see the table vanish from their midst, so that two persons sitting opposite each other were no longer separated but also would be entirely unrelated to each other by anything tangible.[8]

Seung is a designer of these tables, the world of things that Arendt speaks of in such an eloquent, metaphorical manner. Depending on the design of the table, and I remind our readers that the table is a horizontal platform, the relation of the people who sit around it may change. I would argue, on the one hand, that the most fundamental role of Seung as a table-maker is the affirmation of the simultaneous importance and loneliness of the individual man, not as a social being, but a finite entity thrown into this world. On the other hand, Seung understands that he is not only the table-maker but is one of many who sit around the table; side by side with different people in a mass society. He thus adheres to the idea of man as a political being within the confines of society. As I have outlined at the beginning of this essay, with his work as the City Architect of Seoul and Chair of the PCAP, Seung has brought architecture properly into the political and social arena. Politics and aesthetics are an ever-changing process, in Korea as in all places where freedom is as fragile as it is fundamental to the modern human condition. It is clear that architecture has a part in this difficult process. As built work, Seung's projects comprise a landscape that is at once beautiful, tragic, and open to an unknown future. They call for language and thought; they ask the people around the table to sustain its relevance.

7. Hannah Arendt, *The Human Condition* (Chicago: Univ. of Chicago Press, 1958), p. 55.
8. Hannah Arendt, *The Human Condition*, pp. 52-53.

For Seung, work is by definition not something to be given to the public. At the same time, he has thrown himself to the agonism of the roundtable. This is why Seung constantly presents the monastery, the spatial order of monastic life, as the model of how architectural work and the social body may co-exist. Each individual, in the solitude of their existence in the world, come together less as a society but as finite beings within an existence that they cannot fathom. The clarity of the monastic table is the very antithesis of our mass society absent of the order of the in-between world, a Post-Truth society that we see "falling on each other." We can now see why Seung did not feel the need to restate the phrase "giving one's work to the public" from the Hannah Arendt quote that he so cherishes. For Seung, the status of his work is ultimately based on man's solitude and not on the society their multitude forms. Seung the person is involved in work but, as Kim Hyun Kyung has pointed out, is formed through society. Perhaps, it is this very distance between person and work that allows Seung's *vita activa*, to not just co-exist with but also nourish the latter. Work that has the passion of life: that is what also brings Arendt, as well as the existentialism of Kierkegaard and Jaspers together. It was their sense of "philosophy as a passionate and deeply engaged activity, in which the integrity and the authenticity of the human being are decisively implicated."[9] We may bring Seung to this table of thought, exchanging architecture for philosophy. What is certain is that as Arendt has already underscored, humanity is achieved not just by designing the table but by the commitment to sit at the table of the public realm.

9. "Karl Jaspers," *Stanford Encyclopedia of Philosophy*, (First published Jun 5, 2006; substantive revision Tue Jul 17, 2018), https://plato.stanford.edu/entries/jaspers/

—090	Muhakro Methodist Church
—098	Bugye Arboretum "Sayuwon"
—098	— Hyeonam
—106	— Sadam
—112	— Myeongjeong
—120	— Wasa
—128	— Cheomdan
—140	Myungrye Sacred Hill
—148	Graveyard of President Roh Moohyun
—156	Public Cemetery Park "A Thousand Winds"
—166	Korea DMZ Peace and Life Valley
—174	Residence "Moheon"
—182	Korean Medicine Hospital of Daejeon University in Seoul
—190	Myung Films Complex
—198	Design Vita Office Building
—206	Chusa Memorial Museum
—214	Country Club House "360° Earth, Water, Flowers, and Wind"
—222	Traditional Buddhism Center of Jogye Order
—232	Shin Dongyeop Literary Museum
—240	Vanke Residential Culture Center
—248	Humax Main Office Building "Humax Village"
—256	Hyehwa Residential College of Daejeon University
—264	30th Anniversary Memorial Building of Daejeon University
—272	Hyehwa Culture Center of Daejeon University
—280	Gudeok Presbyterian Church
—288	Chaowai SOHO
—296	Boao Canal Village
—304	Commune by the Great Wall
—312	Lock Museum
—320	Welcomm City
—328	Paju Book City
—336	Kyobo Book City
—344	Residence "Soowoojae"
—352	Reed House
—360	Teochon House
—368	Residence "Subaekdang"

The etymology word for the church is ecclesia in Latin, which means those who are called-out. And the Bible says, in the New Testament Book of Ephesians (Chapter 1), "…. the church, which is His (Christ's) body, the fullness of Him who fills all in all." Thus it is wrong to understand the church as a building, and there is no prototype or typical model of the church. Calling out is to expel oneself out of the boundary of the world. Perhaps it seems that Jesus Christ was called-out and expelled himself by himself out of the boundary of the world to immortalize himself. It seems that Christians are those who imitate the life of Christ (*Imitatio Christi*). Although martyrdom is the supreme act of faith, those who are not able to do so are to imitate Jesus in order to live a life of Christian poverty, chastity, and obedience, abandoning greed, envy, and lust of the world. As it is nonsense that the church is the only place where the omnipresent God resides, the church should not be the house of God, but the house of those who have been called-out, and who have been exiled from the desires of the world. So, it will be natural that the church, which houses those people, should be made of only essence and of the simplest form. Paul Valery said that there is nothing as mysterious as clarity. The essence of the church is a clear and simple space, the home of those who want to be free within truth.

Located in *Hayang*, a secluded village with a beautiful name meaning "riverine sunshine," the church is only 50 square meters in area. It is a very small size church in a rural village but good enough to express the essence of the church. A brick company offered red bricks for free, and all the construction work was done only with bricks. In its simplest form, it creates the clearest space and light. The words that there is nothing as mysterious as clarity could be realized here. The space that is not enough has been complemented by the outdoor chapel. This place has become a place of communion where people in the neighborhood can easily come and renew their communal life.

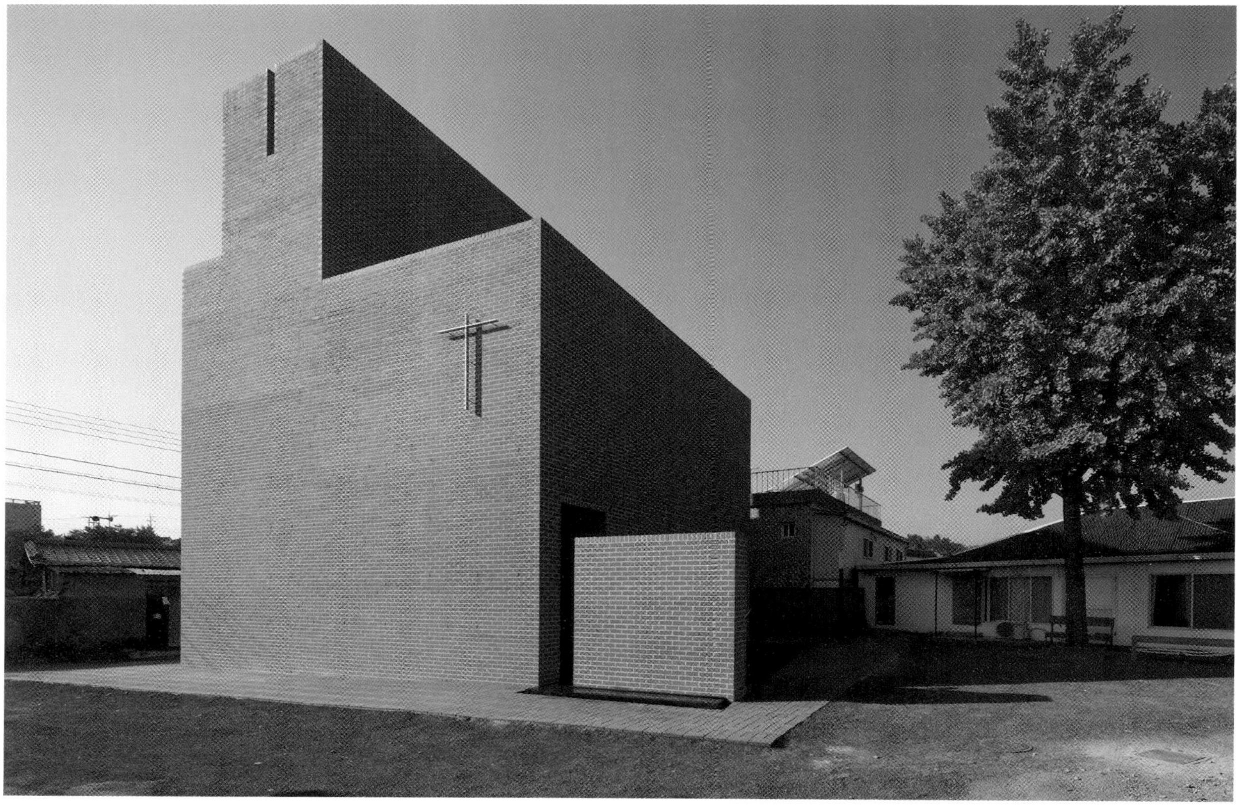

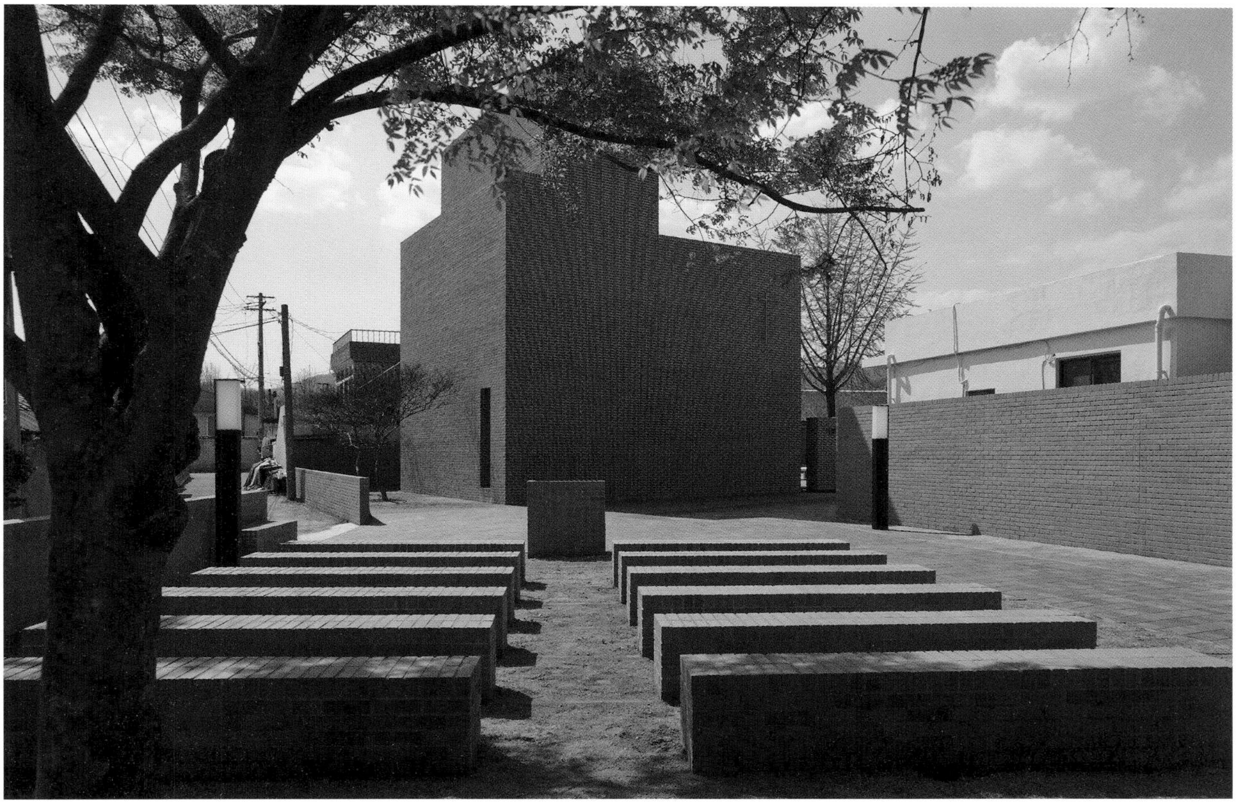

Muhakro Methodist Church

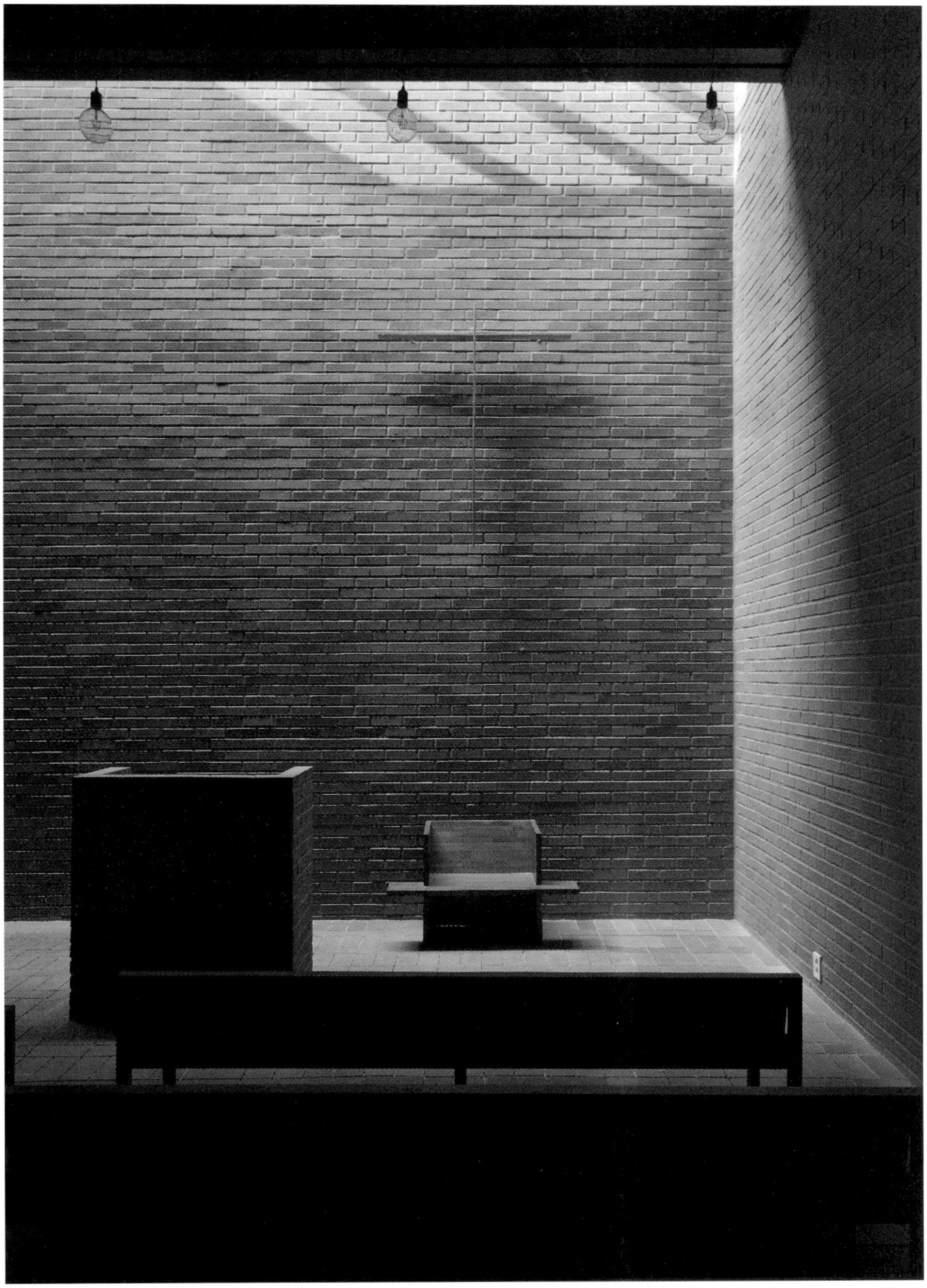

– 96   Muhakro Methodist Church

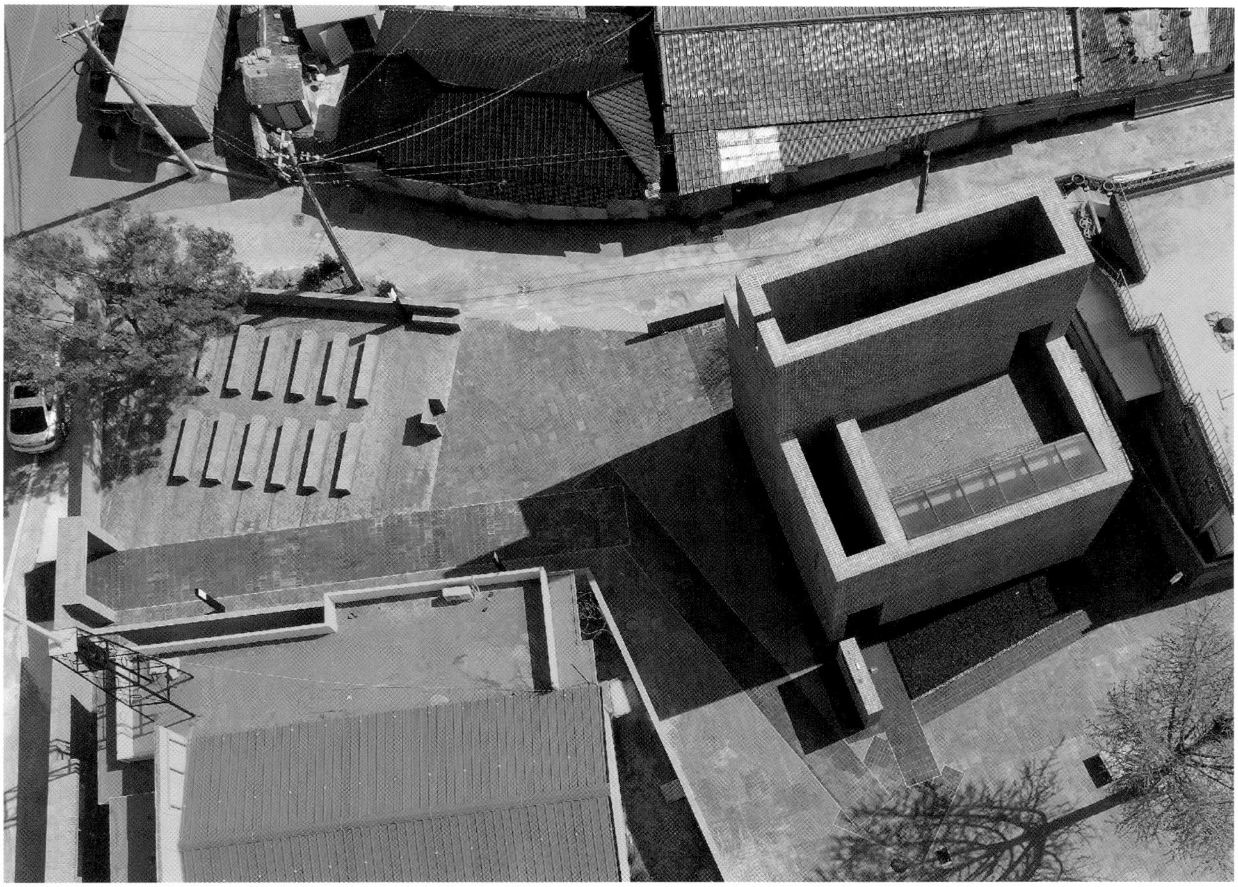

The building owner, or my client who discovered a new joy of life in a small house named Moheon that I designed in the City of Daegu, began constructing an arboretum in a 100 ha mountain area in Gunwi, Korea. While he had long transplanted 600-year-old quince trees, thinned the forest, and observed the change of the nature, he wanted to build the first house to live in there. The site is located in the middle of the mountain where people can see nothing but the rugged terrain and the sky. It faces the west, surely giving us a chance to see the sun going down over the reservoir and giving warmth in the winter season along the path of the sun.

The client hoped that his future arboretum would be a place for meditation. This is why the five small artificial gardens along the access road were made, passing through the dense pine tree forest, to this cottage. While these are all small, it seems that the contrast of the slope and the flatland around each of the gardens would be a trigger for meditation. At the end of the gardens, people will see a Corten steel structure along the straight slope. Above this structure, we will see an artificial hill while seeing the valley below. Entering the structure through the door, people will find themselves overwhelmed by a deep embrace of the majestic natural landscape. No architectural concept exists there, only he or she and the nature remain in complete silence.

If visitors are fortunately there at sunset, they could see the beautiful glow of the setting sun. When they climb on the hill and sit down on a cold Corten steel chair in the middle of silver grass, they will feel like as part of the nature. This is a completely solitary moment, and a moment for philosophy. This is why the house was named *Hyeonam*, which literally means a black and shady cottage.

When people see this house at a distance, they will find it protruded from the ground as if it just came out of the underground into the world after waiting for a long time. That is why this house is yet to be completed and remains still.

「玄庵」
COGURO

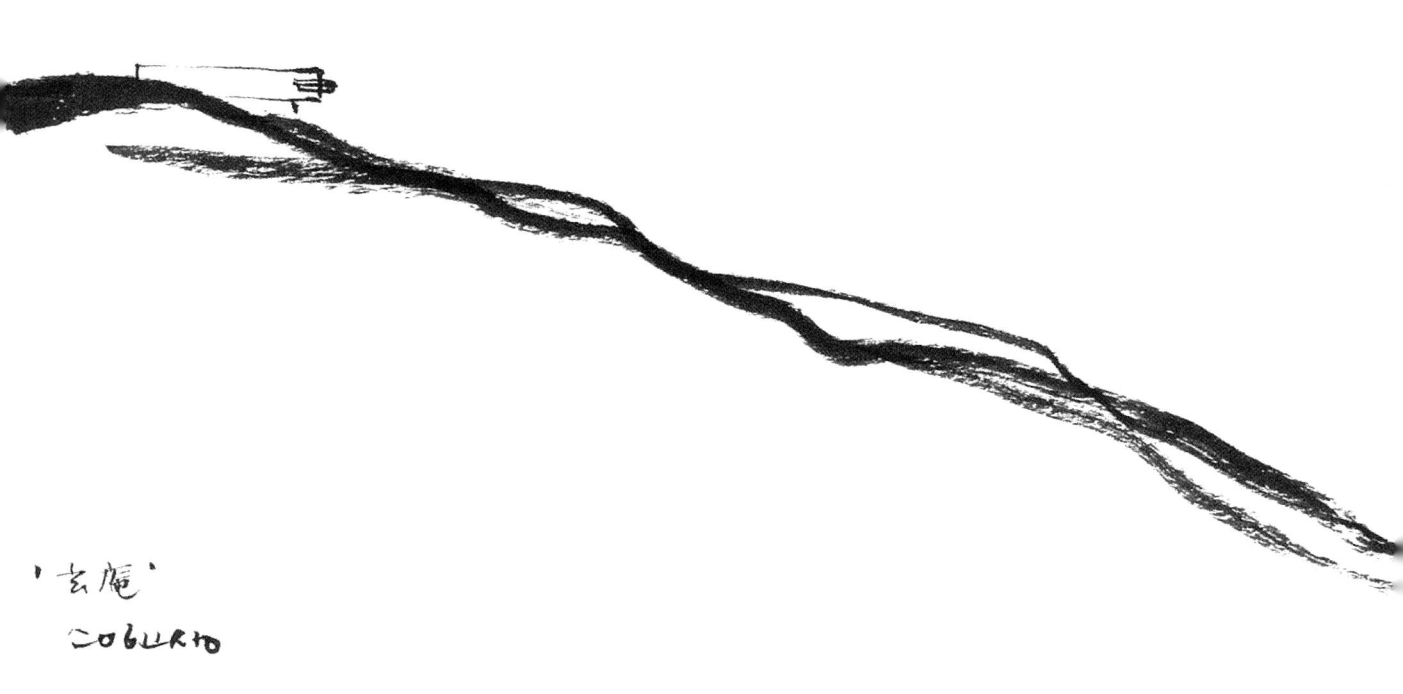

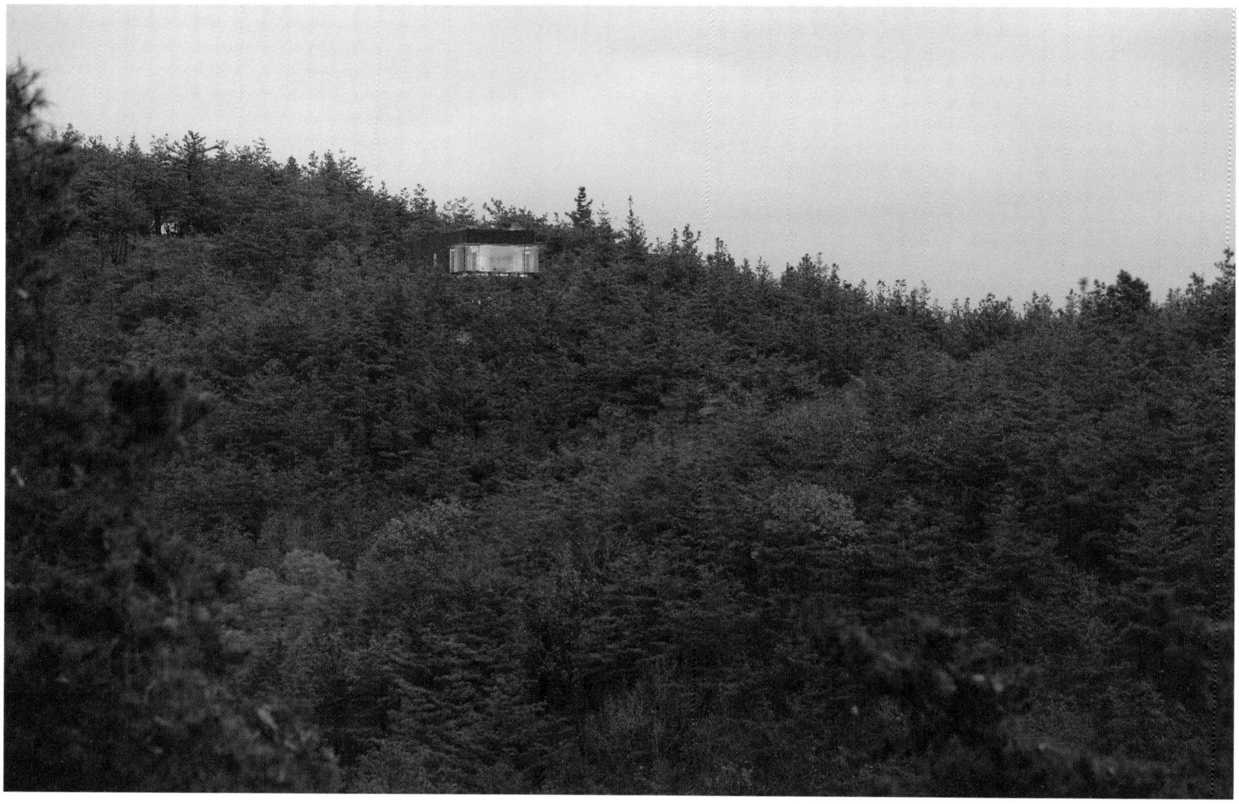

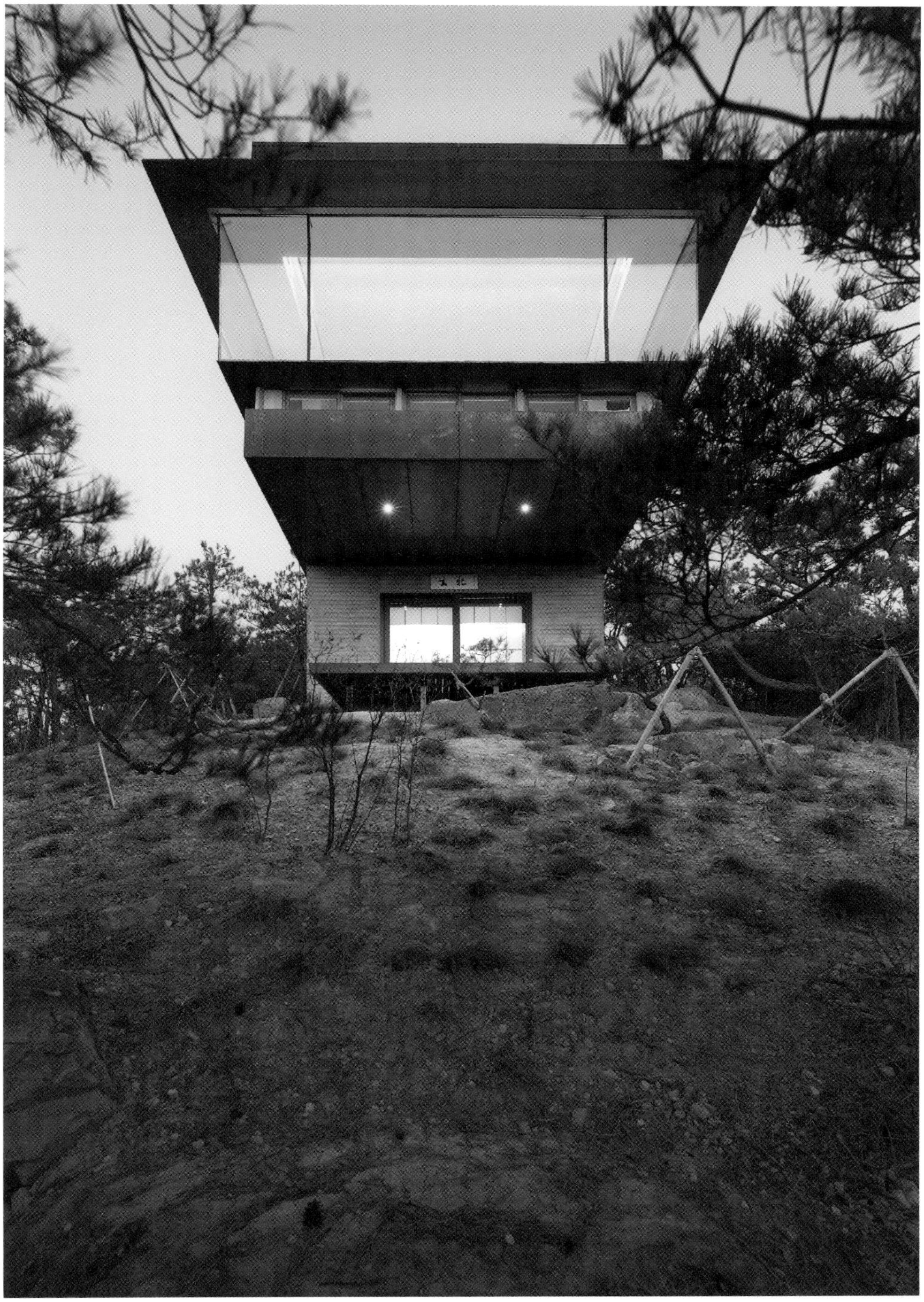

Bugye Arboretum "Sayuwon"— Hyeonam

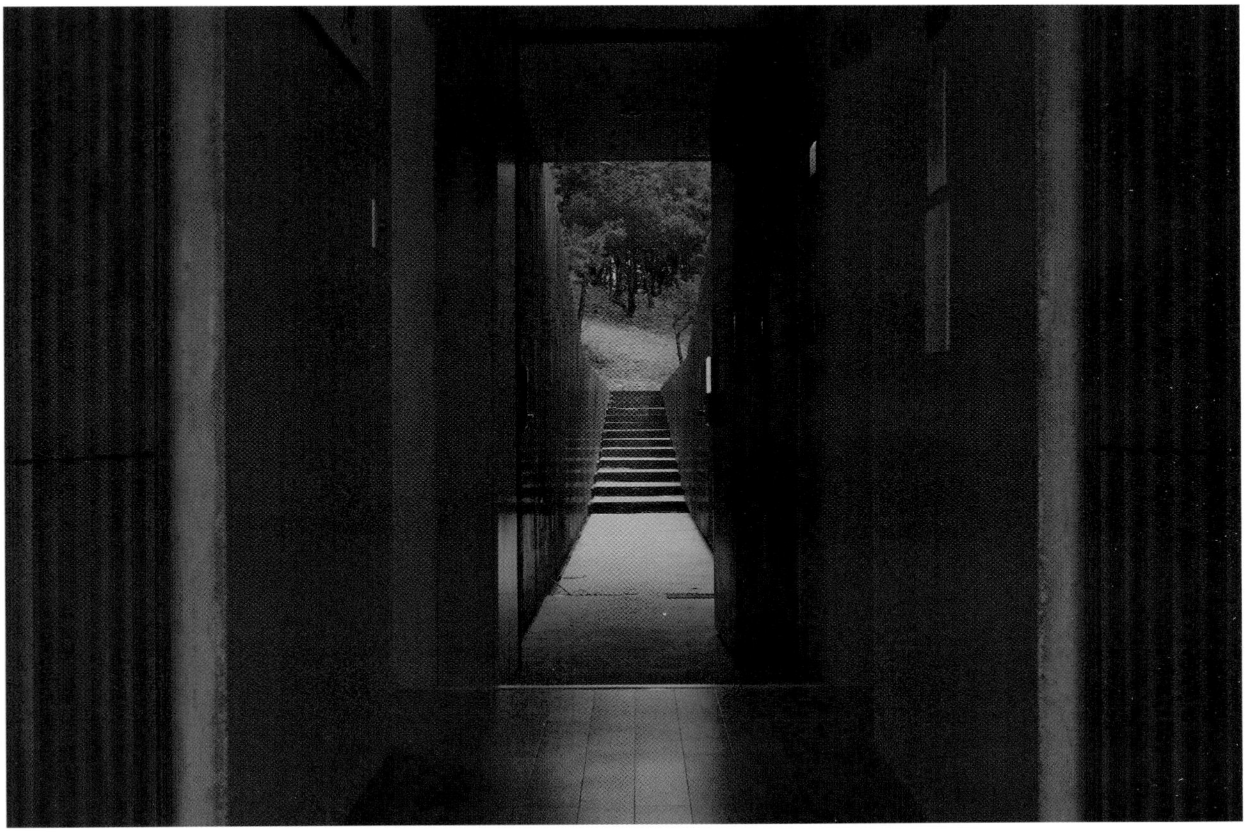

Bugye Arboretum "Sayuwon"— Hyeonam

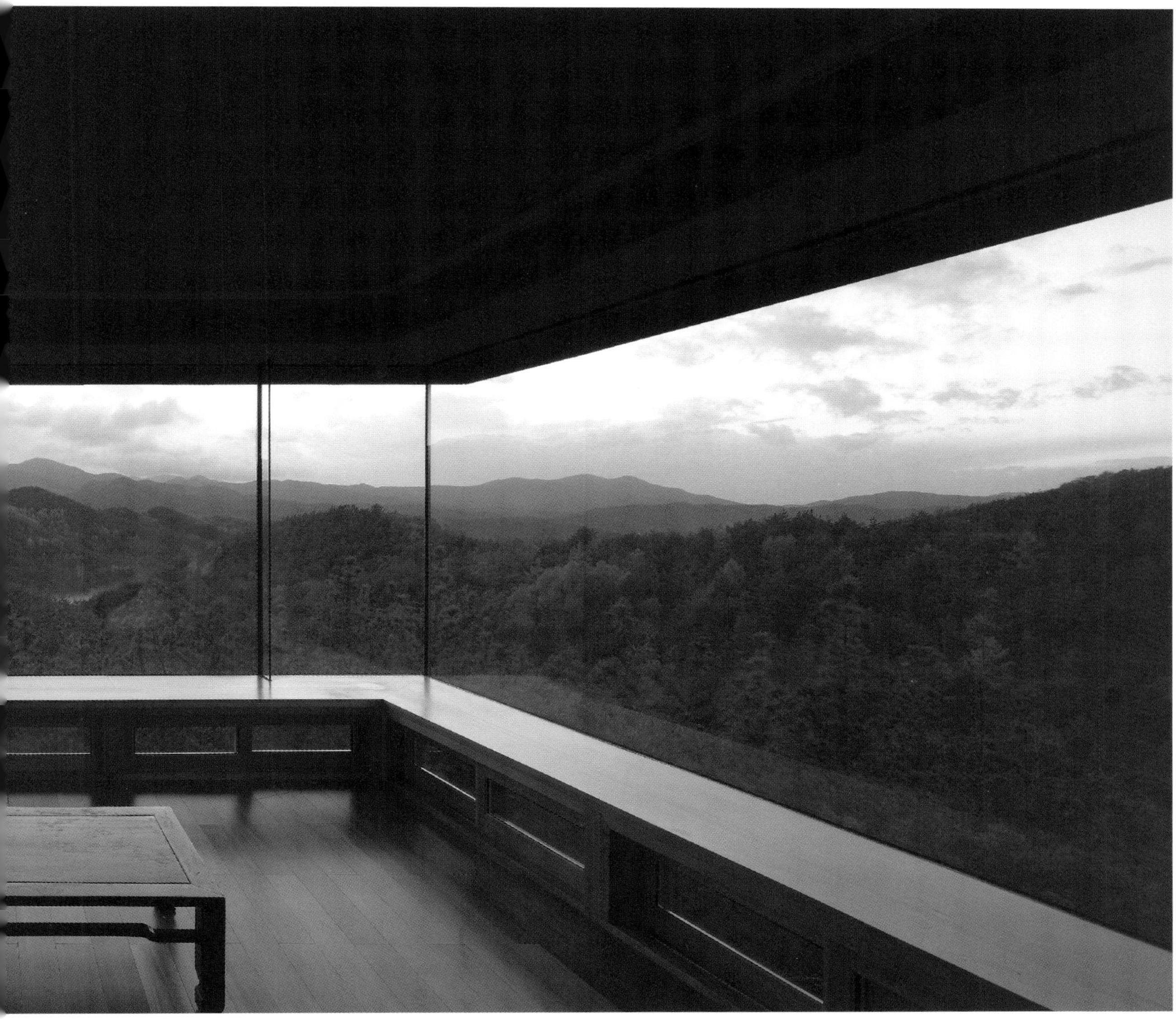

The primary function of this facility for enjoying cultural performances at the waterfront was established by creating a pond is background for a stage. The Corten steel wall, which does not corrode, stands up as if it were pulled out of the hill as the background for a beautiful performance. In the back of the wall, there is a small restaurant as well as subsidiary facilities for the performance where visitors can enjoy the scenery of the waterfront when there is no performance.

The stage is linked to the rooftop along with a steep stairway connecting to one end of the Corten wall. There is another stage on the rooftop which makes a three-dimensional performance possible if needed. Of course, the stage on the rooftop can function as a pavilion or observation deck for watching the surroundings. Especially when the sun sets, the scene of the audience, sitting on a long bench on the slope opposite the pond, watching the performance reflected on the pond looks like a beautiful picture. This project has been named Thinker's Pond.

水

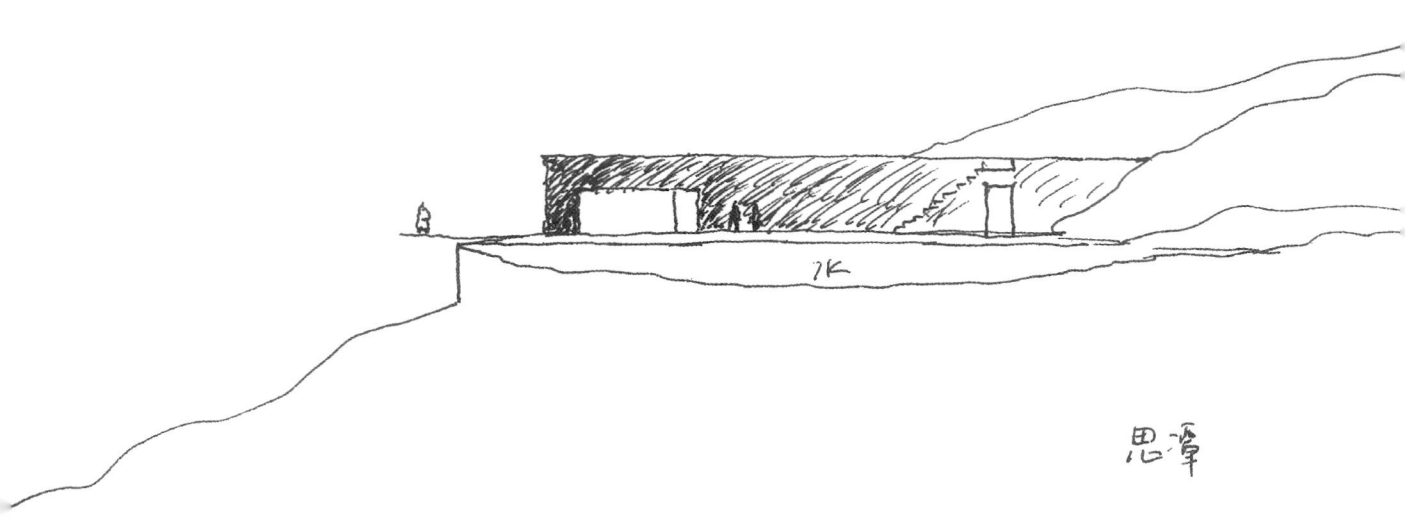

思潭

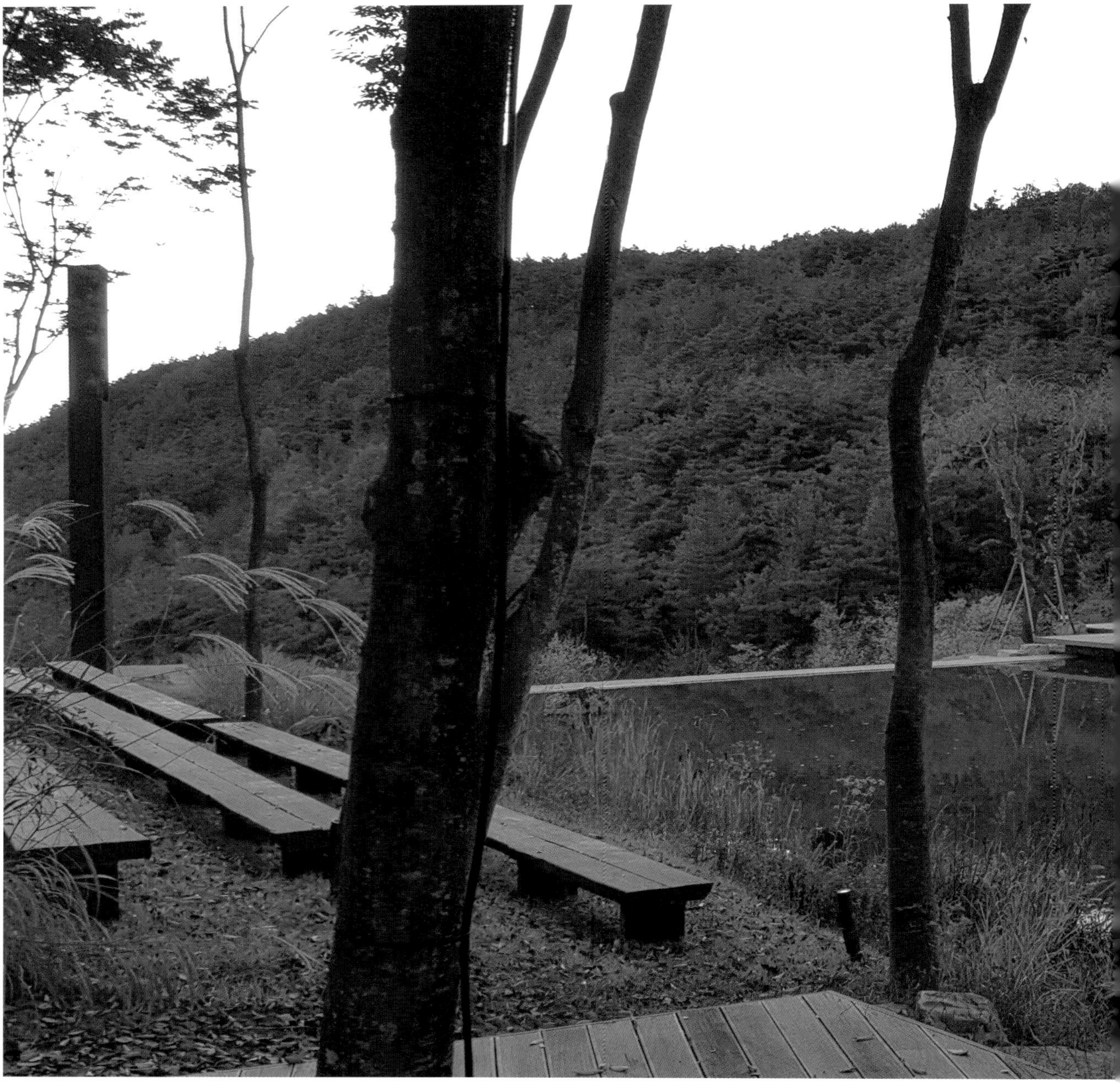

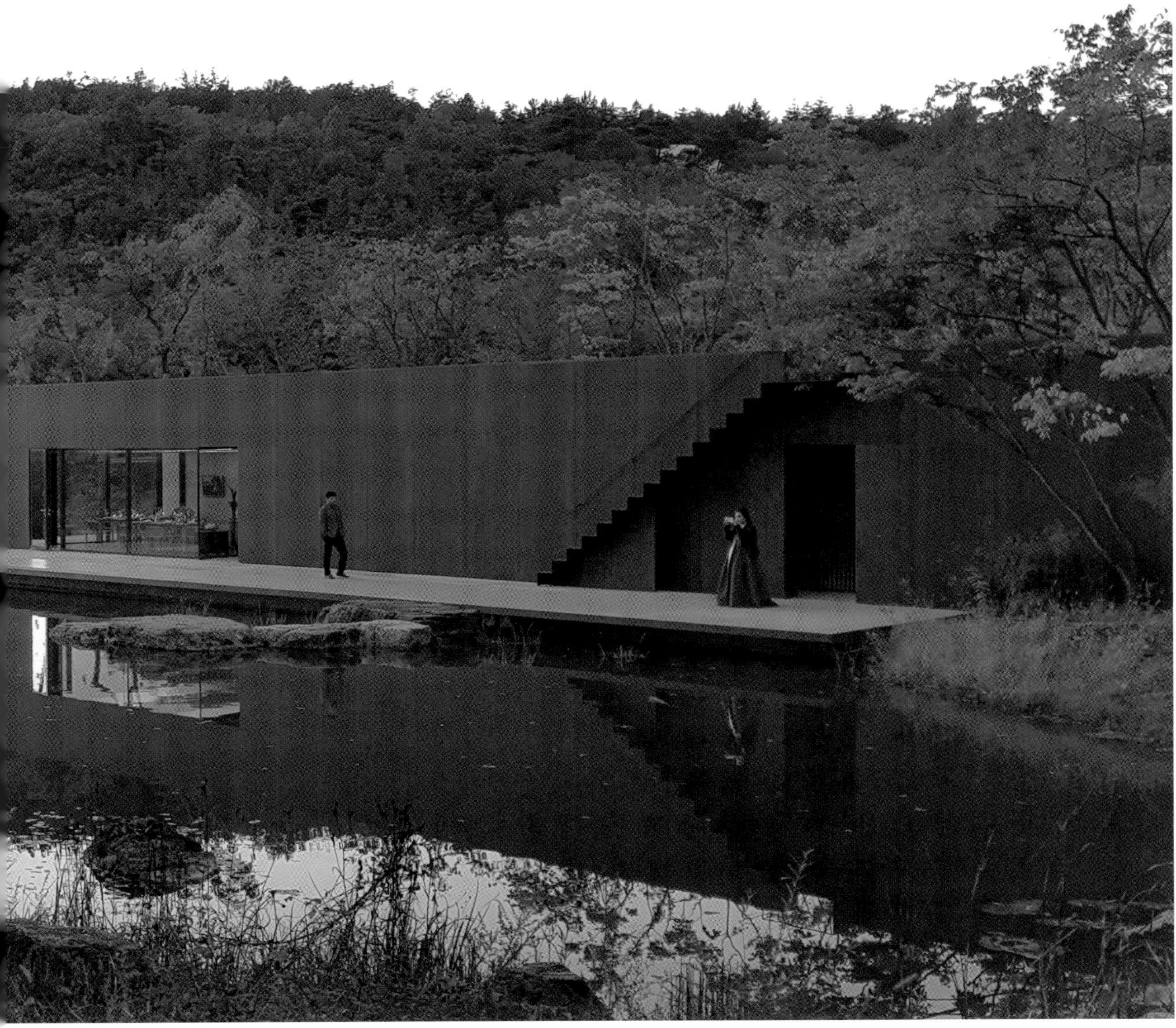

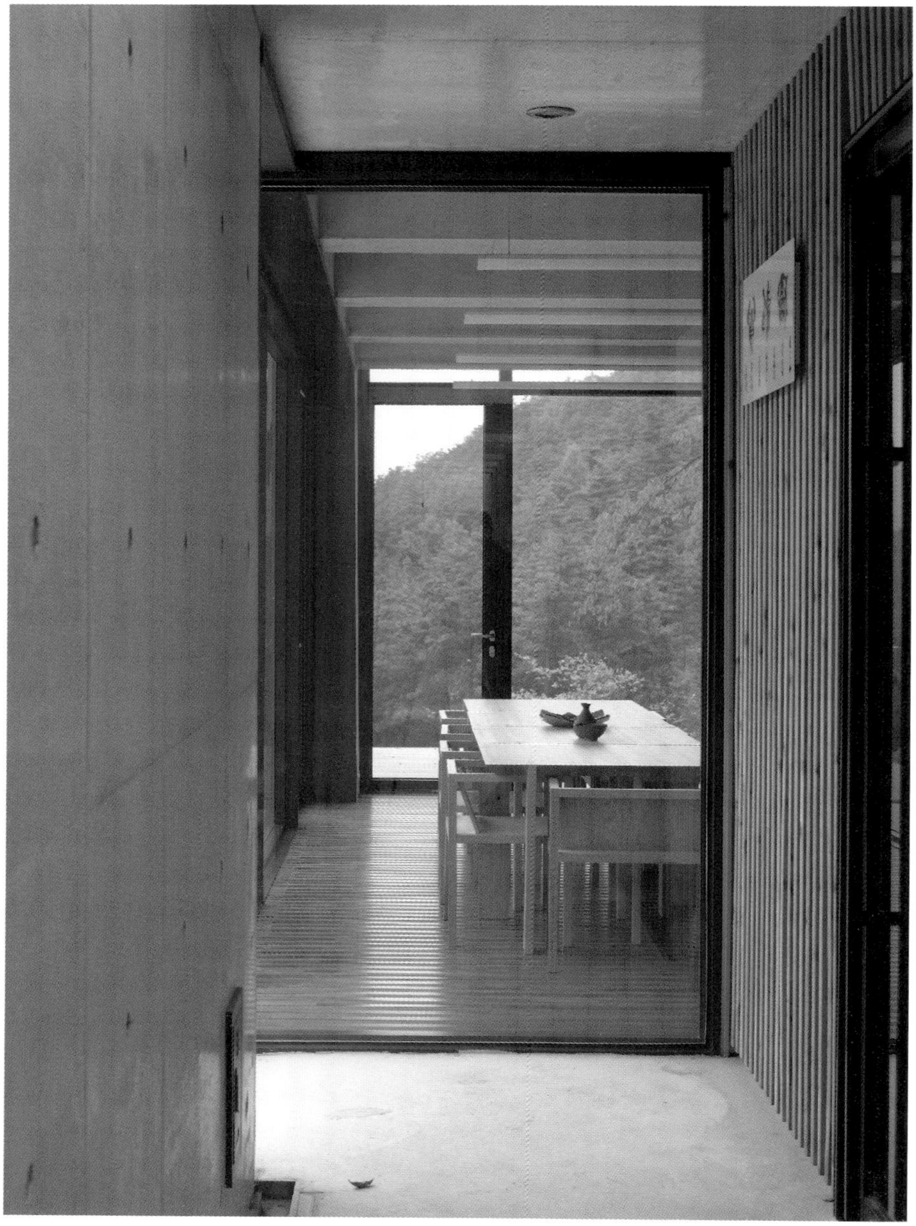

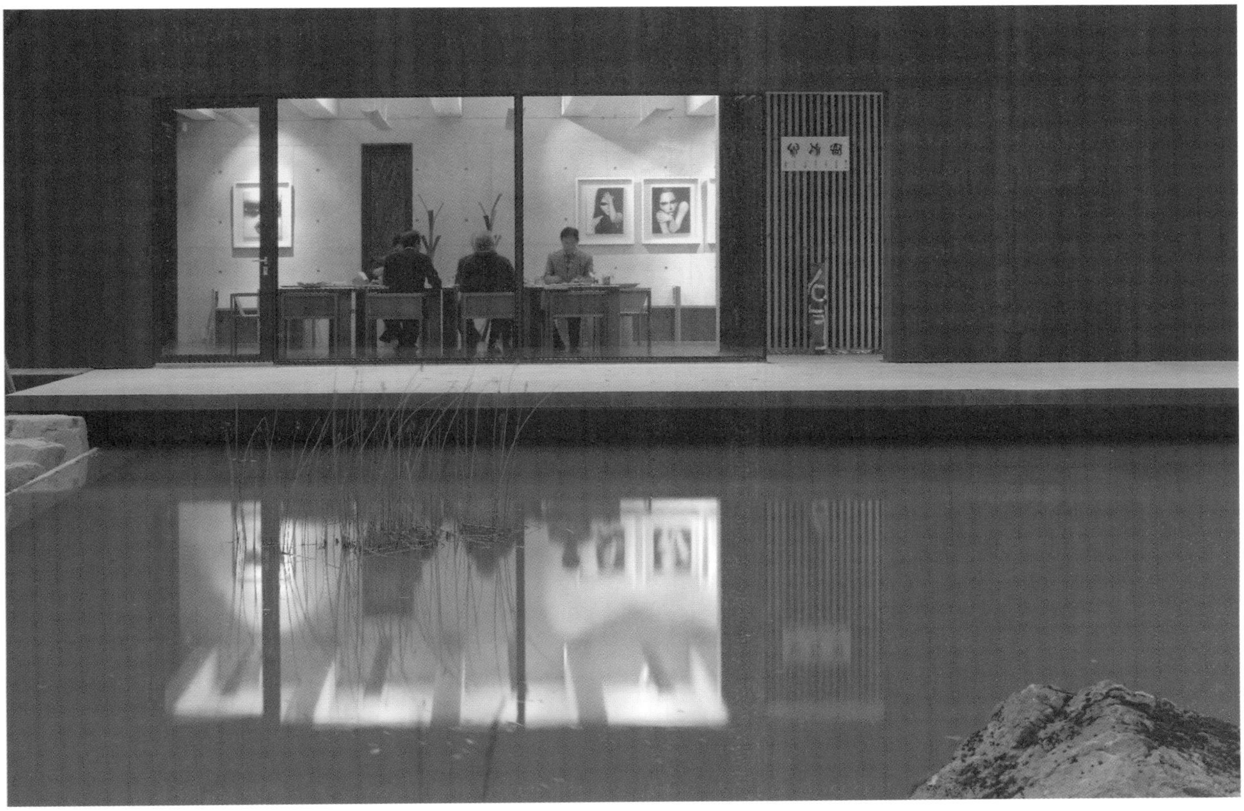

This place, asked for an observation deck on the northern peak of the arboretum, is the place where visitors come after seeing almost all the beautiful scenery of the arboretum. Therefore, in order to make the view of the arboretum more beautiful to those who bring all the memories of the arboretum, it is necessary to keep the memory in mind. This is why this place is not a mere observation deck but a place for the visitors to reflect on themselves. Thus, this place was named *Myeongjeong* (Meditation Garden) at the first beginning of design, and the entire facility was pushed into the ground. Only the concrete front wall is visible, but even the concrete wall is covered by a fir forest. When people go up a slope led by a long wall, they will see a small opening and a long aisle. If going along this narrow passage and turn the direction, the descending stairs is connected. When people go down the stairs 27 meters and turn the direction, they will encounter an unexpected space. There, people will see water running on the stone wall, the floor covered with the water, and the stage on the opposite side connected by a passage over the water. A long bench of concrete awaits them in front of the water. No trees can be seen here.

When people go in passing the water-flowing wall, a long silent space appears, and there are tabernacles like small sanctuaries in this space. They can hear only the mere sound of the water running down the stone wall, but the sound of silence prevails. What lies here is only meditation.

It is truly spectacular to see the landscape of the arboretum spreading to the south and the soft and delicate silhouette of Mount Palgong which seems to have enveloped all the whole world when people go up the narrow and steep staircase made between the stone walls. This landscape is different from the one they saw first and it will be a new world again.

瞑庭

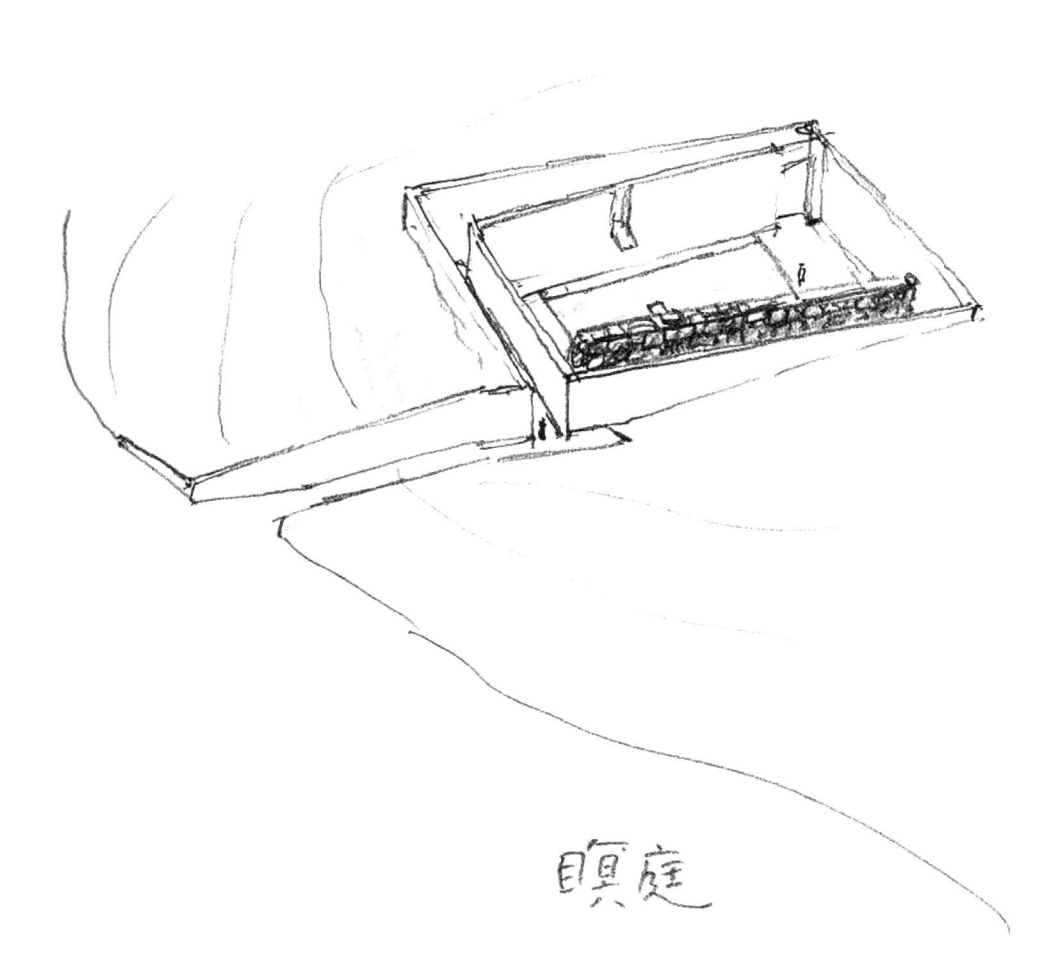

Bugye Arboretum "Sayuwon"— Myeongjeong

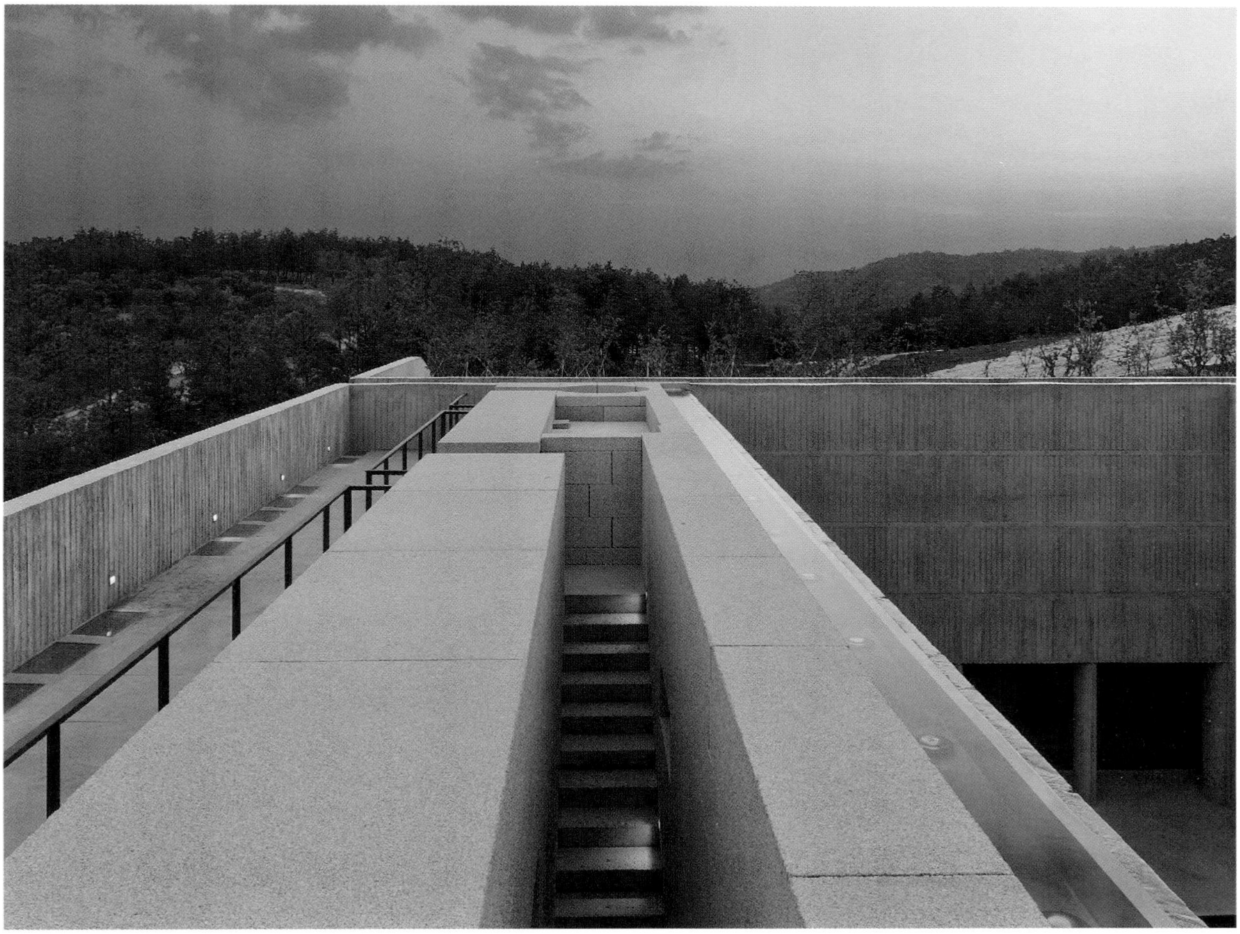

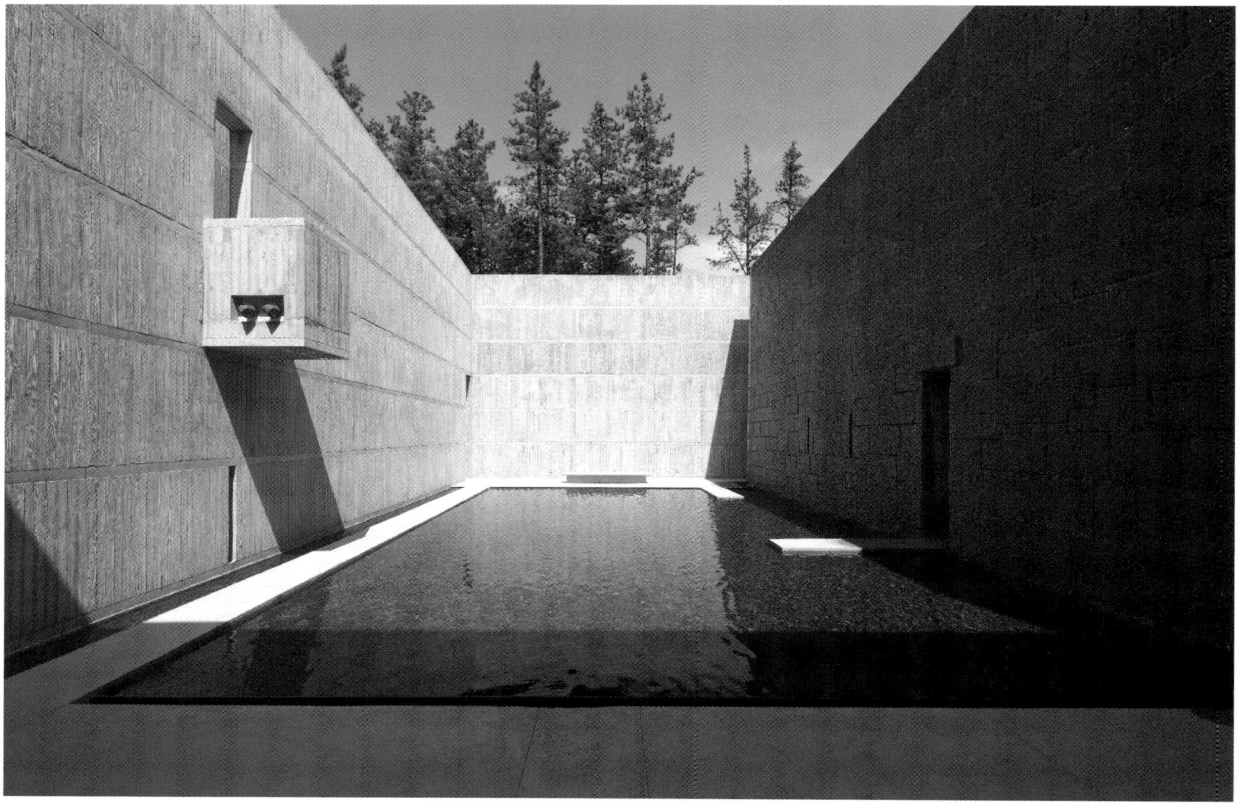

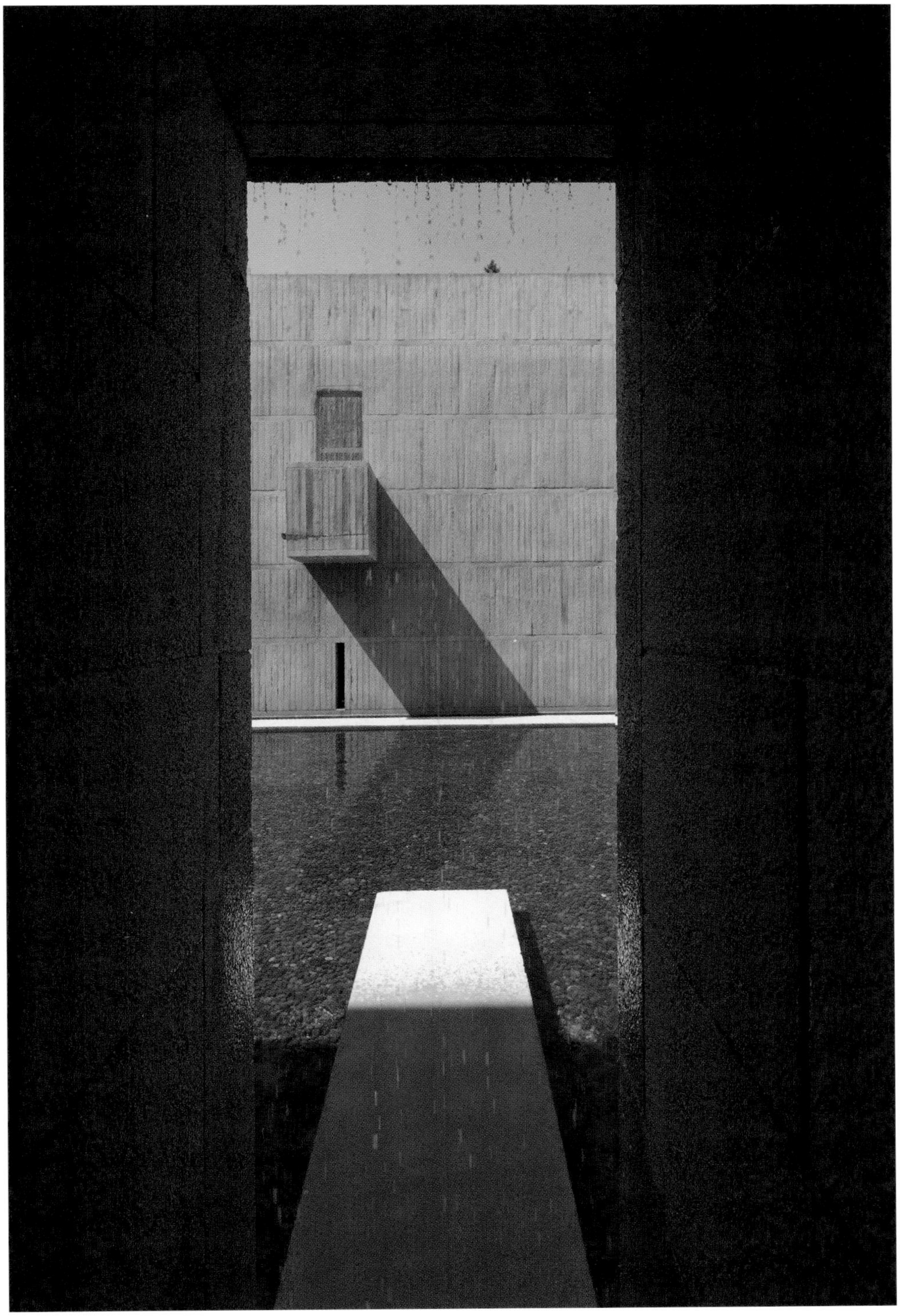

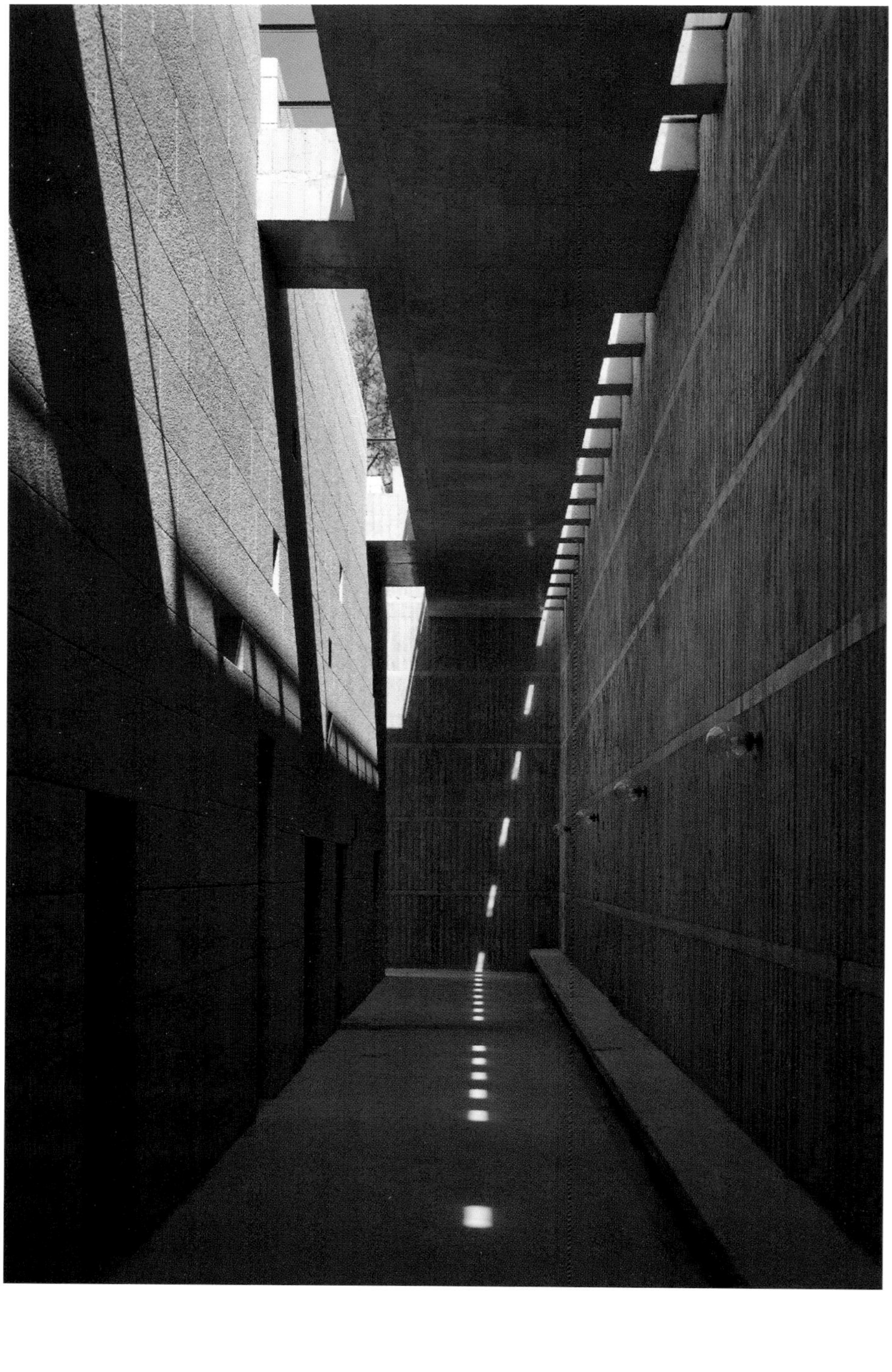

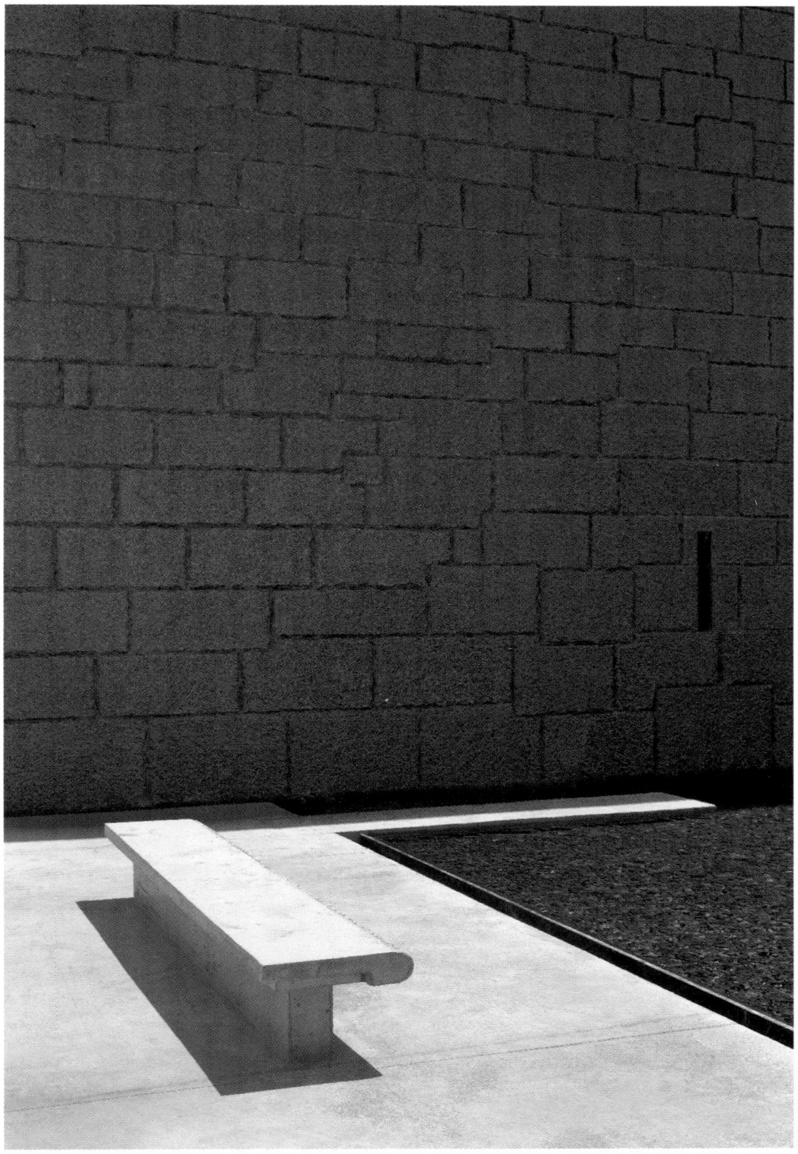

Three ponds were built in the steep valley down the lower part of the arboretum. It was considered that visitors would need resting shelters along the ponds. Although the ponds are different in height and size, some adding facilities should be better if connected. It was, however, the most isolated place in the entire arboretum and needed a special facility worth visiting here. It was a monastery. However, according to the legal requirements, it was not possible to construct an architectural building. Instead, it was decided to build a structure as like an artistic work with space. In the case of an artistic structure with space, it was needless to equip the structure with measures indispensable for living such as insulation and protecting from extreme weather of outside. Instead, it was possible to concentrate on the essence of the space of the structure.

The structure should be long if it can run along the three connected ponds. This concept may lead to an idea of a monastery lying down. As such, the interior space of the long Corten steel box was divided for an imagined arrangement of such places as a chapel, refectory, chapter room, and dormitory. The facility is made to look like an organism with its height changing according to the terrain. The tower on the side of the structure is the bathroom, where small wind-chimes are hung so that visitors can feel that they are in a temple, at the bell sound, in the middle of the mountains. If people take some time to lean on this facility just for a while and look at the water in the pond, they will feel how beautiful the world is.

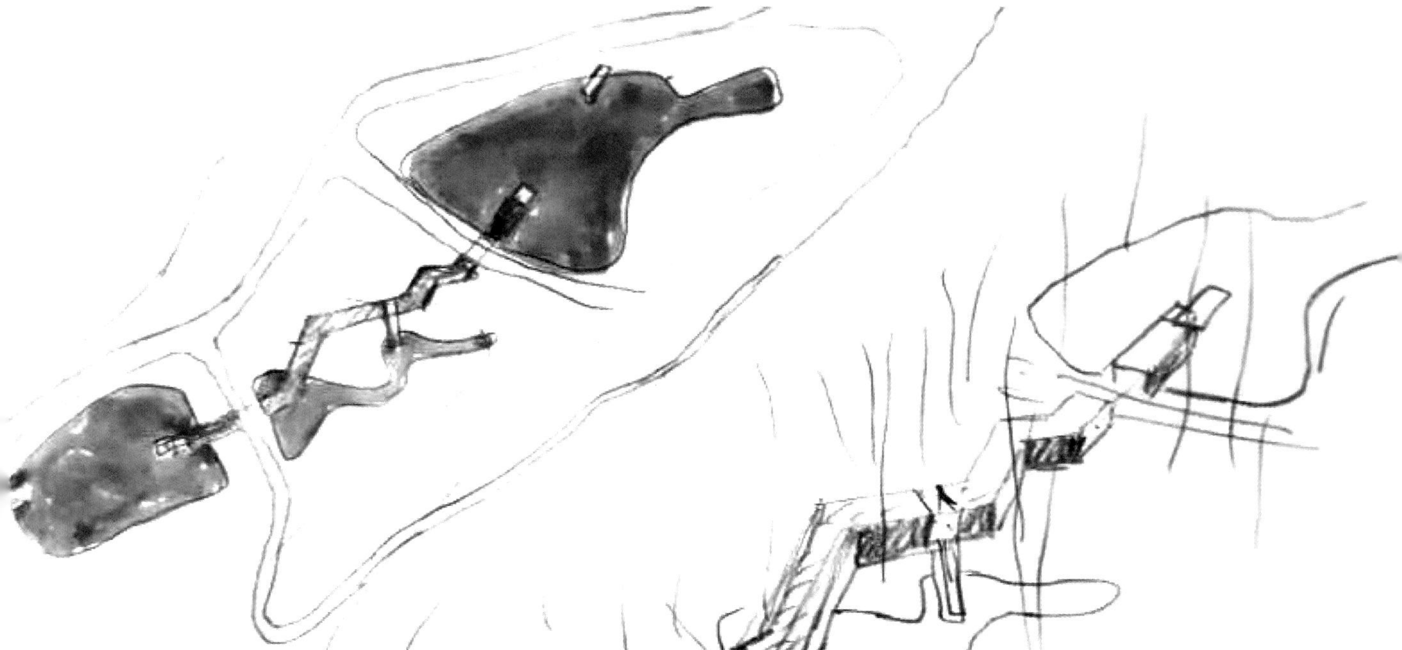

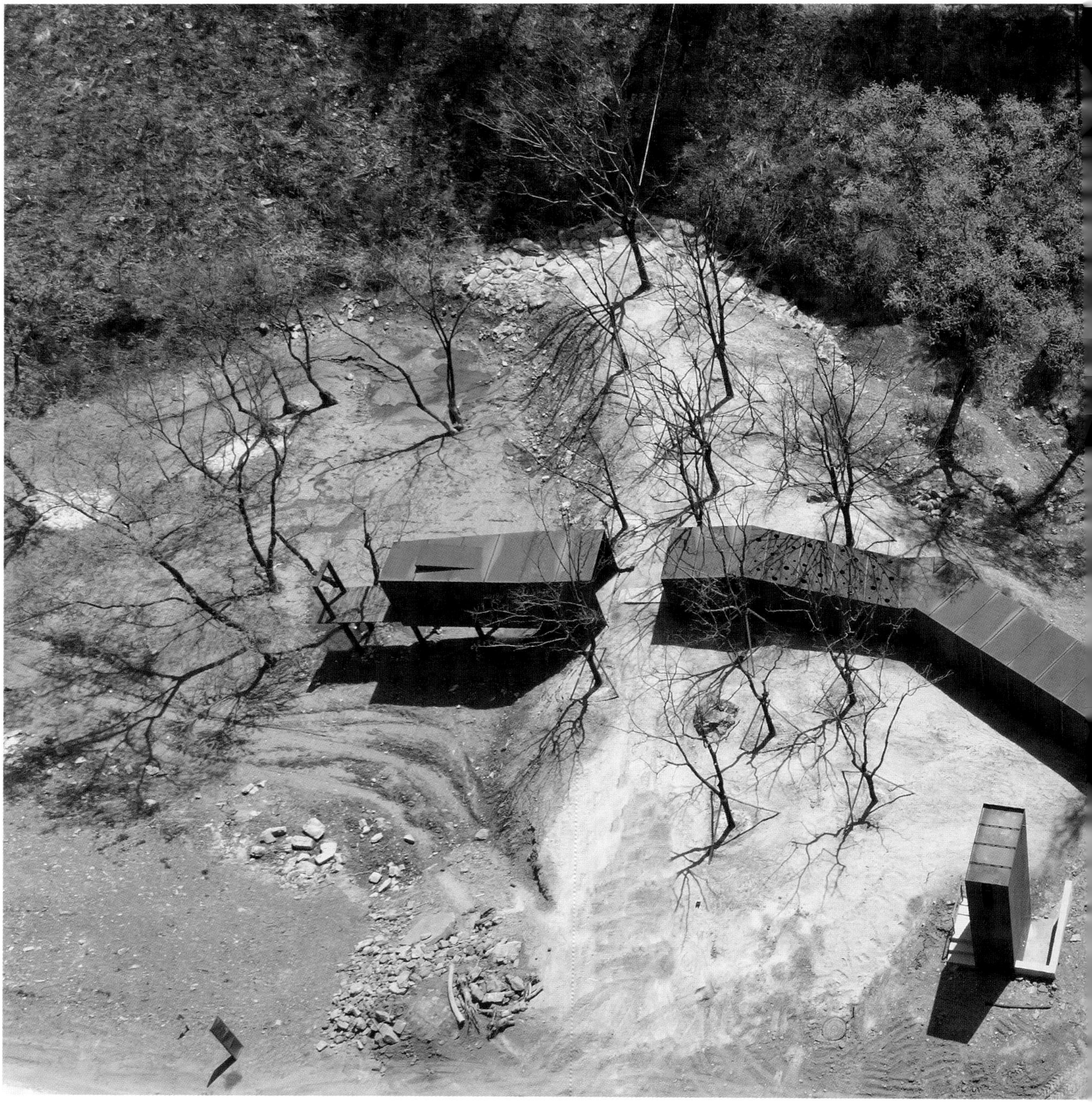

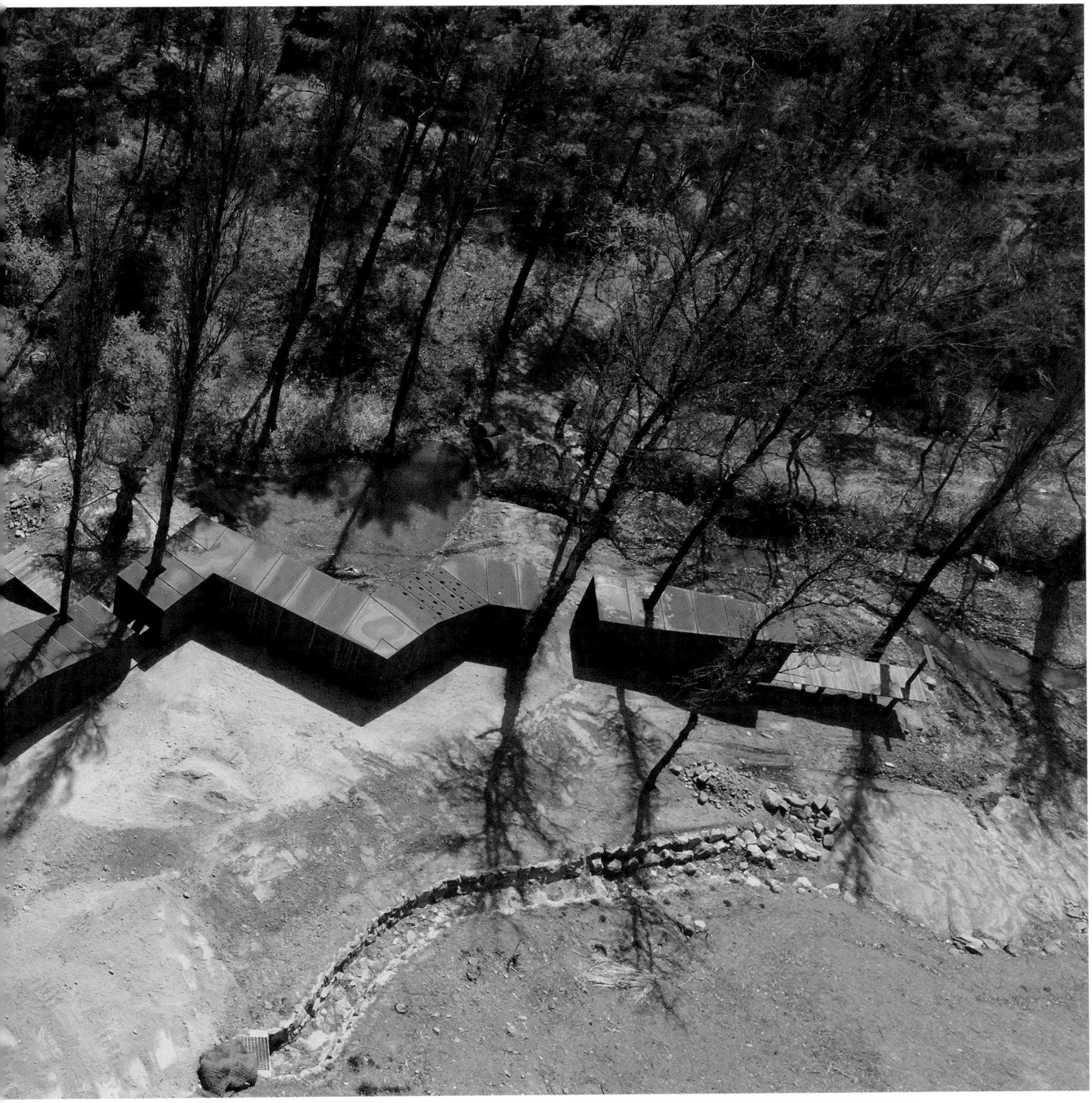

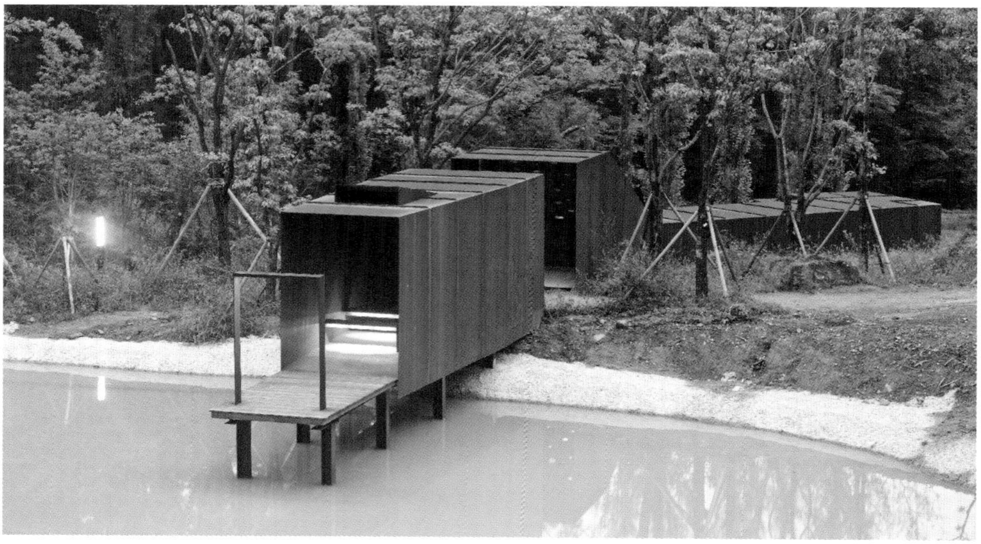

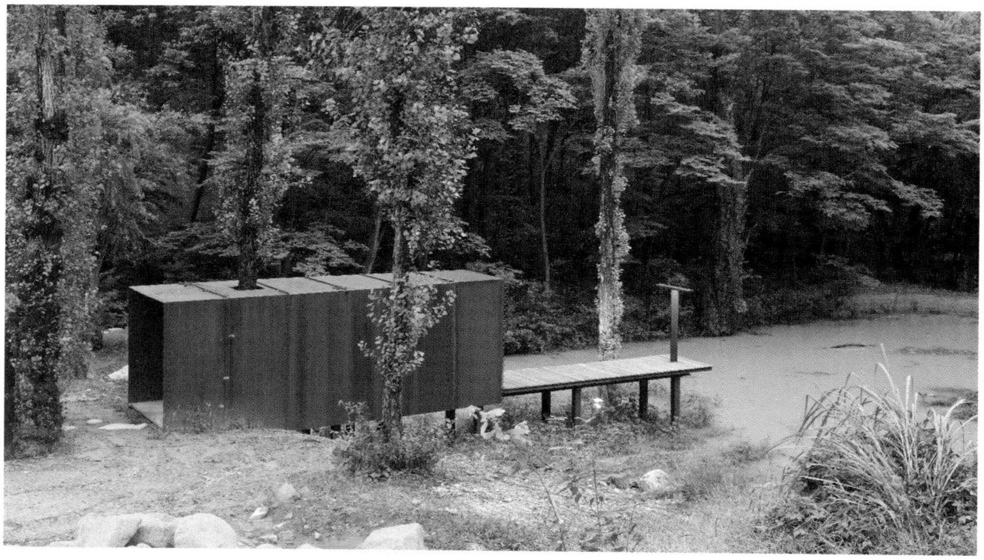

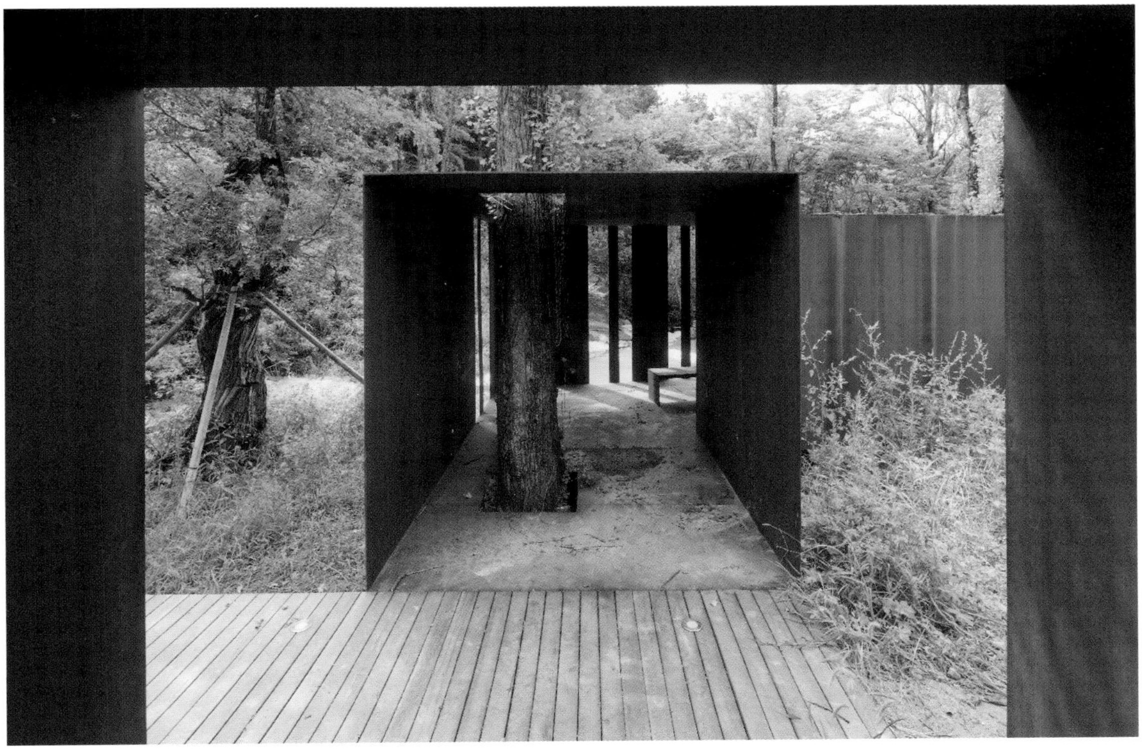

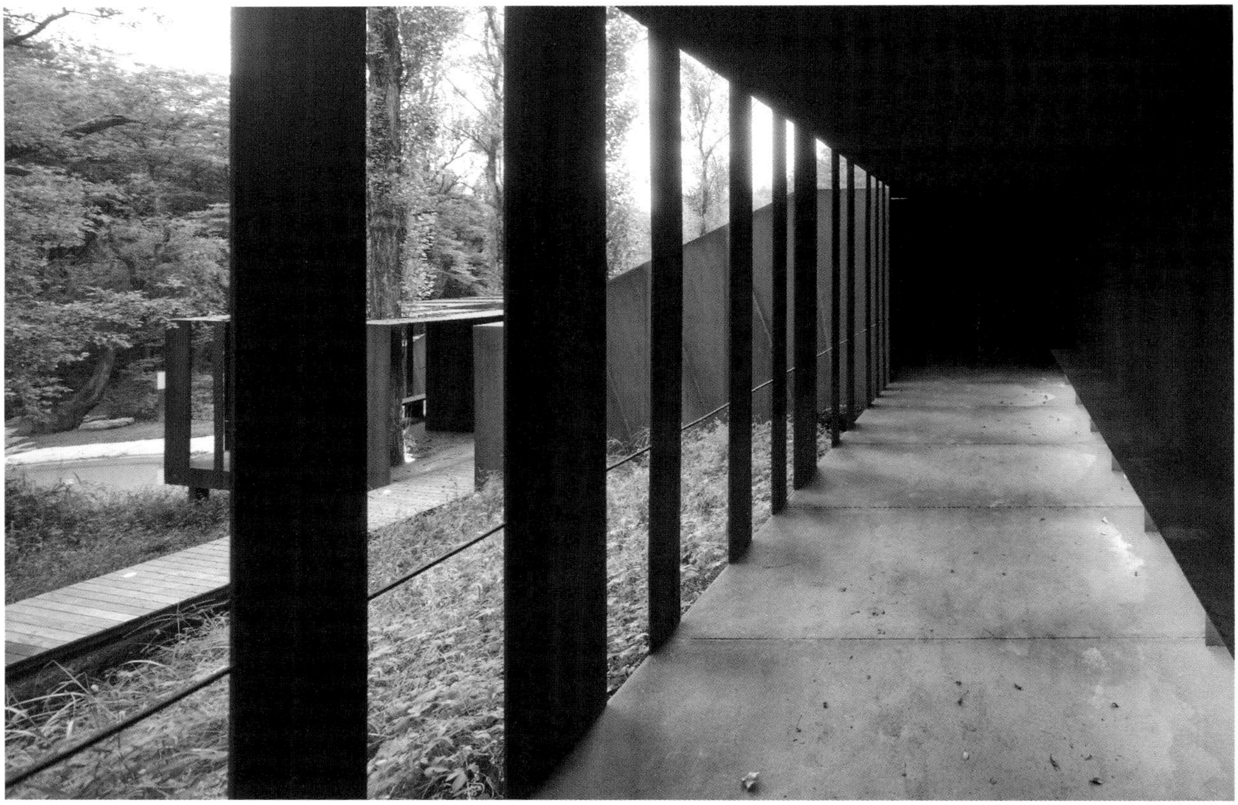

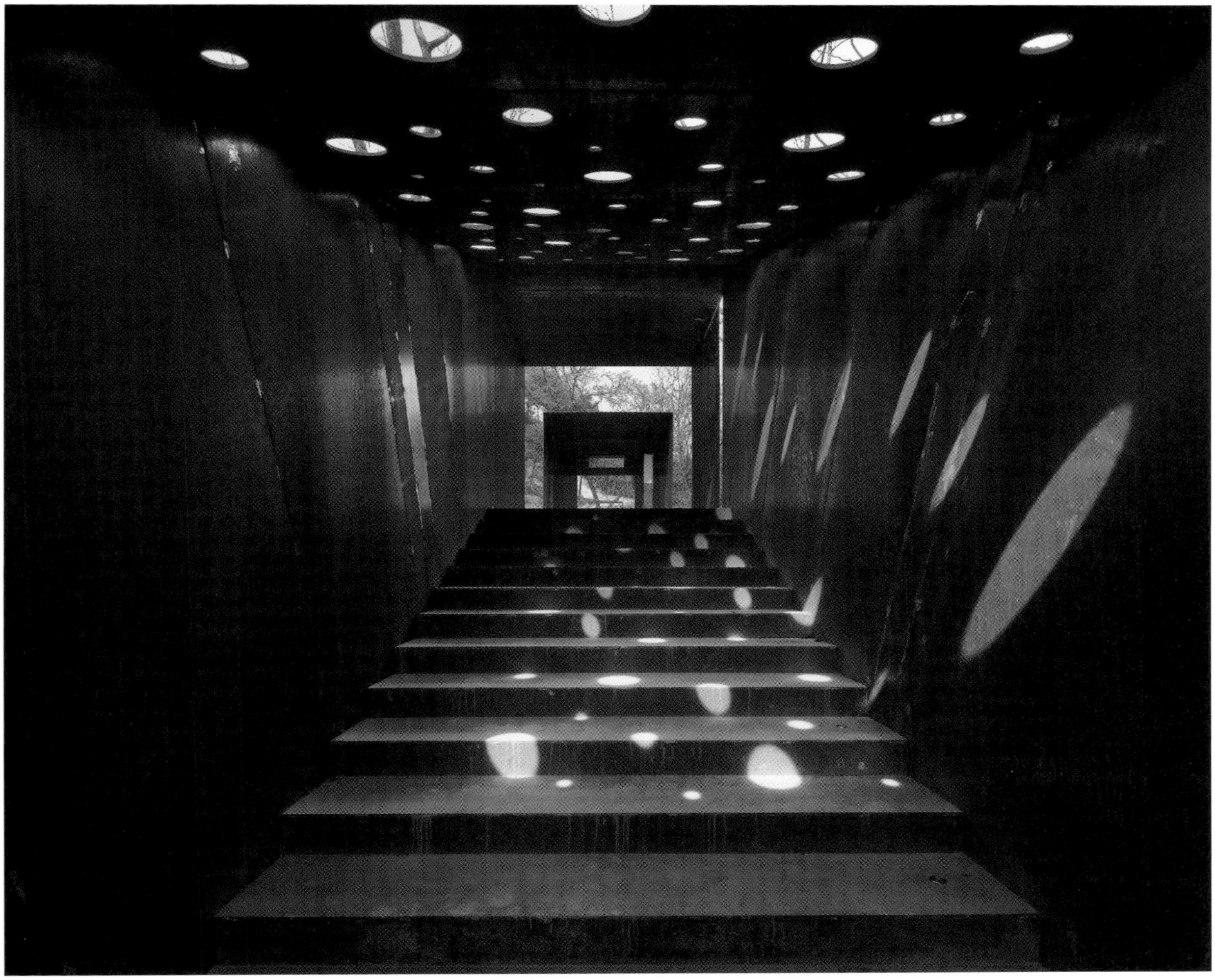

There are several attached facilities in this arboretum: the parking lot around the entrance, the benches along the strolling alleys and makeshift performance stages, as well as the ecological restrooms scattered over the place. Made of Corten steel, wood or concrete, they play a big role in expressing the identity of the whole arboretum.

Besides, two large water tanks supplying water to the entire site were asked to install in two places. One was built in the ground, and its upper surface was made to serve as a viewing platform to take a view of the quince orchard. The other was built on the hill top, and it may be used as another viewing pavilion to look over the east. This concrete structure has a staircase that rises up along the wall, and the structure was divided into several segments that look like a small fort. It also serves as an observatory to look at the stars engraved on the sky chart. This is why the name of this structure is called *Cheomdan* or astronomical observatory. The vicinity of this area forms a special landscape, matching the small doors of the astronomical observatory made of stone with the far-reaching meadow.

PHIMEANAKAS

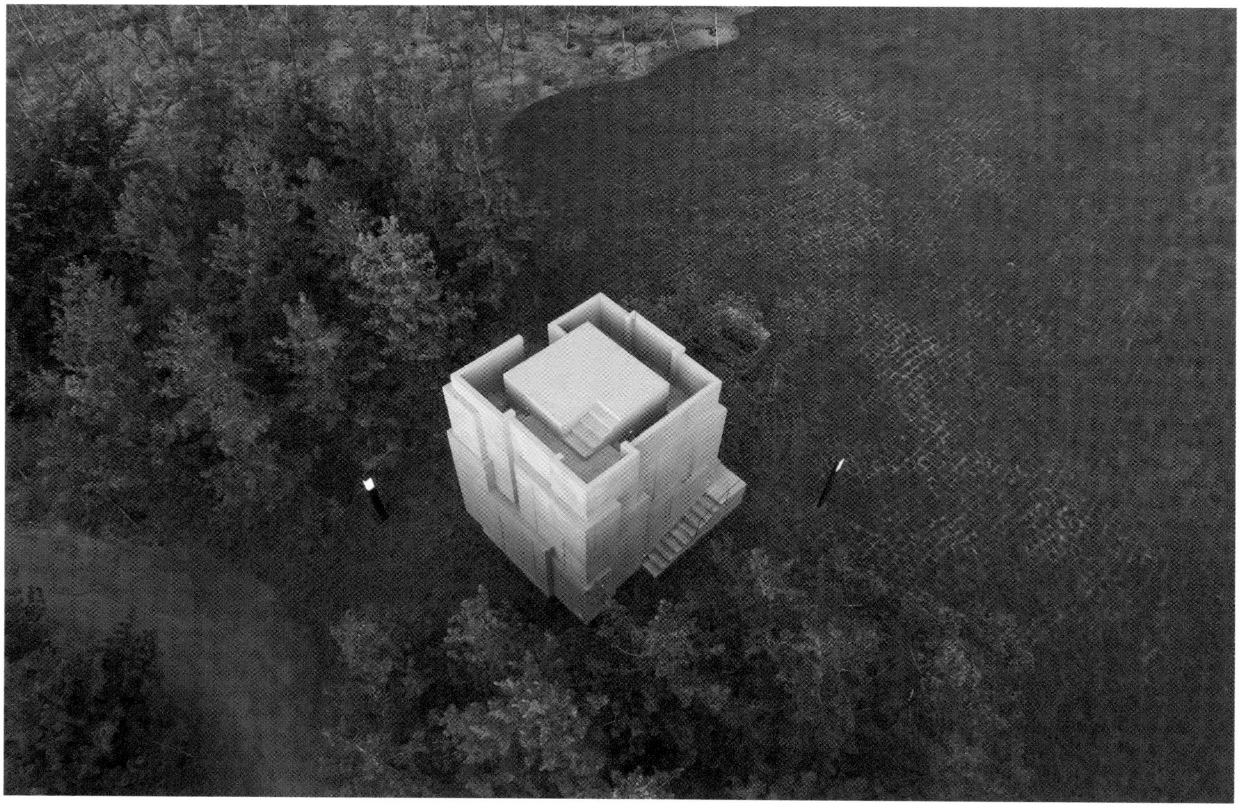

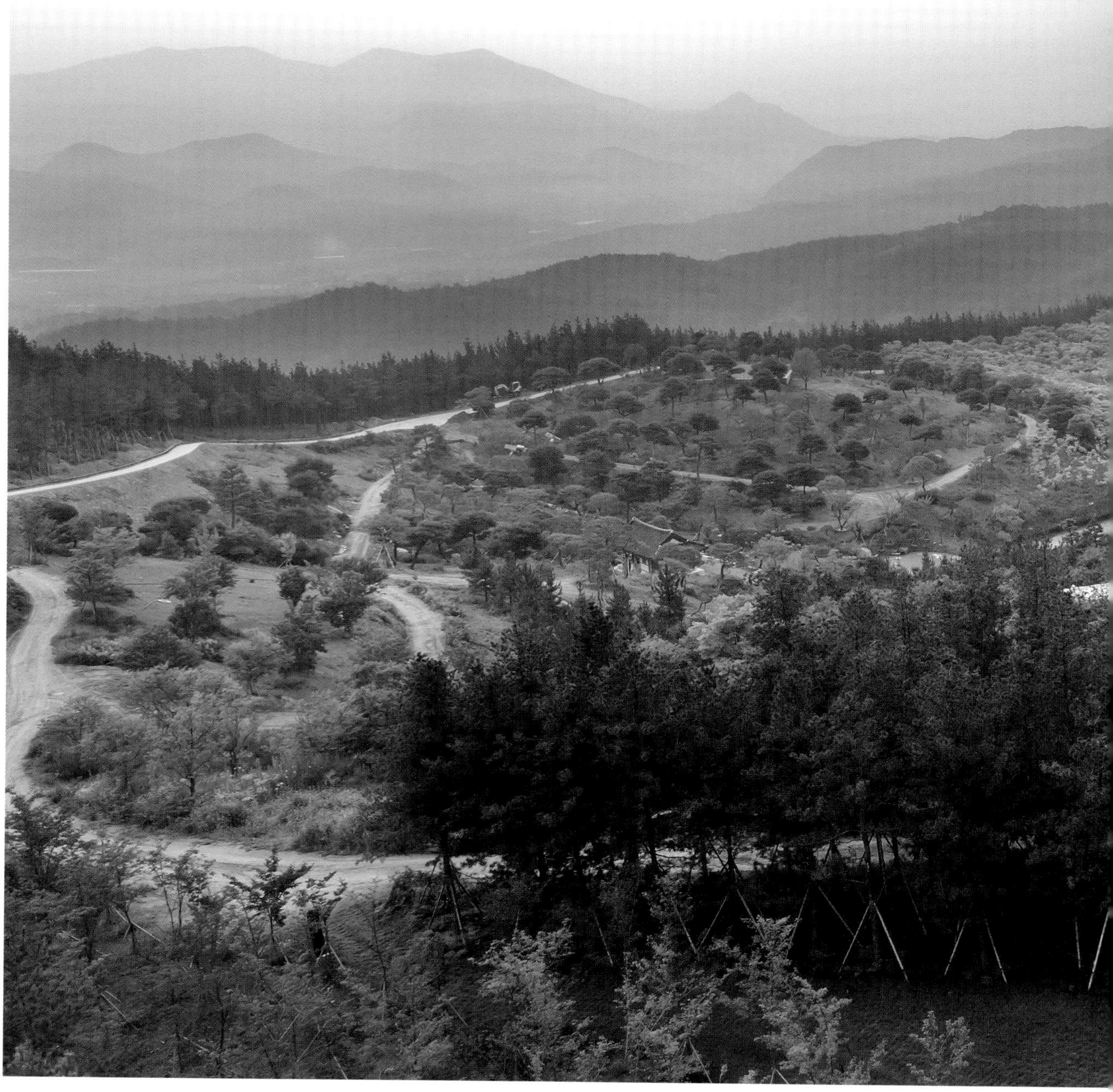

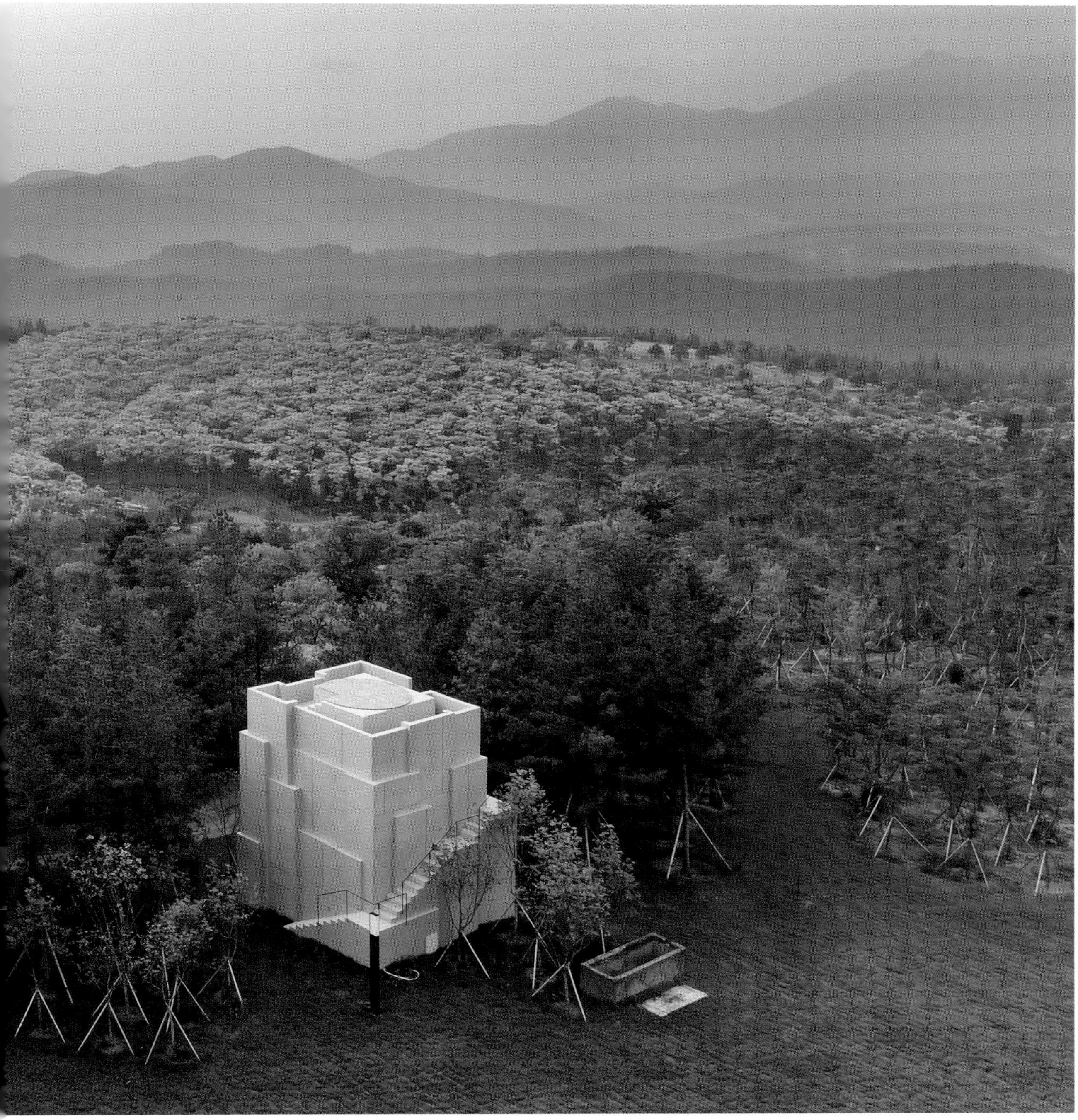

Bugye Arboretum "Sayuwon"— other attached facilities

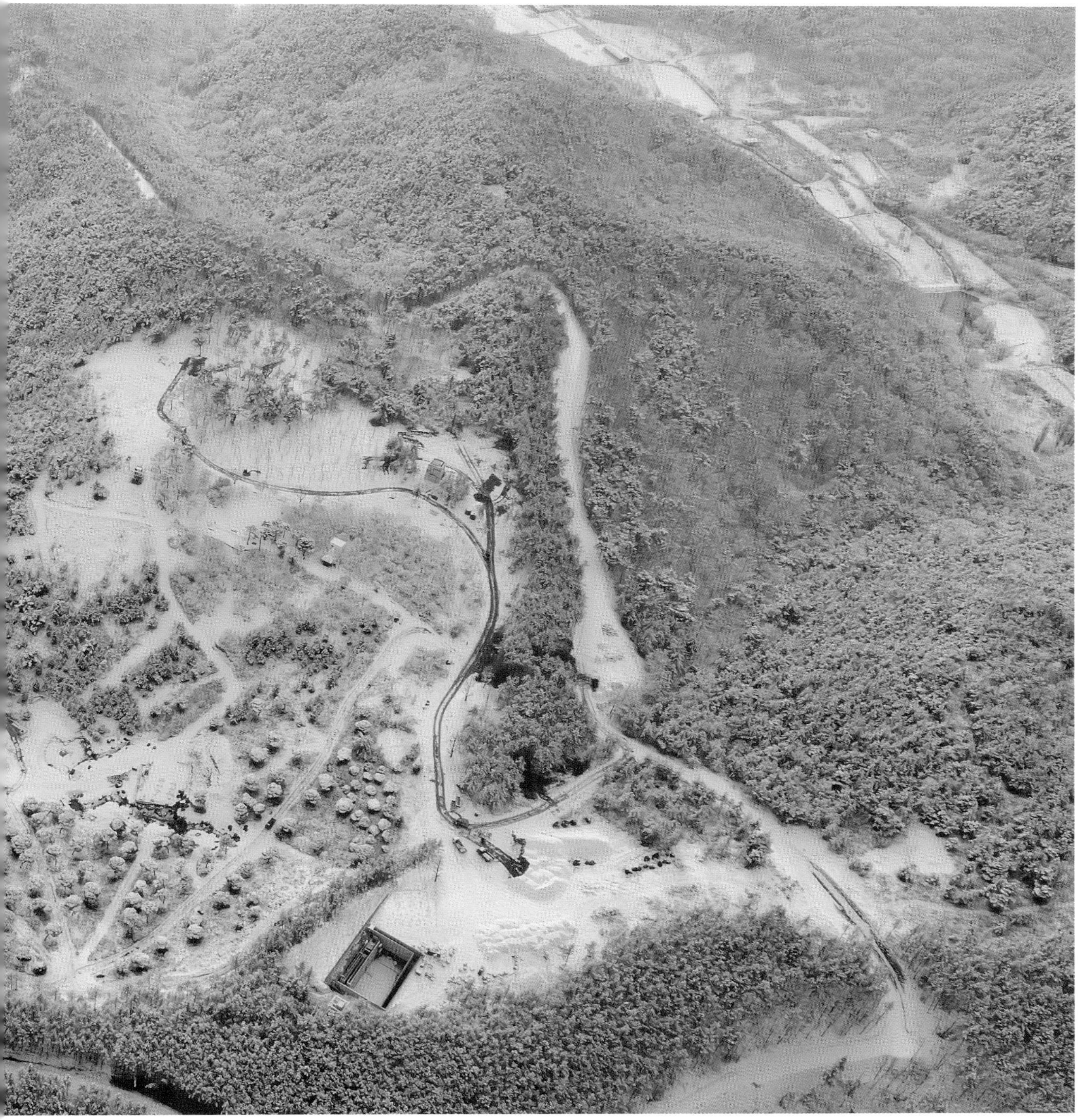

Bugye Arboretum "Sayuwon" — other attached facilities

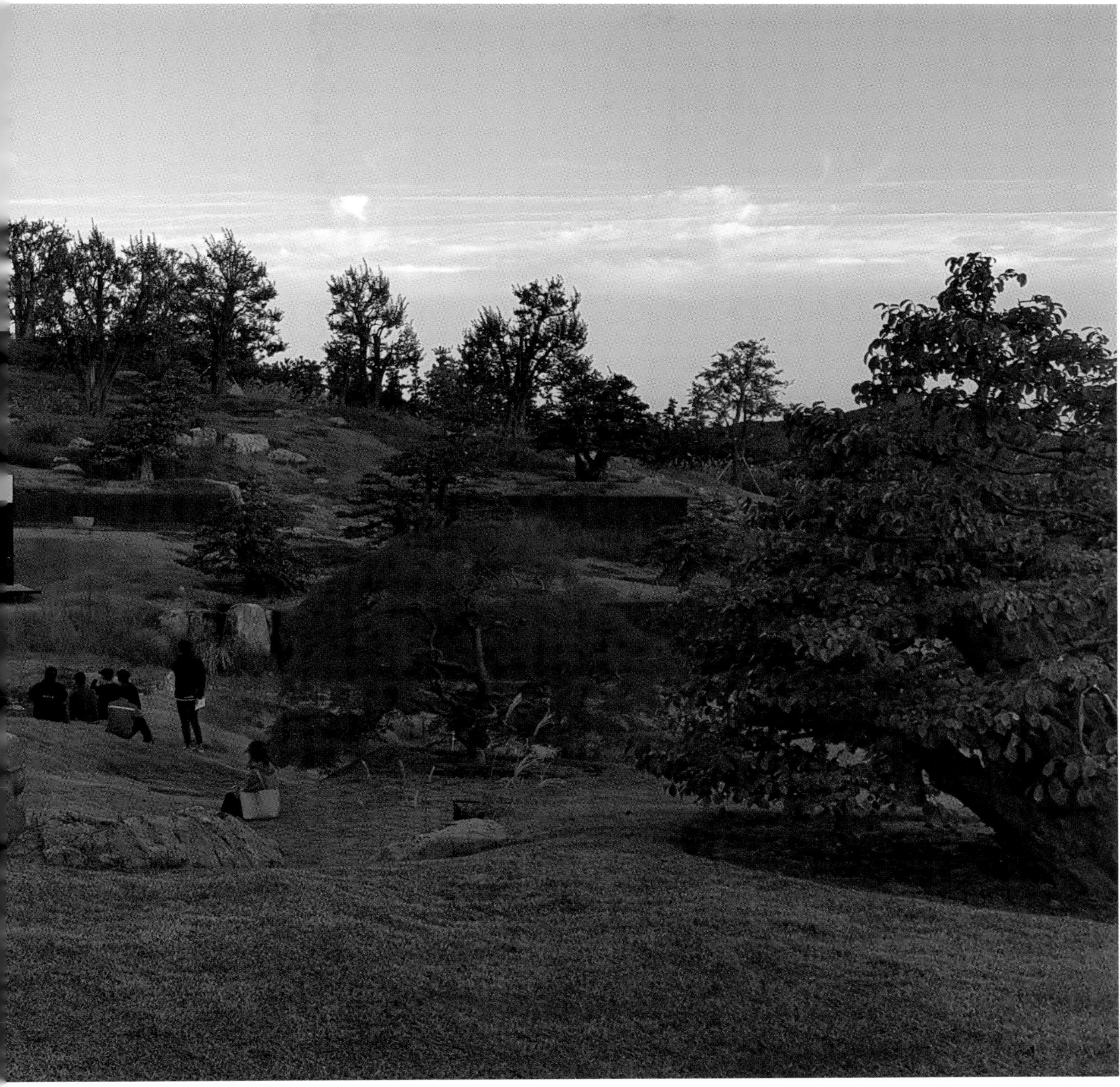

Bugye Arboretum "Sayuwon" — other attached facilities

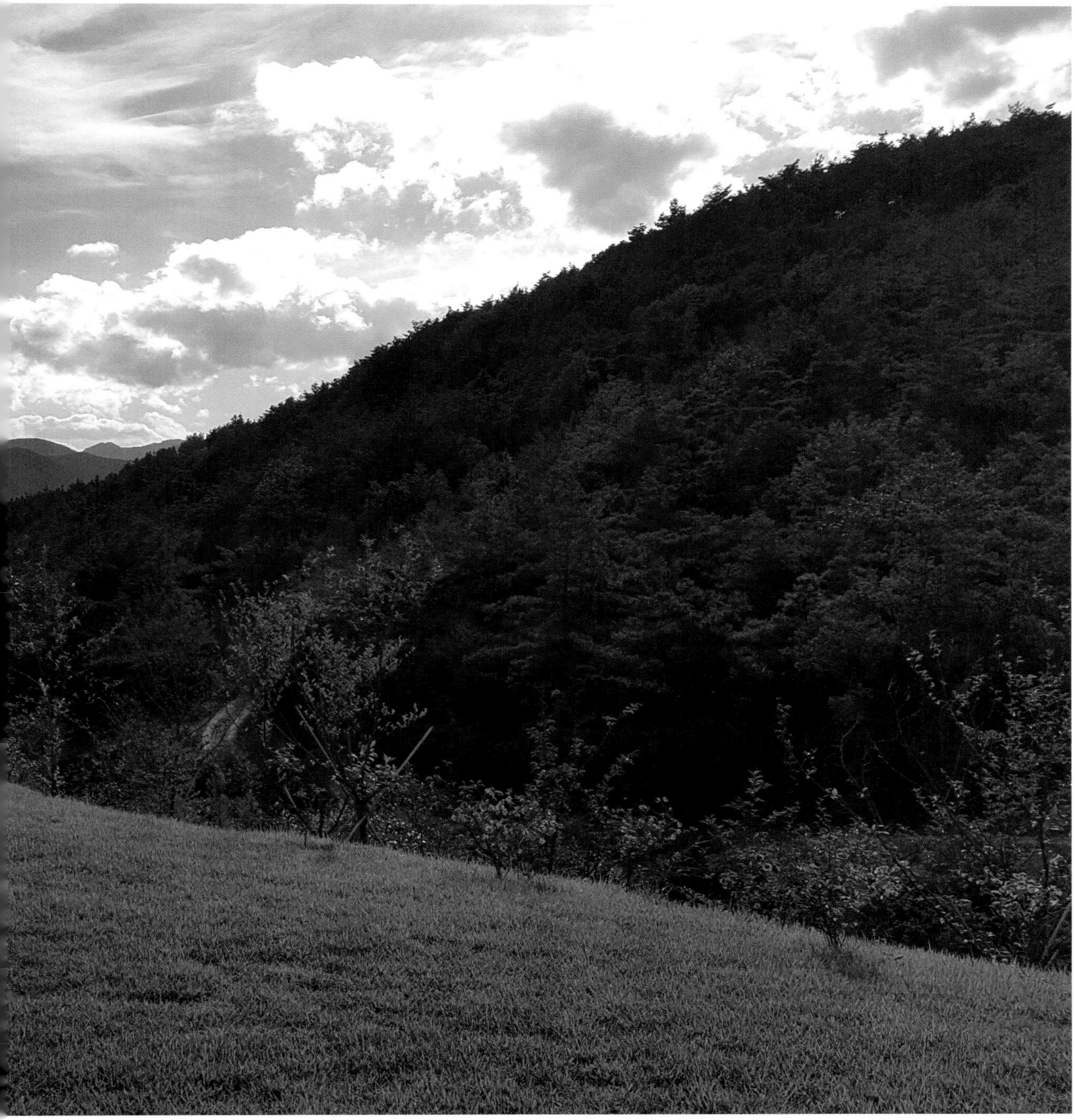

Myungrye Sacred Hill

This is a sacred place dedicated to Marco Shin Seok-bok (1828-1866) who became a martyr at the age of 38 during the Byeongin Catholic Persecution of 1866. Being an ordinary person who sold salt and malt, he was executed because he refused to betray his faith. In 1897, a small Catholic church was first built here in his birth place, but was later destroyed by fire. In 1938, a Korean-style church was rebuilt in a reduced scale of the original church building, and is now placed on the list of local cultural heritage sites. This place was originally a hill around which the Nakdong River meanders. The existing church is small in size and humble in structure, but looks very symbolic and dignified as there remains a superposition of events along the timeline of history in the church. It was dangerous for a new building to be built here to be unusual because the existing small church building should be inevitably central. The premise for the construction of the new building was to create a special landscape and to make it special in terms of sanctity.

First of all, it is very reasonable to divide the whole land to embody the Way of the Cross (Via Dolorosa) and Fourteen Stations which are often hung on the inner wall of the Catholic church in the form of images. Using existing property lines of the land, 14 points for each of the Fourteen Stations could be connected as the Way of the Cross for pilgrimage. For the final section of this pilgrimage, it would be good to utilize the existing useless water tank around the boundary of the site, thereby completing the Way of the Cross along the whole area of the hill.

The new memorial church was to be built on the western slope as part of the cliff side landscape. The interior of the church was designed to provide an experience of light and darkness and of relaxation and tension. A relatively large yard created close to the church would be used for pilgrimage events. Steps, banisters, a bell tower, among others, were structurally installed to increase spatial tension, especially when the church is vacant. The journey from the entrance, through the Way of the Cross, to the memorial church, to this yard — a long encounter with different events and scenes — will serve as a road of asceticism, completing the biblical landscape. The way becomes, therefore, the most important theme of the Myeongrye Sacred Hill.

Myungrye Sacred Hill

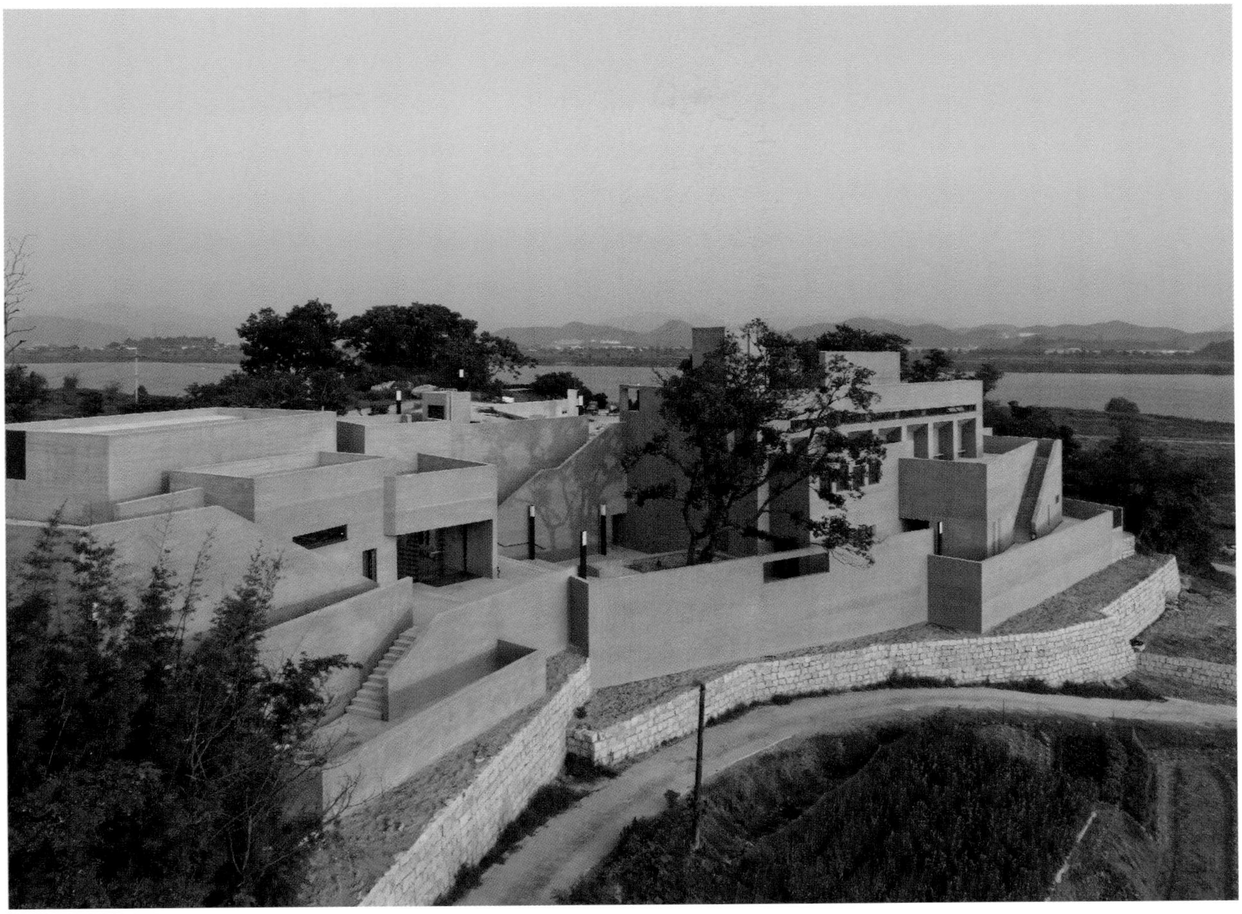

Myungrye Sacred Hill

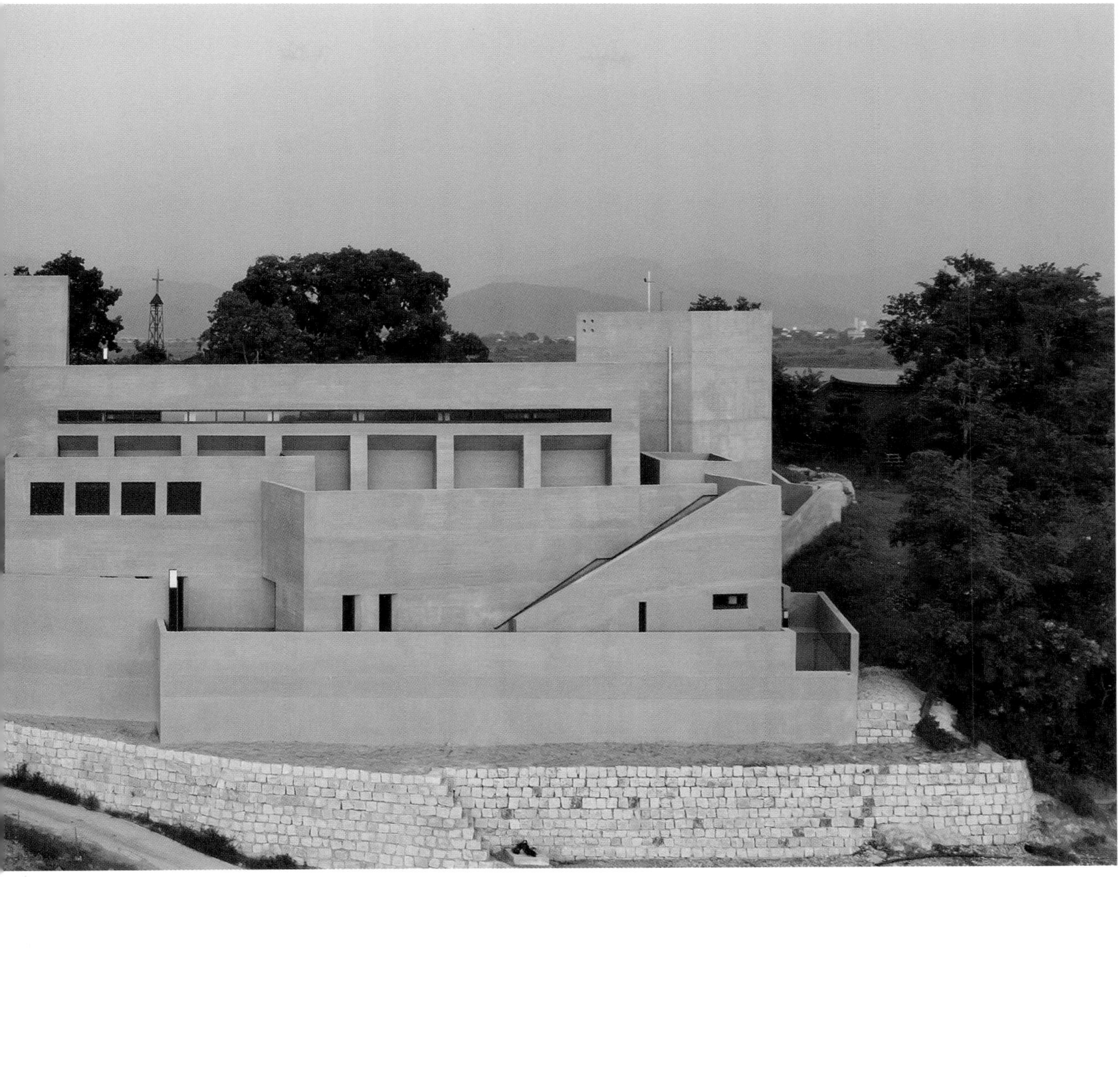

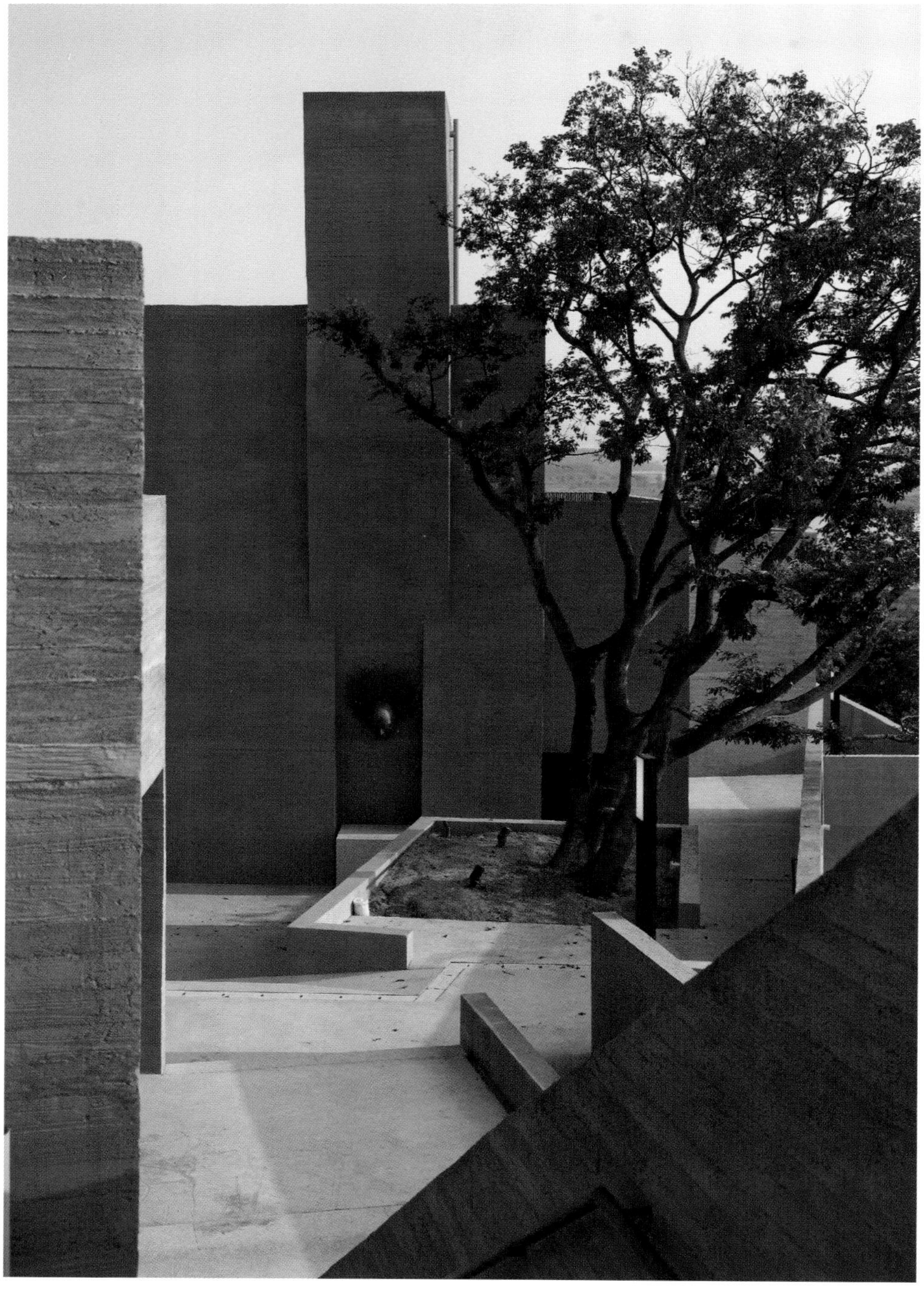

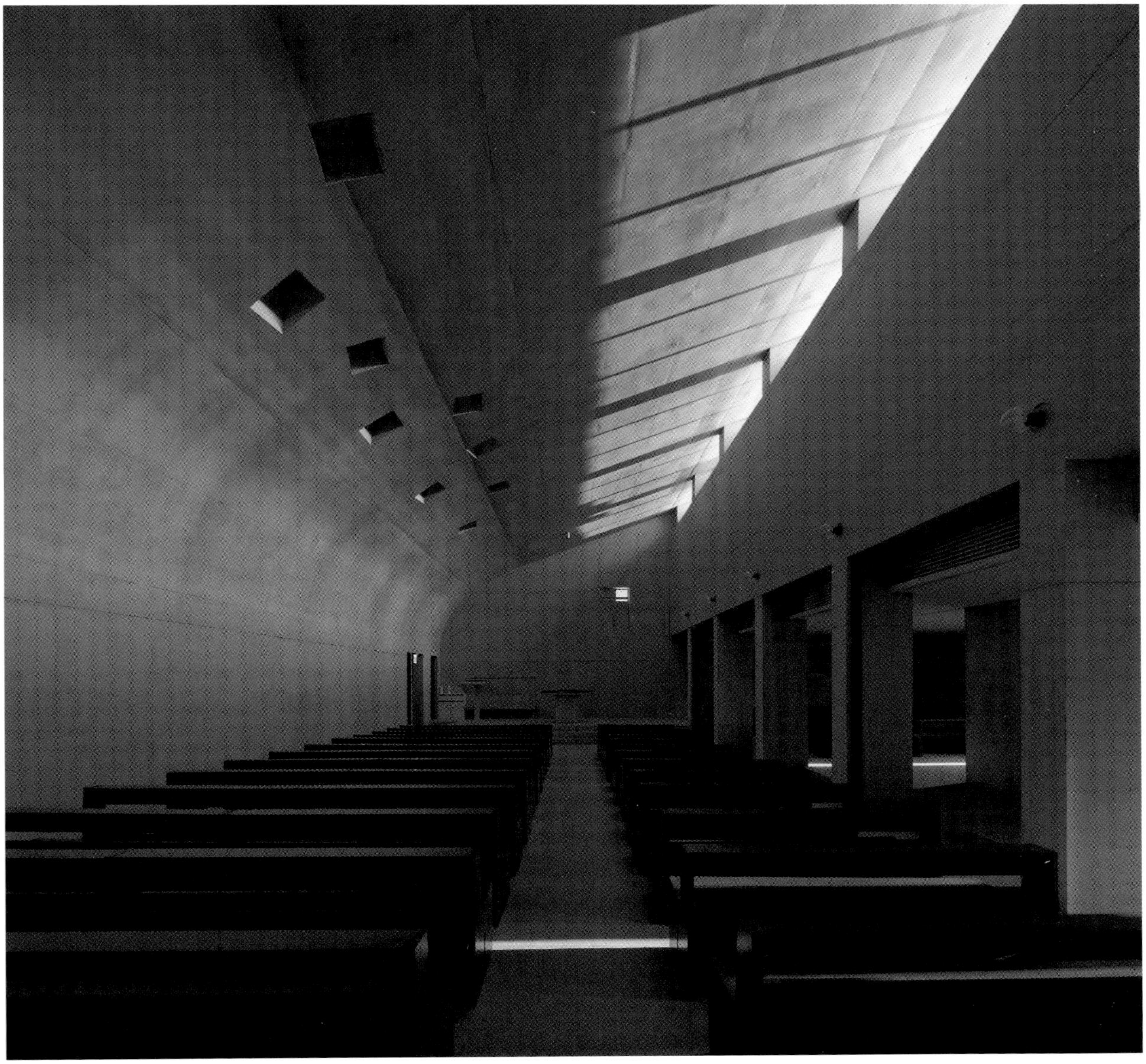

On the morning of May 23, 2009, former President Roh Moo-hyun committed suicide by jumping from a mountain cliff in his hometown. Regardless of the political background and process of this incident, everyone living in Korea began to rethink his or her relationship with the late Roh. He was a stranger in our society. He was able to enjoy a rich life like other people with vested interests, but he always drove himself out of the boundary and criticized what was established within the boundary. According to Edward Said, author of *Representations of the Intellectual*, " …… intellectuals should be the ones to question patriotic nationalism, corporate thinking, and a sense of class, racial or gender privilege." And, Roh Moo-hyun's decisive life was really a life an intellectual ought to live. Accordingly, his death was a reflection of the times to everyone.

The death of such a man should not match the hackneyed form of the National Cemetery on the visible high ground. Furthermore, he had already rejected this place in his last will, and asked for the burial of his body with a small gravestone in his hometown village. Upon the request of the funeral committee to fulfil his las will, I suggested a flatland below the rock from which the late president jumped, for a place where his cremated remains would be interred. As this triangular flatland lies at the point of connecting village and mountain, as if reality and eternity, it could nicely become the location of a graveyard where the living and the dead meet. Moreover, two streams flowing to the flatland seemed to have already set the character of this land.

The new ground was lifted and adjusted the elevation to create an emotional terrain so that the graveyard could look like a place far from the reality. Lots of granite stone pieces were laid on the surface of the floating land shaping a village map, and each piece was inscribed with a memorial statement of each of the citizens who paid for the cost. The stone floor, which 15,000 people voluntarily paid for, became a grand installation art.

This area as a national graveyard gathers a million people visit to pay respect to the late Roh each year. Most of visitors used to look here and there, and stand still for a long while as if they were lost in thought. It is the scene of their reflection. That is a landscape for the people who are voluntary gentiles. When people want to ask about the meaning of their being, and when they feel lonely and desolate, standing here on this square and looking for the noble value of the voluntary gentiles is highly recommended.

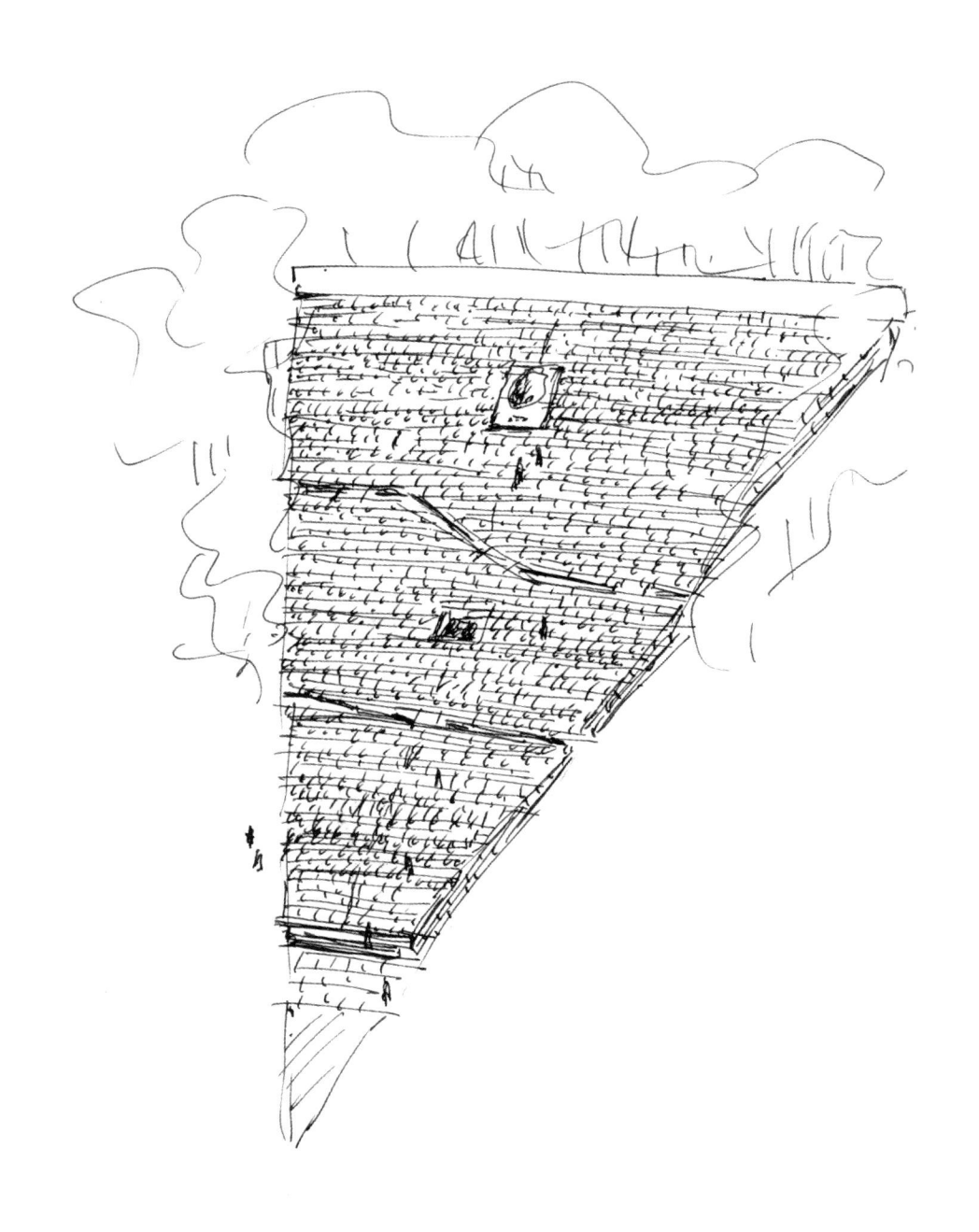

NMH MONUMENT
- A VOLUNTARY GENTILE ON STREET
090630 Soleri

Graveyard of President Roh Moohyun

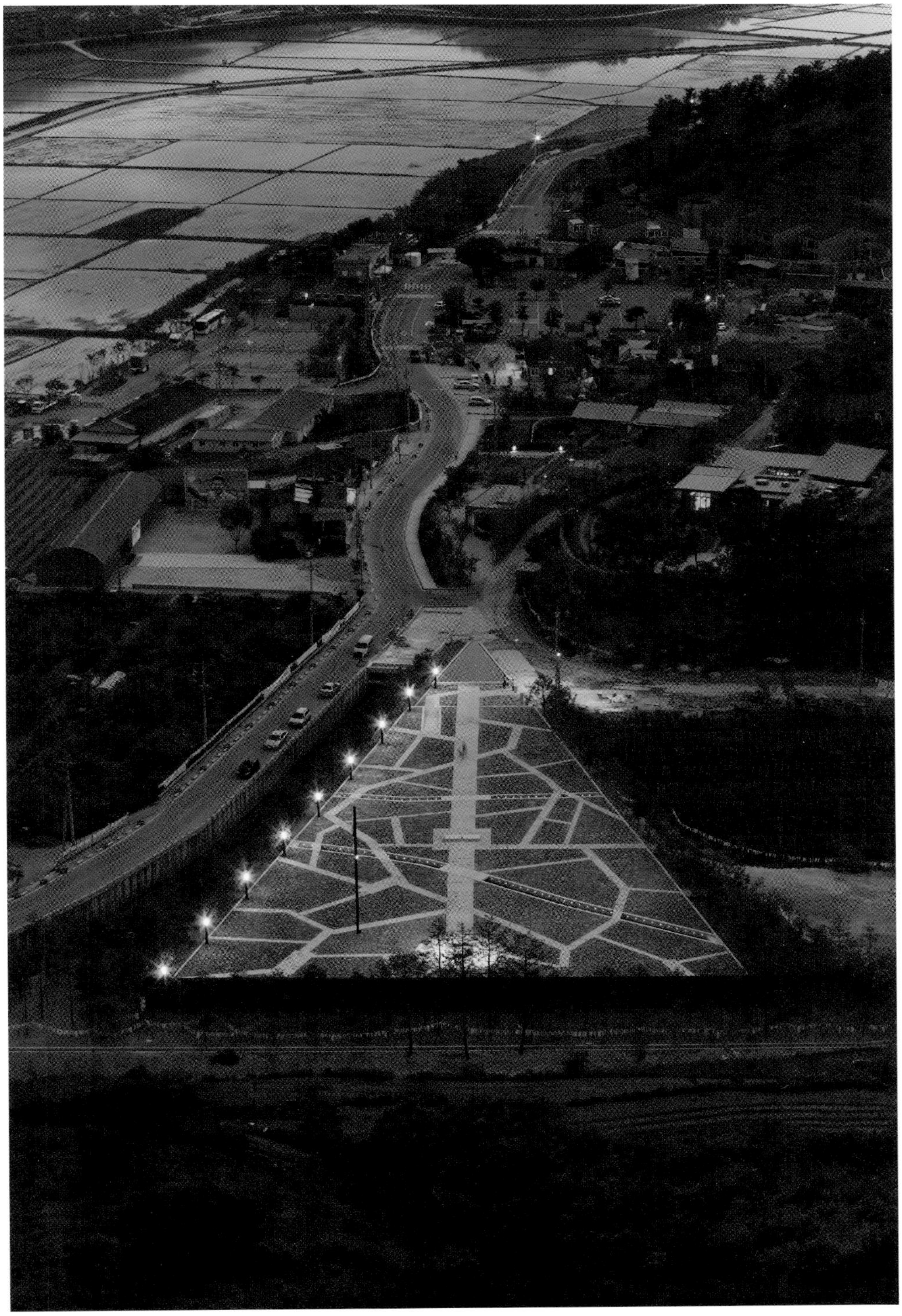

Graveyard of President Roh Moohyun

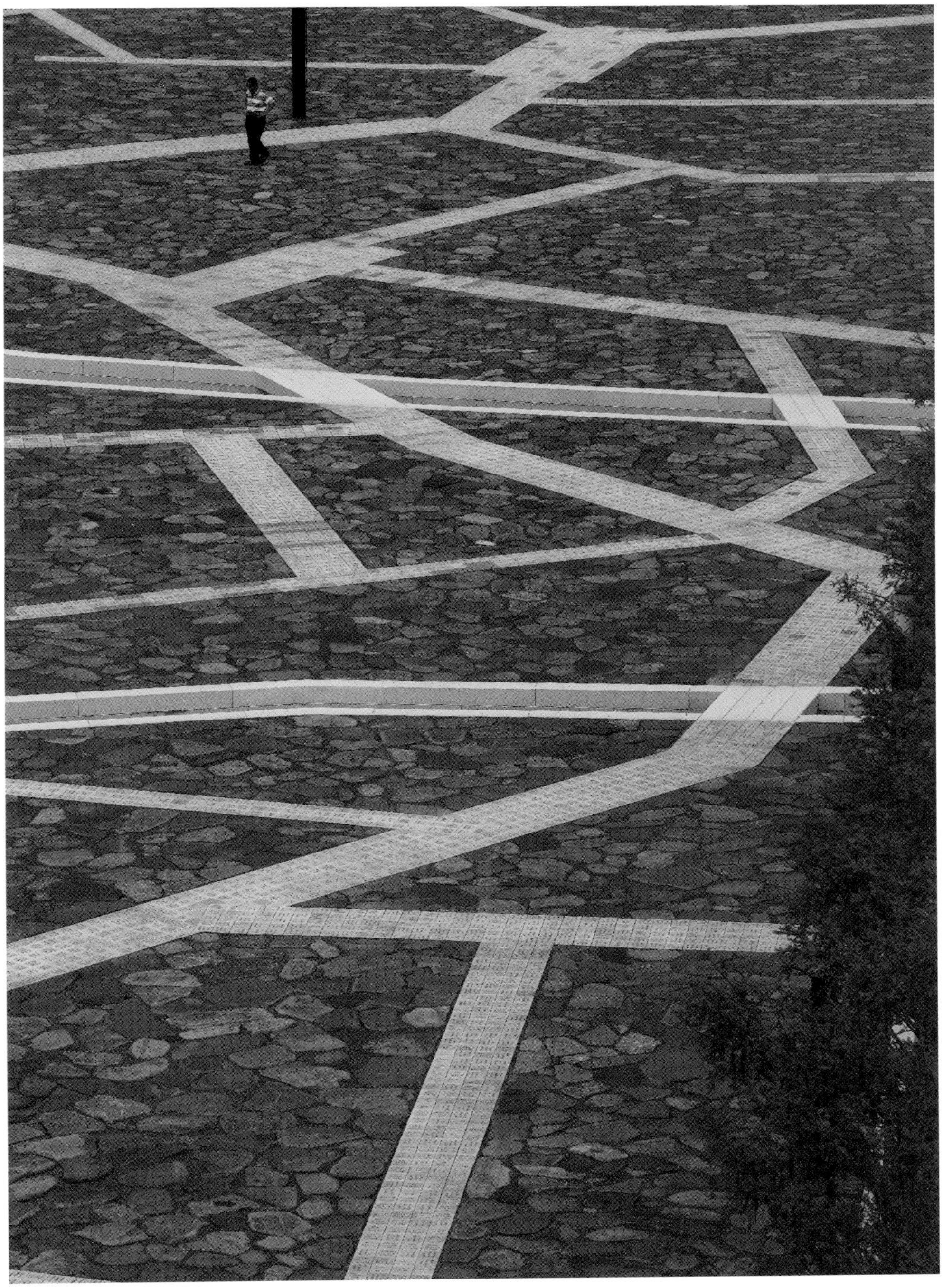

Graveyard of President Roh Moohyun

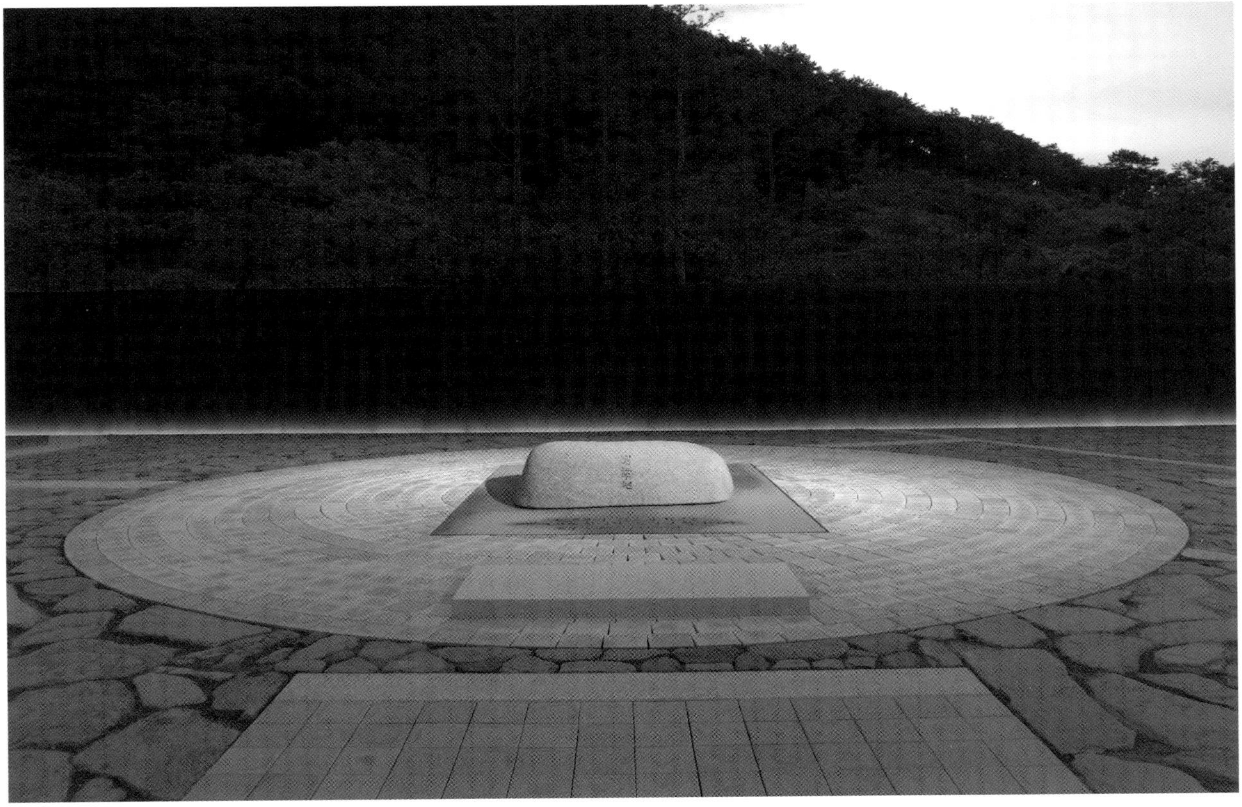

Being a place where ten thousand lives are gathered in the form of death, it is a community and city of the dead. So designing the whole structure as a complete set of required facilities for a city is top priority. With a city located on a slope, it was a rule to make each individual shelter follow the format of a terraced house. Due to the grass covering the roof of terraced house below, the front side of each terraced house is an independent area. From a bird's eye view, the whole place looks like a unique park completely covered with green area. Small communities of terraced houses of varying sizes are connected to each other through the paths on the slope or staircases. Shared facilities including small parks and squares as well as the sanctuary of each community are located at the junctions of paths. The main square for the whole city is located around the bottom entrance. With its floor covered with water and surrounded by high walls made of weathering steel, this place eventually tells its visitors that it is a new city of silence.

As a matter of fact, however, the, graveyard is not a place for the dead. A human being consists of four things: body (體), flesh (肉), spirit (靈), and soul (魂). While body and flesh become a corpse and are buried in a grave, they dissipate and cease to exist in the end. When cremated and put in the charnel house, they are merely a symbol and cannot represent the existence of the person. Soul, which represents human mind, emotion, and passion, also goes extinct at the point of death. What remains is spirit: it is an unconstrained being that freely comes in and out of the human body from the first place. However, once a spirit loses its body and flesh, it cannot remain in this world. It does not exist, therefore, in the grave, but is ousted to another world.

Here is a poem that is said to have originated from a song of wise Indians, *A Thousand Winds*.

> *"Do not stand at my grave and weep,*
> *I am not there, I do not sleep.*
>
> *I am a thousand winds that blow.*
> *I am the diamond glint on snow.*
> *I am the sunlight on ripened grain.*
> *I am the gentle autumn rain.*
>
> *When you awaken in the morning's hush,*
> *I am the swift uplifting rush*
> *Of quiet birds in circled flight,*
> *I am the soft stars that shine at night.*
>
> *Do not stand at my grave and cry;*
> *I am not there. I did not die."*

What the poem says seems to be right. It is not the dead who dwell in the graveyard; it is our memory of the deceased that lingers there. As such, the graveyard is not a space for the dead but a place and landscape where the living look into themselves, bringing back the memory of the dead. Therefore, visiting a graveyard or having it nearby is a way of ensuring the sincerity of life. Everybody should be encouraged to come here for a moment of reflection on the beauty of life, strolling in silence.

CITY OF THE DEAD
FOR LIVING US

Public Cemetery Park "A Thousand Winds"

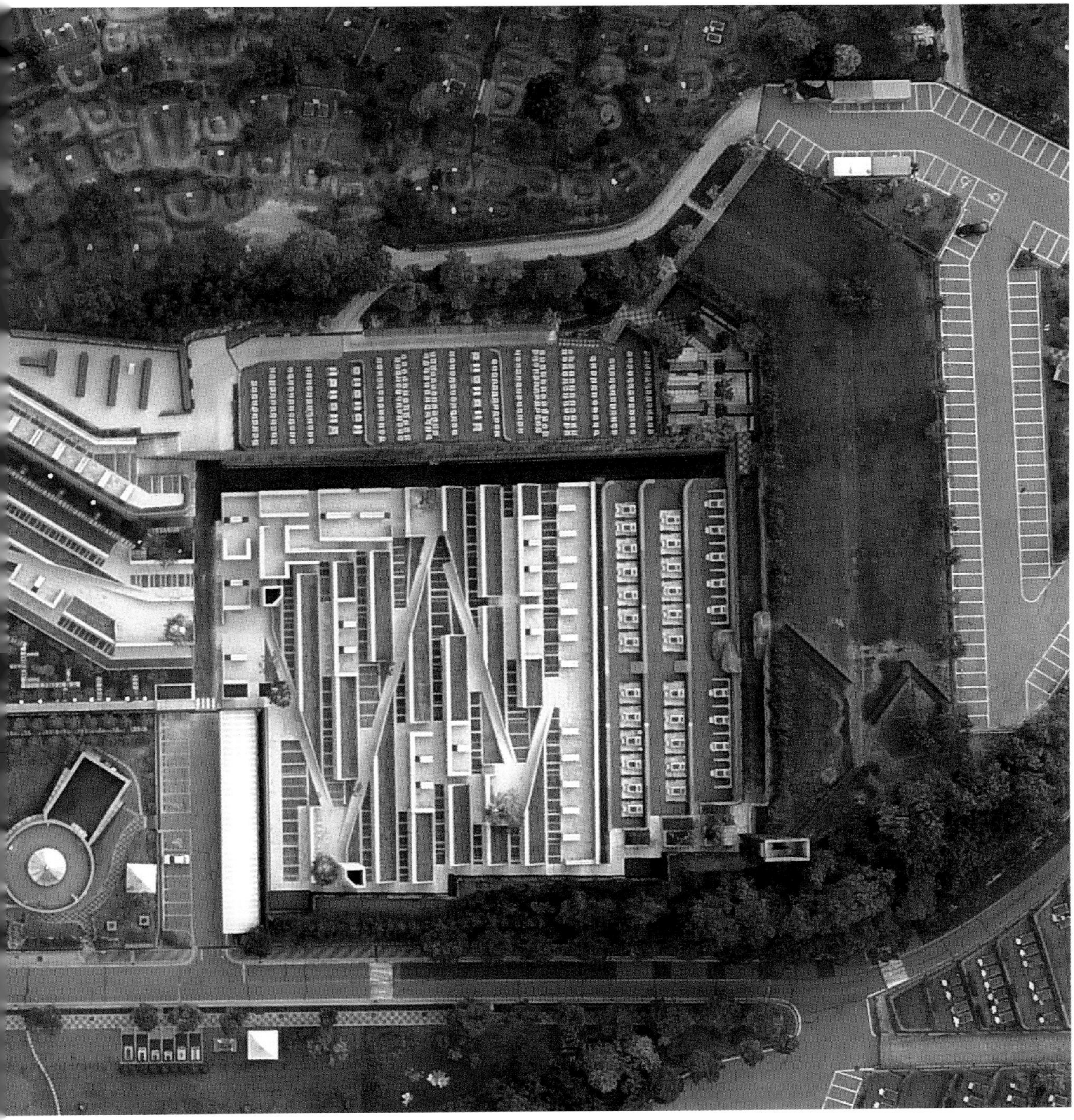

Public Cemetery Park "A Thousand Winds"

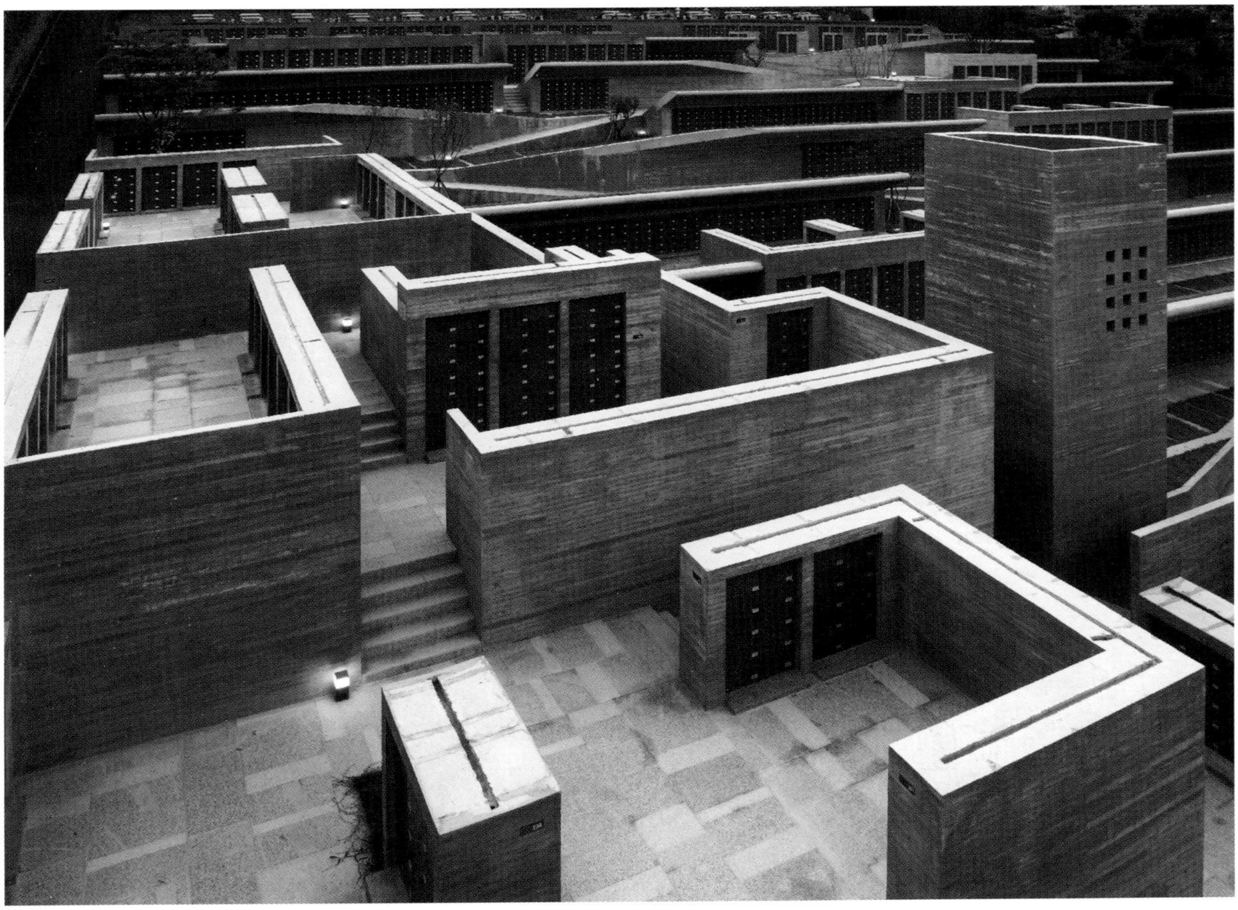

Public Cemetery Park "A Thousand Winds"

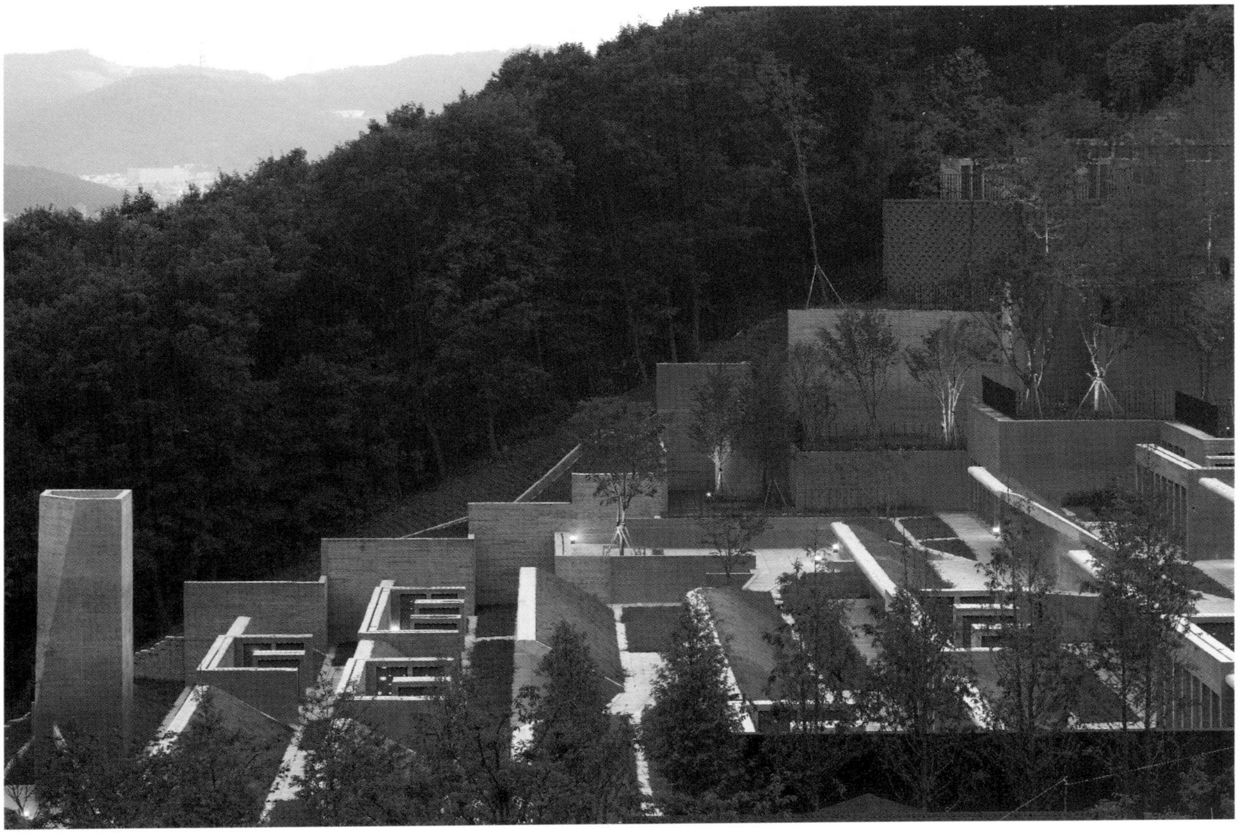

Public Cemetery Park "A Thousand Winds"

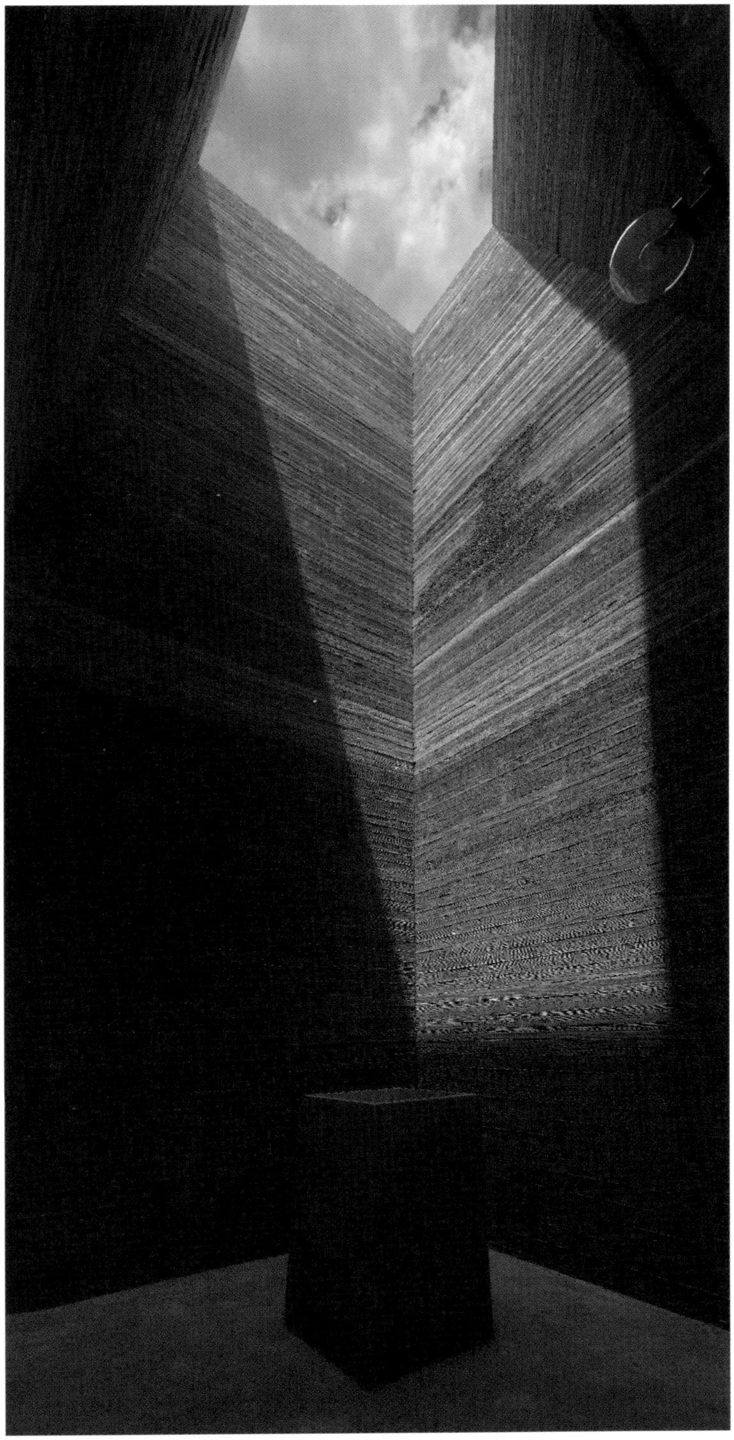

The Korea DMZ Peace and Life Valley, a uniquely named incorporated association, has a slogan which goes "Open the Door of Peace with the Key of Life." Noting how the demilitarized zone (DMZ), a remnant of the Korean War, paradoxically became a scene of life restoration, this organization was founded to campaign for contemplating contemporary history as well as introspect about the dignity of life. Some proactive intellectuals of the times gathered to found this organization with extensive support from Gangwon provincial government.

This organization mainly serves as a base camp for the exploring tour of the DMZ, but it also promotes life-respecting movement by doing farming activity in addition to its emphasis on lectures, seminars, and meditation programs. Thus, the facilities of the DMZ Peace-Life Valley themselves were regarded to maintain a harmonious relationship with the nature. From the onset, any of the facilities not allows to look hostile against and dominating over the nature.

The plot for the DMZ Peace-Life Valley is located in a mountainous area in the County of Inje, which is close to the DMZ. This mountain has a depression in the middle that faces the west. This landform is considered to promote an important concept as it connects the natural mountain range to the motorways or a symbol of civilization. As an architectural structure ought to serve as a medium linking all these things, it should be both an artificialized nature and a naturalized artificial structure. If viewed from the mountain, it appears as if the land were cleaved; if viewed from the road, the scene looks like a mountain flows in through the vacant gap. Thus, the architectural structure here should not exist. In other words, the architectural project is what has been made by the land and what comprises the landscape. Buildings sometimes look ephemeral.

사라지는 마을

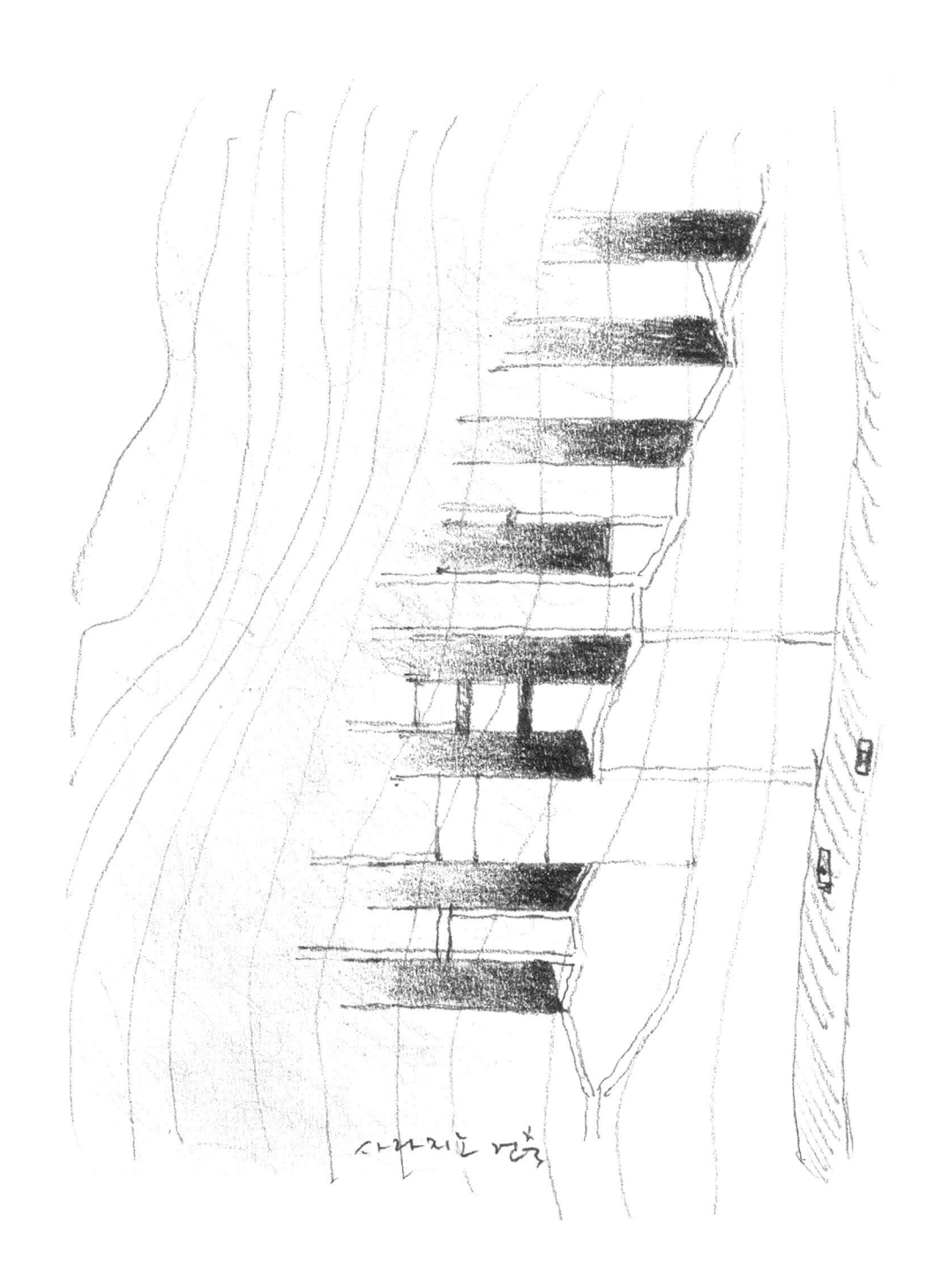

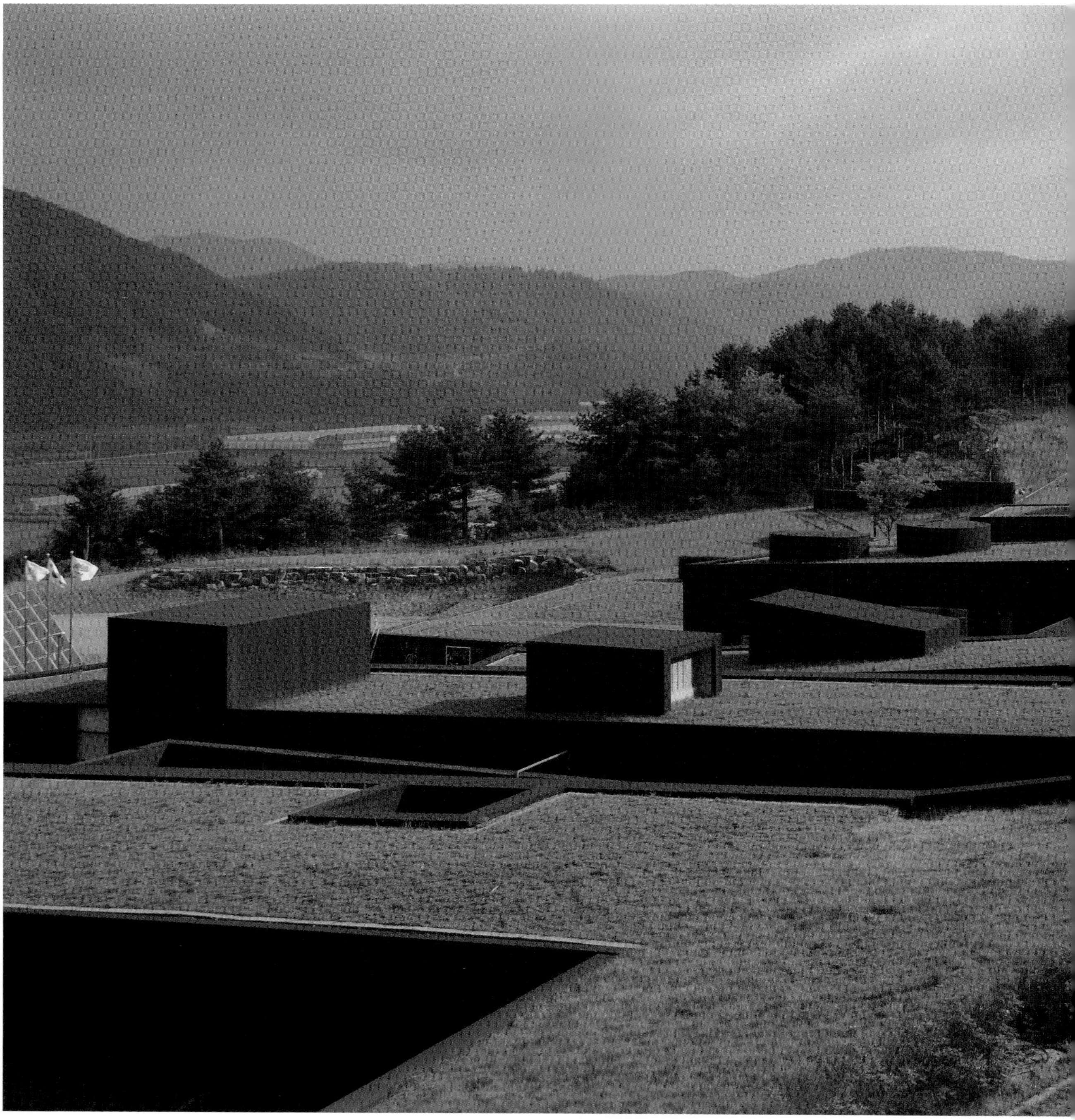

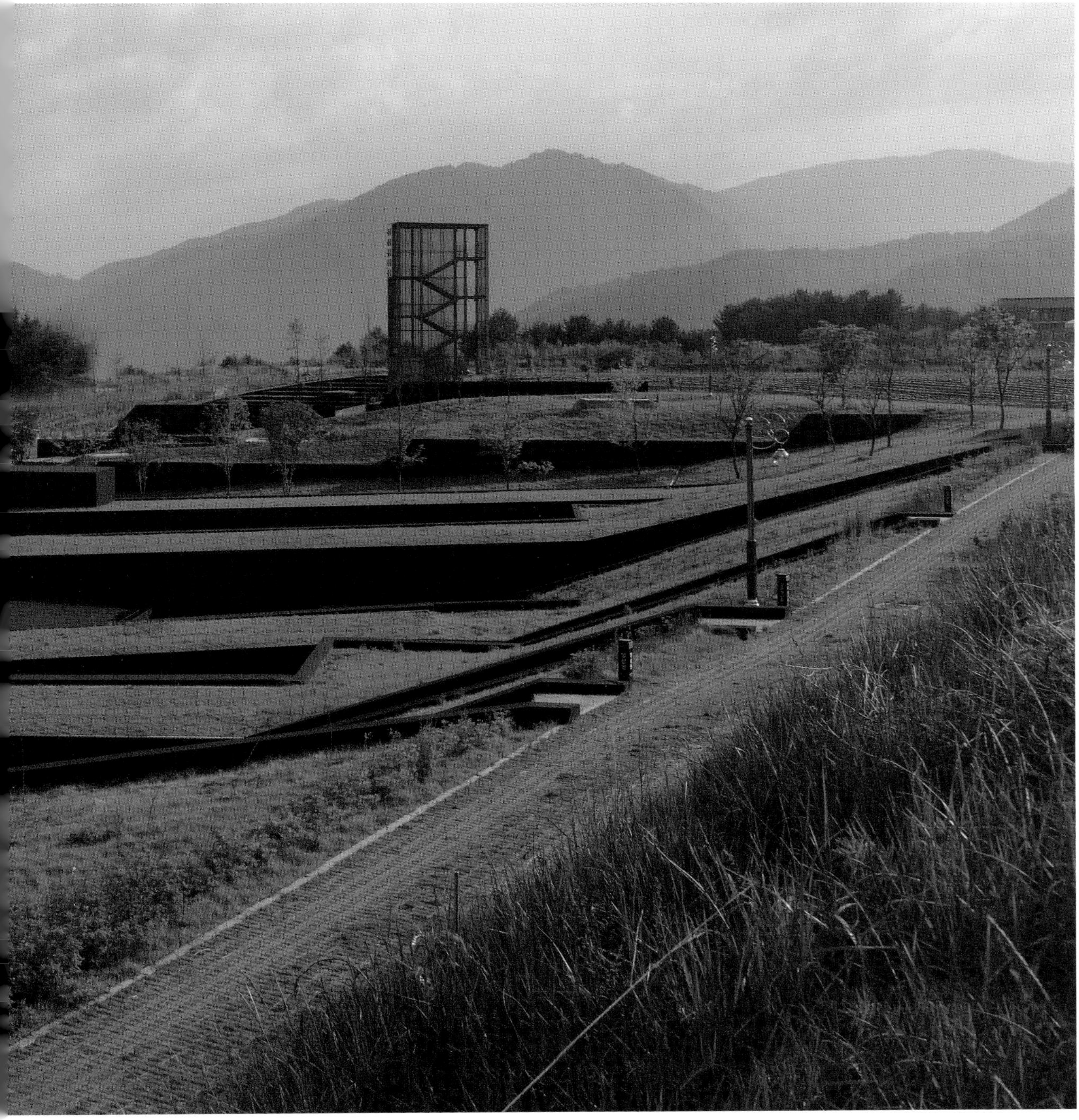

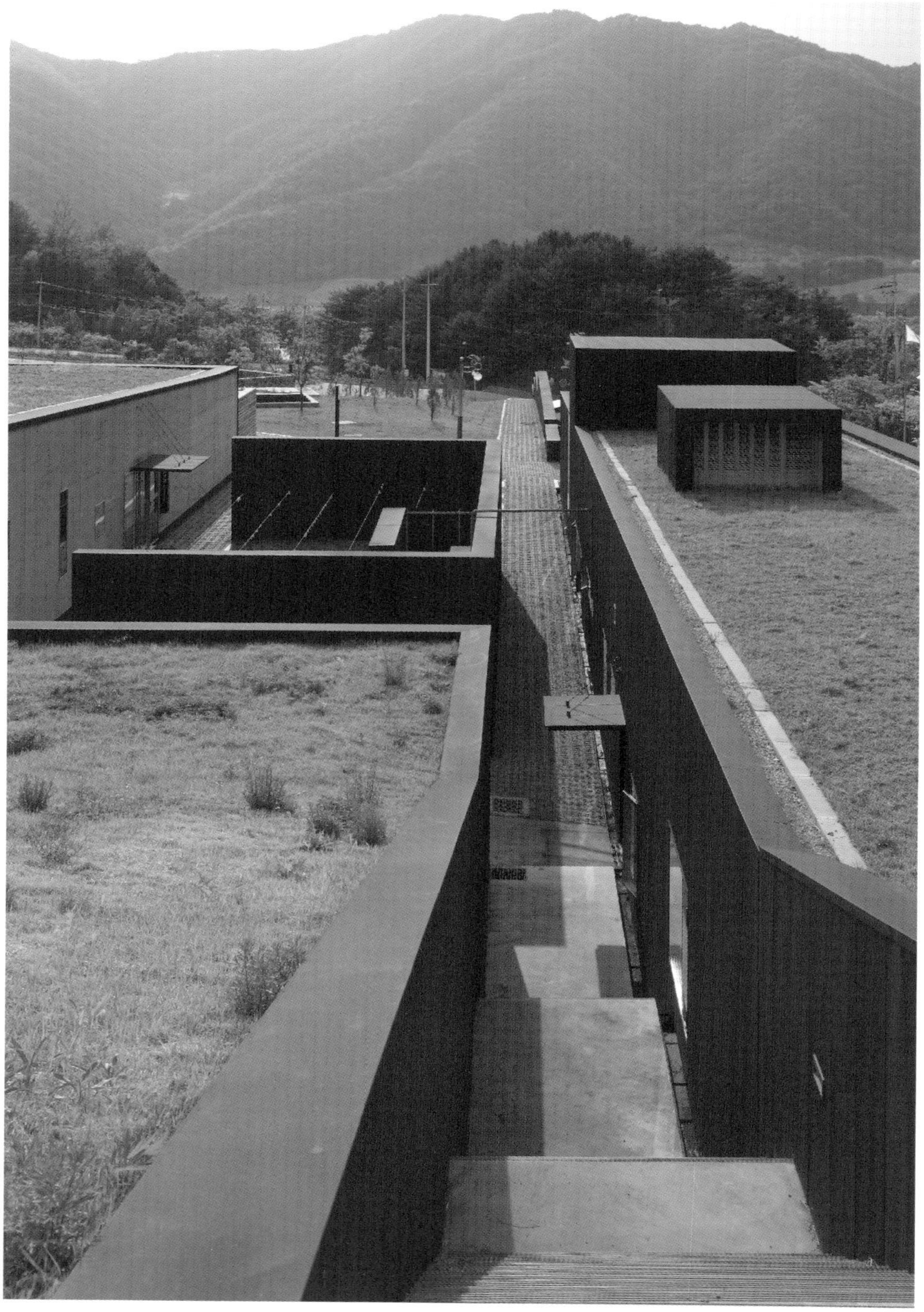

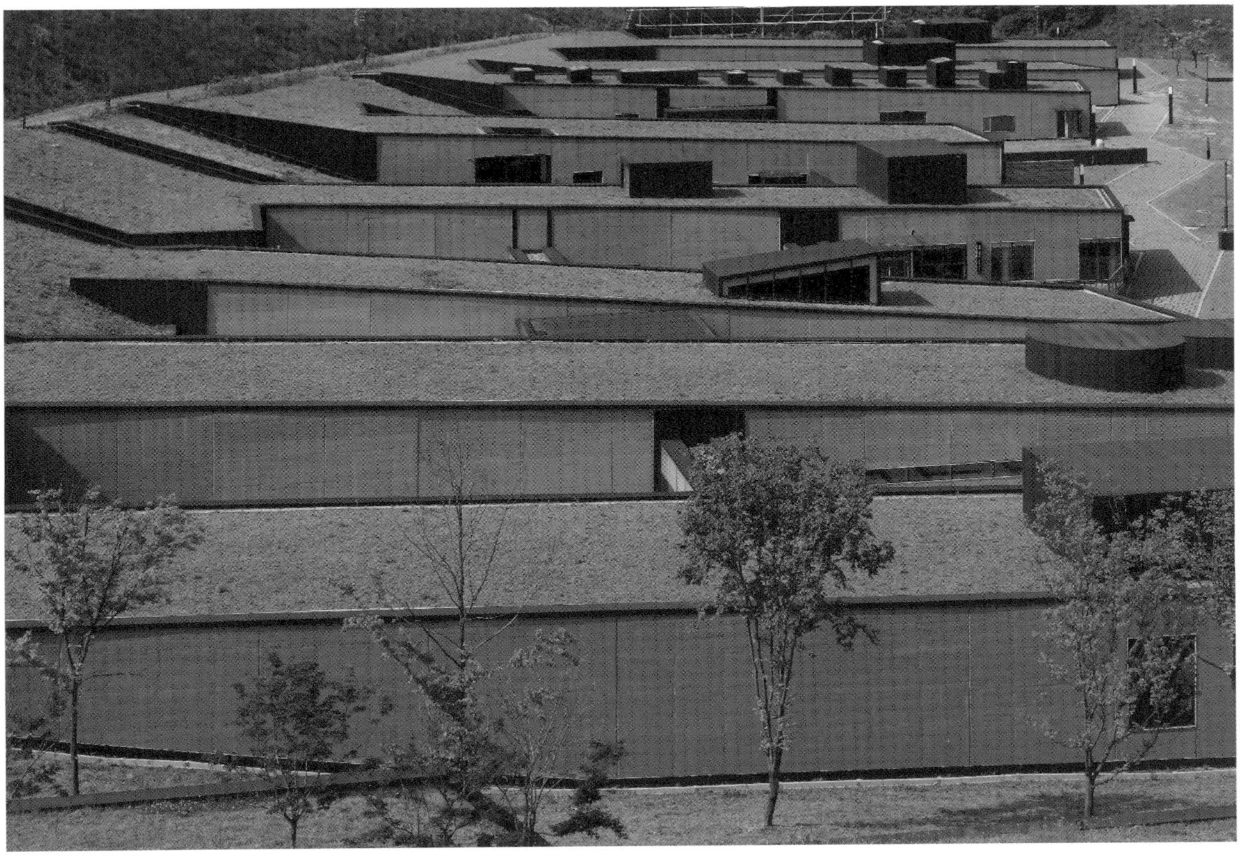

Korea DMZ Peace and Life Valley

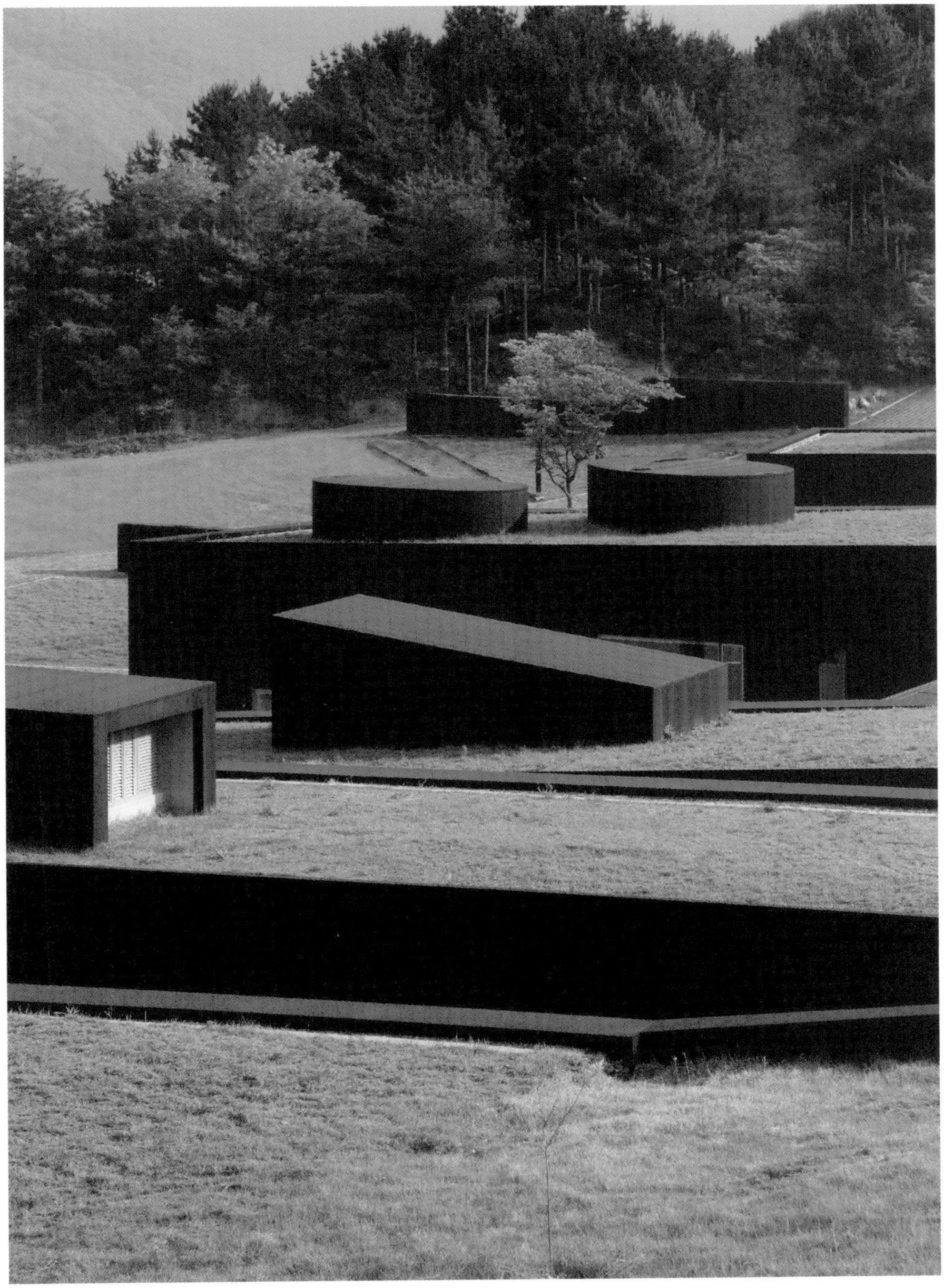

Residence "Moheon"

When construction was approaching completion, the client asked to name this small house. A word popped into my head instantly, and it was "Moheon," literally meaning someone's house. Moheon means a non-existent house as it is not a particular person's house. This house ought to be called this way.

This small facility is attached to client's old house built 40 years ago. It is composed of a bedroom and a restaurant where people eat meals, enjoying the view of the garden. As an important purpose of this house was to create a beautiful garden, the presence of the house should not be exposed. Although the plot for the house was just 300m² wide, four courts were created. To maximize the area for the front court, the building, composed of two sections, had to be set back. The walls of the frontal section, or a dining hall, was made of transparent glass, thereby making a view of the front yard visible through it from the bedroom or the back section. A connecting passage was laid between these two sections, thereby creating two courtyards. One was made to be a garden of water while the level of the other was sunken for the basement get light from outside. From the bedroom, people can see a small bamboo garden over the window. This kind of visual connectivity makes the space much deeper and richer. The dining hall has movable walls that allow flexible space. What is more, however, is that the dining hall, which is transparent to all the directions, has power to make the surrounding area look wider than actual. The entire building site was surrounded by Corten steel walls with special treatment as high as the height of the house to increase the tension of the enclosed space as much as possible, and to emphasize the empty space up to the hilt. Jeong Yeongsun, a landscape architect, planted wild pear trees densely in the front yard which is 165m² wide and 9m deep. She, then, put rough gravel all over the ground. The front yard, with all these landscaping efforts, looked like a forest of an enormous scale or part of the primeval nature. The wild pear trees, which had been usually considered useless, splashed splendid red colors over the yard. It was magic. Architecture should disappear and only landscape should remain.

If a guest to this house, the atmosphere of which is of traditional Korean architecture, sitting on the floor, opens the push-up window and follows his or her vision to the dark gray wall of Corten steel through the garden of water and the transparent dining hall, he or she will happily encounter a deep and rich landscape of the stone yard. This is surely the result of what architecture has abandoned itself. Being so sensitive, the client gives a call or text message to inform about how touched he is whenever the sound of rain, wind or snow falls down the ground of the house.

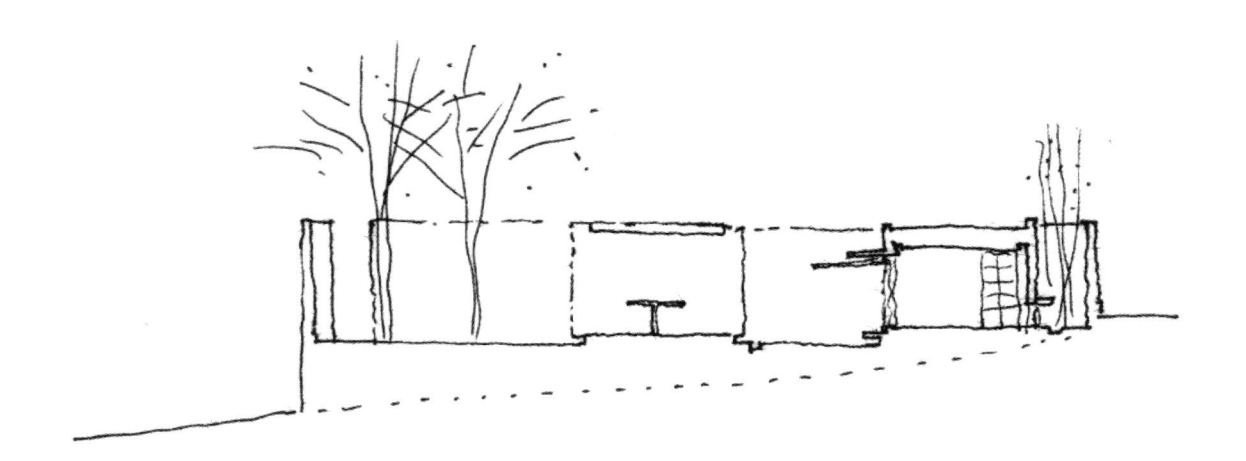

Residence "Moheon"

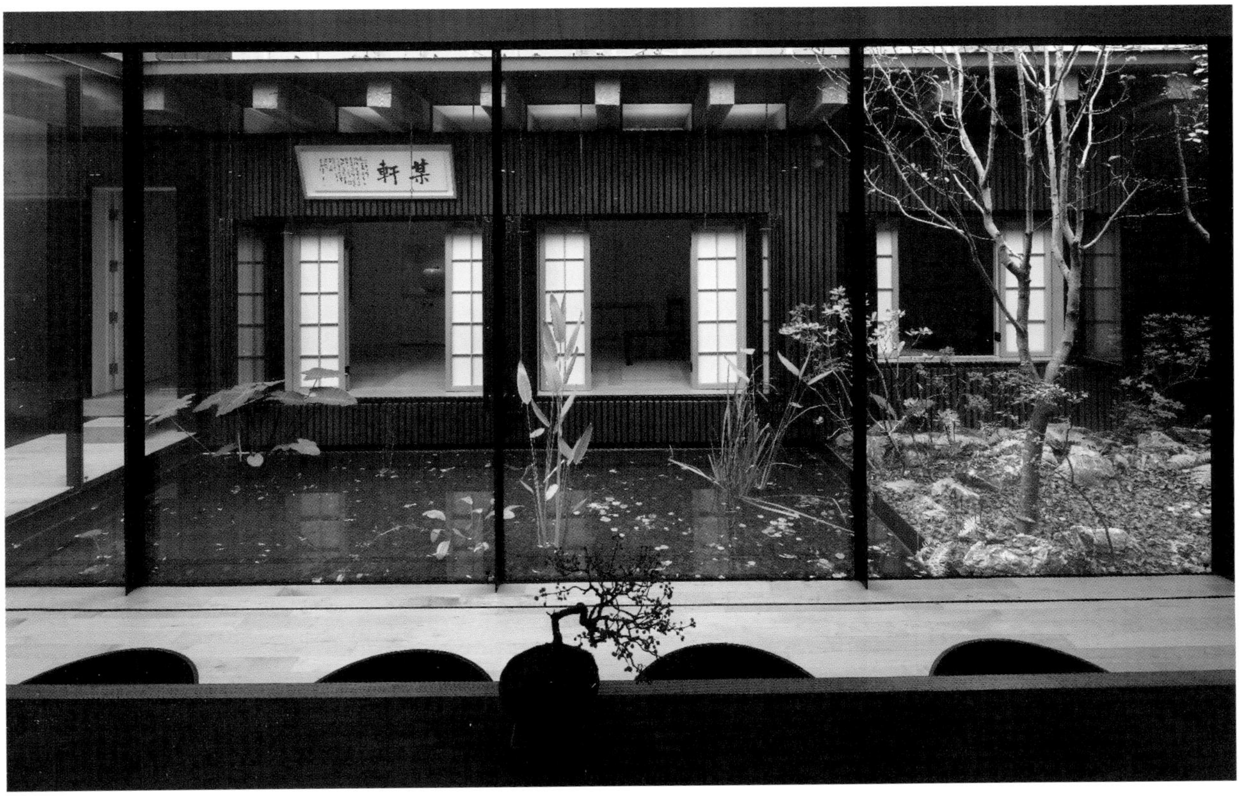
某軒

Residence "Moheon"

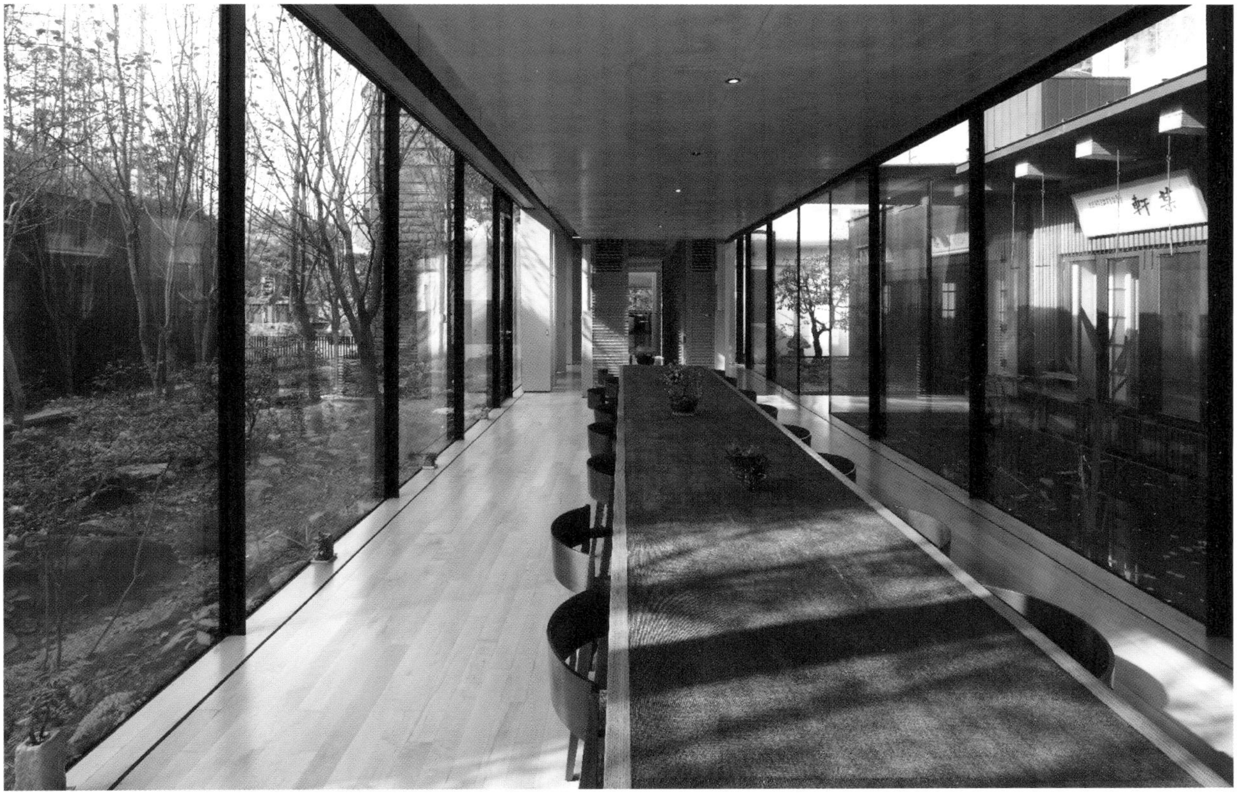

Residence "Moheon"

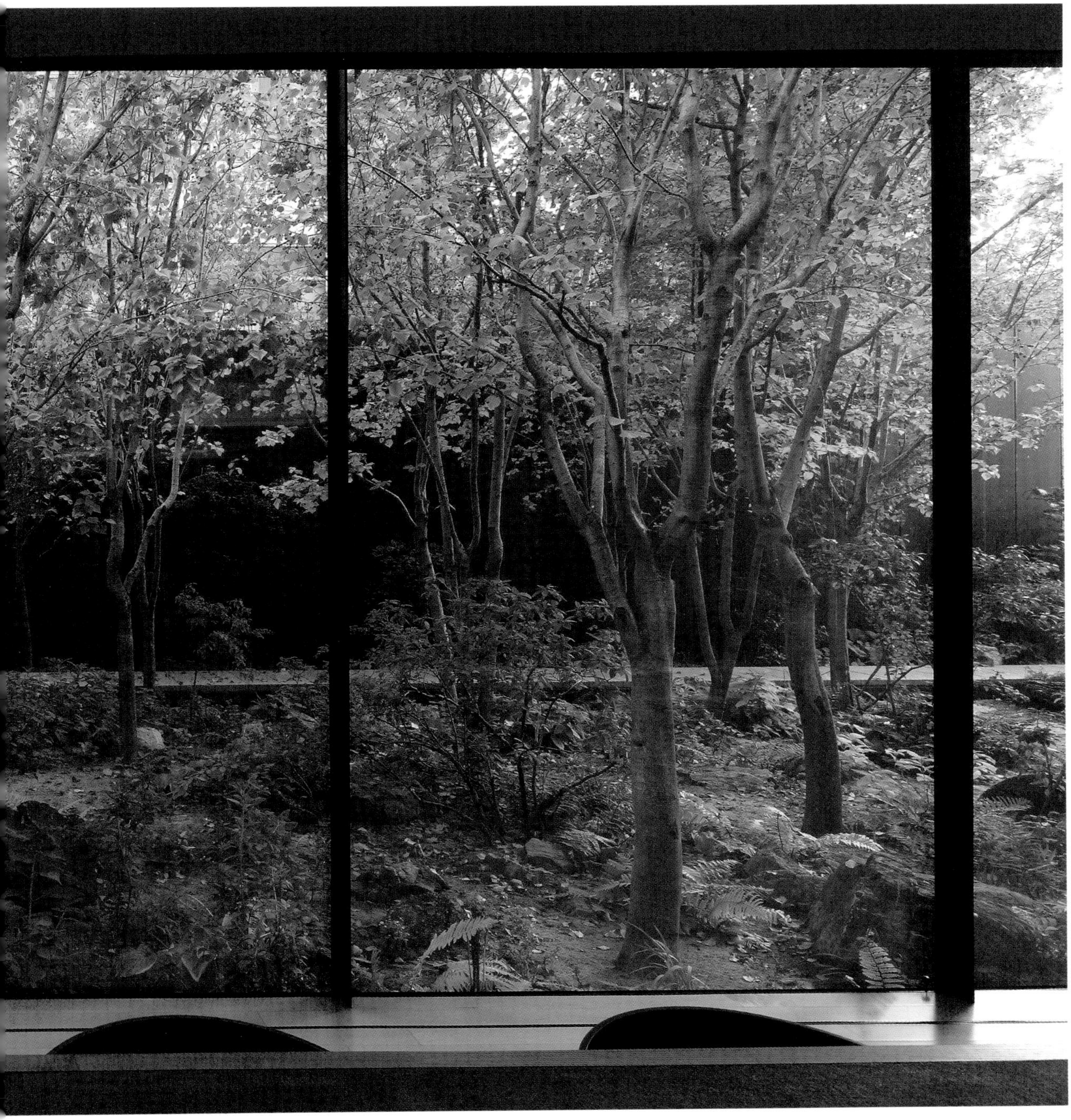

Korean Medicine Hospital of Daejeon University in Seoul

Munjeong-dong, an outskirt area of Seoul, where had remained a farmland for a long time, is a place of drastic change where high-rise buildings have been constructed for the past ten years. As this area has a strategic value of the future for a local university like Daejeon University, the Seoul Korean Medicine Hospital of the University was built here. This facility would function also as base camp in Seoul.

As the site of the buildings is in touch with the intersection, the location is good enough. In particular, while only one side of most of the neighboring high-rise buildings faces the road, three sides of the hospital building face the roads. Since the internal functions of the hospital are different for each floor, the façade should have various patterns related to internal functions. In addition, the sides of the hospital building, which face the intersection, were designed as if a vertical garden.

While most of the other surrounding buildings are finished with curtain walls or metal material, giving an impression of hurried and expedient construction, the exposed concrete as prevailing material, is adequate in order to enhance the characteristics of the area and express the internal space of the building.

High-rise buildings are monuments of a city, and in some cases, they are the images that represent the city. Though this building is just an architectural structure, if it feels familiar because of its vertically differentiated and integrated properly, it may help this new development area be an intimate one.

VERTICAL ARBORETUM FOR ORIENTAL H

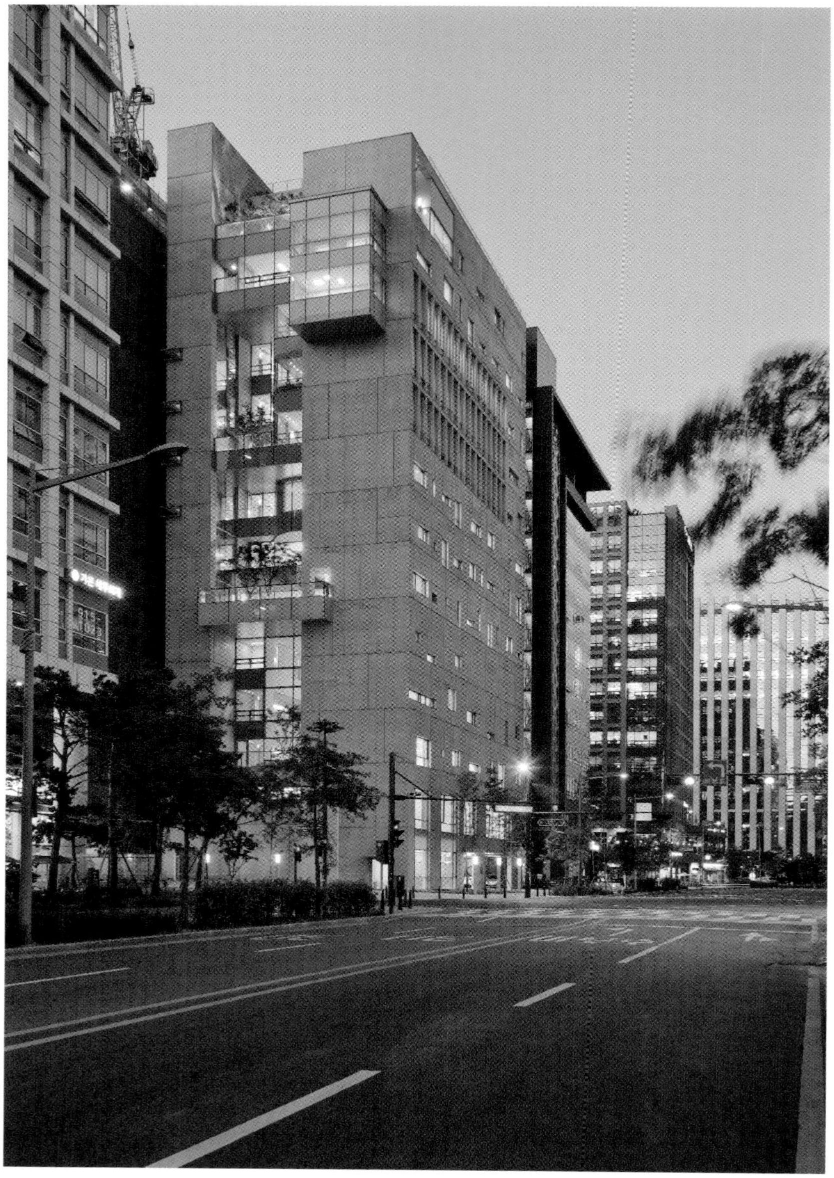

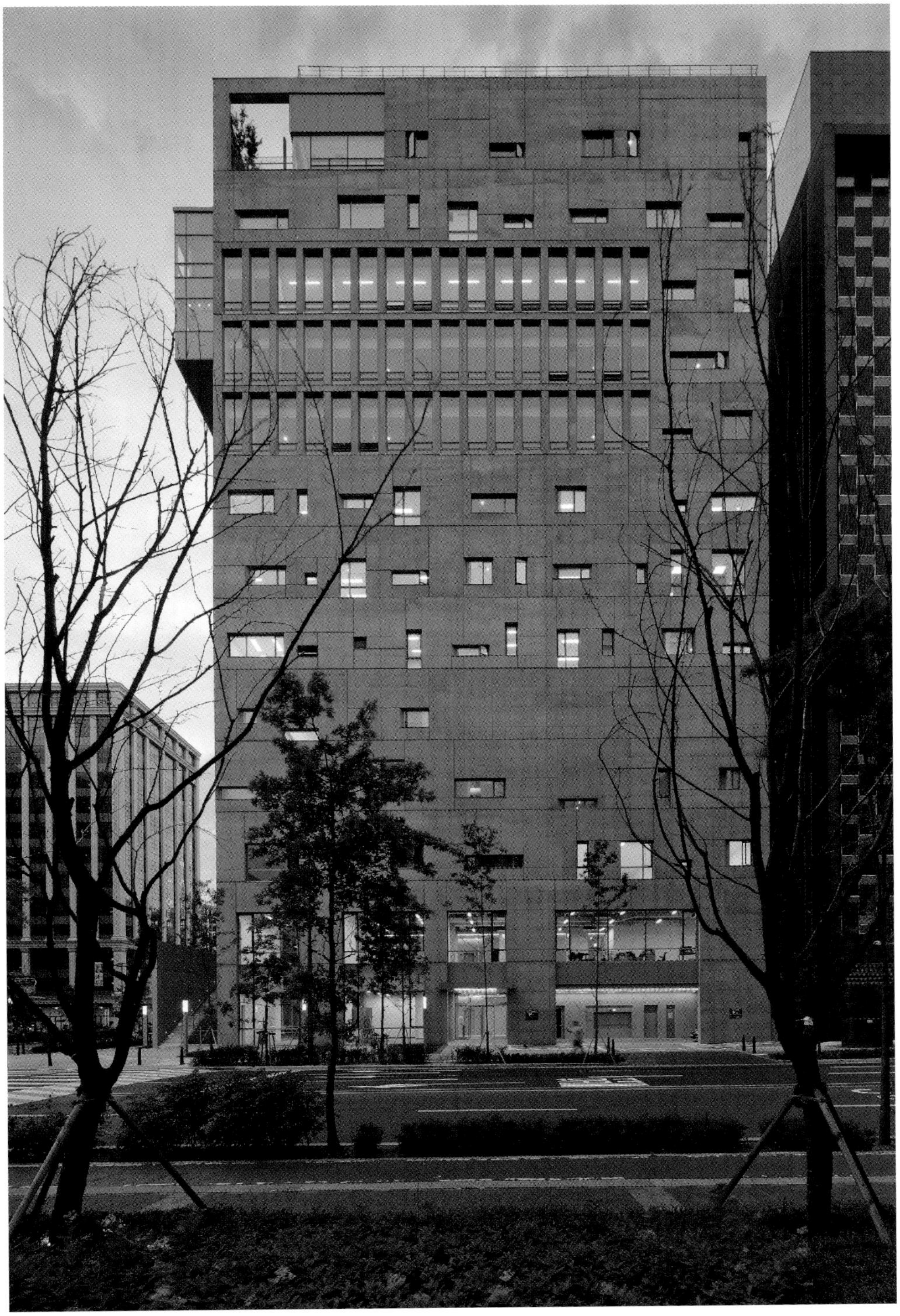

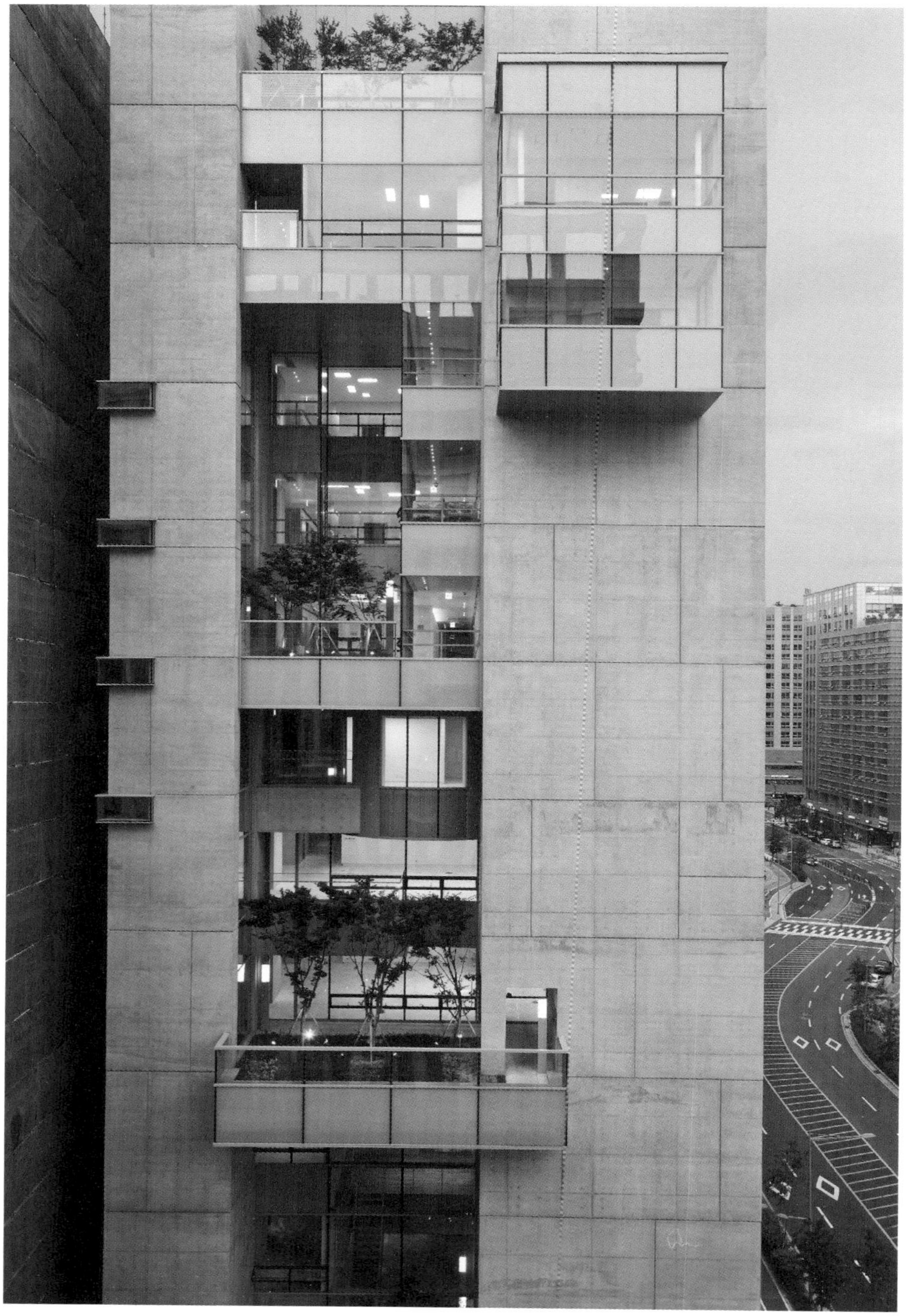

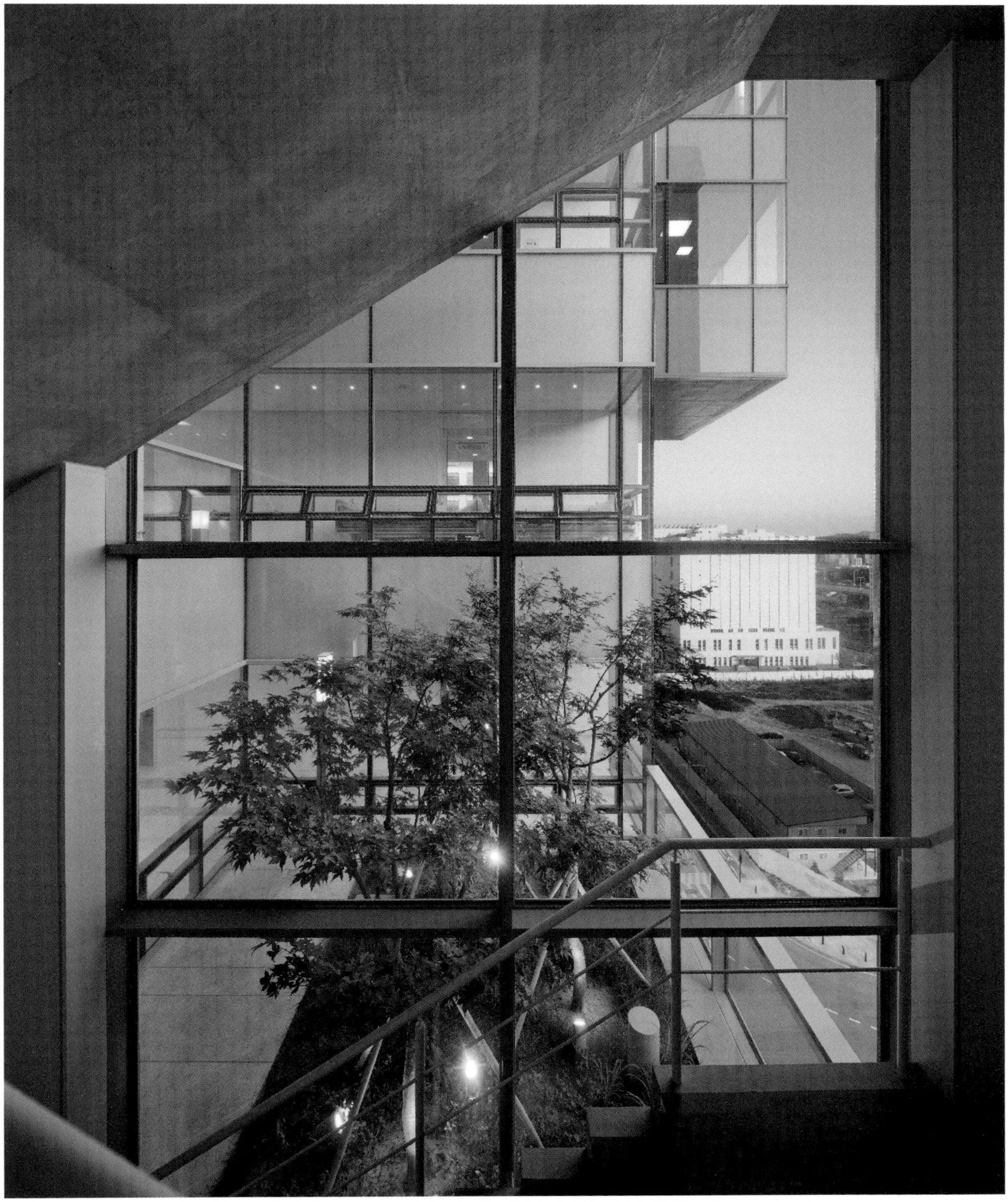

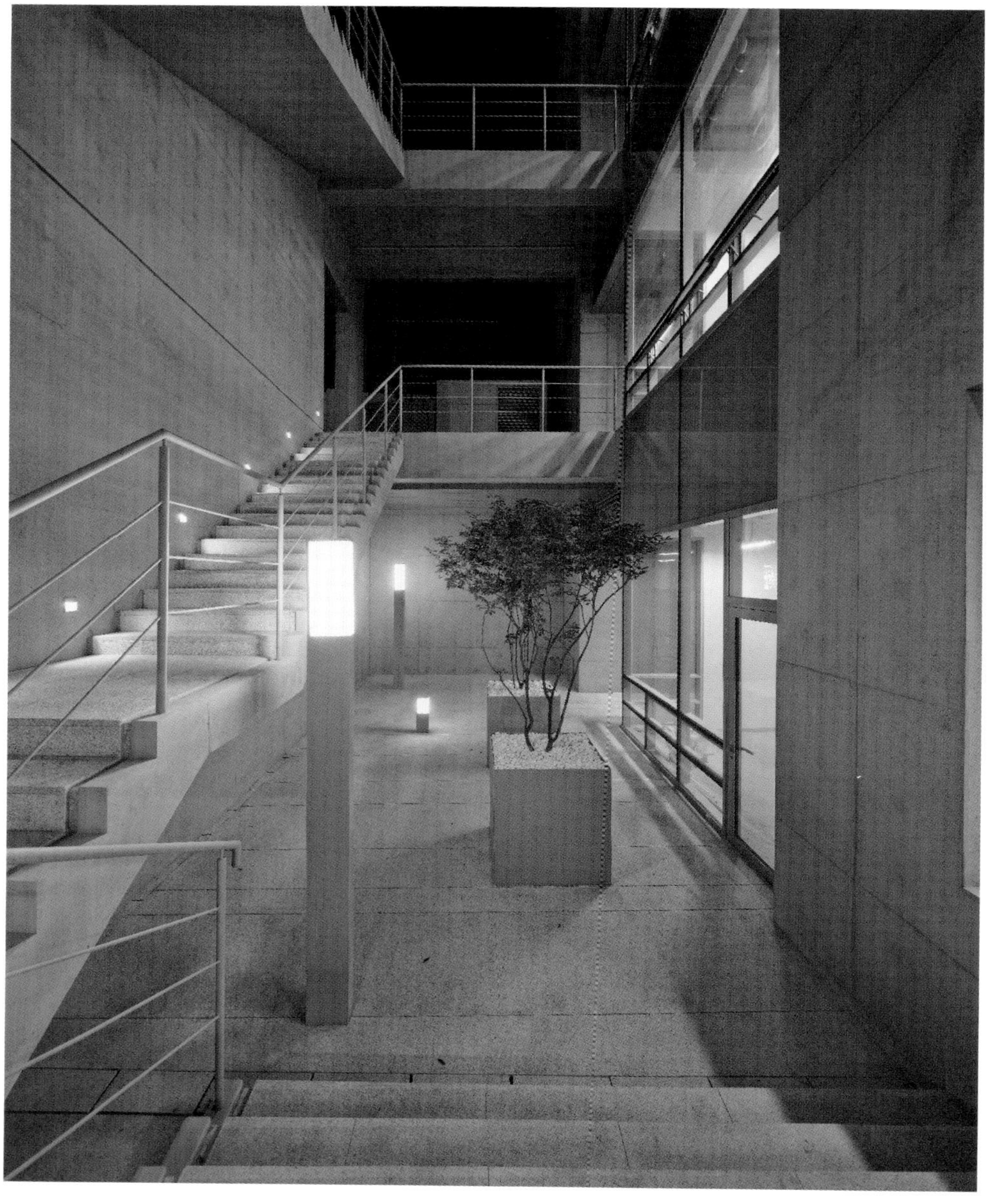

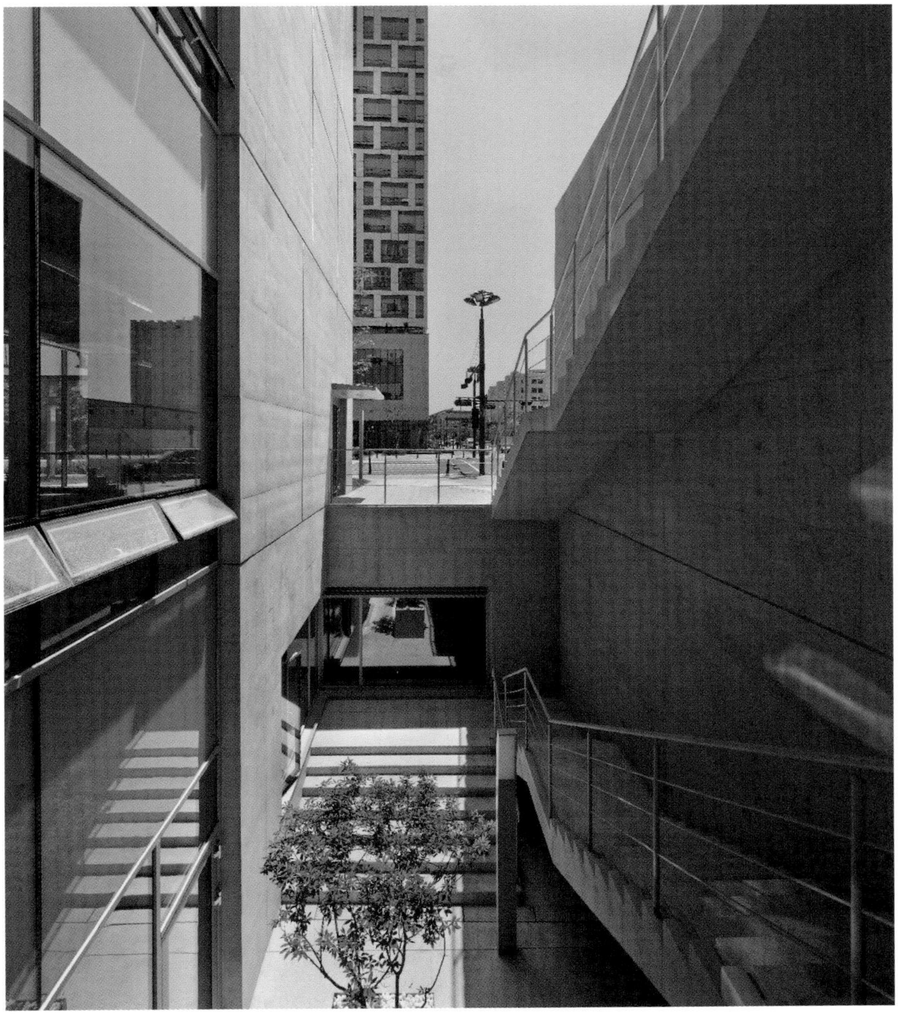

Myung Films Complex

Myung Flims is a relatively young and successful film production and distribution company. They did not just intend to have a building with only the functions of film-production in 2nd phase of Paju Book & Film City, but wanted to have more facilities as like a film-making school, multipurpose spaces for performing arts, movies, and exhibitions which would be open to outsiders. In addition, they wanted to build housing for individuals, and a dormitory and guest rooms for students and long-term visitors at the same time the office building was constructed. The basic concept of this project was, accordingly, to design a small city which has complex functions such as production, consumption, culture, and residence.

Based on the construction guidelines of Paju Book City on the promotion of pedestrian streets within the premises, it was highly required to get rid of the demerits of the road system with more emphasis on vehicles for designing this architectural structure. For instance, dividing the entire mass into two parts, and providing a pedestrian route in the middle as the main square of this small city must be a good strategy for anyone to freely meet, stay, and part.

The mass divided into two parts are connected by a bridge and a deck so that people there can look over and respond to what's going on in the square and the street in this small city. The inside of the main mass facing the street is visible from outside because it is covered with the transparent glass wall. This way, the landscape of life in the mass is exposed. The inside is more like an urban area. Passages, like streets, travel through the inside of the mass where the spaces with various functions are positioned. There are small parks and resting places here and there. Of course, all of them are designed to have close relationship with the outside, and are open to each other.

As the residential section at the top is a private area, maximum emphasis has been placed on privacy. The residential section for owner's families is also a community which consists of spaces with different layers. Therefore, the diversity of layers, which is noticeable, should be respected.

It's natural that this architecture exists as an ever-changing landscape. With the memories of the changing landscape piling one over the other, the buildings change; with the dimension of time, this small city becomes an architectural structure. It is made by the residents. Perhaps, like some scenes of a movie, caught by a 3rd camera and not intended by the movie director, a true movie or a real architecture may be worthy enough only if they are predicated on the objectivity of the real world

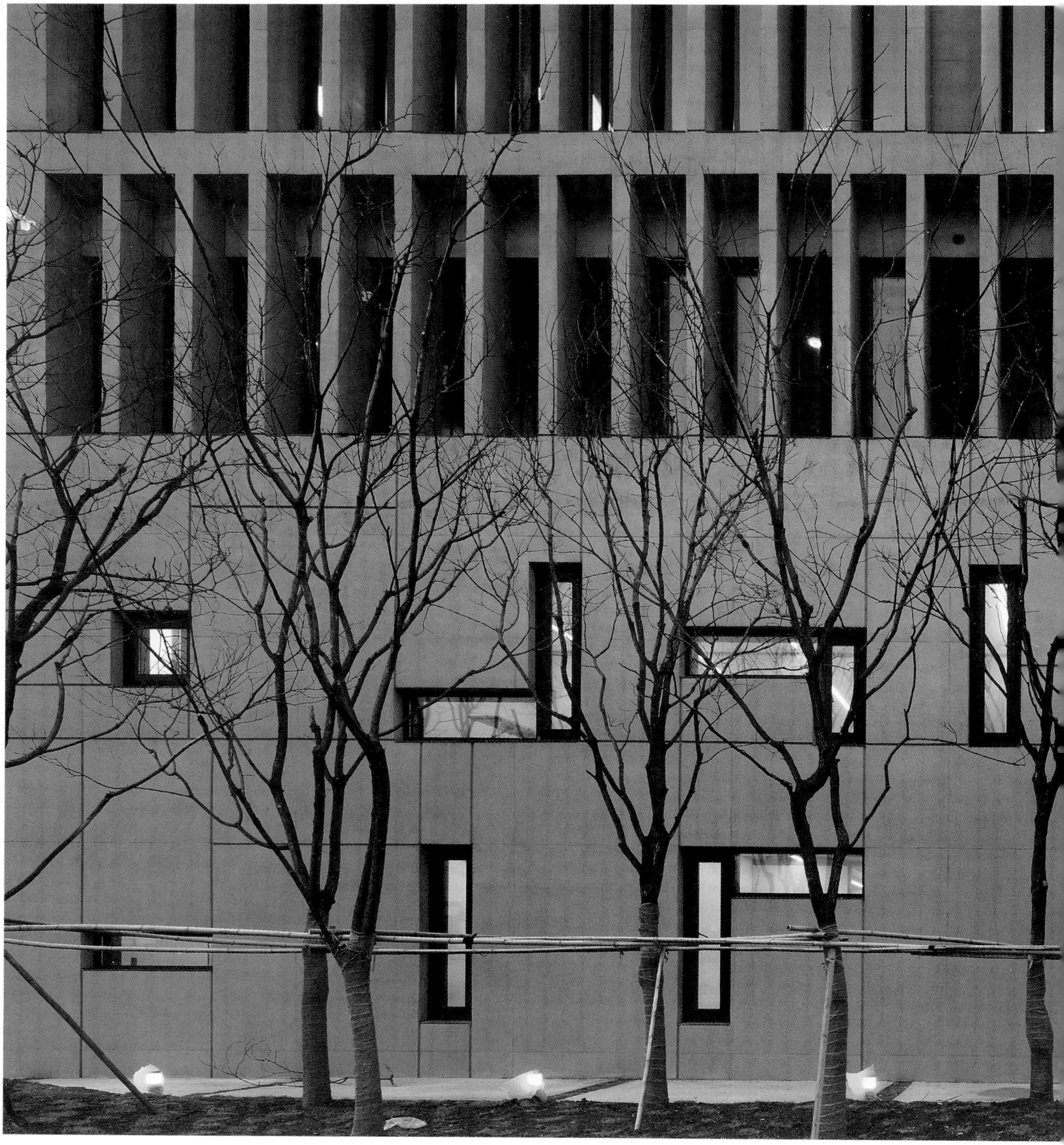

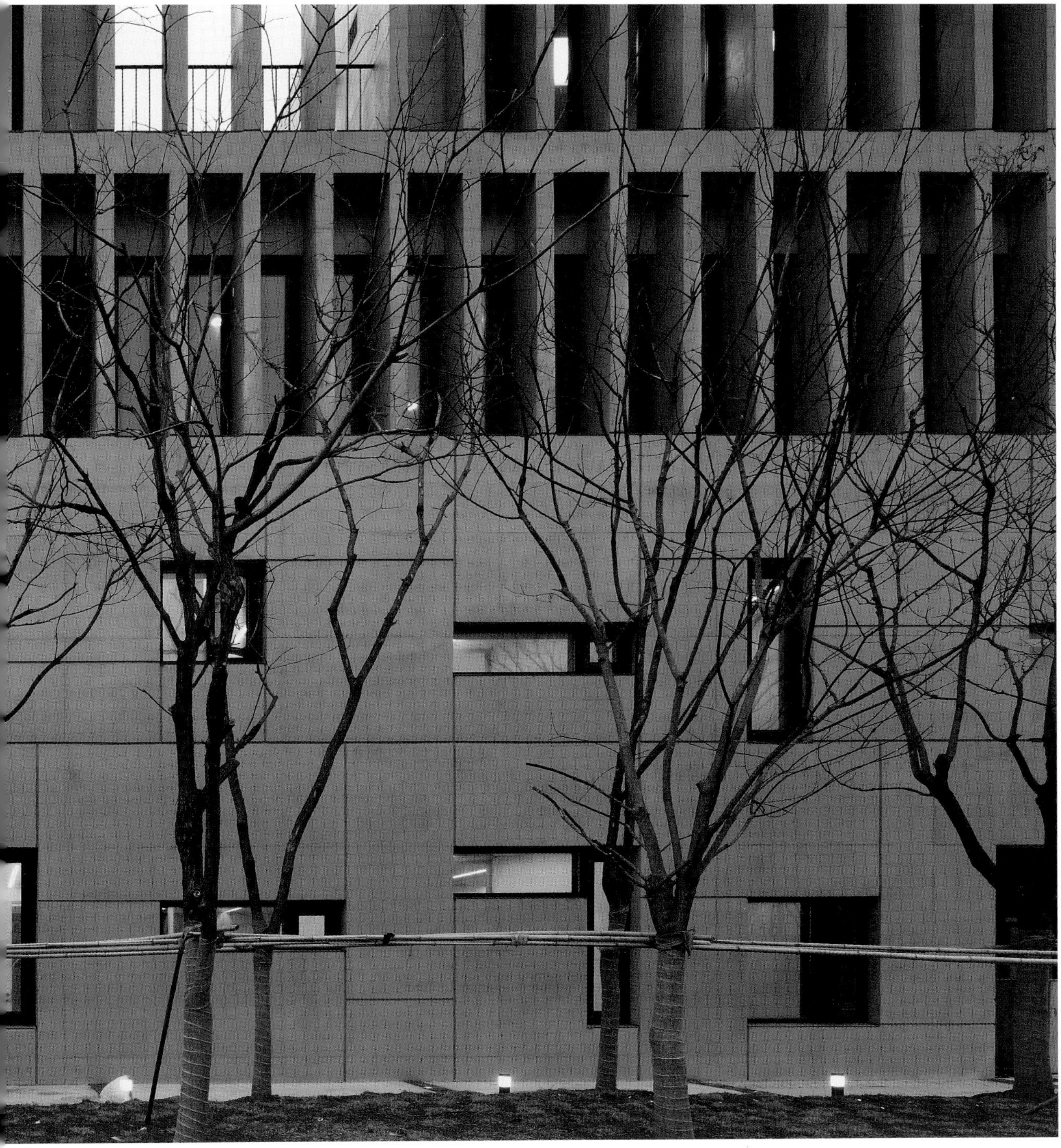

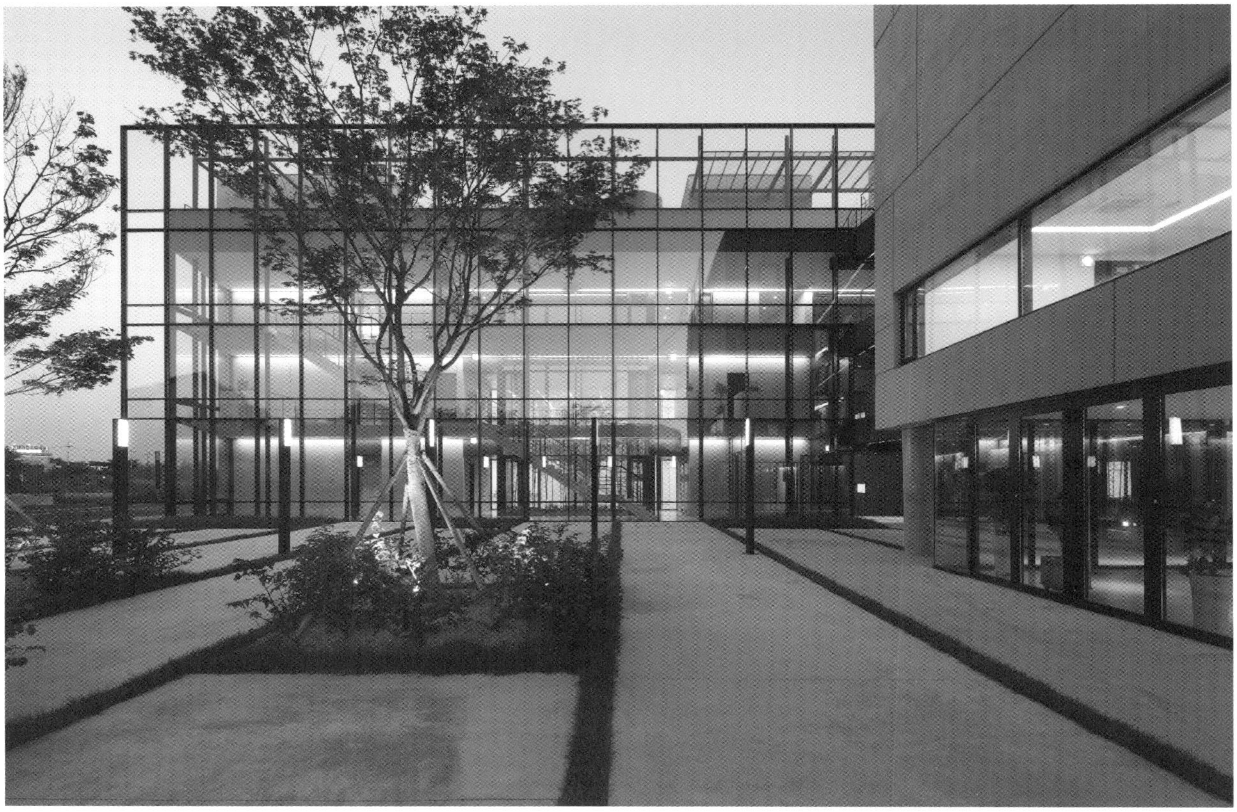

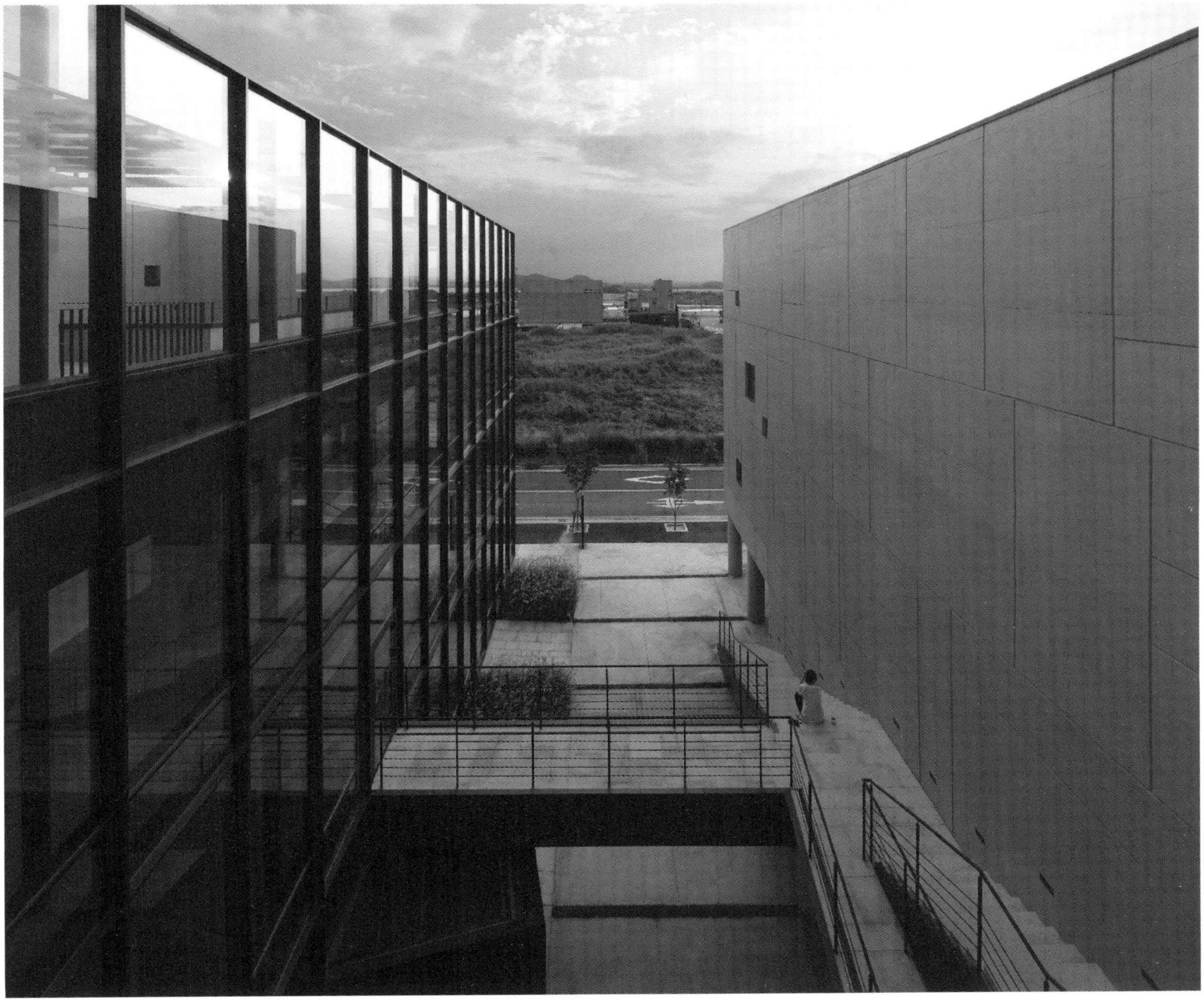

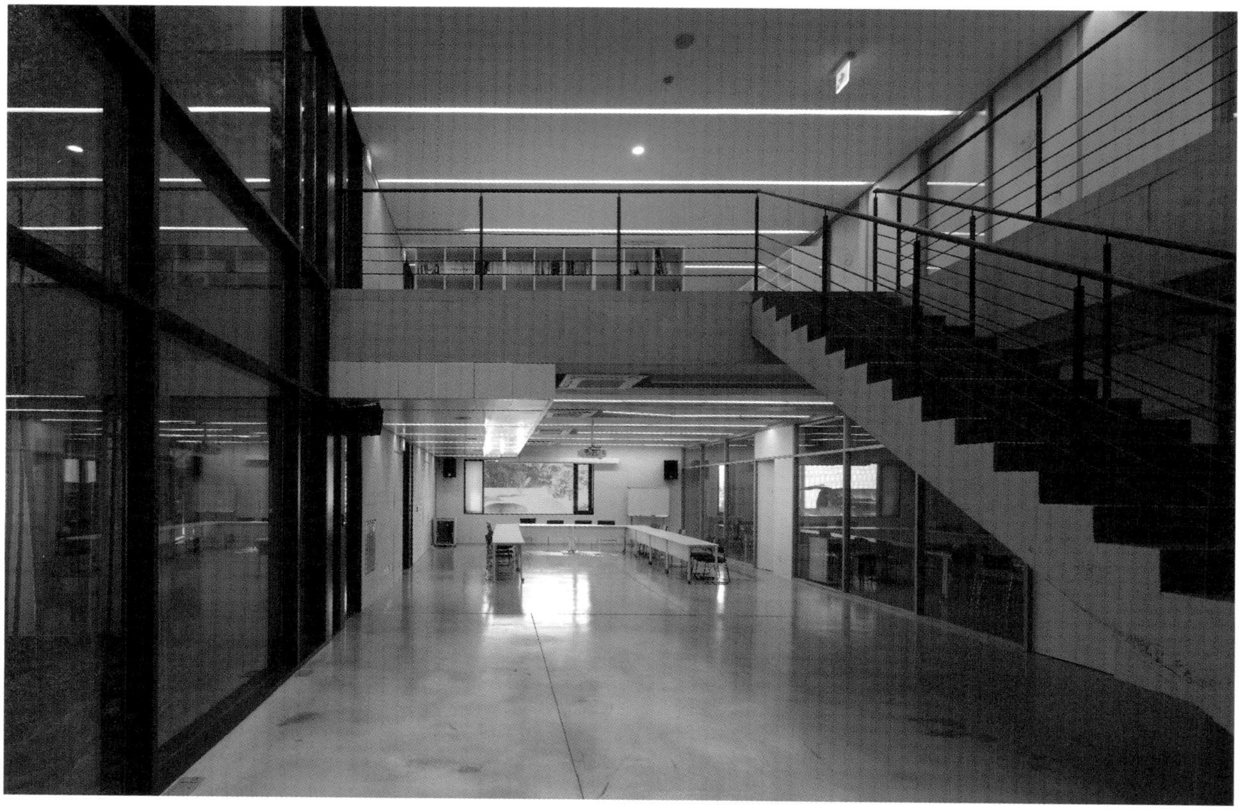

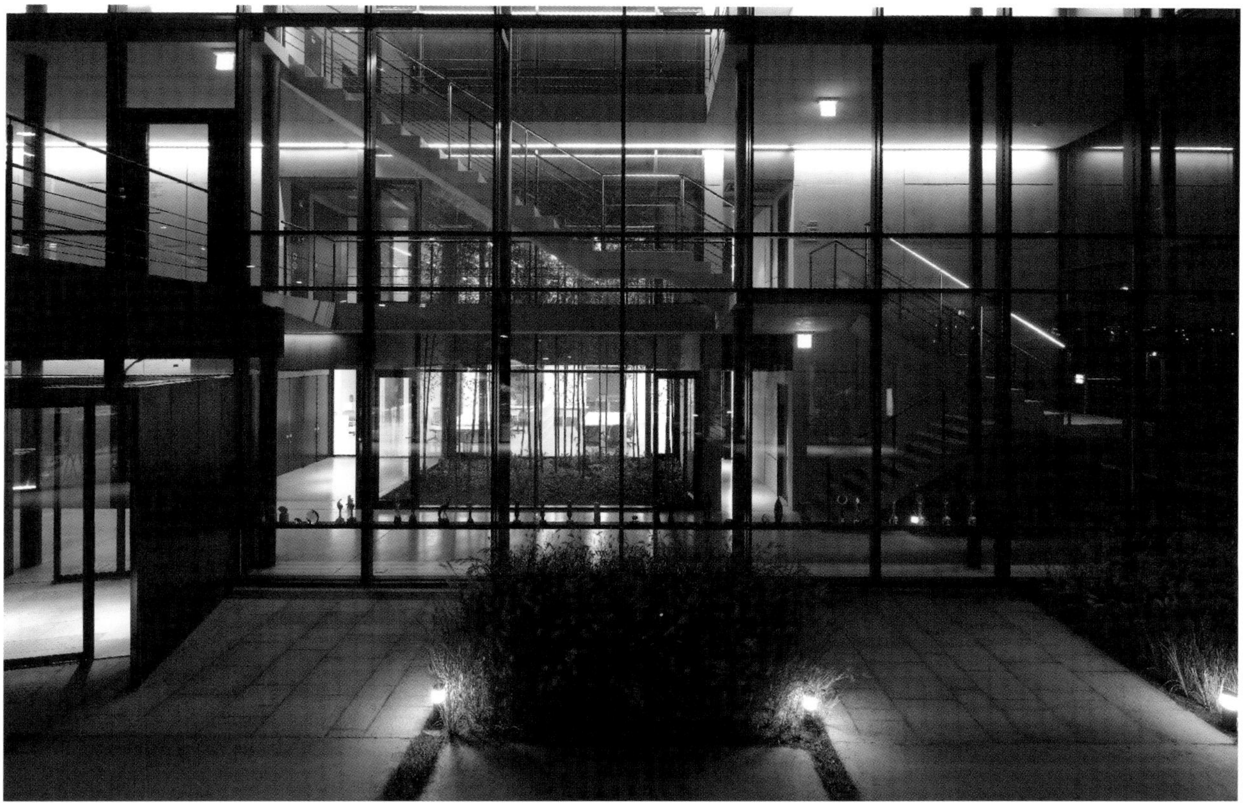

Design Vita Office Buillding

For the first phase of the Paju Book City master plan, many people had consistently argued for changing the existing conventional road system, or the greatest impediment to the formation of commonality of the phase. Unfortunately, however, nothing changed and the second phase began. The second phase included the film industry in the land almost same in area as the first phase. The second phase differed from the first one only in name -Paju Book & Film City. The project site of the second phase sits on the land right across from Lotte Outlet, a very large outlet shopping center that did not seem to suit the city's vision from any perspective. The challenge was to make this small building maintain its presence in an area dominated by large-scale commercial buildings.

The first thing was setting up a big wall on the road side for the promotion of stability and calmness in the inside of the wall. Although it was a concrete wall, it looks like a bookshelf frame. The volume of the building, centered on the building site, is small in scale but filled with various spaces. There is a café adjacent to the communal yard, a workspace dedicated to book design, a space for exhibitions or conferences, a uniquely shaped meeting room, a small park, and a meditation room. All the functional spaces have different conditions of light and darkness and vary in shape and size. As they are all independent and harbor different energy, meticulous arrangements have been made to ensure that a walk through this place becomes a pleasant stroll. The exterior has been finished with concrete which need not be of good-quality exposed concrete. Though using ordinary plywood for form work, strict verticality and horizontality was kept. It would then manifest the spirit of those who worked on its construction. Covered with a thin layer of white paint, it tells the truth.

WORM'S EYE VIEW

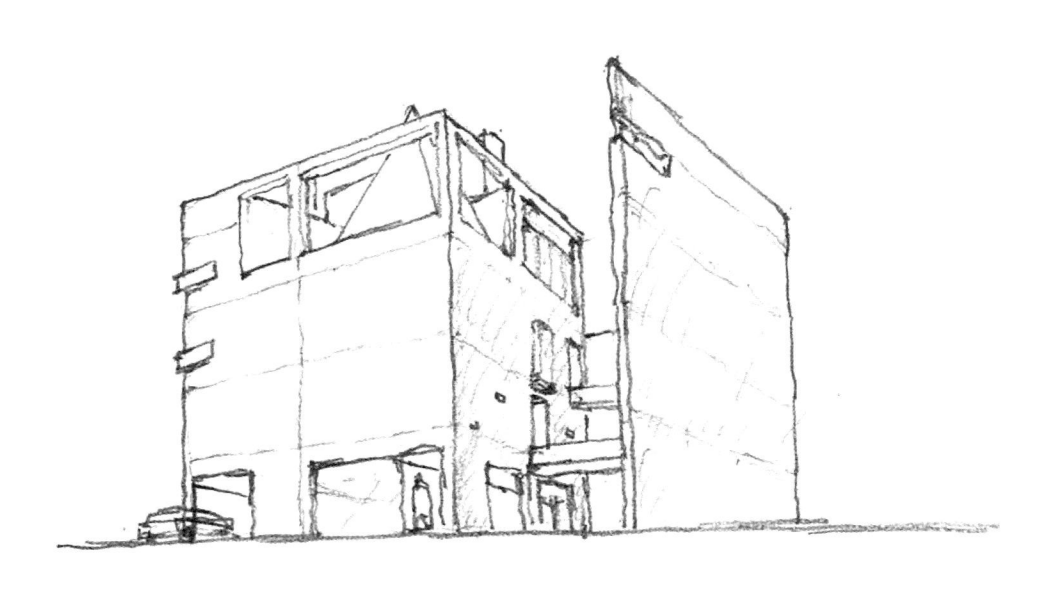

Design Vita Office Building

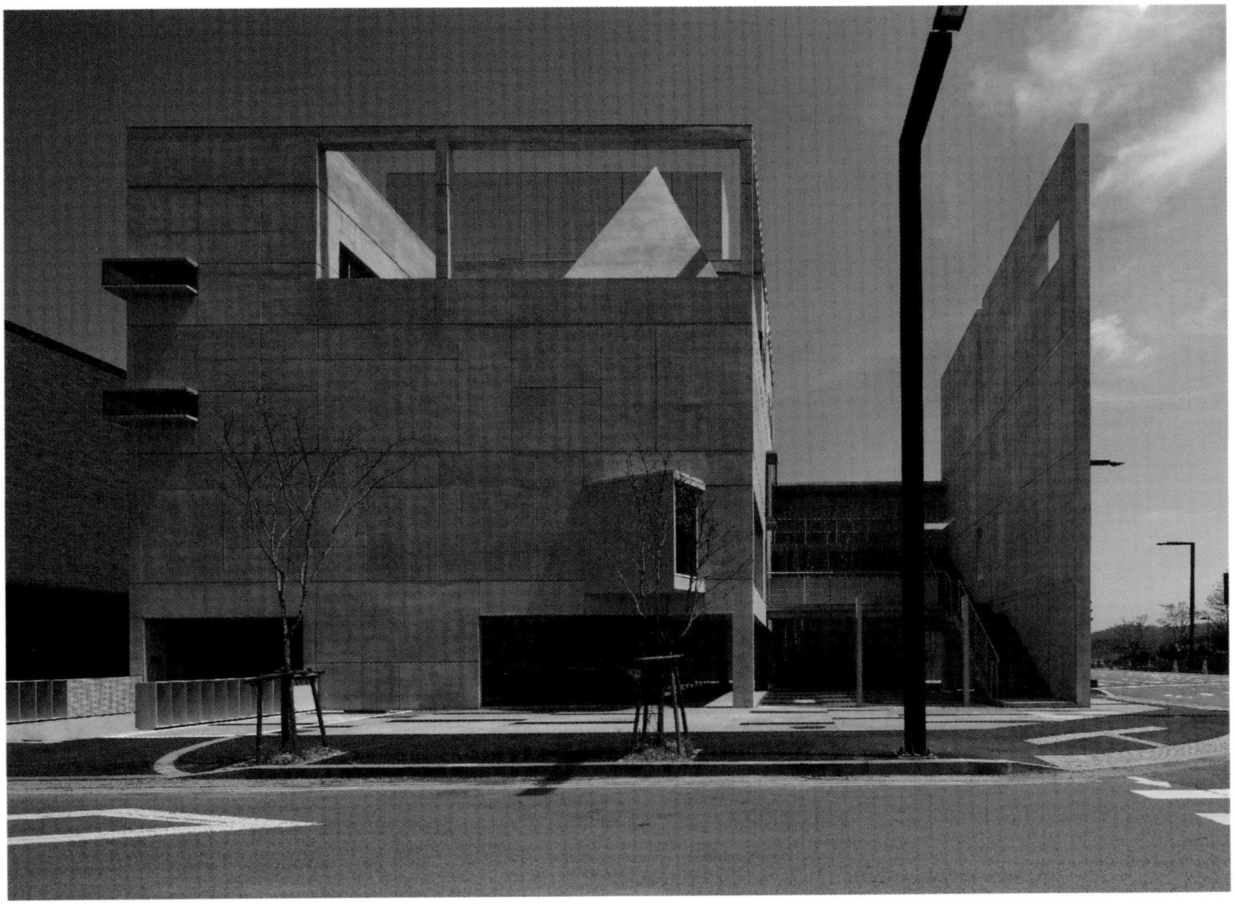

Design Vita Office Building

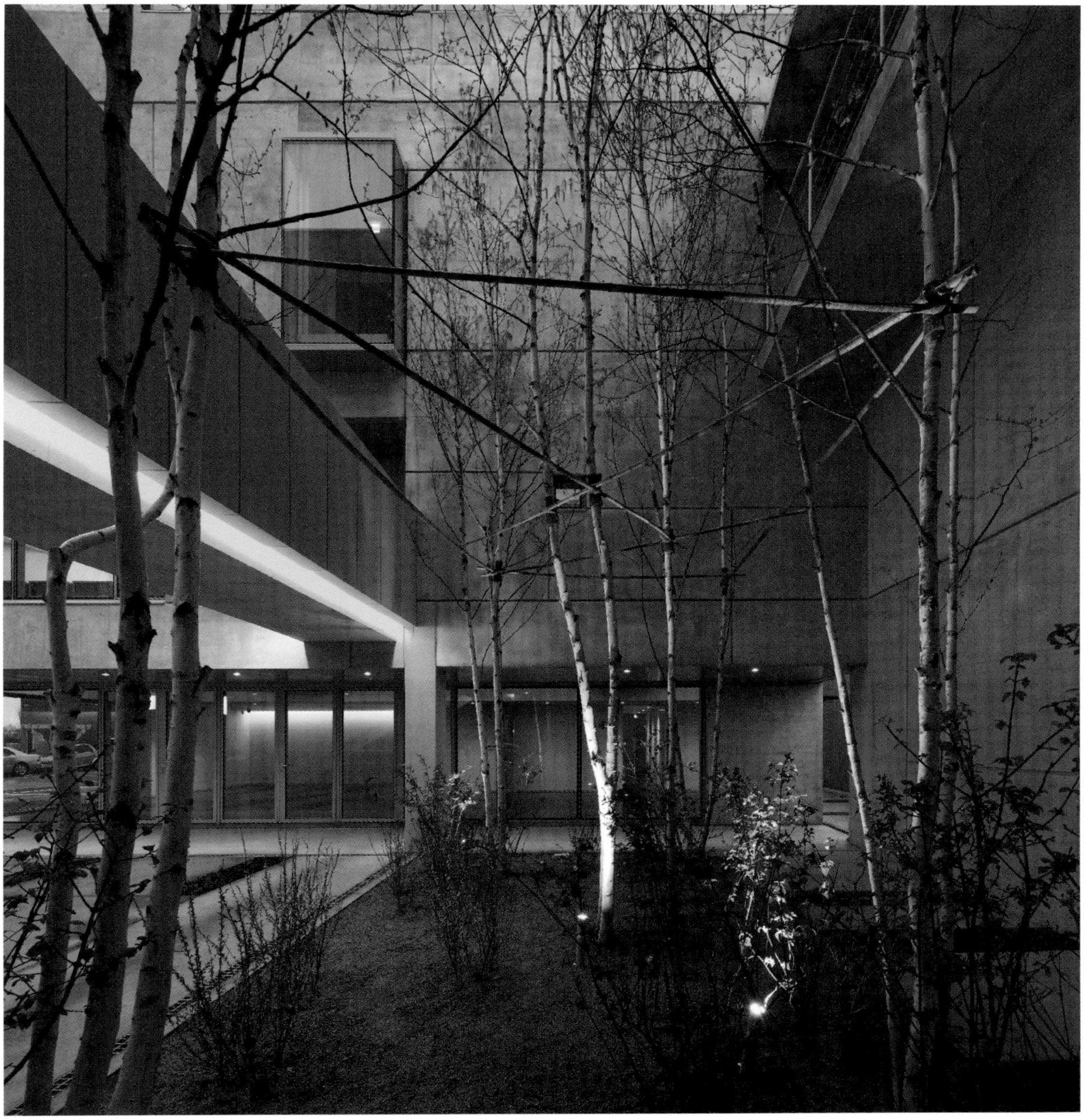

Design Vita Office Building

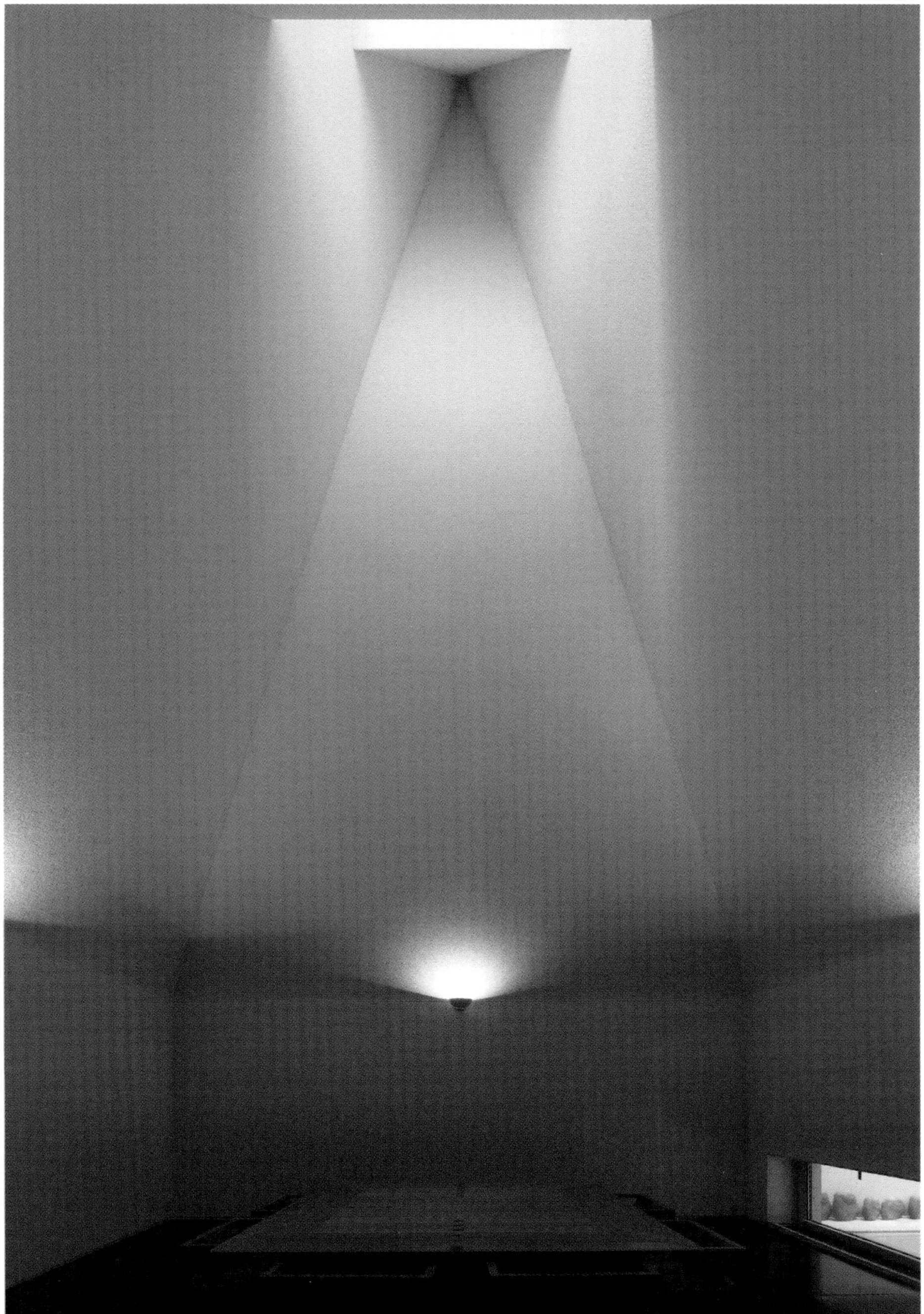

Chusa Memorial Museum

Behind the beautiful scenery of Jeju Island are deeply-furrowed traces of sad history. The island had to be exploited for hundreds of years as an attached territory of the mainland, and even before that, the invasions by the Japanese left deeply-cut wounds on all over the Island. In the modern era, the tragic events caused by the ideological conflicts between the left and the right political factions still remain as a traumatic experience that cannot be erased. In addition, Jeju which had long been a very tough place of exile in the past, is a place where the culture of exiles who should live with resentment and sorrow, still remains. Kim Jeong-hui (1786-1856, well known as his pen name *Chusa*) was the central figure of the exile culture. Chusa, who was one of the highly-respected intellectuals during the late part of the Kingdom of Joseon, drove himself to the highest artistic level by sublimating solitude during the eight years of exile in the island. His sharp and powerful calligraphy was the product of such loneliness.

Because this was the architecture in commemoration of Chusa, representations of all the sloppy desires should be removed. Moreover, the site was adjacent to the remains of a fortress in Daejeong, and the village in the fortress remains looked plain and simple due to the small and humble houses in the village. The gross floor area of the Chusa Memorial Museum was about 1,200m², which was rather too large in terms of the surrounding environment. Because of its size, such a relatively big museum would surely fail to keep a balance with the surroundings. First and foremost, it was crucial to make the architectural least visible. It was highly required to place almost all the volumes underground, and make the Museum appear on the ground as small and simple as possible. For the underground space, sunken yards were created to secure lighting and ventilation. When the visitors finish watching the exhibits, they are to reach a space open to the top. Reaching the space walking up the stairs, they encounter a totally empty space where nothing but silence remains. It has been arranged for them to personally meet with Chusa there.

秋生
ôure
2010

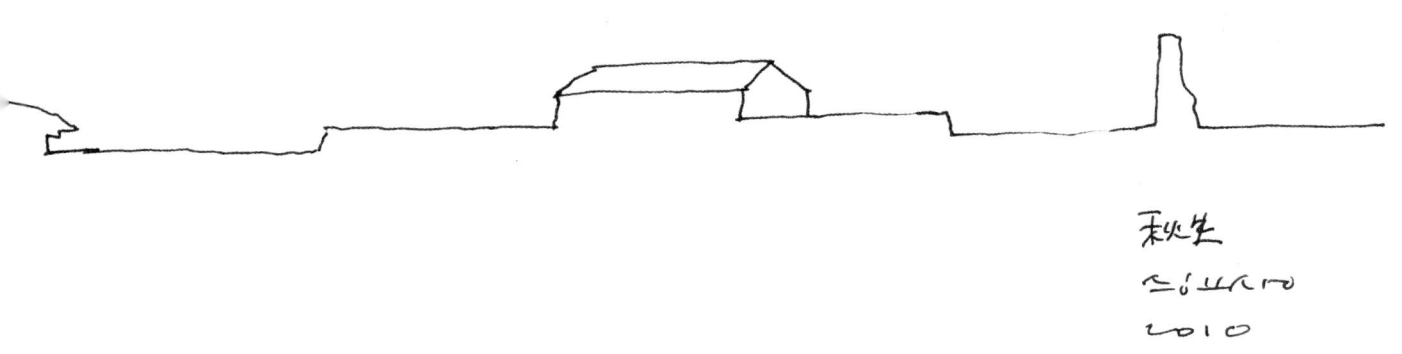

Chusa Memorial Museum

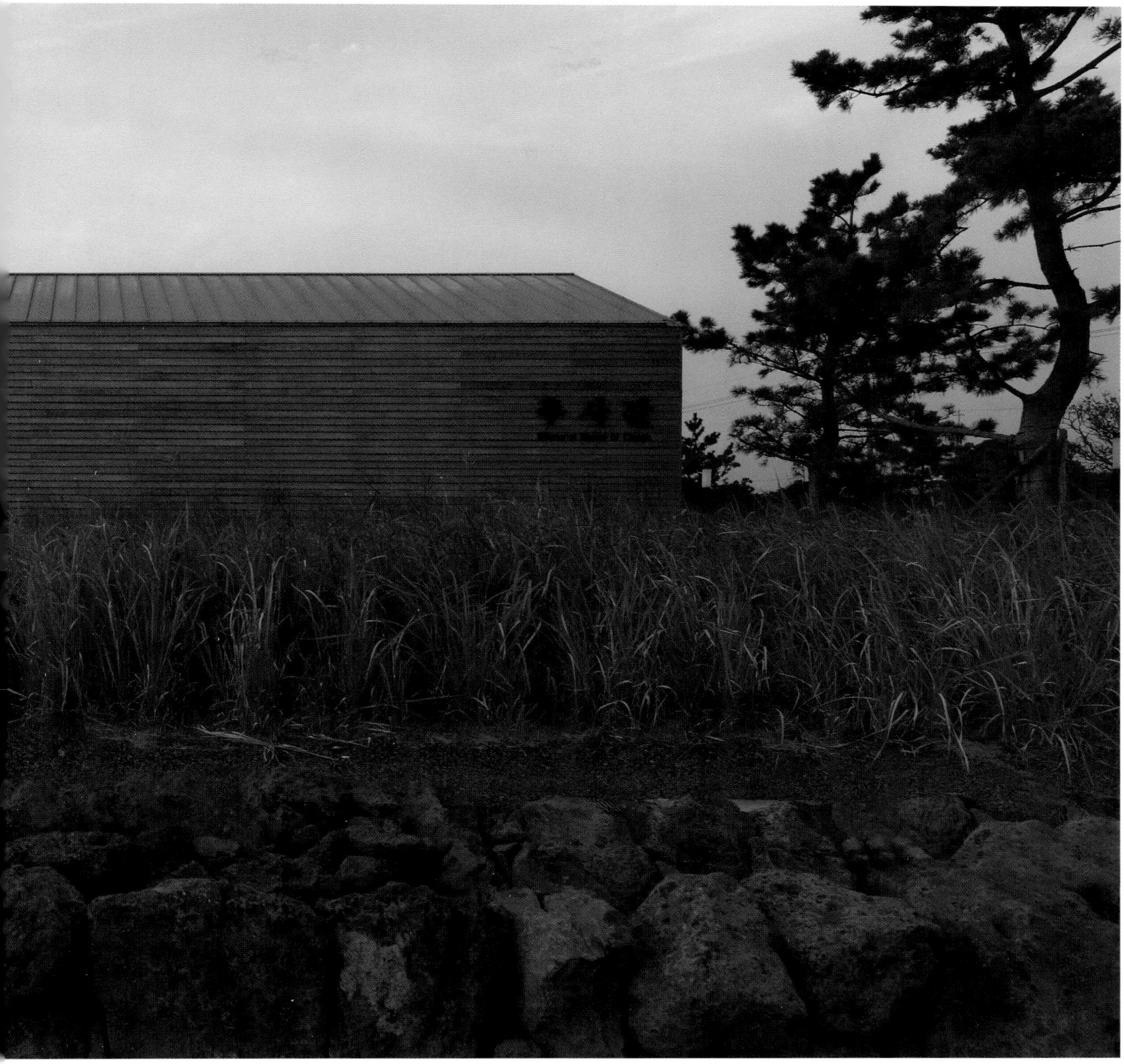

Chusa Memorial Museum

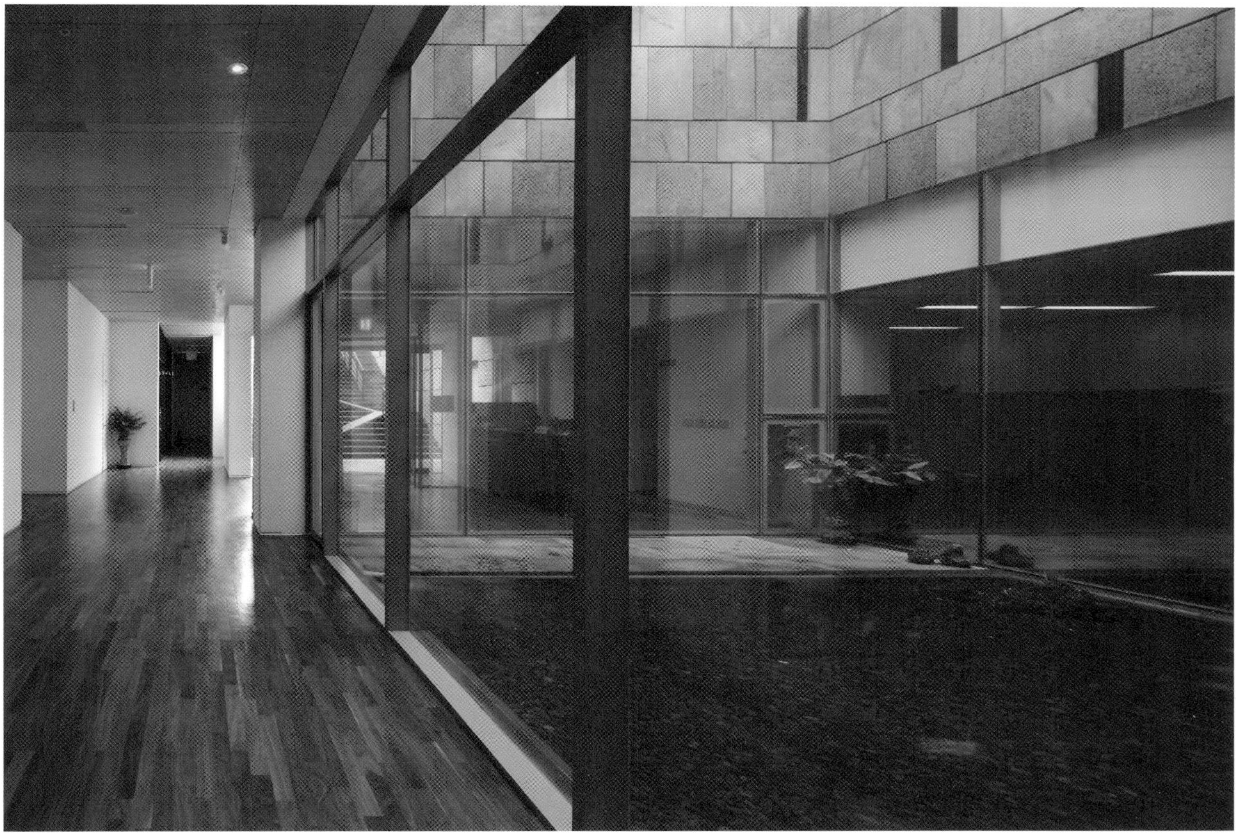

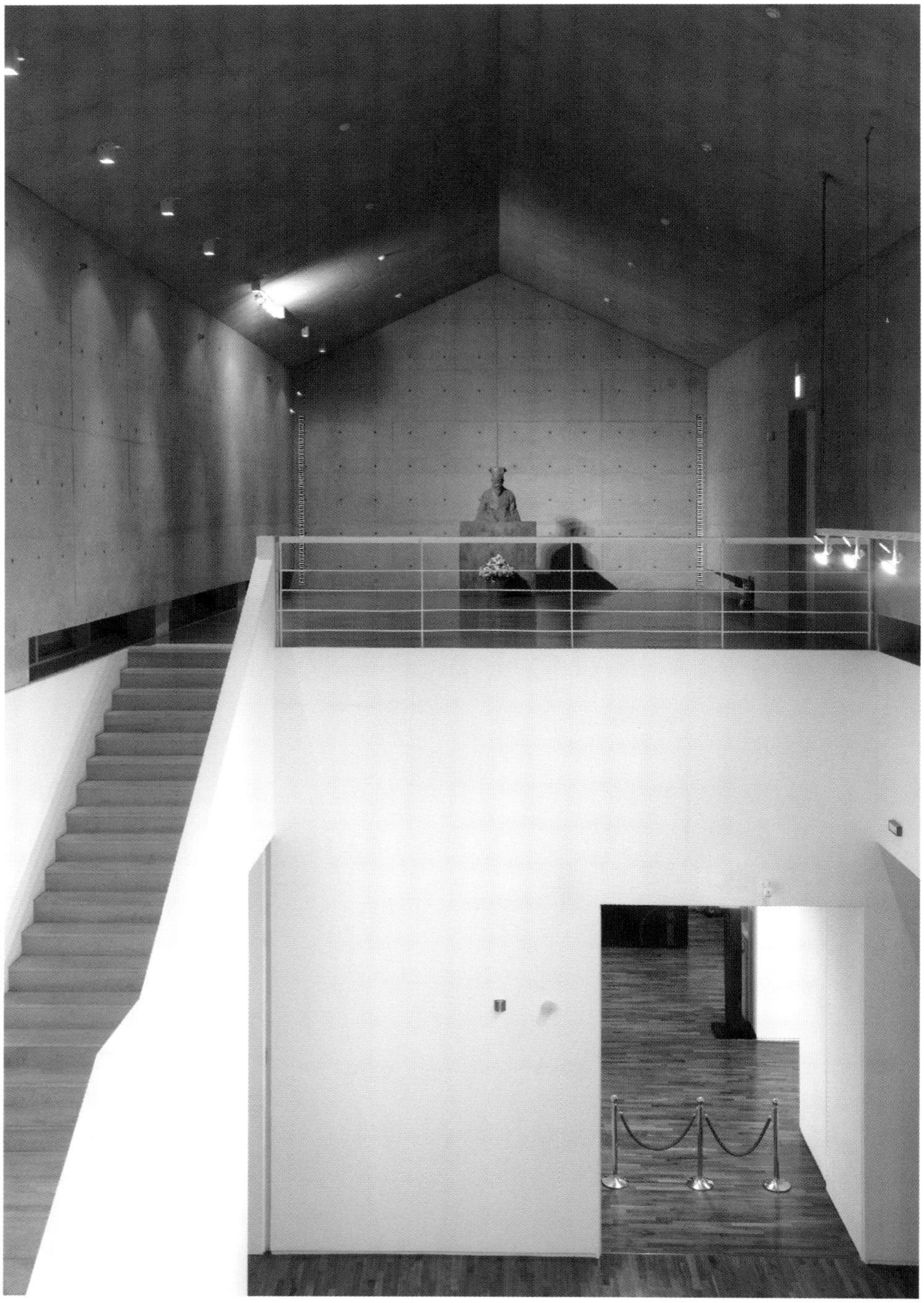

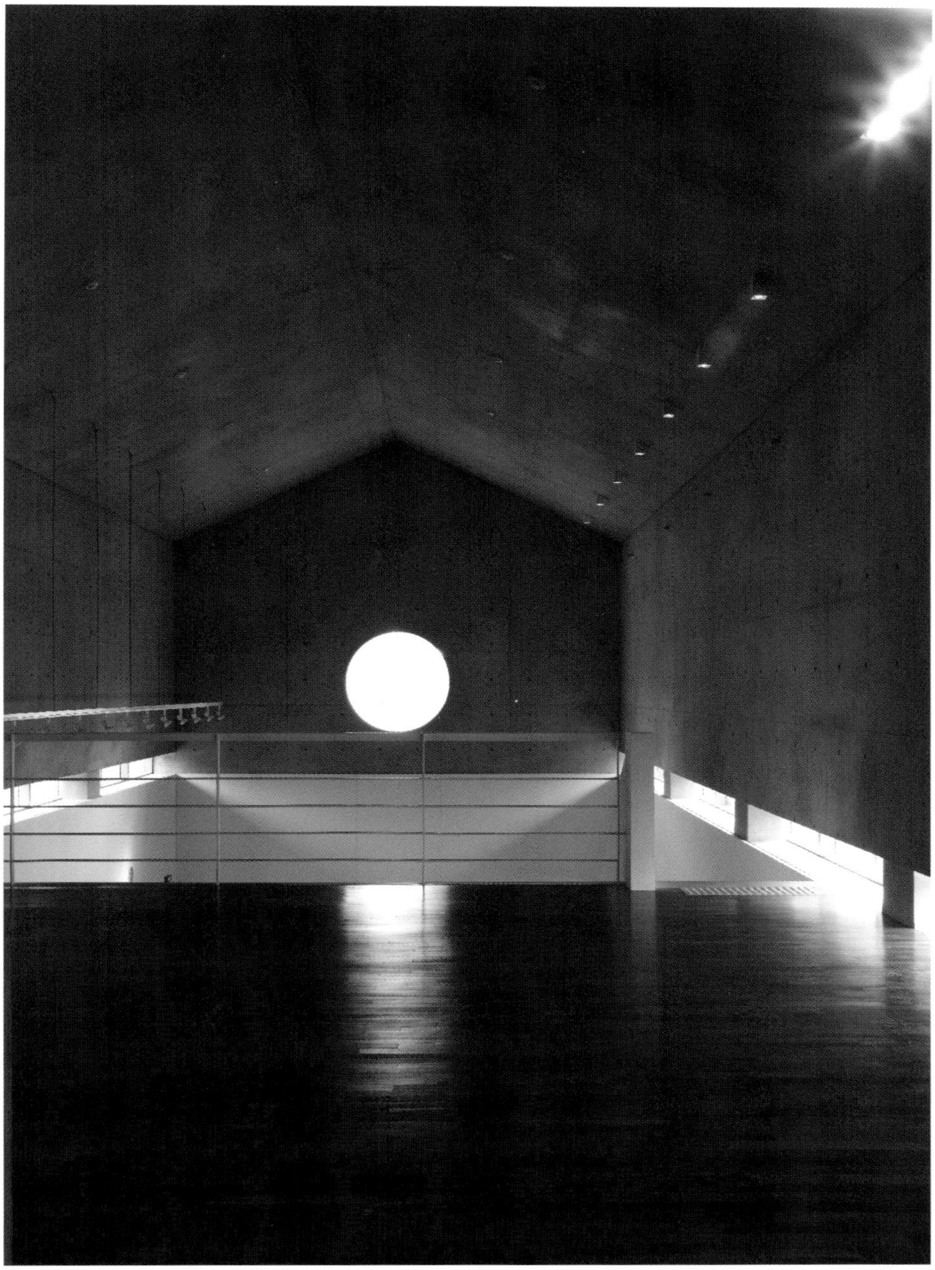

Country Club House "360° Earth, Water, Flowers, and Wind"

This 360° golf club has another unique name as "Earth, Water, Flower, and Wind". The club house is an urbanites' gateway to nature and a space where routine changes into exception. The club house, where transition takes place, is a community where people, unknown to each other, share the same space. It was fair, therefore, that the club house or a social building, should be shaped as a village and town.

The club house, which is composed of several buildings, also should satisfy the functional requirements for the system of the golf club which needs rapidity in responding to the requests. For this purpose, an appropriate volume for each house unit was suggested for optimal functioning, and the house units were placed for maximum functioning. As such, they look as if they were arranged randomly. This randomness resulted in a natural cluster of house units. What is noteworthy is that the spaces between the house units look like courtyards. In addition, such spaces contribute greatly to natural ventilation, light, and both visual and spatial richness.

The golfers will feel like they drive through a village as they approach the golf club. The guest house adjacent to the club house embraces the access road, thereby intensifying such feeling. In case some golfers who arrive late for a round, a route of sequential shortcut movement is offered so that they can be ready for the tee-off as early as possible. On the contrary, for those who have enough time, meticulous arrangement has been made for them to take time even in the locker room, enjoying the view of surrounding courtyards.

Approaching the last hole in the field, the golfers encounter the lustrous titanium roof coverings of the town. The club house remains as a town of vivid memory of earth, water, flowers, and wind for those who return to their ordinary life after finishing a full round of golf.

Country Club House "360° Earth, Water, Flowers, and Wind"

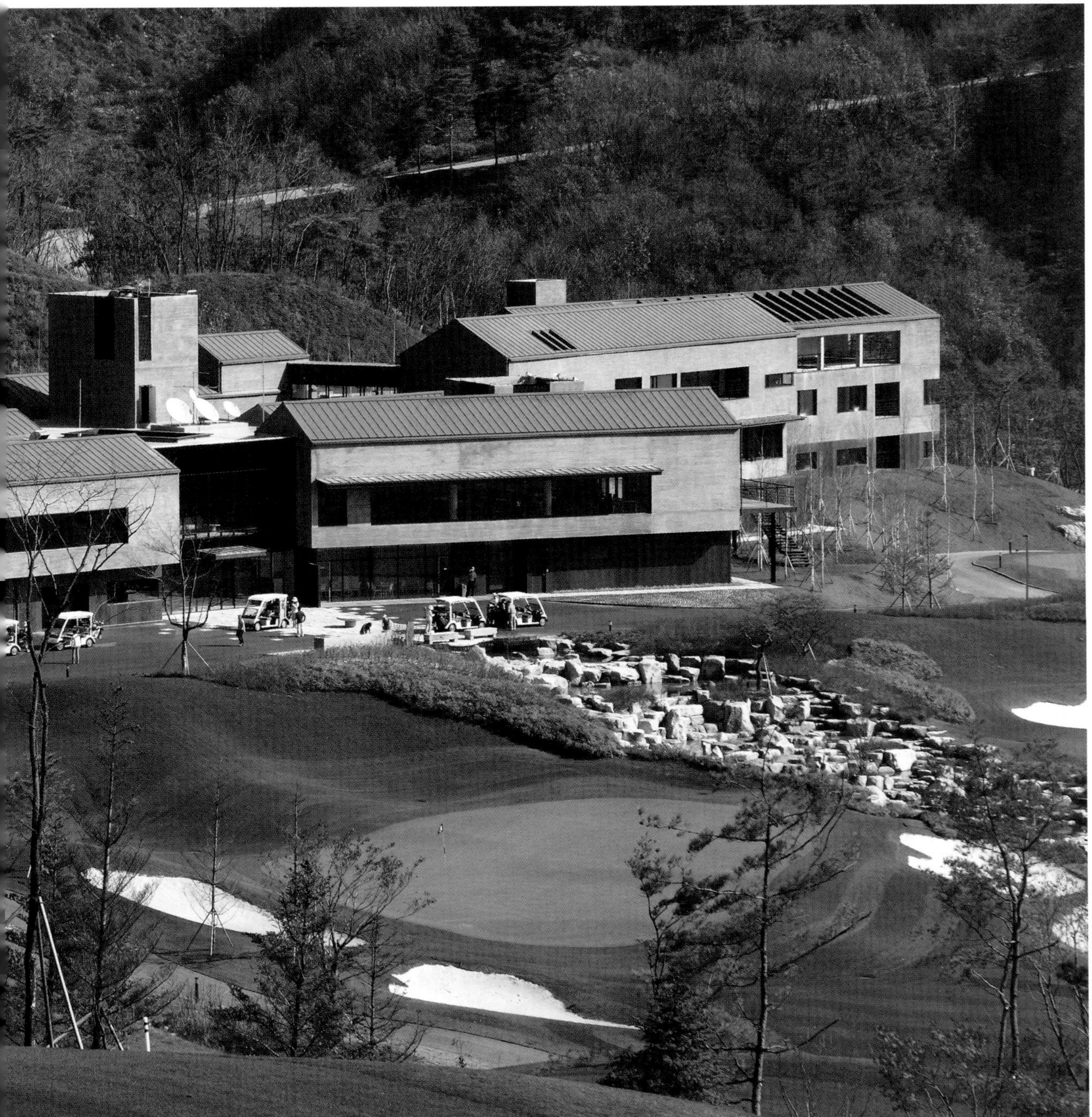

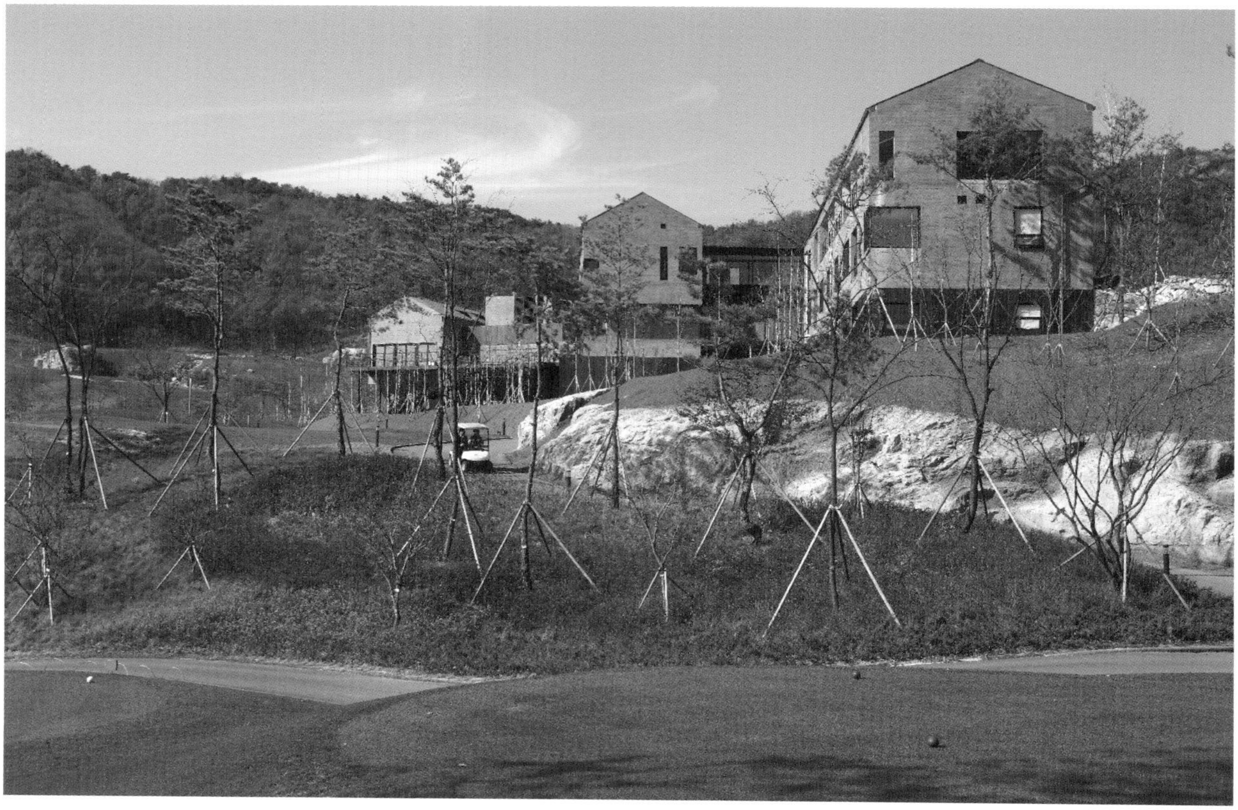

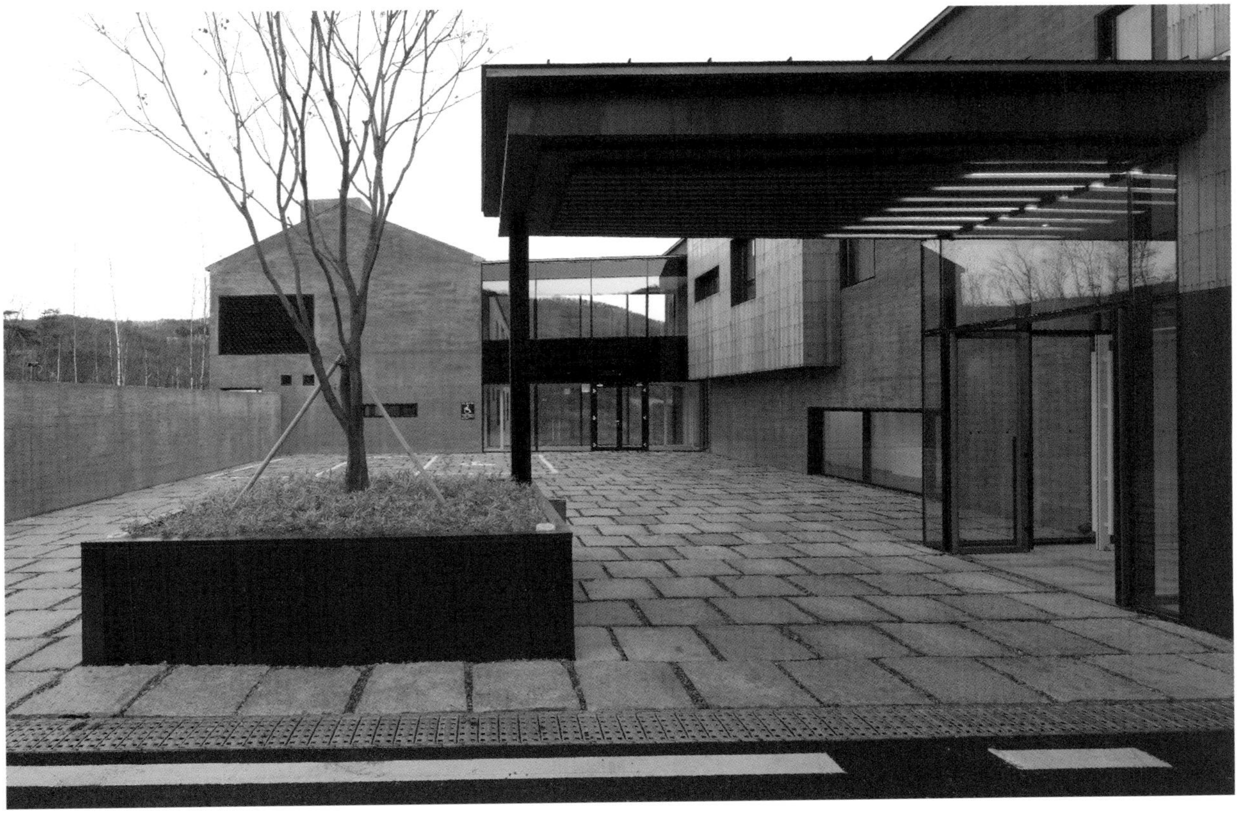

Country Club House "360° Earth, Water, Flowers, and Wind"

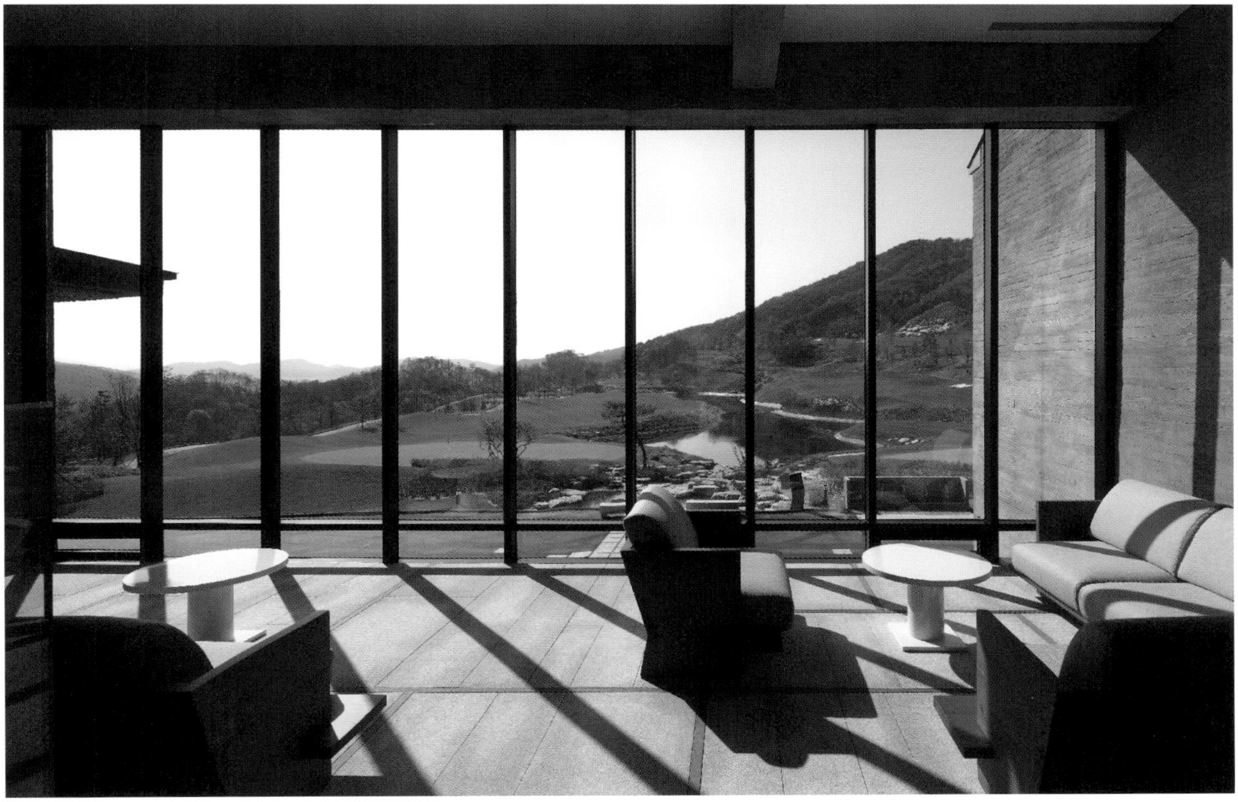

Although the traditional Korean Buddhist architecture remains blank in contemporary architecture and the influence of the pro-Confucianist and anti-Buddhist policy of the Kingdom of Joseon (1392-1910) remains largely untouched, the Buddhist circle seems to be obsessed with the old forms of architecture even today. Would not it be contrary to the respect of the Buddhist teachings and the essence of Buddhism? As such, whether or not who would be chosen as the architect of the project was a critical moment of leaving away from the established practices. After a difficult process, the leaders of the Jogye Buddhist Order made a progressive decision and accepted this architectural project.

What is the most important in the Buddhist architecture? It is nothing but "emptiness," and this is the essence of Buddhism. So the newly embodied emptiness had to be an important concept of this architectural structure despite all conditions and requirements. Much of the site of this architectural structure was already designated as a prohibited area of construction because many roof tile kilns of the Kingdom of Joseon were found before starting design. The Buddhist circle seemed to be a bit disappointed, but it was rather fortunate. Naturally, the central part of the site should be emptied widely, and the architectural structure was driven to the edge of the site. This lead to the beginning of a dramatic sequence of emptiness.

There are a lot of courtyards in this architecture. Here, several buildings are the factors that limit the yard, and the yard around here is connected to each other by its own way of existence, and carries traces of beautiful scenery and habitation around it. And the passage to the space of emptiness often touches the nature, and gives the visitor the beauty of life and a moment of reflection on himself. Could it be a religion in itself?

Wood, stone and earth – they are the building materials. They all eventually change in form, and disappear into the earth. What remains is emptiness.

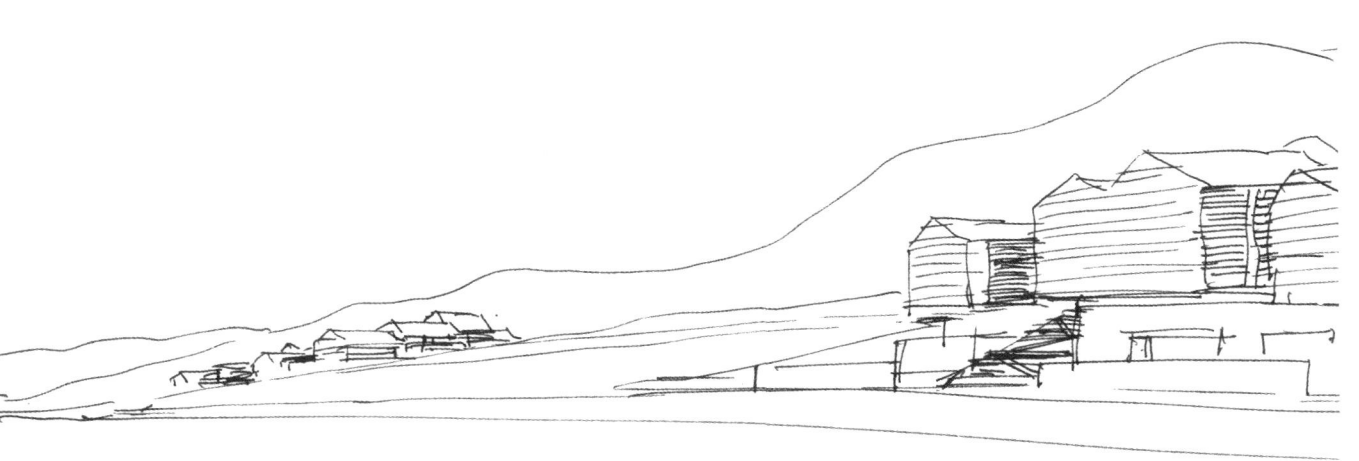

Traditional Buddhism Center of Jogye Order

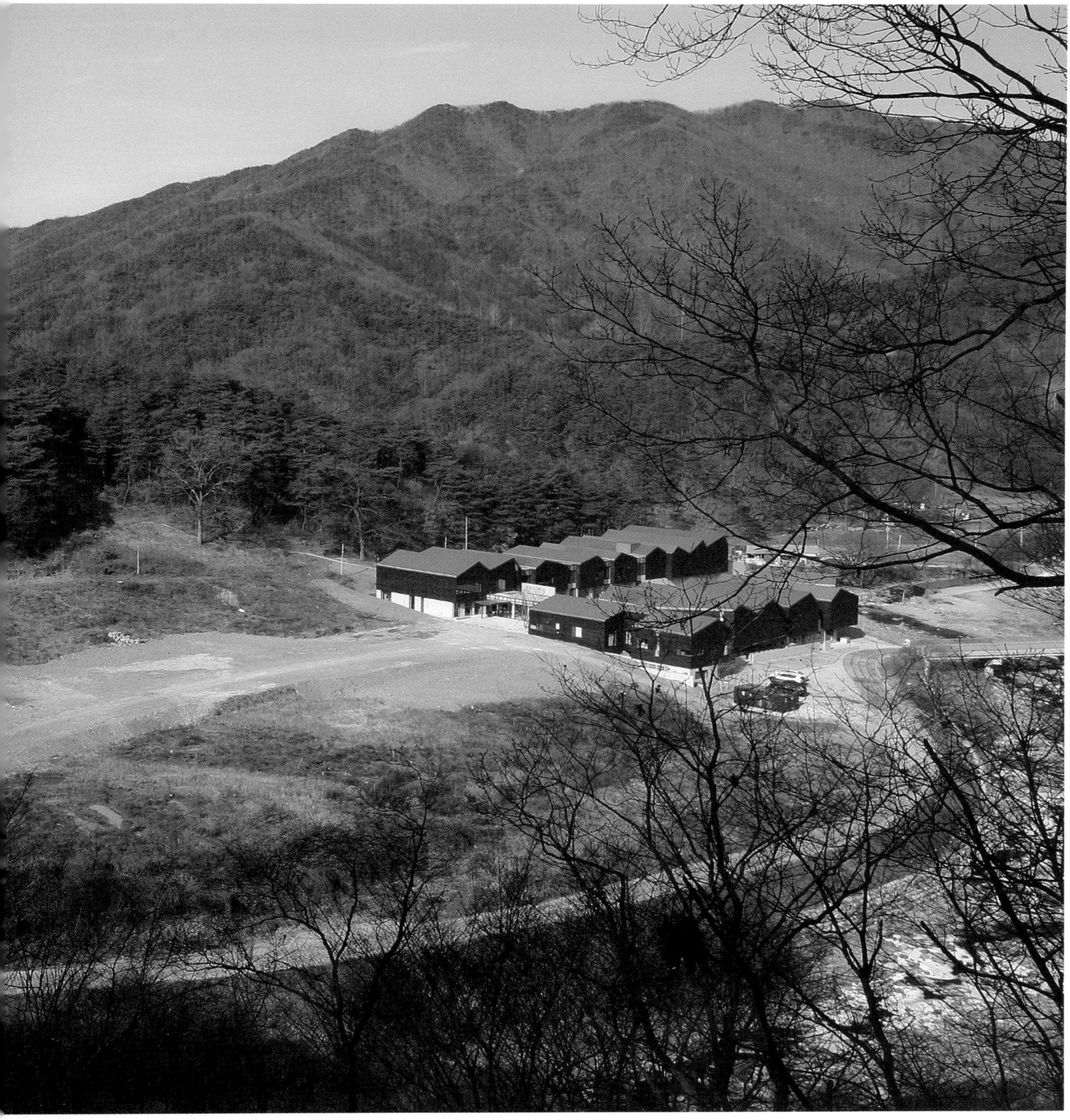

Traditional Buddhism Center of Jogye Order

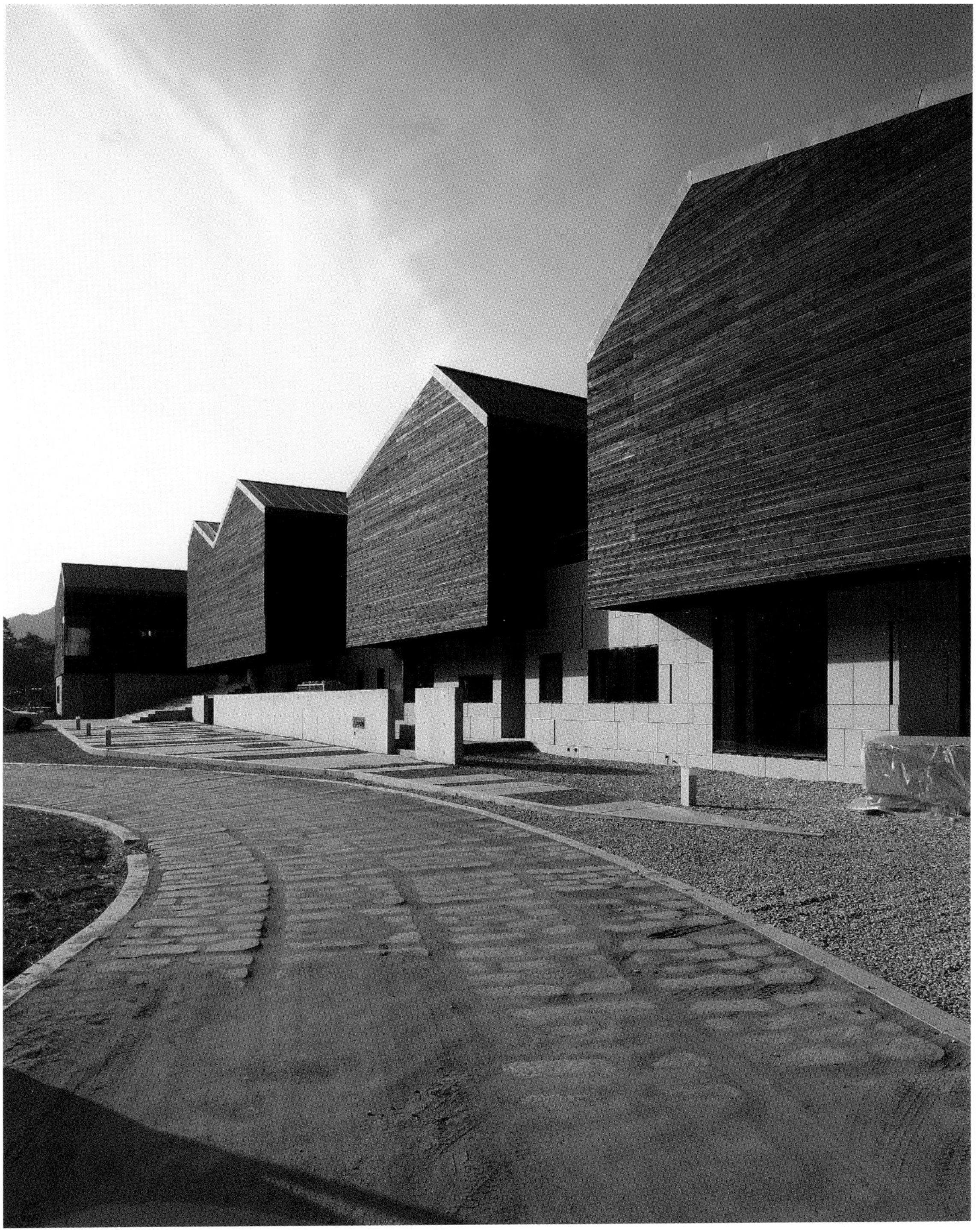

Traditional Buddhism Center of Jogye Order

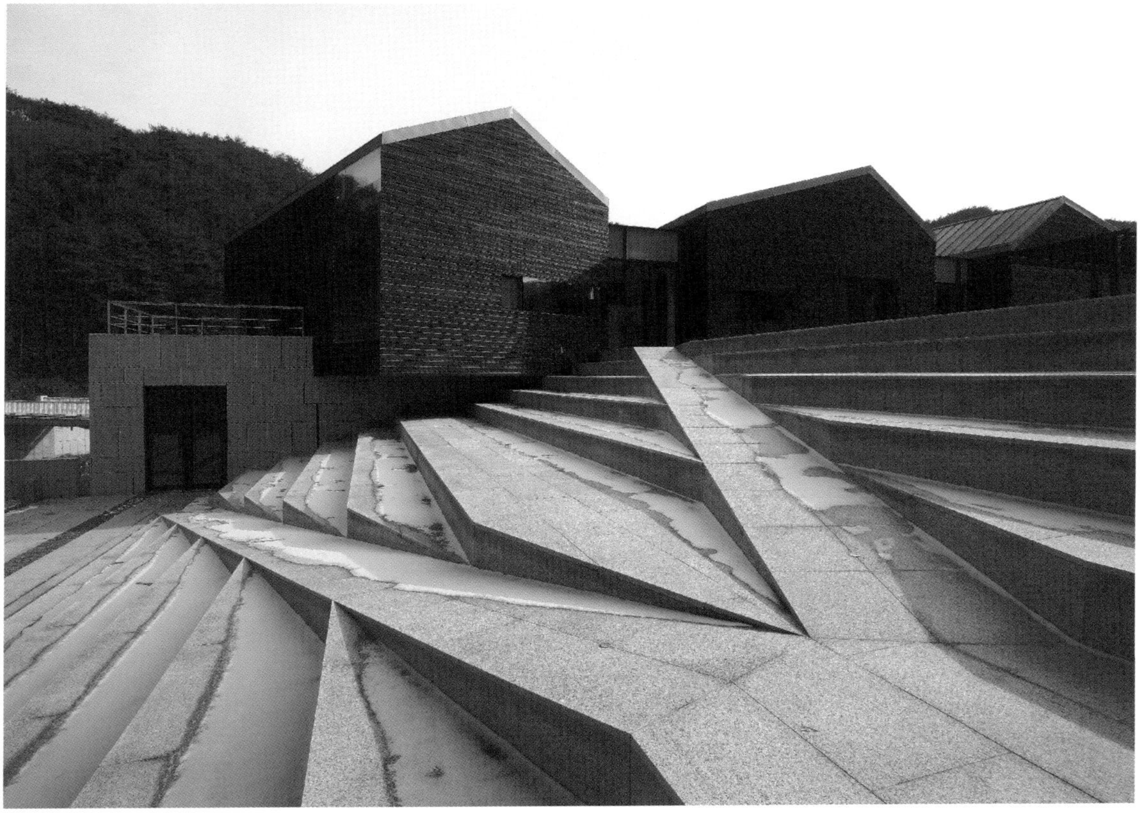

Traditional Buddhism Center of Jogye Order

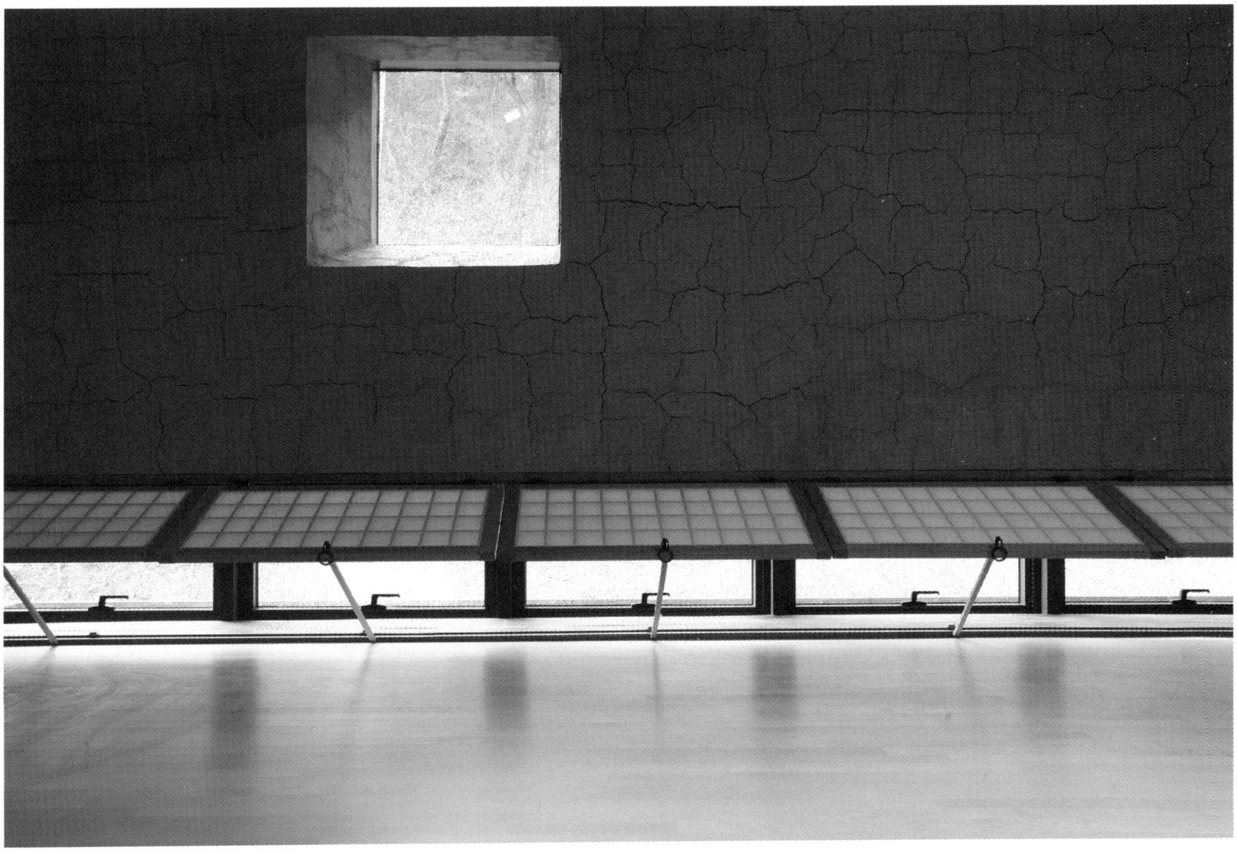

Shin Dongyeop Literary Museum

The literary museum in commemoration of poet Shin Dongyeop (1930-1969) was built in Buyeo, right next to the house where he lived. It was once a thatched-roof house with three rooms, and then, changed to a shabby slate-roofed house, which seems to show the sadness of the poet who lived his life in disharmony with his contemporaries. However, it is not the only purpose of this memorial to commemorate the poet who screamed about the irrationalities of the times of dictatorship, saying "Go away! You, empty shell!" This memorial must give us a chance to commemorate ourselves and the land where we are now standing. So, it would be meaningful for the visitors to have an opportunity to discover their inner selves, approaching to the start point after following the suggested route of sequential movement for the visitors. This way could increase the possibility of finding out what the poet is in our innermost mind.

For this reason, this route of sequential movement for the visitors to this memorial is of a circulating structure. Once people enter the museum premises passing by the poet's old house, they are requested to see his works and other exhibits in the museum. Leaving the memorial building, people are greeted by a courtyard. When they go up the stairs there to the top, they will be intrigued by several pieces of new land. All of lands are connected, in a circulating structure, with each other, but at a different level. People walk down the piece of land of the lowest level to the ground of everyday life. There, they see a square that is full of flags on which the poet's poetic words are written. Visitors surely will be fascinated by the scattered poetic beauty up in the air. While happily intoxicated with the beauty of language, visitors will be surprised at themselves who have already arrived at the place where they started.

This memorial museum is merely a medium that gives people a chance to have this kind of experience, and thus it is natural if it does not exist in its own form. In this sense, there is just rough concrete as the background, and the building does not commemorate itself.

CIRCULATING LAND
FLAG OF POEM

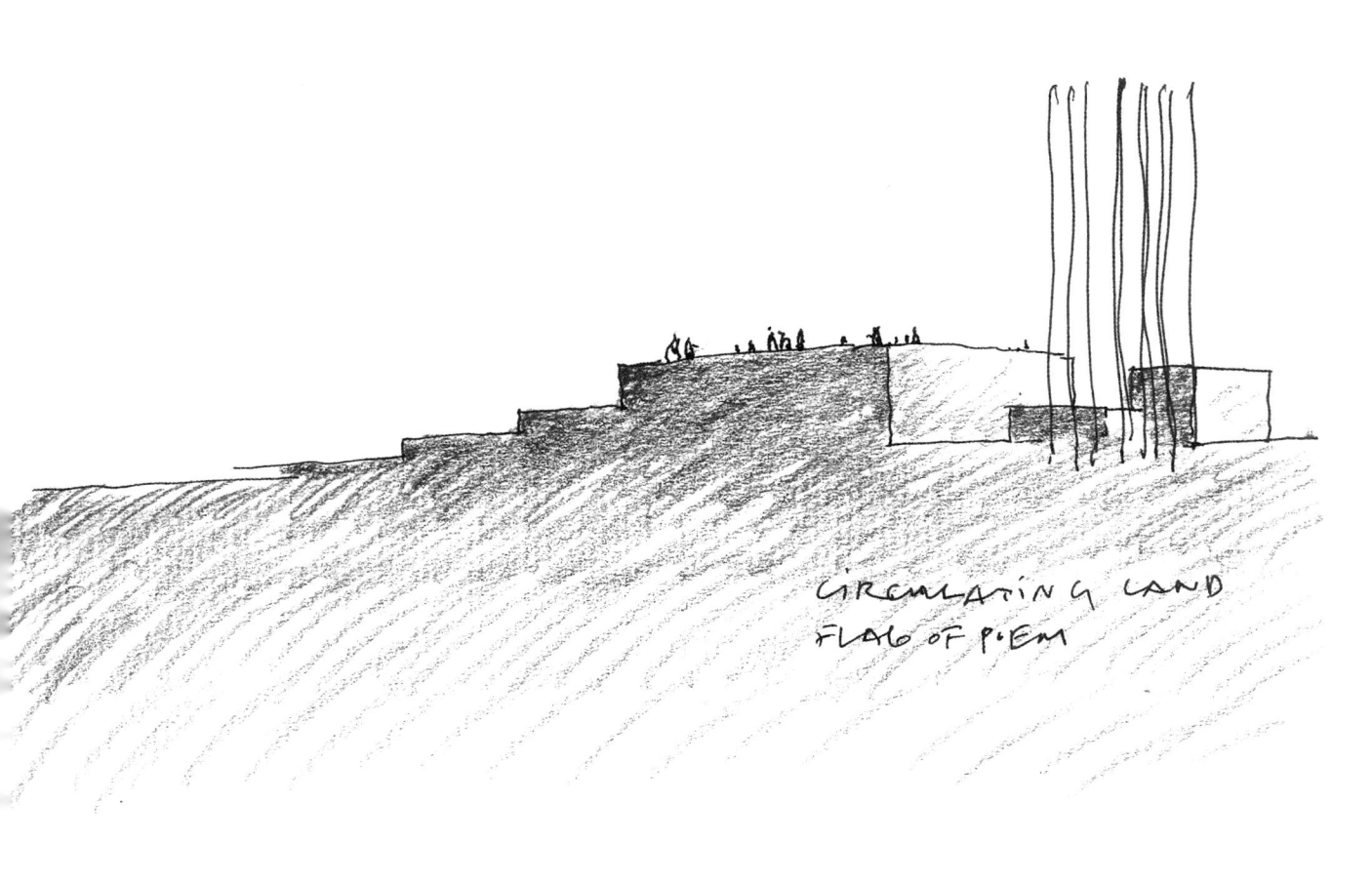

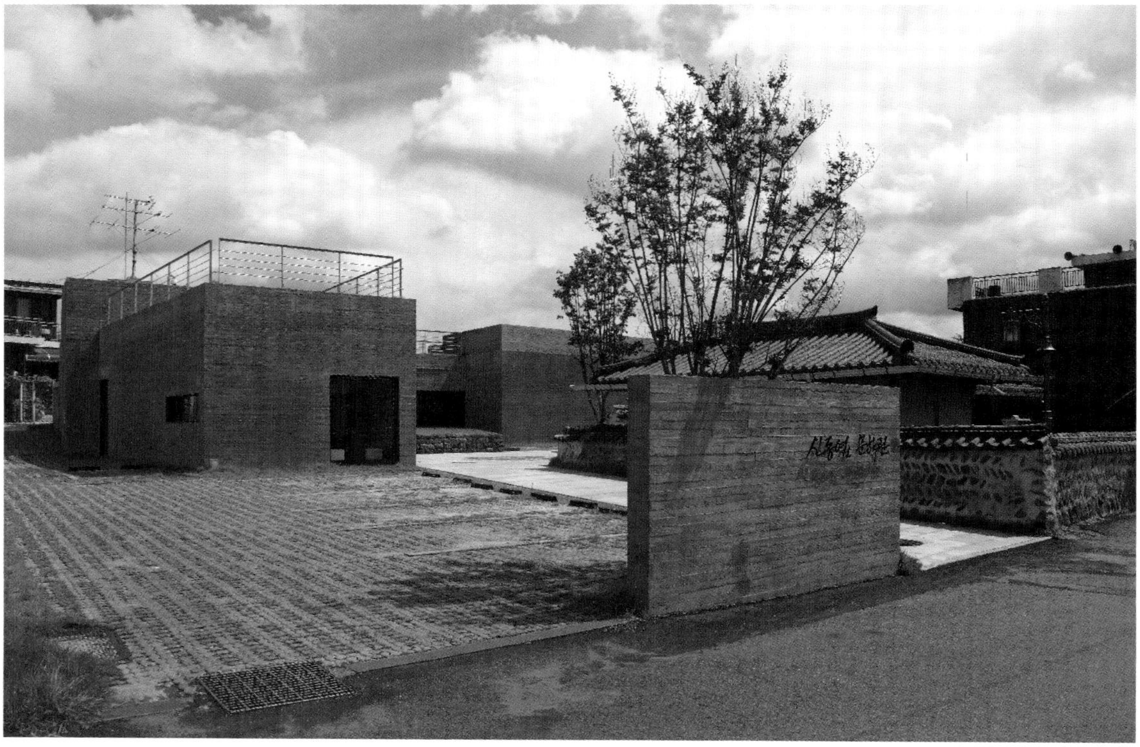

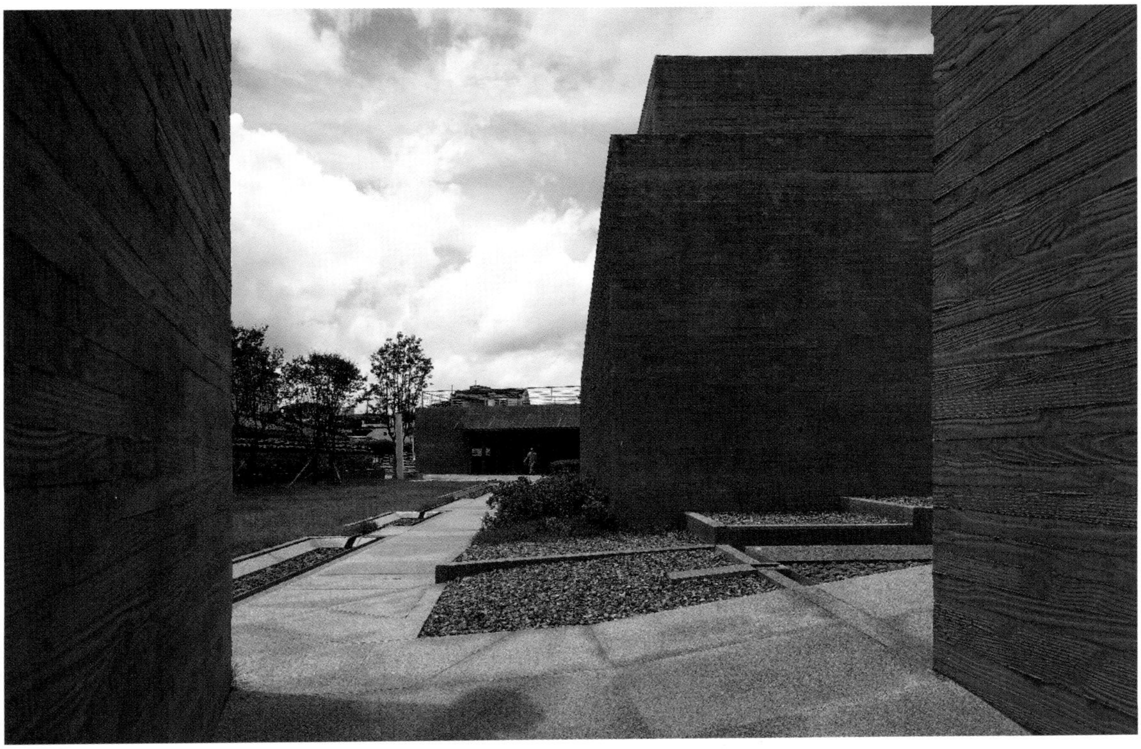

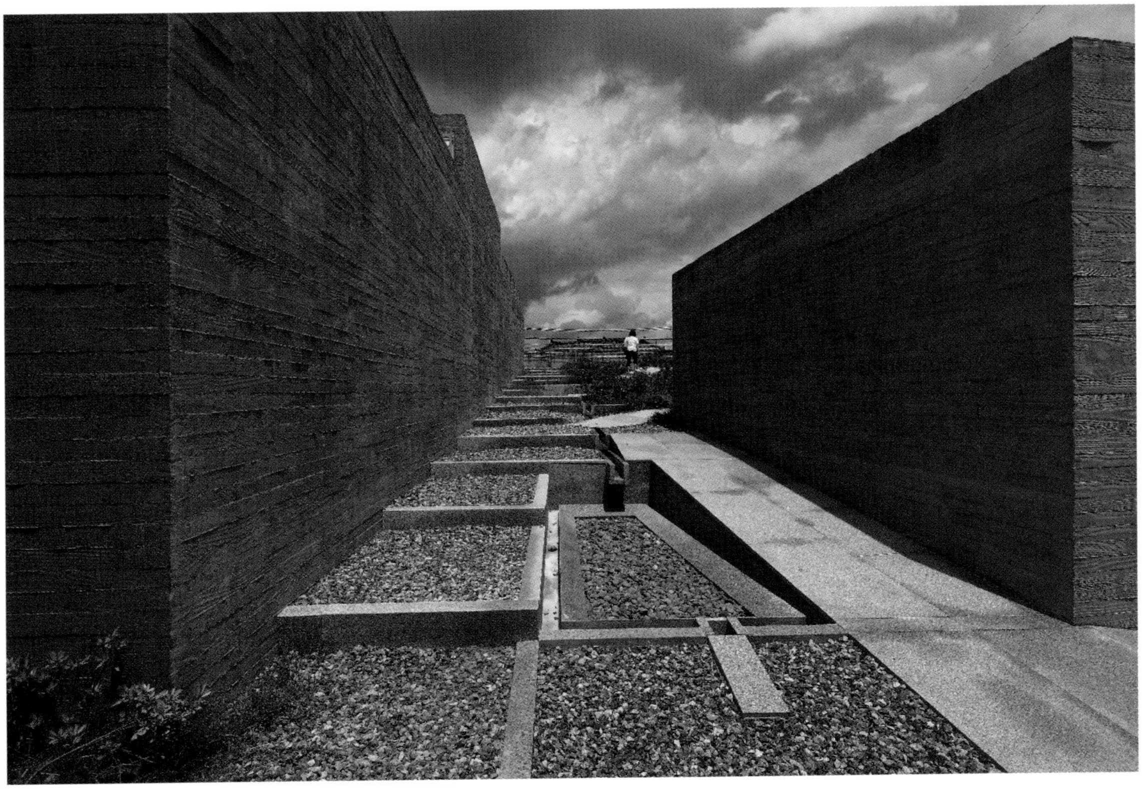

Shin Dongyeop Literary Museum

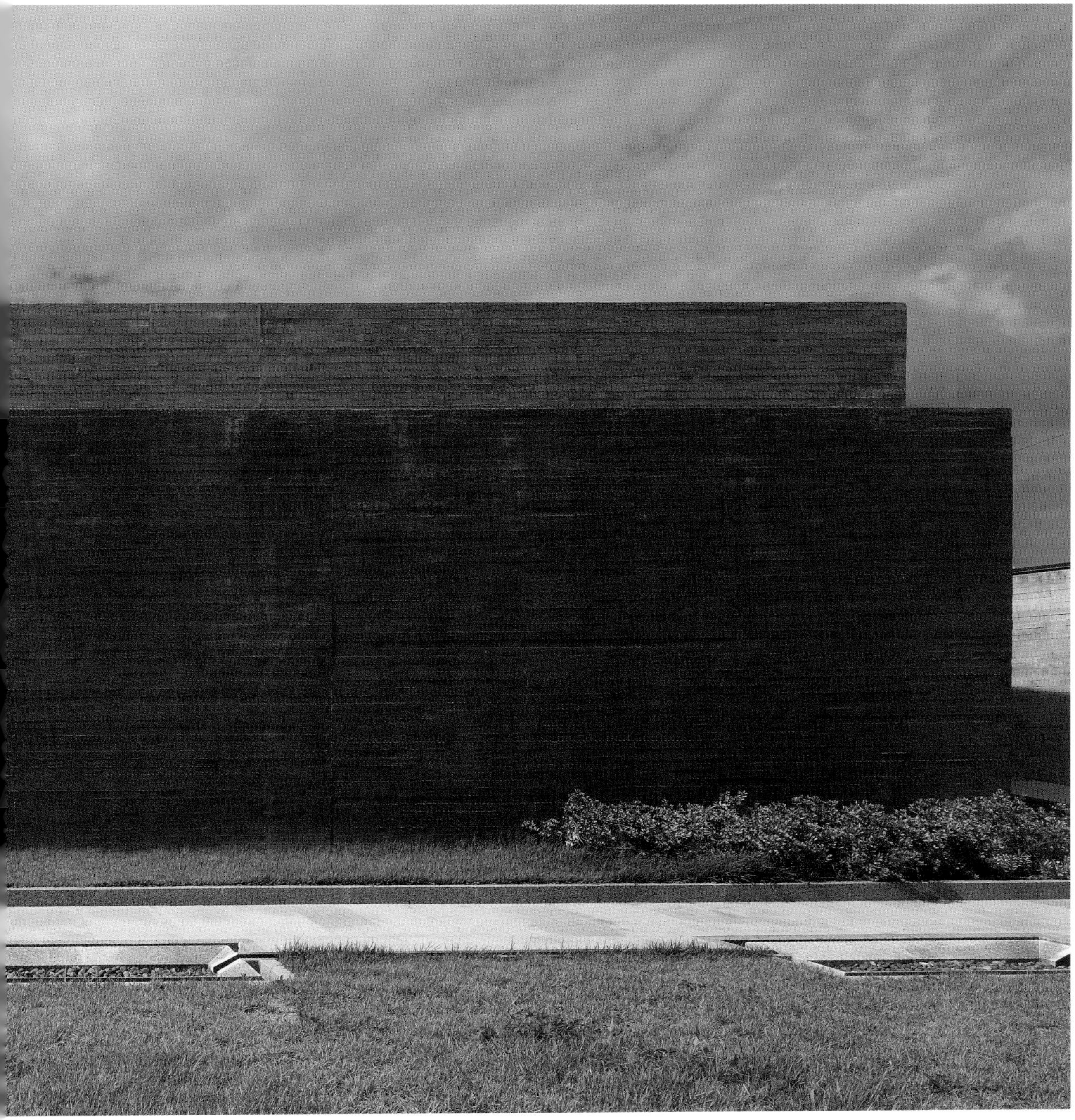

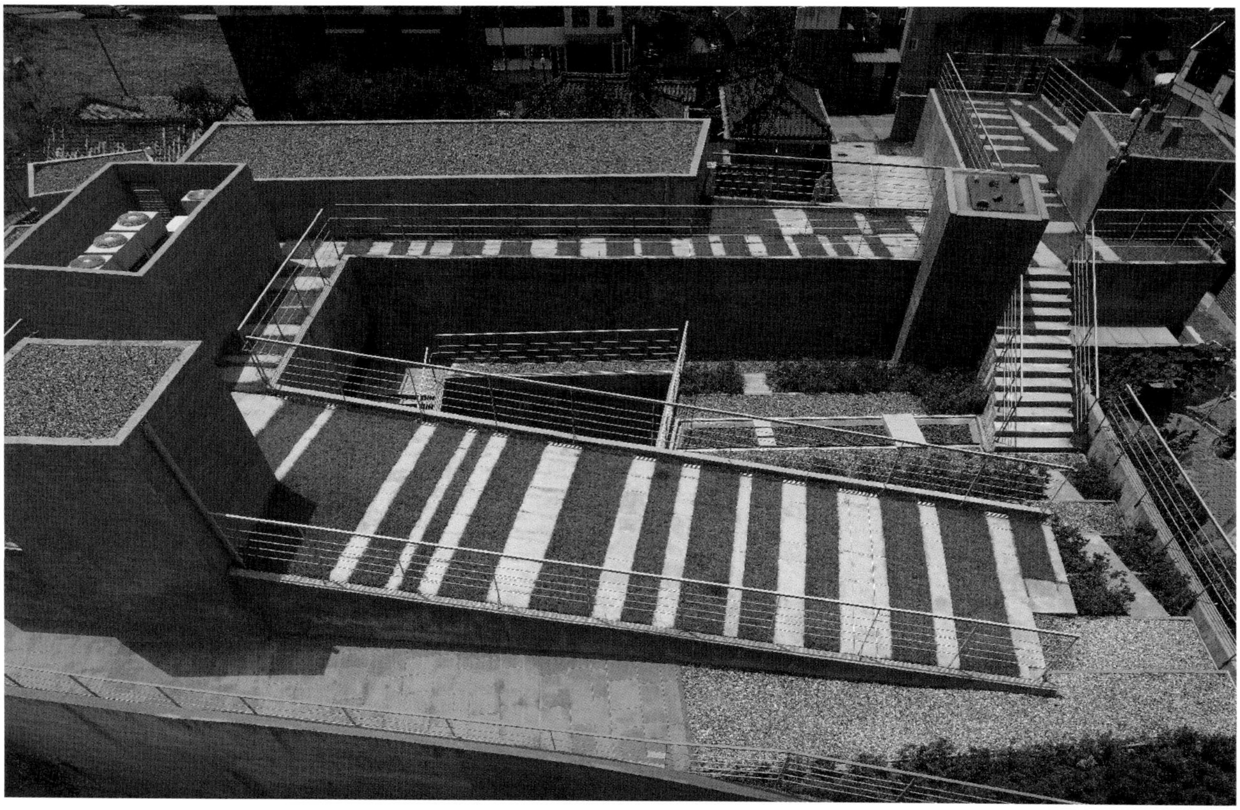

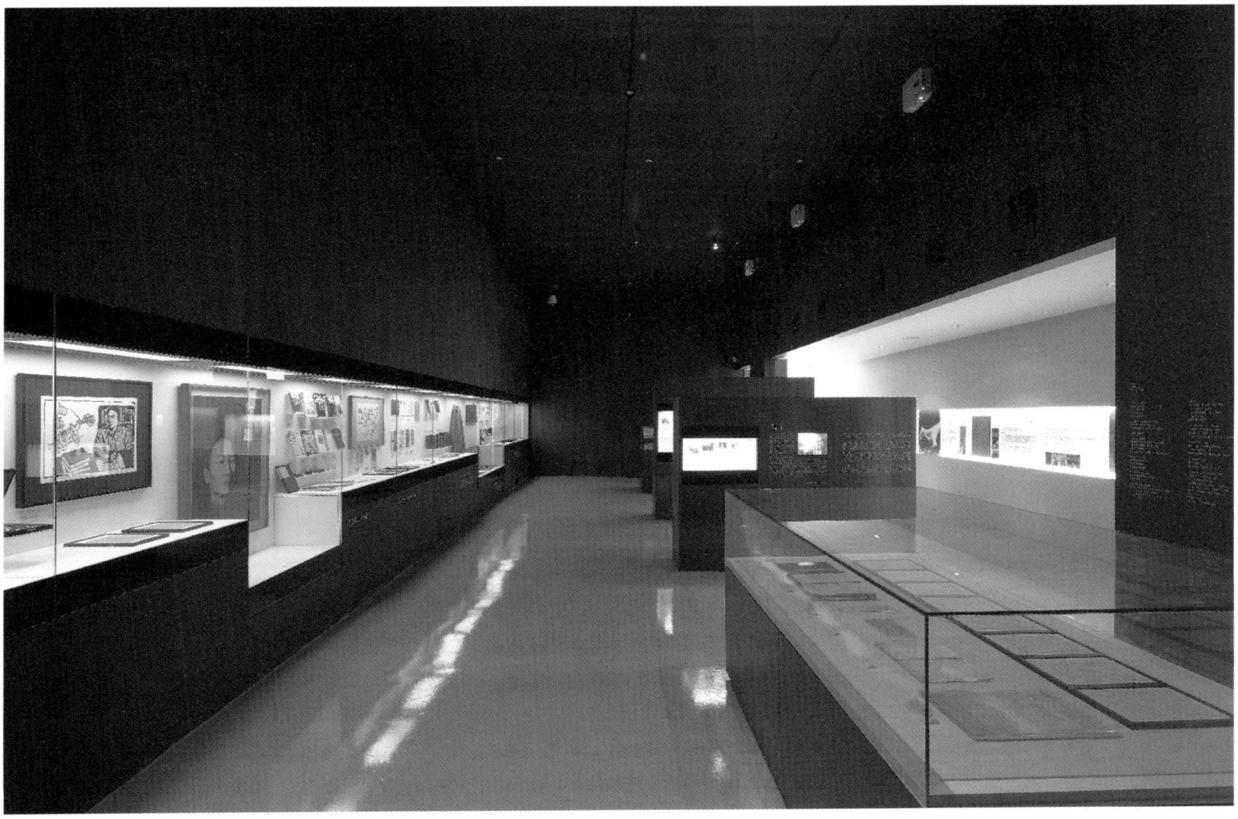

Vanke Residential Culture Center

Pingdu is a city in China with a population of 1.5 million people and with a rich history of 3000 years. Located around the northern outskirts of Qingdao, this city has recently experienced rapid urbanization under the heavy influence of Qingdao. In detail, the government offices moved from the downtown area to the newly developed one, and a master plan to develop the old center of the city has been implemented.

People expected that they would find relics of ancient times in this old city of several thousand years' history. Unfortunately, however, the apartment houses and government offices built there since the period of the Republic of China (1912-1949) had been constructed, destroying all of the relics. It was fortunate enough to find rarely-seen old maps telling that many of the ancient roads were still in use. Accordingly, based on the old roads, a master plan with "landscript" as a theme was completed and named Pingdu Historical Area Regeneration Plan.

Vanke Group, a large residential real estate developer in China that took charge of the regeneration project, requested to design the first building in the plan area which would be used as the promotion hall of the whole project and a residential culture center. The site for this building was part for a small building attached to the city hall with densely populated trees. As the trees were all 200~300 years old and required to be preserved, it was mandatory for the residential culture center to build on a remaining empty land. What should be seriously considered was that this new building should be connected to the road ahead so that citizens could easily recognize it. For this, concrete frames were put up along the boundary line of the road. These concrete frames were given a function as a street gallery and designed to connect the new building deep inside the land and the gallery around the entrance to the access road. However, all these structures are merely tools that define the spatial boundaries of the beautiful trees around the building, and they do not exist in terms of architectural concept.

A model house was to be built in the building so that visitors could see what would their future homes look like. As it was just a model house, it was placed diagonally against the walls of the hall to be in in contrast with the actual space of reality, thereby adding more interest to the interior space of the building. Nevertheless, the most overwhelming factor here is the trees around the building that witness the past. They were like what was given and should remain as they were. This should be regarded as one of the most important principle for all architectural works in the future.

TRAVEL TO PAST

GLADE

TRAVEL TO TIME

overlap box in Boxes in GLADE

URBAN FRAME

URBAN FRAME

ARCHAEOLOGY
FOREST
INTRA-ASPHALTE FRAME
URBANITY

Vanke Residential Culture Center

万科城
老市府大院
万科住宅文化館
89-116平毛坯新品
总价45万起
实楼样板间9月盛情绽放
8735 8888 红旗路上 荷花湾畔

Vanke Residential Culture Center

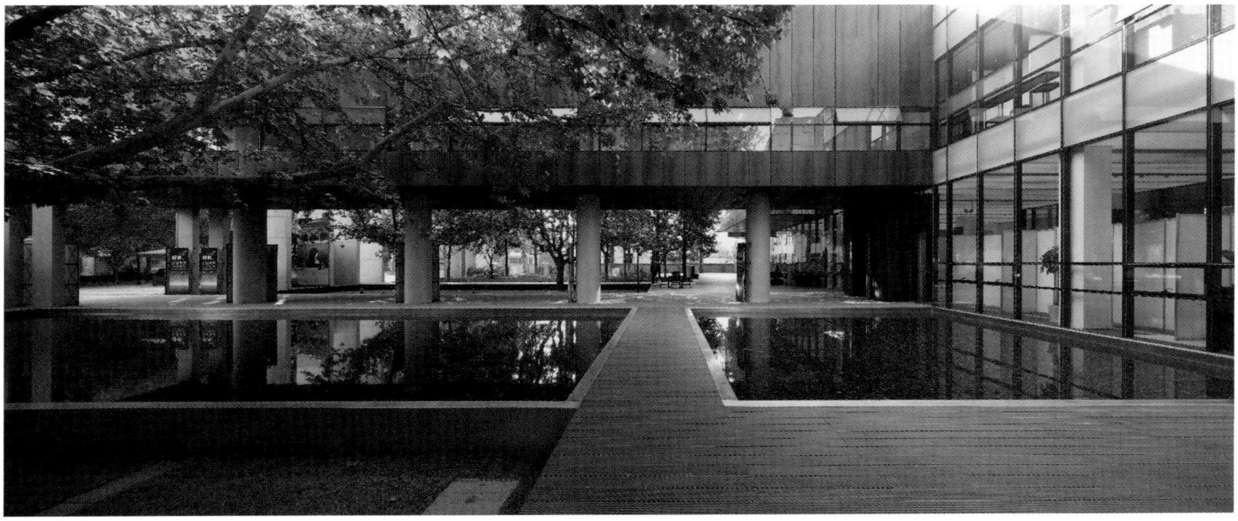

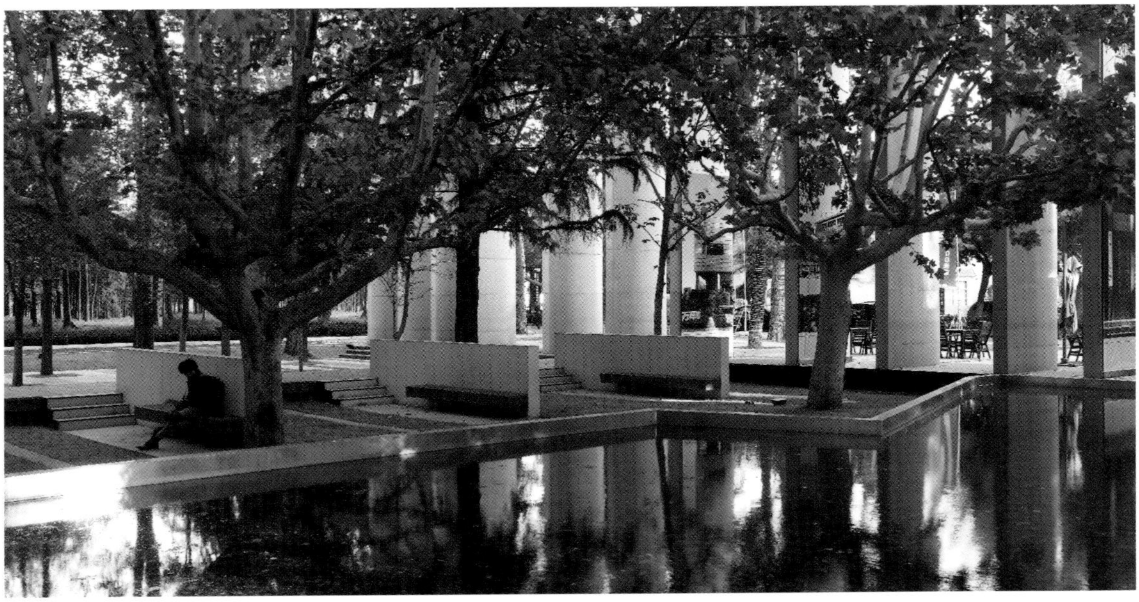

Vanke Residential Culture Center

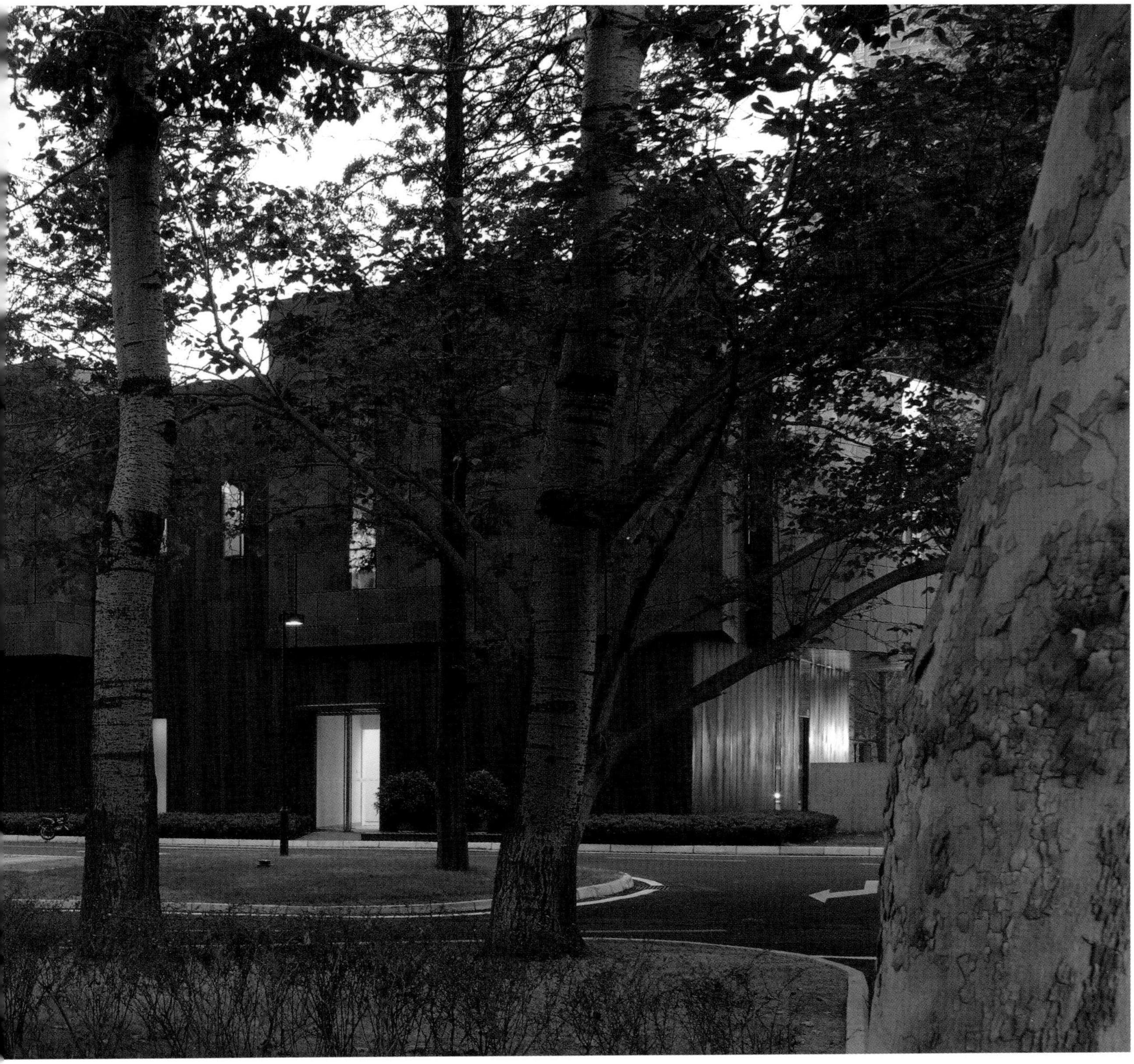

Humax Main Office Building "Humax Village"

People working in the same office building tend to have a strong homogeneity. The homogeneity is, however, not so permanent, everlasting or absolute as the one which is seen in a society based on geographical and blood ties. A society that is formed in the same office building is a time-limited and discontinuous community based on certain contracts effective for a specified period. It is a temporary society. People belonging to the community of Humax are generally very young. Being young, they are full of hope and enjoy challenges for the future. They reject inertia while they are adventurous and look for something new all the time. As such, the conventional ideals of office planning details will be an old relic to such people.

The site was located on the border of Bundang, a planned city. In detail, the site was around the edge of Bundang, where the area of Bundang looks crooked, and on the bank of the Tancheon, a tributary of the Han River. Most of the buildings adjacent to the site looked like black boxes, which seemed to isolate Bundang from the Tancheon and the nature behind. This last piece of empty land seemed to be the only exit to the nature.

This Humax building as like a window to Bundang is transparent as it was supposed to serve as a frame connecting the cityscape to the natural surroundings. There are more reasons that this building should be transparent. The people working for Humax are oriented to an open community. And, they thought that the way they pursed such a beautiful life would contribute more to a better cityscape when exposed. Commonality in this open society is achieved in the interior space. As such, an indoor courtyard in the middle of the inside of the building should be provided, and the space above should reach the sky. This space is defined differently at each story, connecting the 13 stories vertically. Physical means of connection are the stairs like Jacob's ladder and the elevators like a time machine. This courtyard has various functional features of a small park and a small square, and would be the most important place for creating the identity of the Humax community.

Humax Village has the structure of a reduced urban community. Inside Humax Village are thoroughfares, crossroads and cul-de-sacs. parks, and trees and grass as well. Rain and snow fall down through the interior space, and bright sunray reaches the deep corner of the building. Not only because the building houses as many as 2,000 persons, but also because those young people working in the building and forming a non-permanent society should have a vivid and beautiful memory of their life in this building, this architectural structure was designed not as a building but as a village. This is why it was named "Humax village."

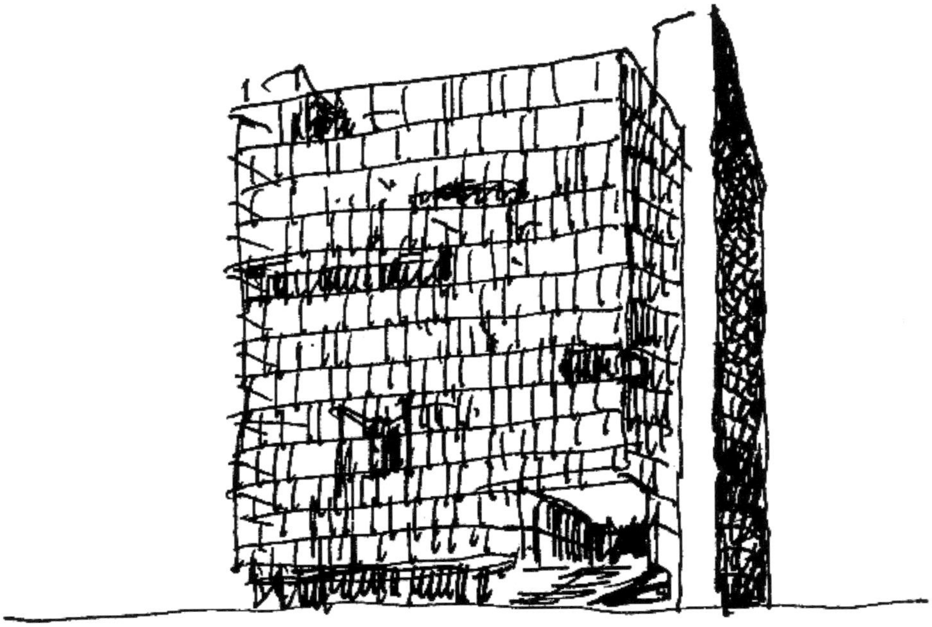

Humax Main Office Building "Humax Village"

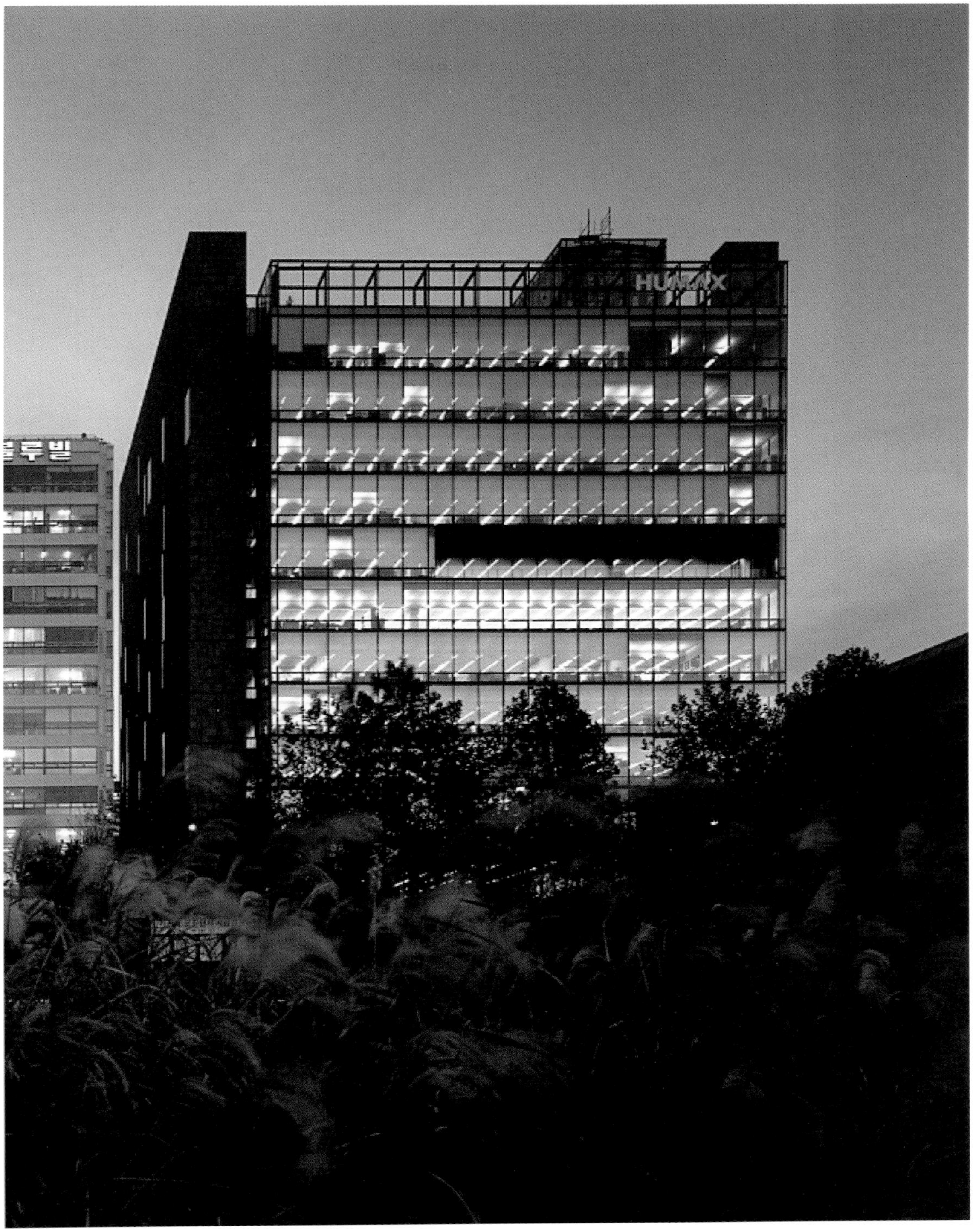
HUMAX

Humax Main Office Building "Humax Village"

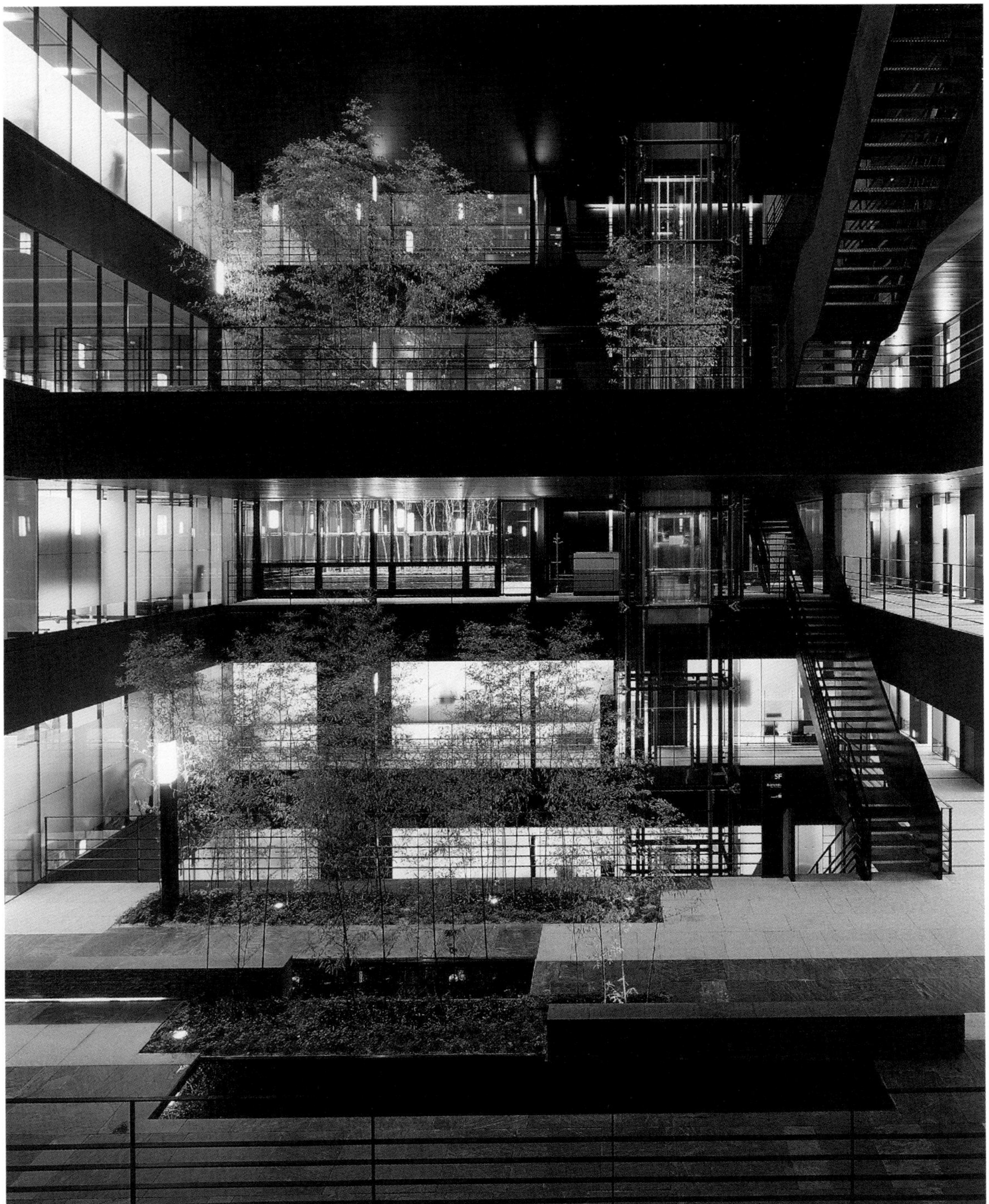

– 254   Humax Main Office Building "Humax Village"

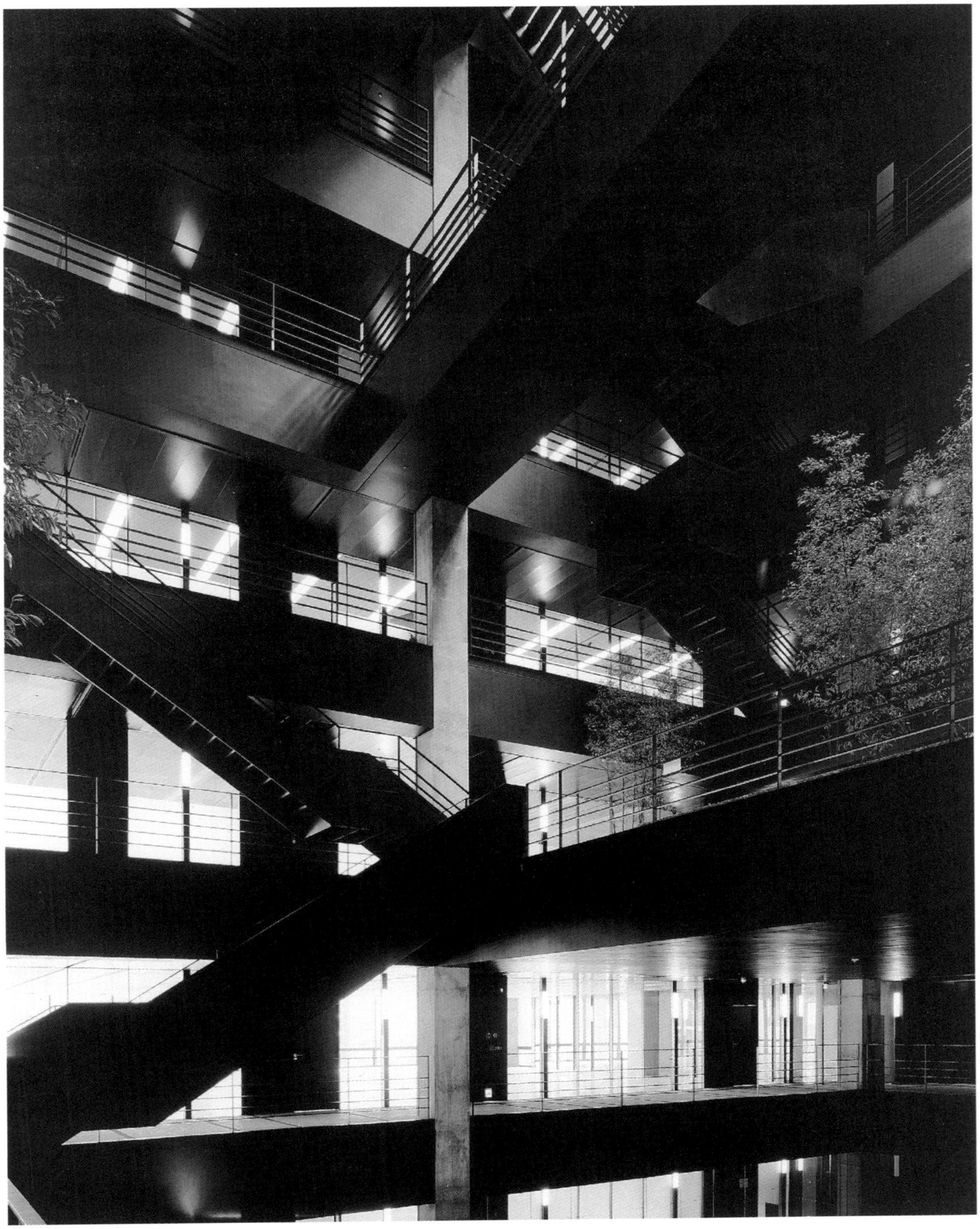

University is an academic institution pursuing universal values as the word "university" itself clearly denotes its meaning. Whole-person education is needed for this goal, and it would be achieved not by simply acquiring knowledge but by making efforts for self-development and learning from living in the real world. Under this understanding, the residential college was shaped as a very effective means. For students, coming into the residential college, even though they live there for a limited period of time, means that they cross the boundaries of the world they have lived so far. In some sense, it may mean that they renounce the worldly life and live a life of monks or nuns looking for physical, material and spiritual freedom. That's why 'academic monastery' was named for this project. The monastery should have clear boundaries off from the secular world. The long wall is for such a feeling of seclusion from the outer world. Though the monastery is open to the existing campus areas, it is difficult to guess about its inside as it is not properly visible from the terrain outside of the university. The inside, however, is unexpectedly free. The residential buildings have freely-deployed shared places between them. The shared places are always very expressive of life and vigor derived from the flow of pedestrians. In the beginning of this project, 'Academic monastery in forest' was name of this project but the existing forest disappeared for the convenience of construction work. Newly planted trees are very young and small, but they will grow up in time. Therefore, this architecture has not been finished yet. It will be realized when the trees are well grown and the students living here become part of the landscape.

Hyehwa Residential College of Daejeon University

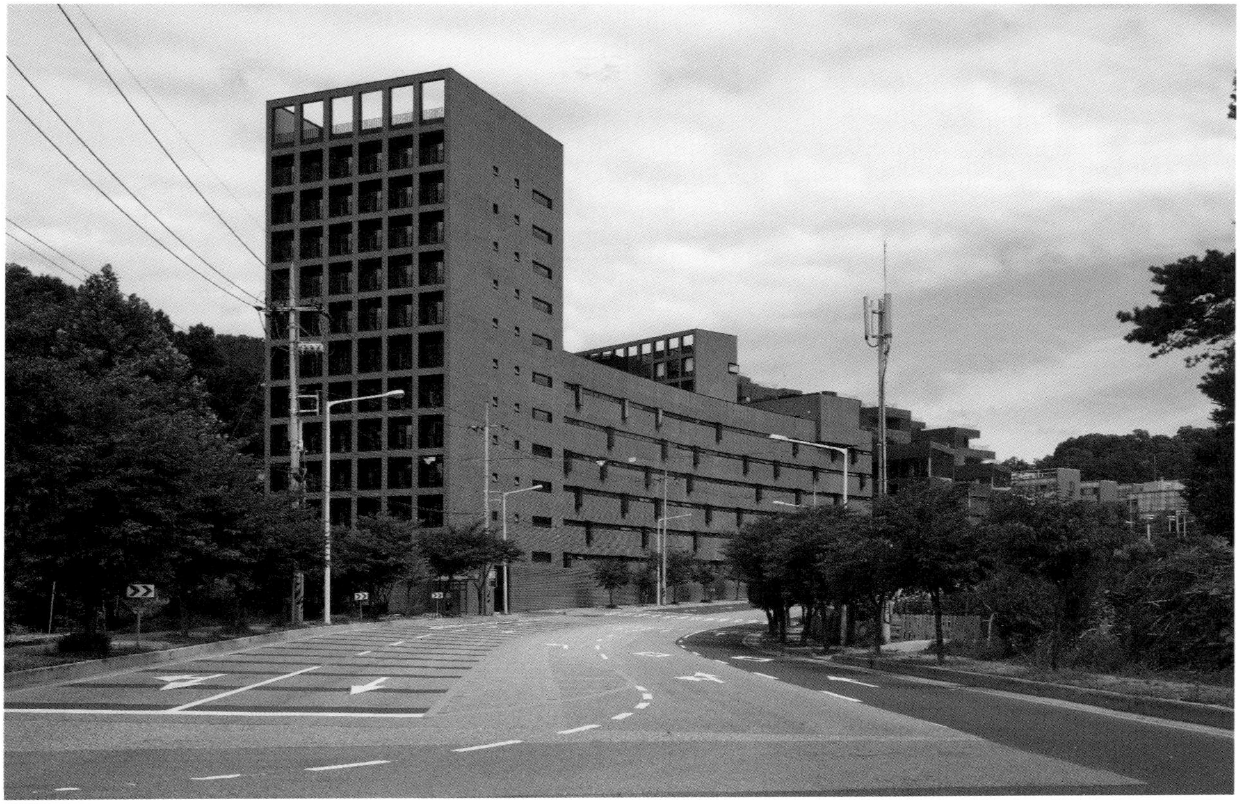

Hyehwa Residential College of Daejeon University

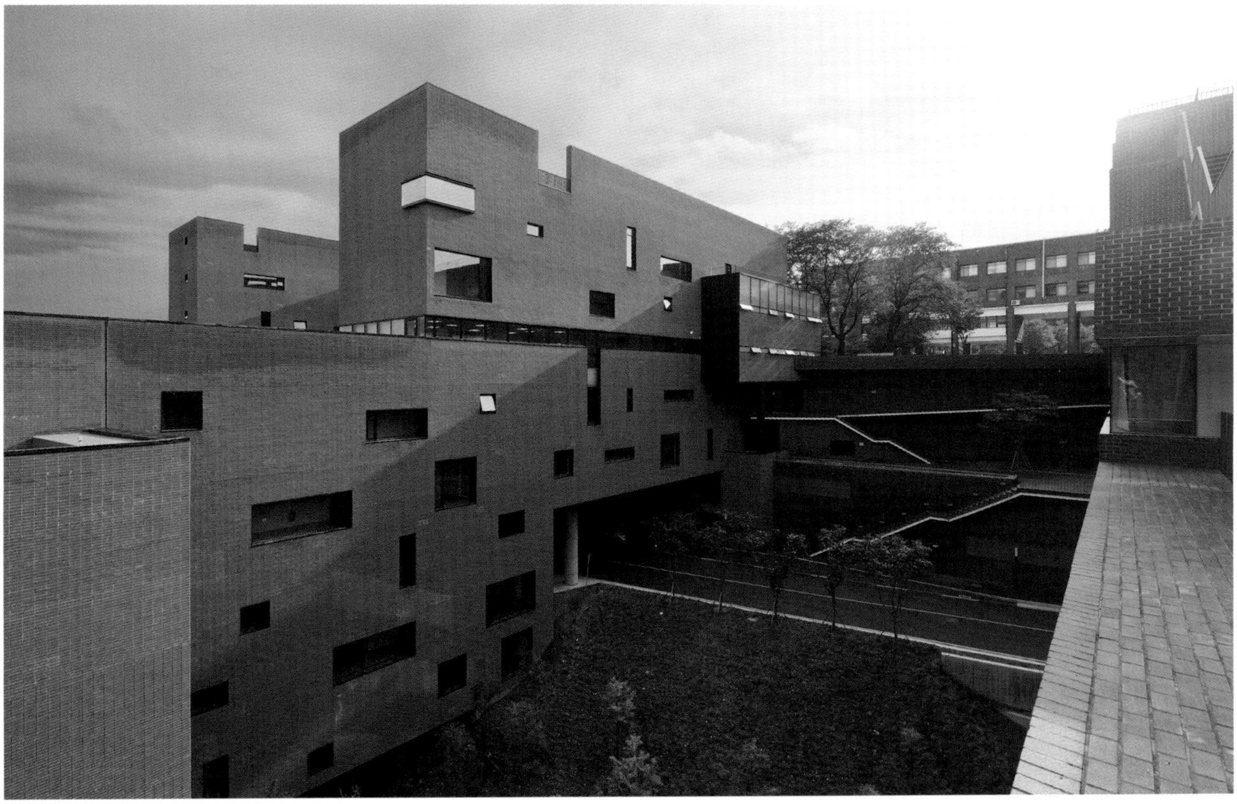

Hyehwa Residential College of Daejeon University

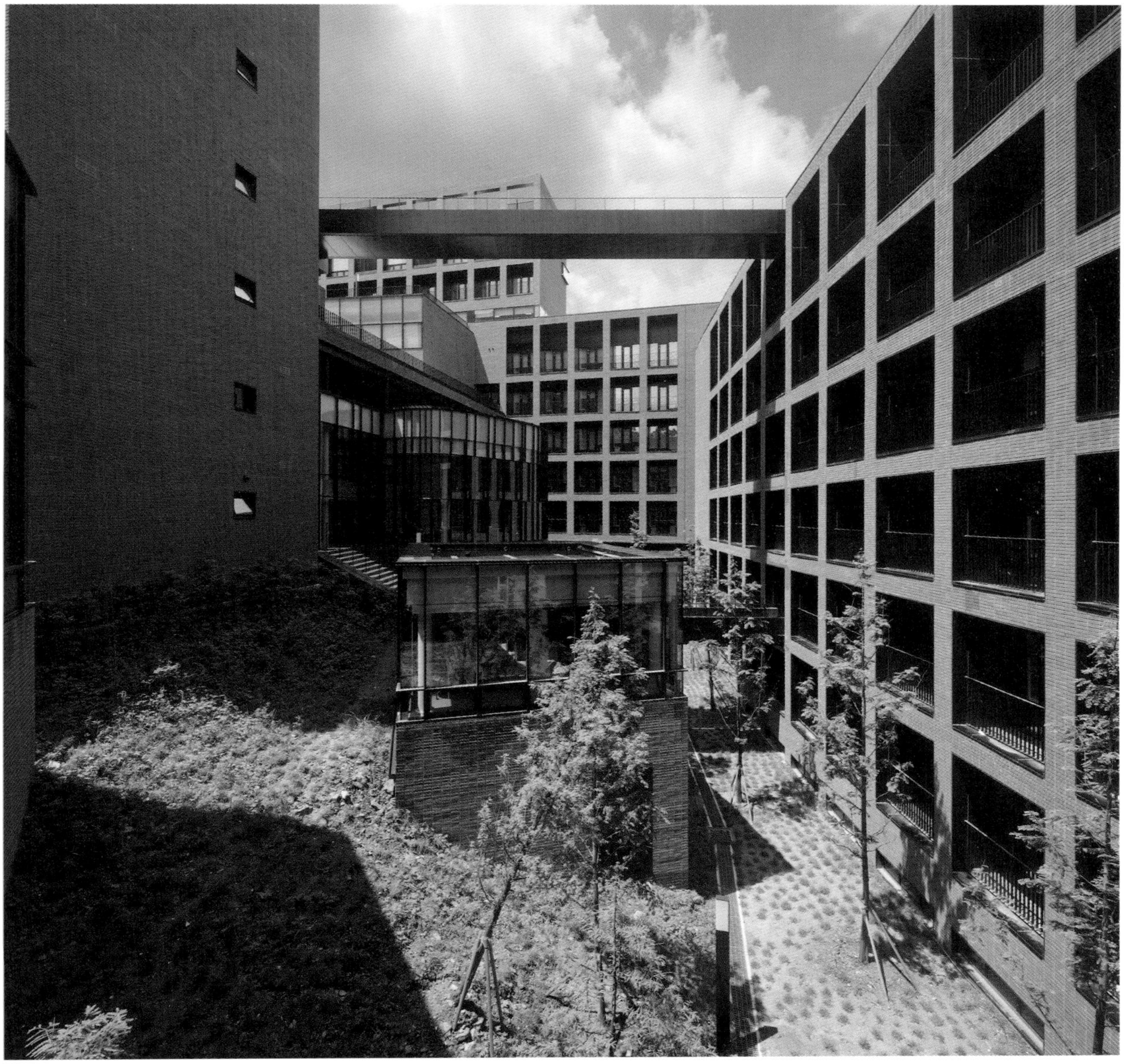

The completion of the 30th Anniversary Memorial Building marks the culmination of the campus development plan. The site was located in an artificially flattened area. Yet, according to the master plan, it seemed obvious that the site could function as a strong axis that led to the west gate and to the pedestrian way that starts from the south gate. Placed right behind the campus library, a well-defined campus spine could be created. The twin tower, described in the masterplan, was not a building in harmony with the terrain. Nor was it in line with the essence of universities which seek universality.

It's regarded also important matter to restore the deformed features of topography through architecture. Thus, the given program was analyzed, and several mass units were worked out and arranged according to the original topography. And also an access ramp suggested by the master plan which departs from the west gate was extended into the building. As the result, it looked like a man-made valley. This valley becomes the most crowded place of this architecture and a dynamic scene by linking the separate sections of the building at the top and at the bottom. Though the administration part is ten stories high, it does not look dominant against the surrounding buildings because its volume is not big. On the contrary, it contributes to harmony with the all surrounding buildings by keeping a balance with the big volume of the adjacent library. The rooftops become new land, and they are always in connection with yards between the separate mass units. Spherical and rectangular volumes occupying the rooftops may arouse curiosity or about the inside of them.

Once again, the form itself means nothing. What matters is the inspiring space that motivates our will for action. Nobody knows what will happen next, nevertheless, the result would be positive as long as a romantic and academic university occupies the land. This belief made free arranging the mass units and spaces with unspecified characters, though they are of proper size and location. And the collective landscape may be said to be this architectural landscape. This should be what the land has longed for.

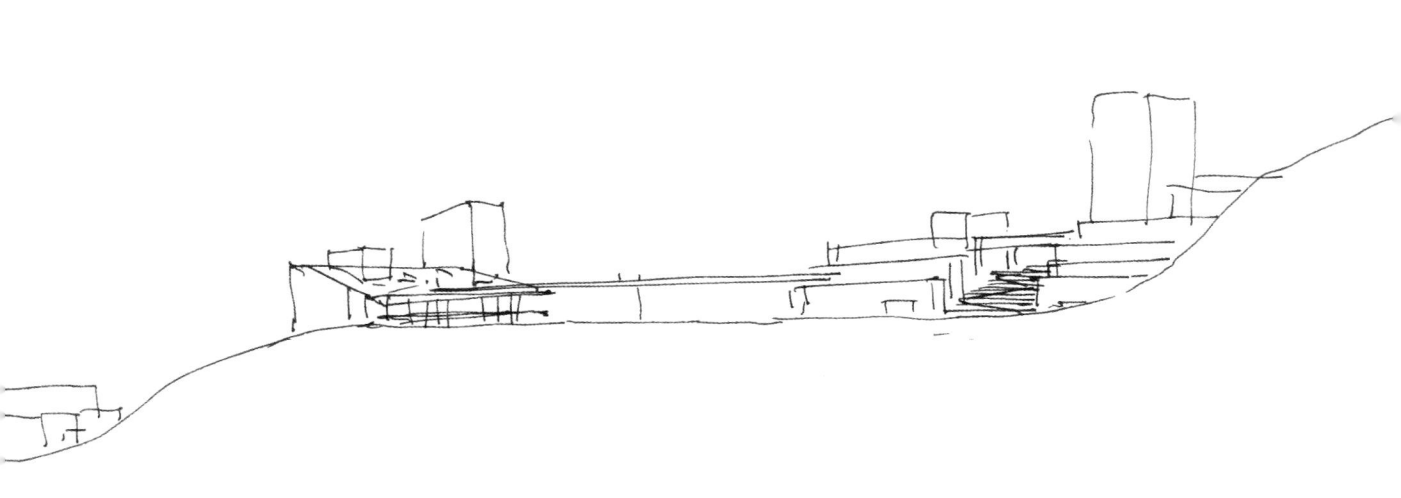

30th Anniversary Memorial Building of Daejeon University

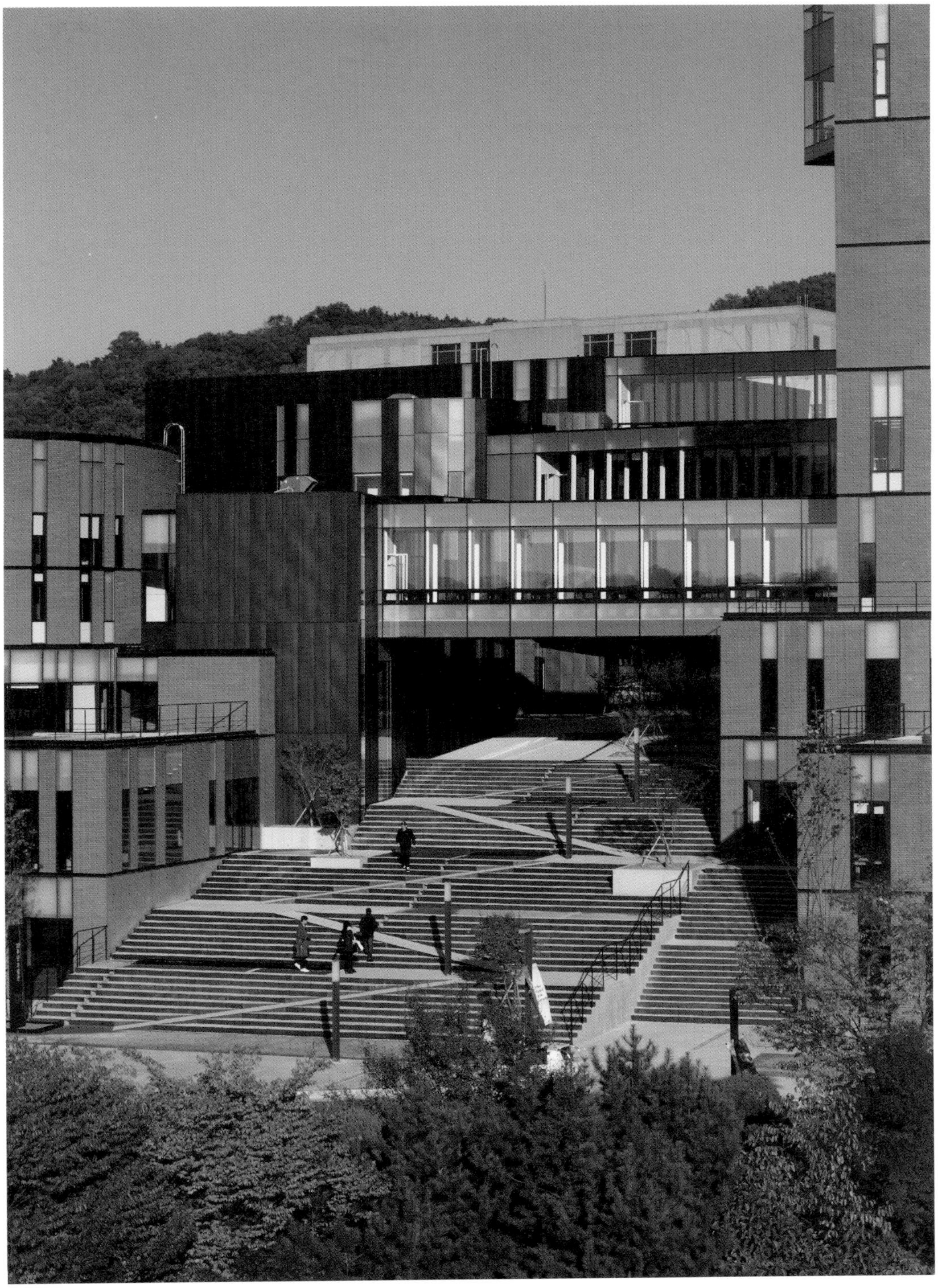

30th Anniversary Memorial Building of Daejeon University

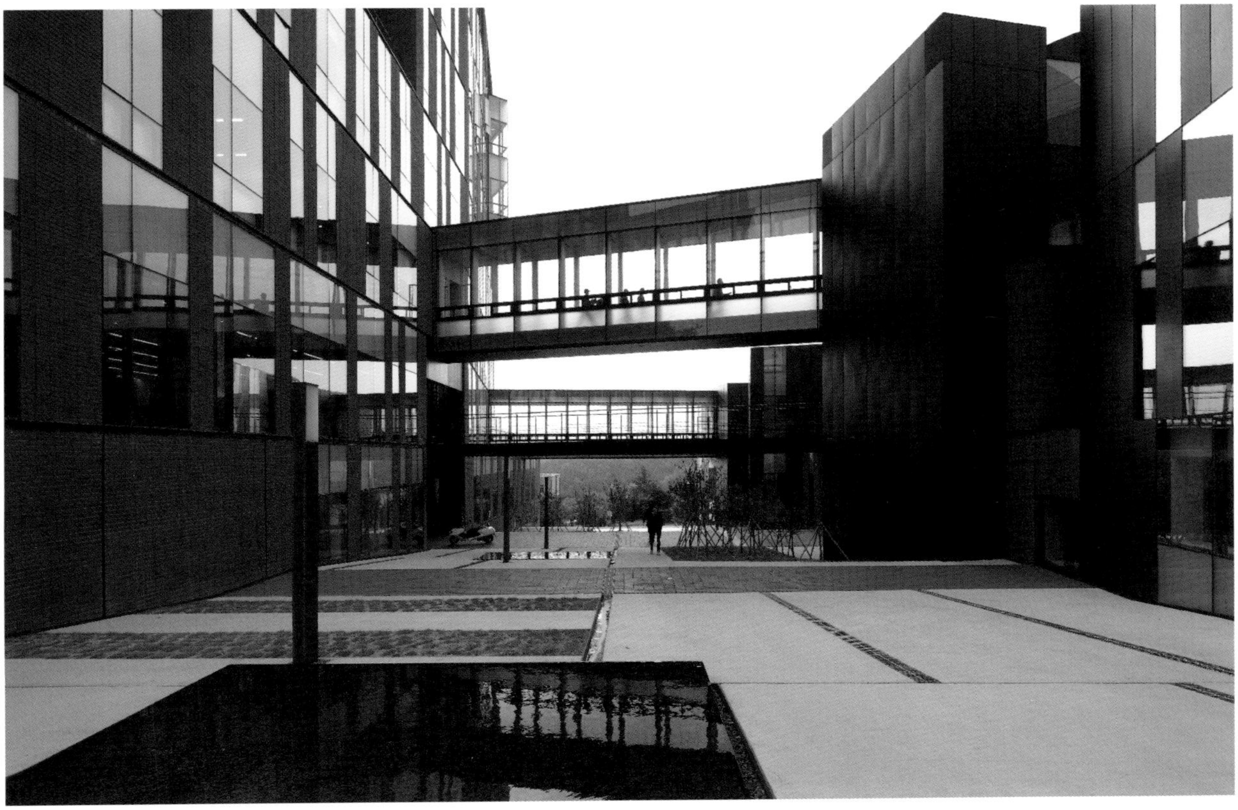

30th Anniversary Memorial Building of Daejeon University

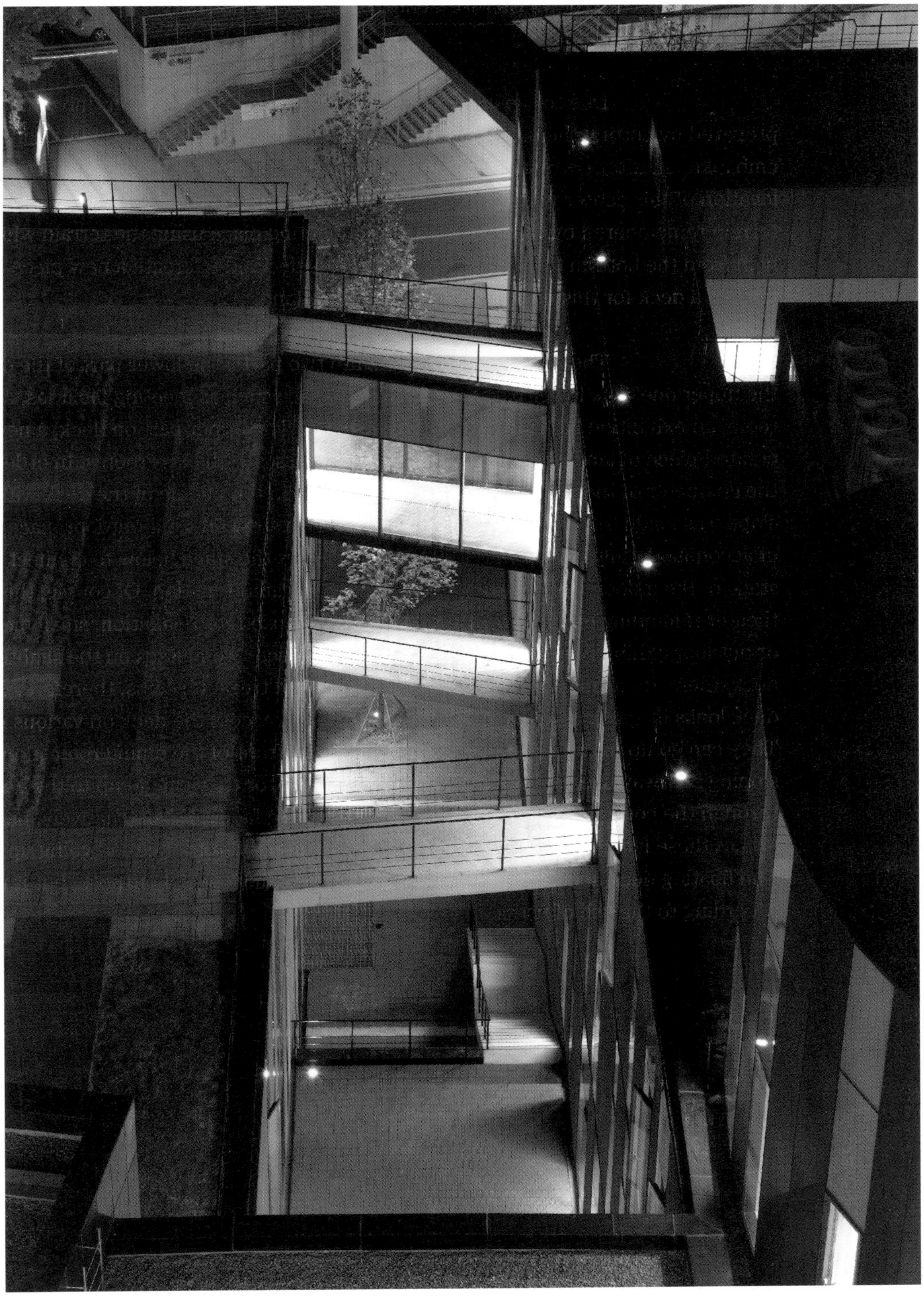

Due to the lack of flatland, the land plot of Daejeon University was prepared by cutting the hillsides since long time. All the existing buildings built on embankment after cutting of hillsides or filling of valleys were, of course, unnatural. The location of this center was in a valley. As such, it was, first of all, a priority to make the terrain remembered by creating an outdoor meeting place using the terrain which is 12m high from the bottom to the top. And also it was decided to create a new piece of land by making a deck for this university which lacks flatland.

The project was divided into two parts: the lower part of the deck and the upper one. The lower part houses shared space such as meeting facilities, a dining room, an exhibition hall and a multi-purpose hall. The upper part on deck, a newly created piece of land, was assigned for 2 glass masses with class rooms. In order to make the character of the deck special, a large stairway in the middle of the deck with a gentle slope was made to serve as an amphi-theater. This stepped semi-outdoor place, capable of accommodating a whopping 1,000 people, allows the stage below to connect to the stage of the indoor multi-purpose hall for an integrated function. Of course, this amphi-theater reminding original topography can also be used for relaxation, small meetings or outdoor exhibitions on an everyday basis. Between two masses on the slightly-tilting deck, there are a small meeting stage, benches, and trees. It seems, therefore, that the deck looks like a park, plaza, or garden. People can access the deck on various routes. They can go up to the deck passing the balcony in front of the dining room along the sloping stairway used as the outdoor meeting place, or they can go up to the deck through the courtyard of the exhibition and meeting facilities. Alternatively, people can access these facilities through 2 glass boxes, or directly from the road going up the stairs. The floating deck above all levels of ground has not any special purpose, but it is used according to the will of users.

Hyehwa Culture Center of Daejeon University

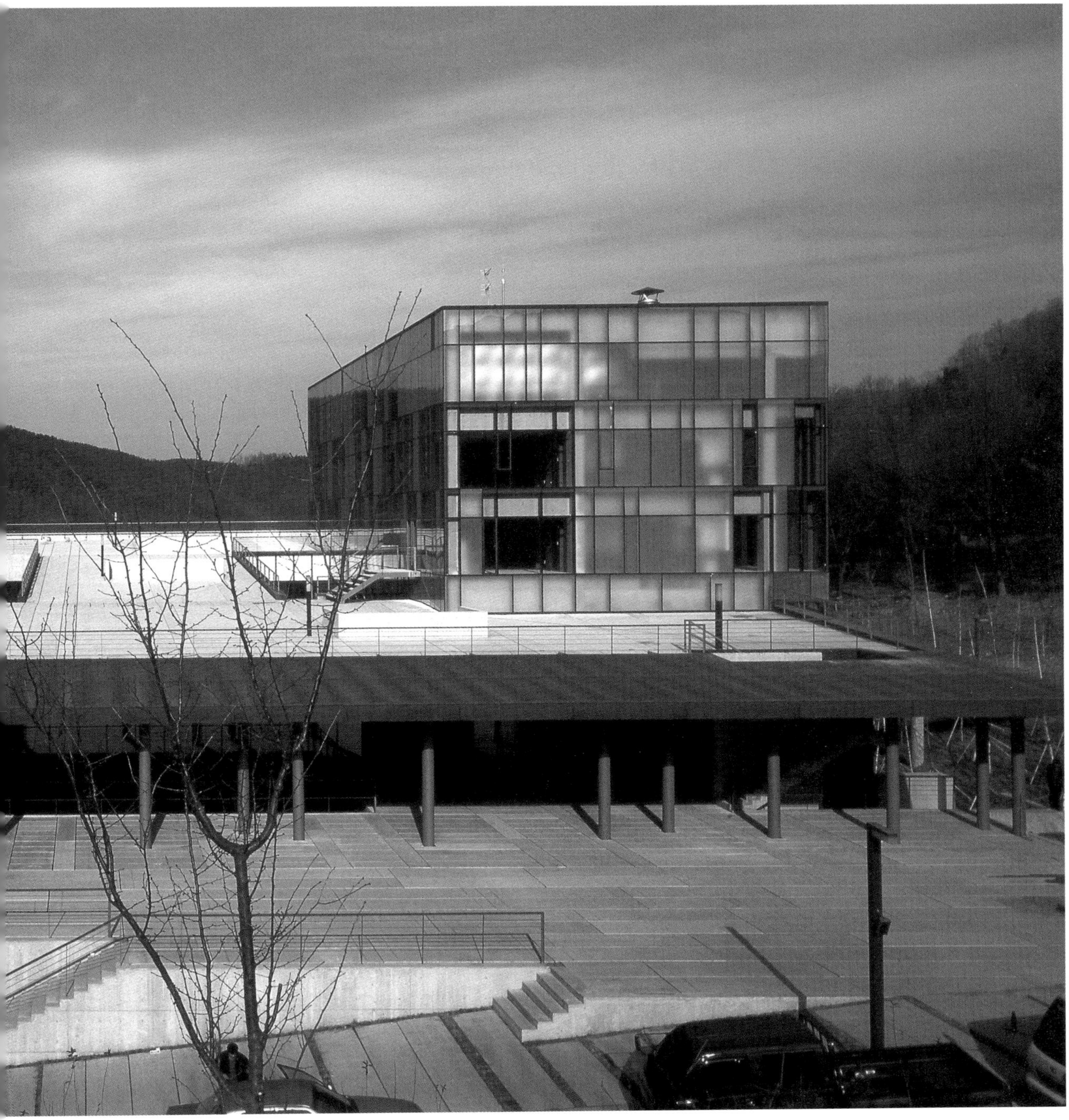

Hychwa Culture Center of Daejeon University

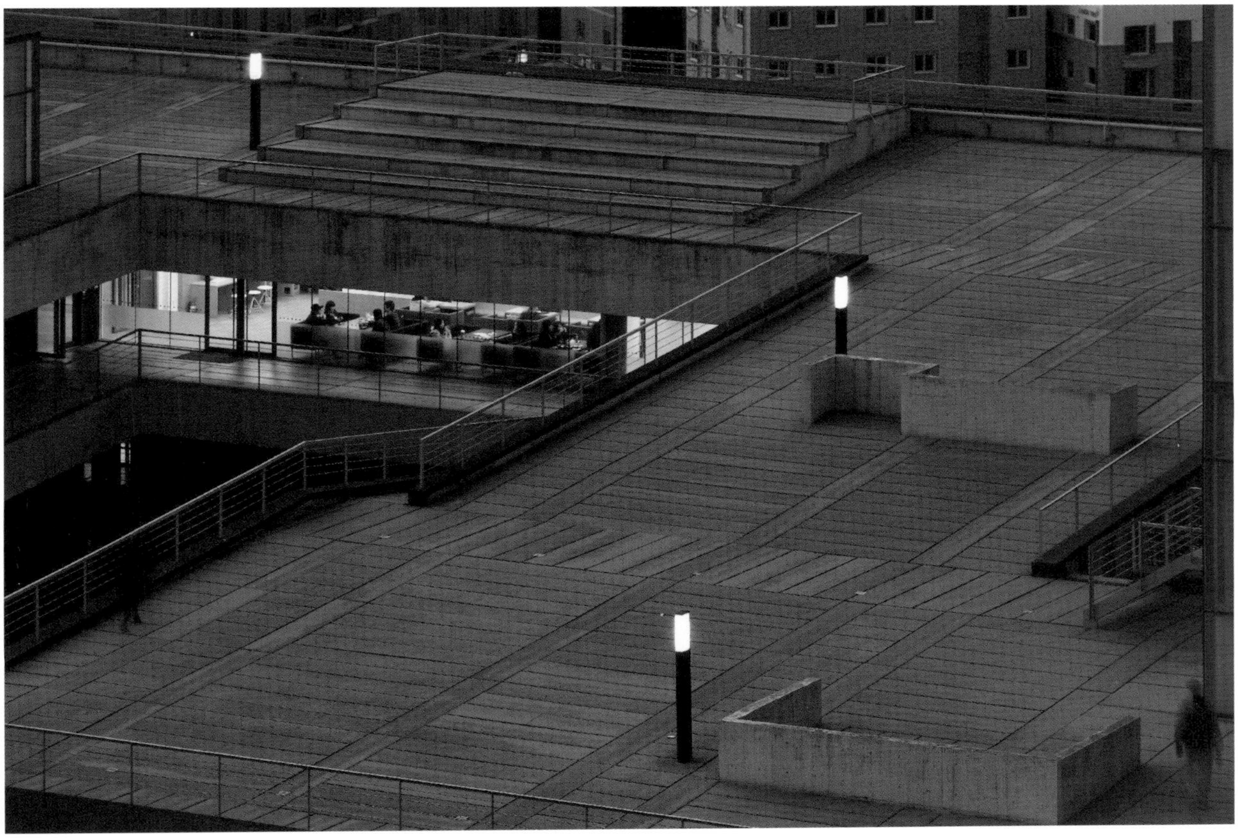

Hyehwa Culture Center of Daejeon University

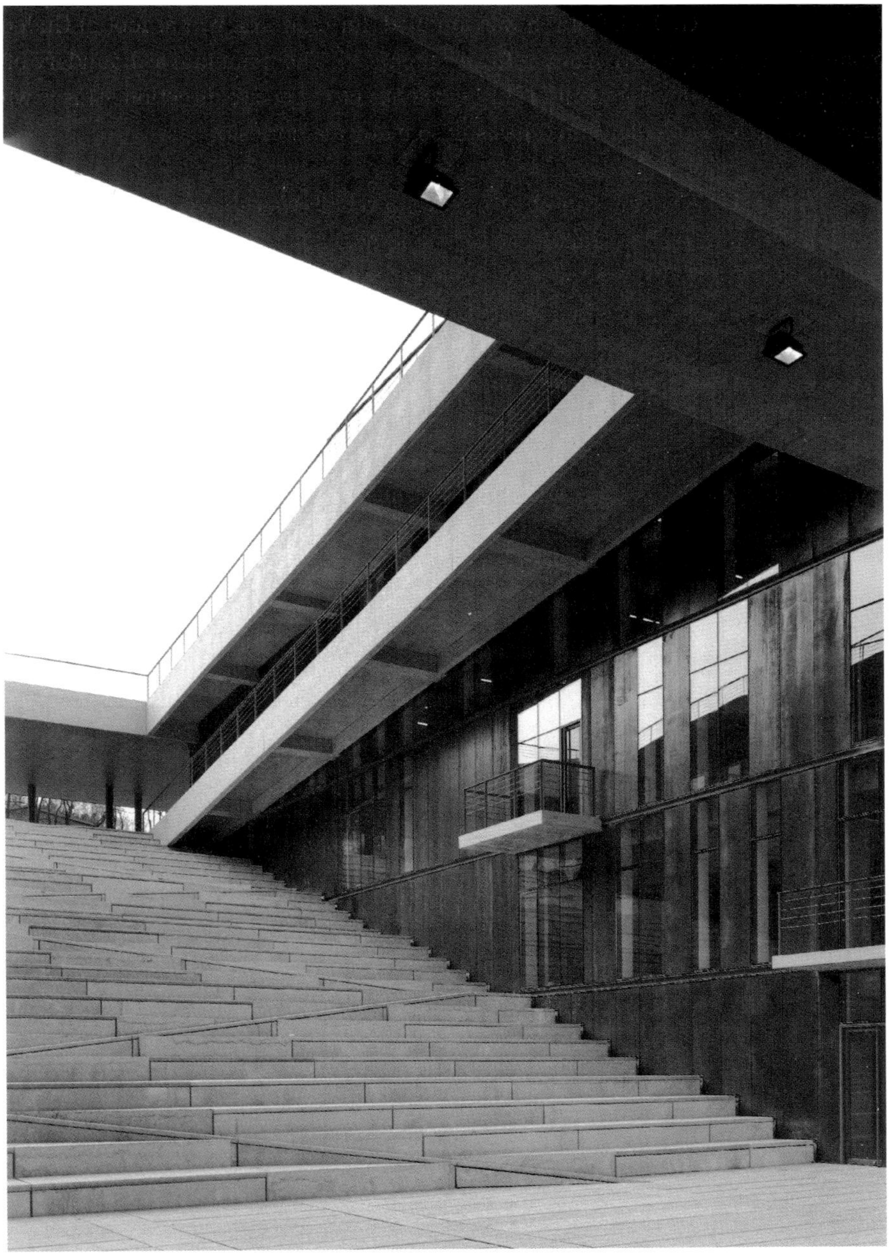

Gudeok Presbyterian Church

Gudeok Church was founded during Korea War at foot of Gudeok mountain in Busan where many refugees migrated. The mountain as boundary of this area made urban development of Busan oriented to opposite direction. This is why surroundings of Gudeok Church has still so many memories of past.

Existing church after several rebuilt was enlarged and included many small houses as attached facilities in surroundings. Some of them are more than half century old. But they were to be demolished for new church building. Keeping even a memory of the houses as a 'modern remains' is regarded important factor to design.

Thus, some old private houses were to be incorporated into the new plan of this church as well as the small alleyways as memory. So most of the elements of the new architectural work –the yard, the stairs, the masses arranged at non-aligned angles, among others – are abstracted and transformed, but they are embodied from the rumination of the memories. Above all the most dominant here is the mountains. It is highly regarded any architecture should have respect to it.

Gudeok Presbyterian Church

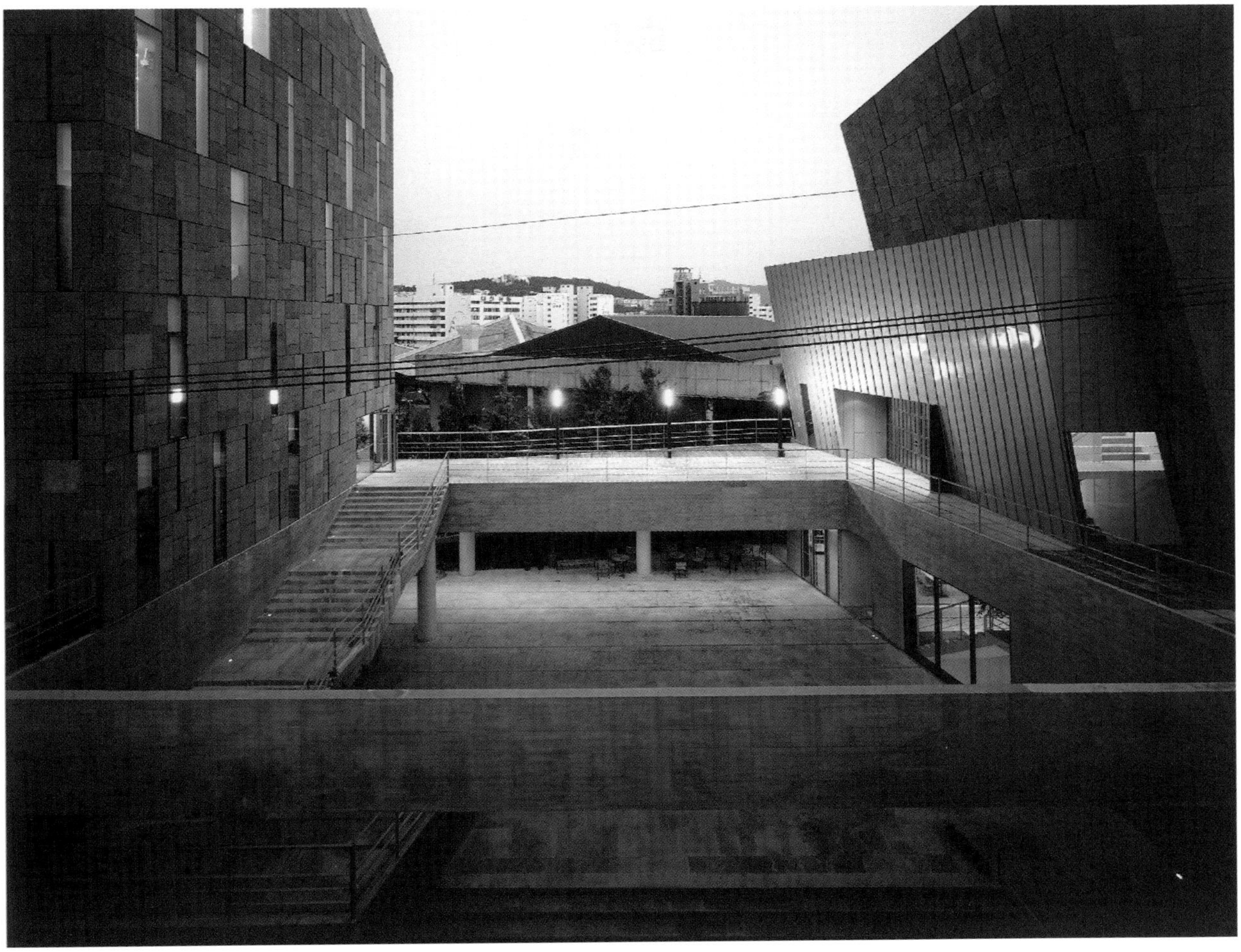

— 284 Gudeok Presbyterian Church

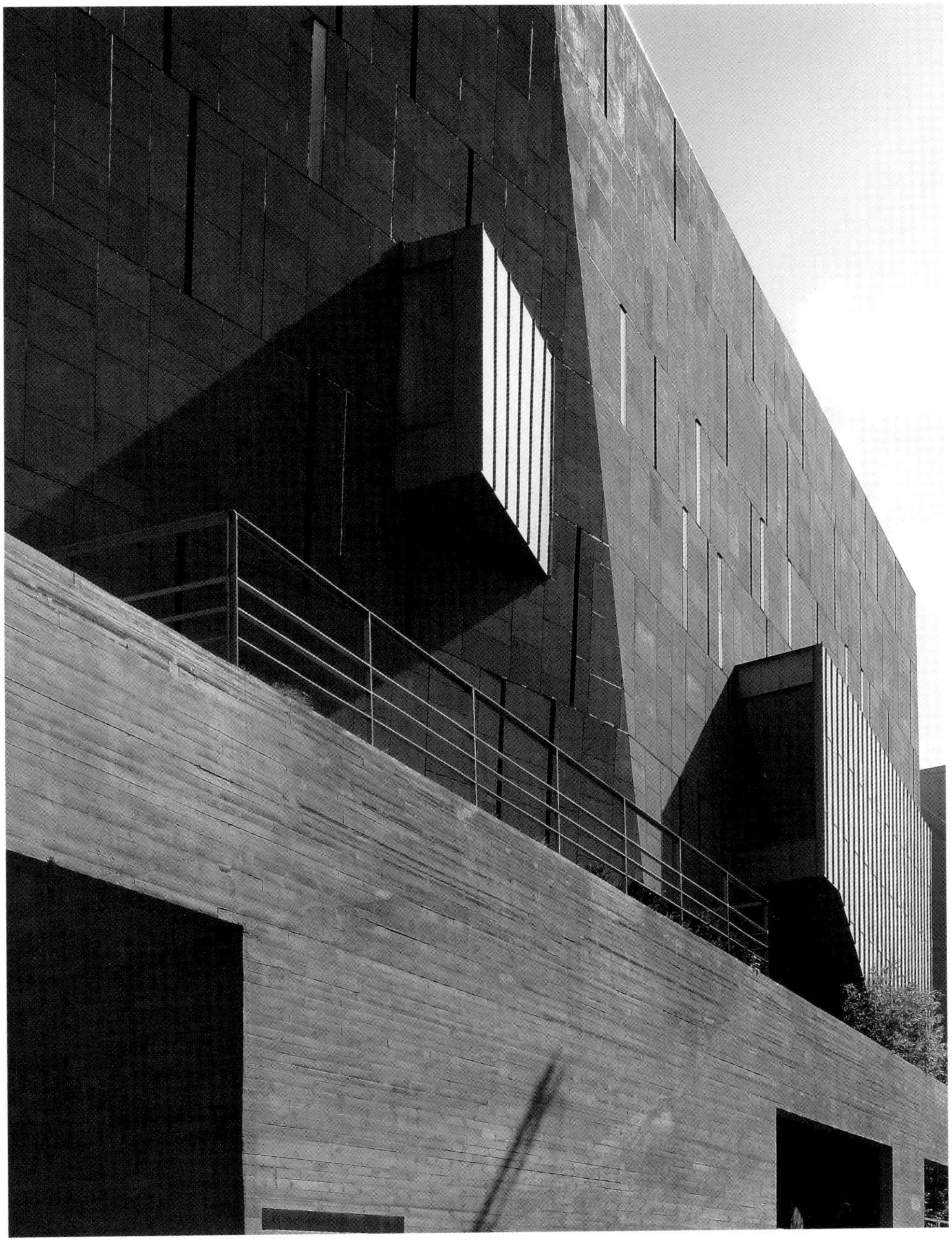

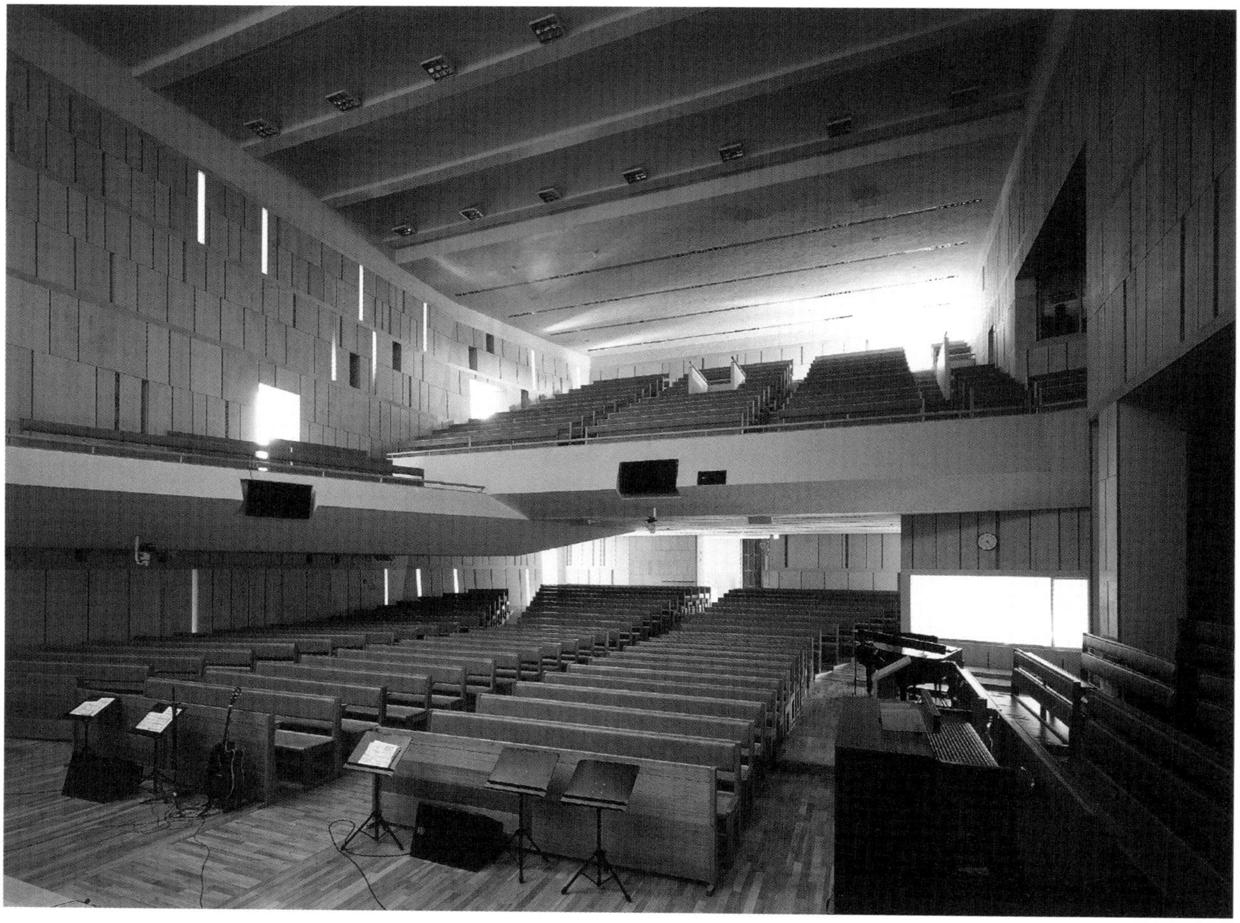

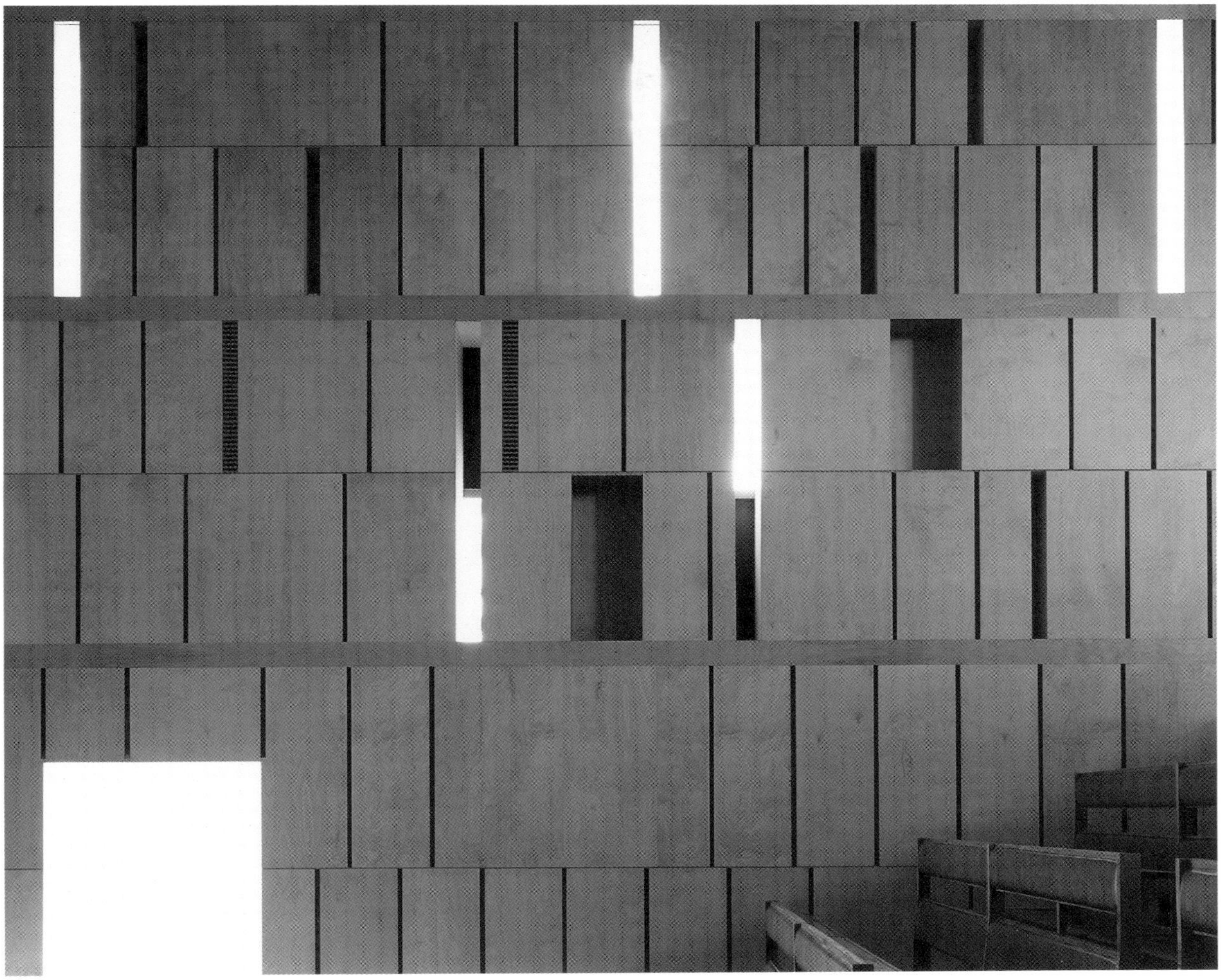

Chaowai SOHO

This commercial complex in Beijing was a design competition among invited architects conducted by SoHo China, one of most successful developer in China. Just a period of two weeks was given for the competition. And it took slightly more than two years to completion of building this 150,000m^2 and 25-story building. In 2005, everything was done at a speed of light in Beijing, and the project was part of the CBD (Central Business District) – the fastest changing region in Beijing. It might be a crisis of losing identity of Beijing.

It was important to make this building a small city in Beijing which seems not to be a city for pedestrians. The most important idea was to make a lot of small alleys("hutong" in Chinese) and streets, and squares and parks inside the building as if they looked like a landscape of a city. In addition, the vertical configuration was not based on the same height of each level. Though it was unconventional, the height of each level was different here and there. The result was the whole landscape looked more dynamic. The surface of the entire building was covered with basalt which seemed to signify a community of strong bonds inside. A square called the bazaar, which was a linear-type square, penetrated the whole site of the building, opening its way to the outside. The functions and roles of the bazaar are not simply shopping facilities or business facilities; they are not clearly distinguished like that. It seemed look like a mess, but it was a strategy to positively accommodate the variety of life. Of course, it is certain that this variety will guarantee a dynamic life in this small city. The material for the outer wall of this city is dark gray stone. The color is the traditional color of Beijing, and plays a faithful role to make the brilliant colors of our life more visible against a dark gray backdrop.

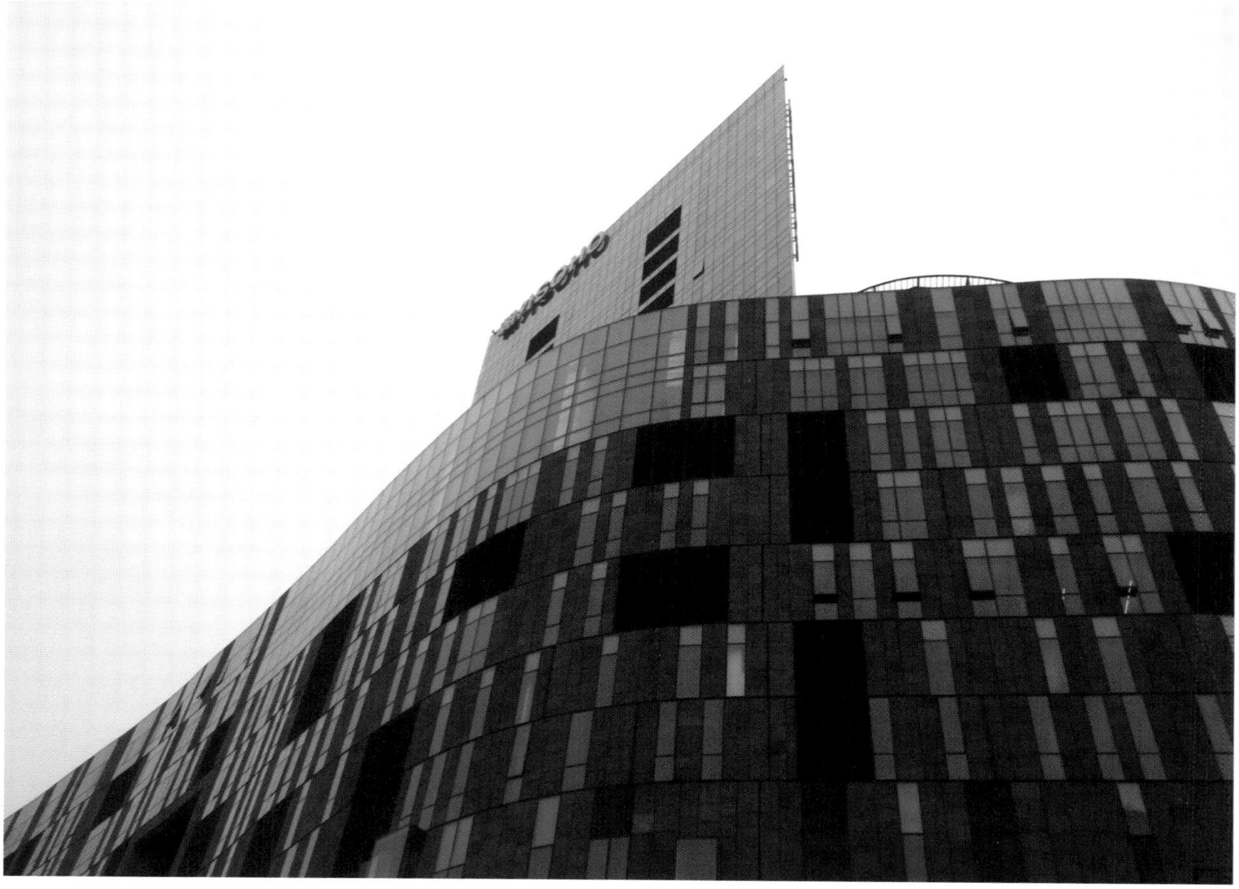

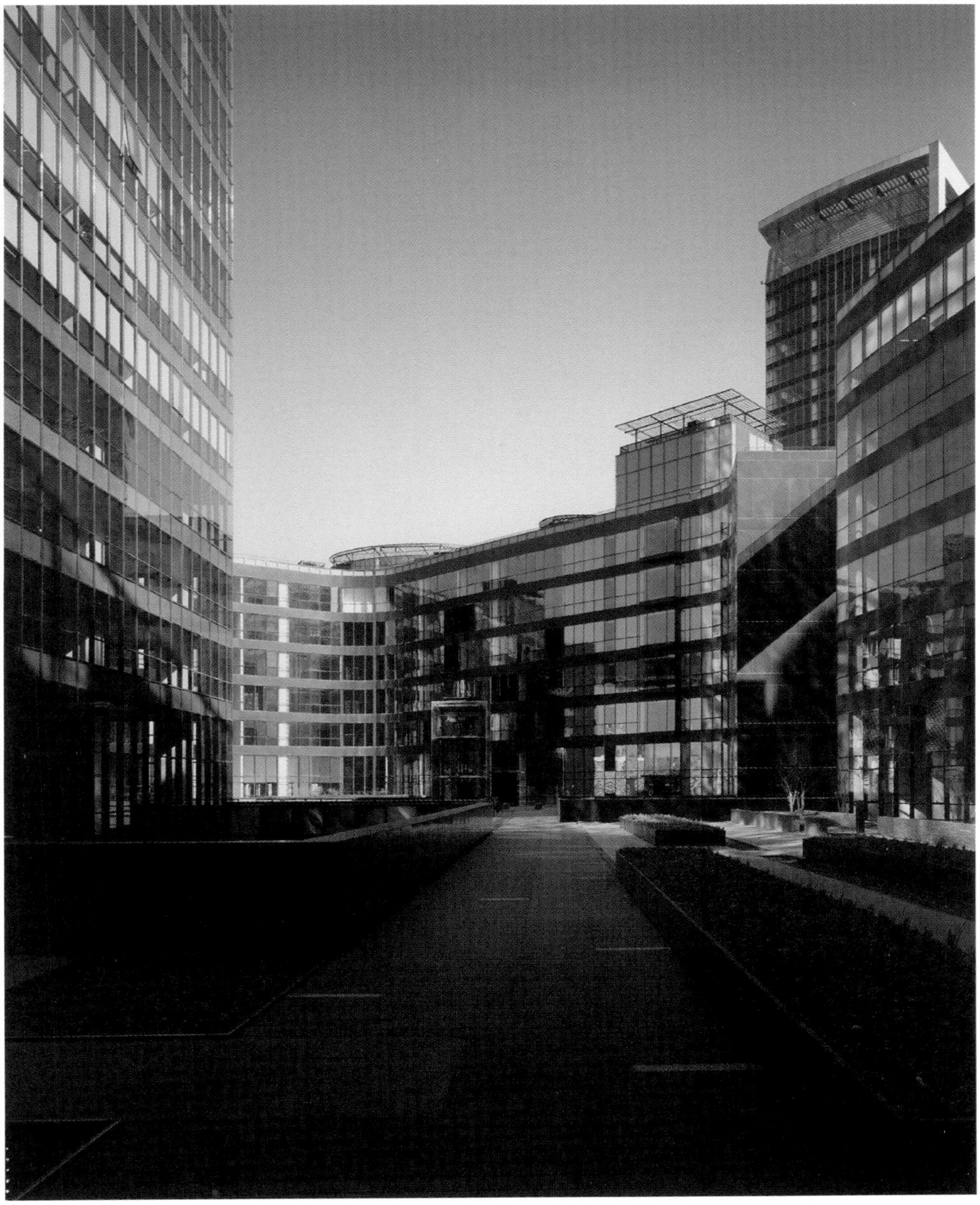

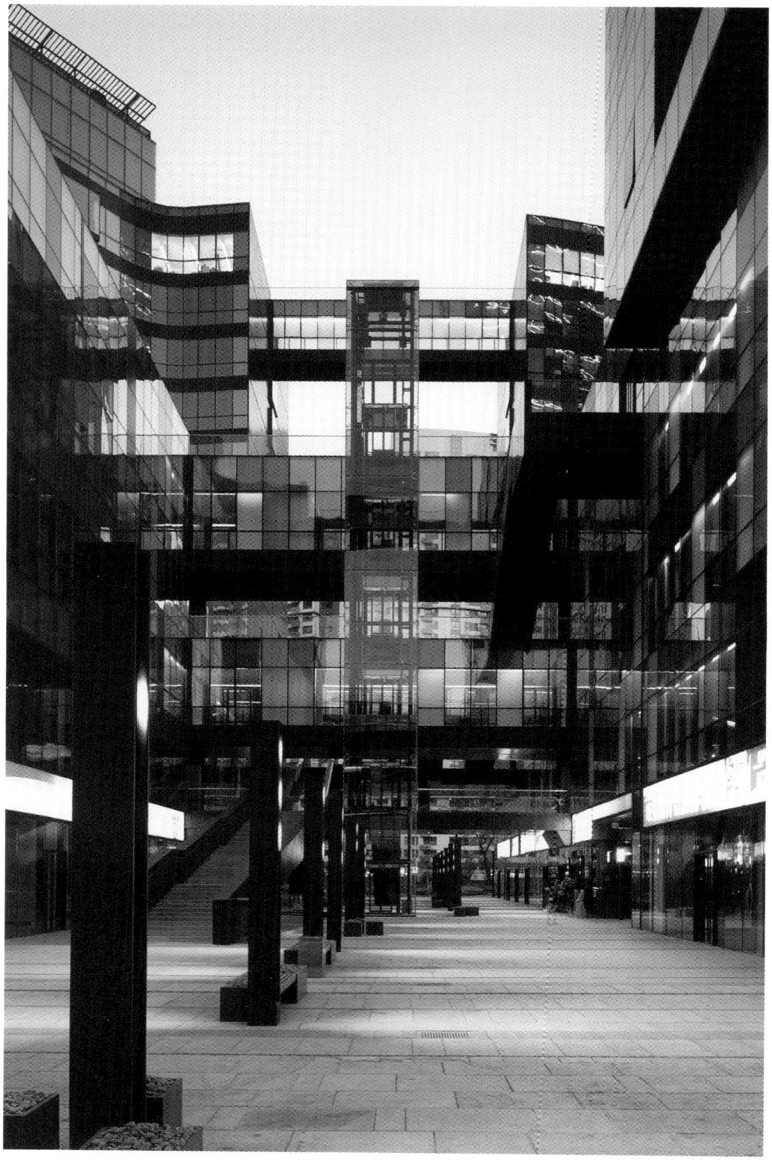

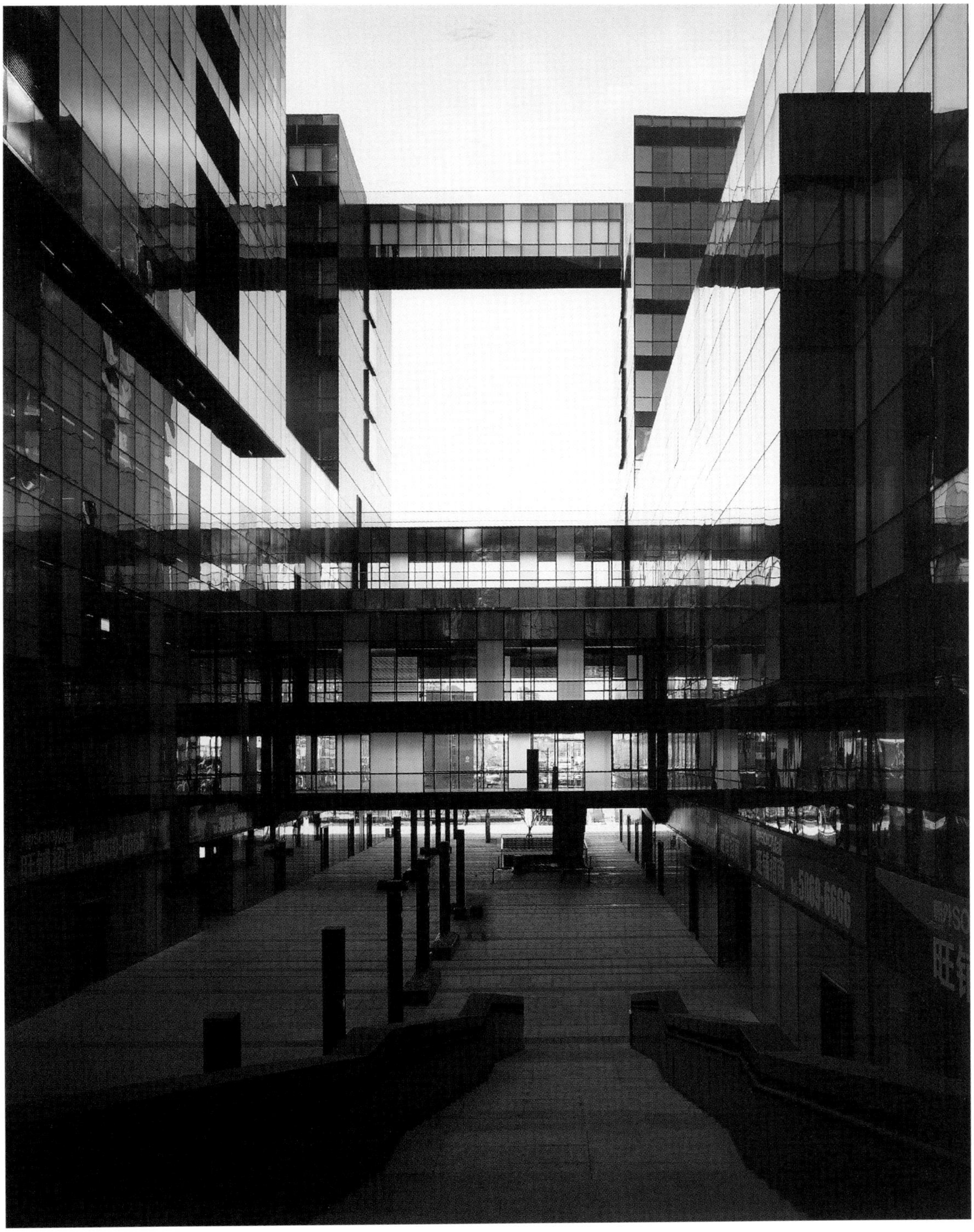

Chaowai SOHO

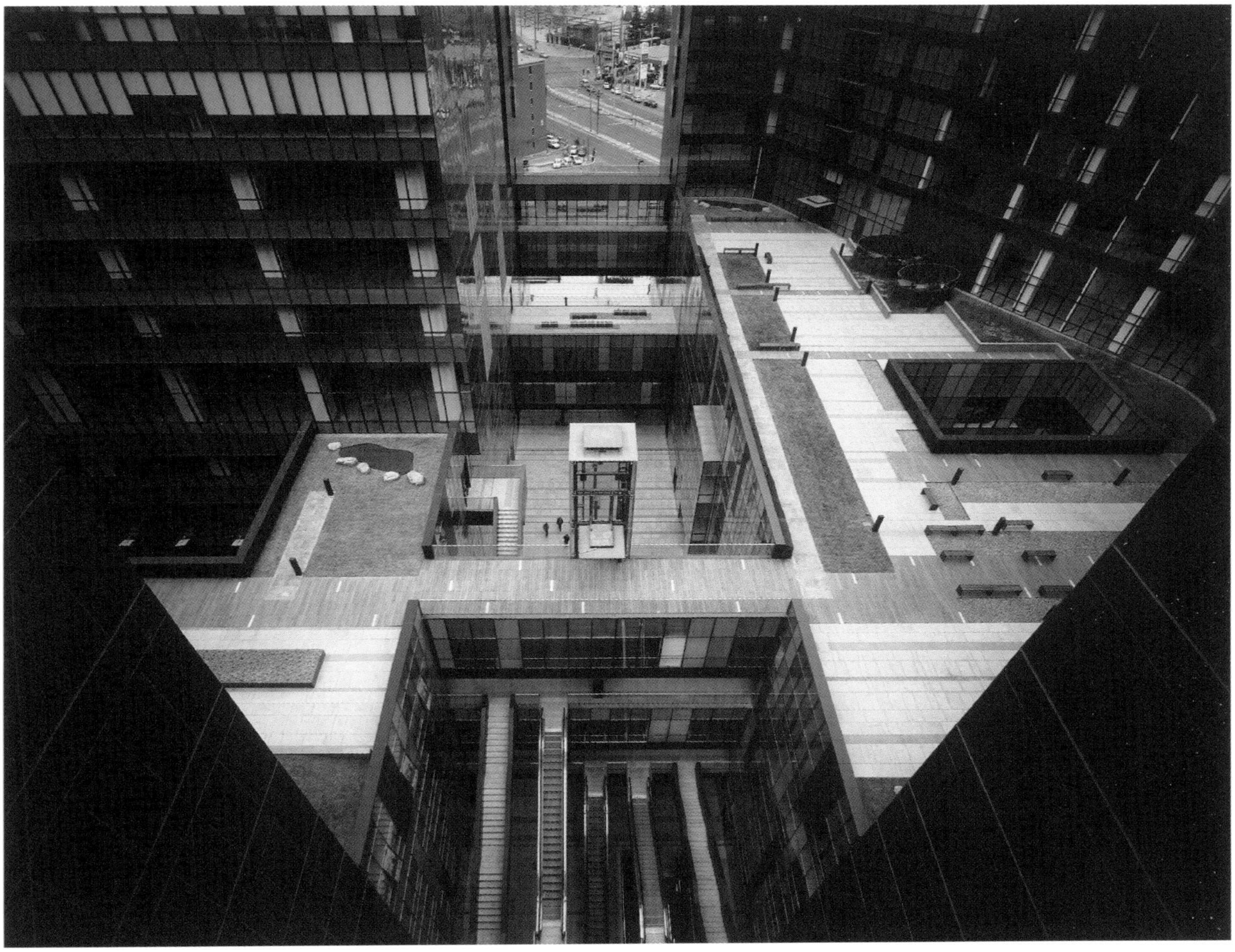

Boao is a small town located in the western seashore of Hainan Island in China. SOHO China, a developer of China, decided to build 400 villas to meet a need to accommodate the coming visitors to attend the newly created Boao Forum. In July 2002, SOHO China invited some selected architects to devise a masterplan in one month. To my surprise, they said the village would be used as the main accommodations for the participants of the Forum to be held in April 2003. Their timetable seemed so far-fetched from all points of view.

The site was extremely beautiful. It was a virgin forest. Luxuriating palm trees and wild tropical plants were entirely exotic by themselves. Crystal clear water and white sand wiped out a stranger's mind that is covered with dust and dirt of the city. The beauty of the sunset that paints the evening sky with diverse colors must enrapture everybody. It was fascinating, spectacular.

There was, however, very stuffy humid. Wind was mostly needed here and it should be a theme of the architect. A pleasant shade was also necessary. The shade would act as a passage to woods from the sea, and at the same time, demonstrate the substance of void. So the floor level of every house should be lifted one meter above the surroundings. While considering water level at high tide, it is required to preserve the original topography as much as possible. As the result, the wind was expected to blow through the house and under the house as well. Two basic types for the villas were suggested: a house facing the water and the other facing the forest. A courtyard was placed in the middle of the house, causing wind to blow through. A rhythmic arrangement was made along the water, and along the forest.

The construction plan was slightly revised, and 100 houses were built first. It was still a very difficult construction work, but in the end the visitors could stay in the villas, as planned, in April. It was magic.

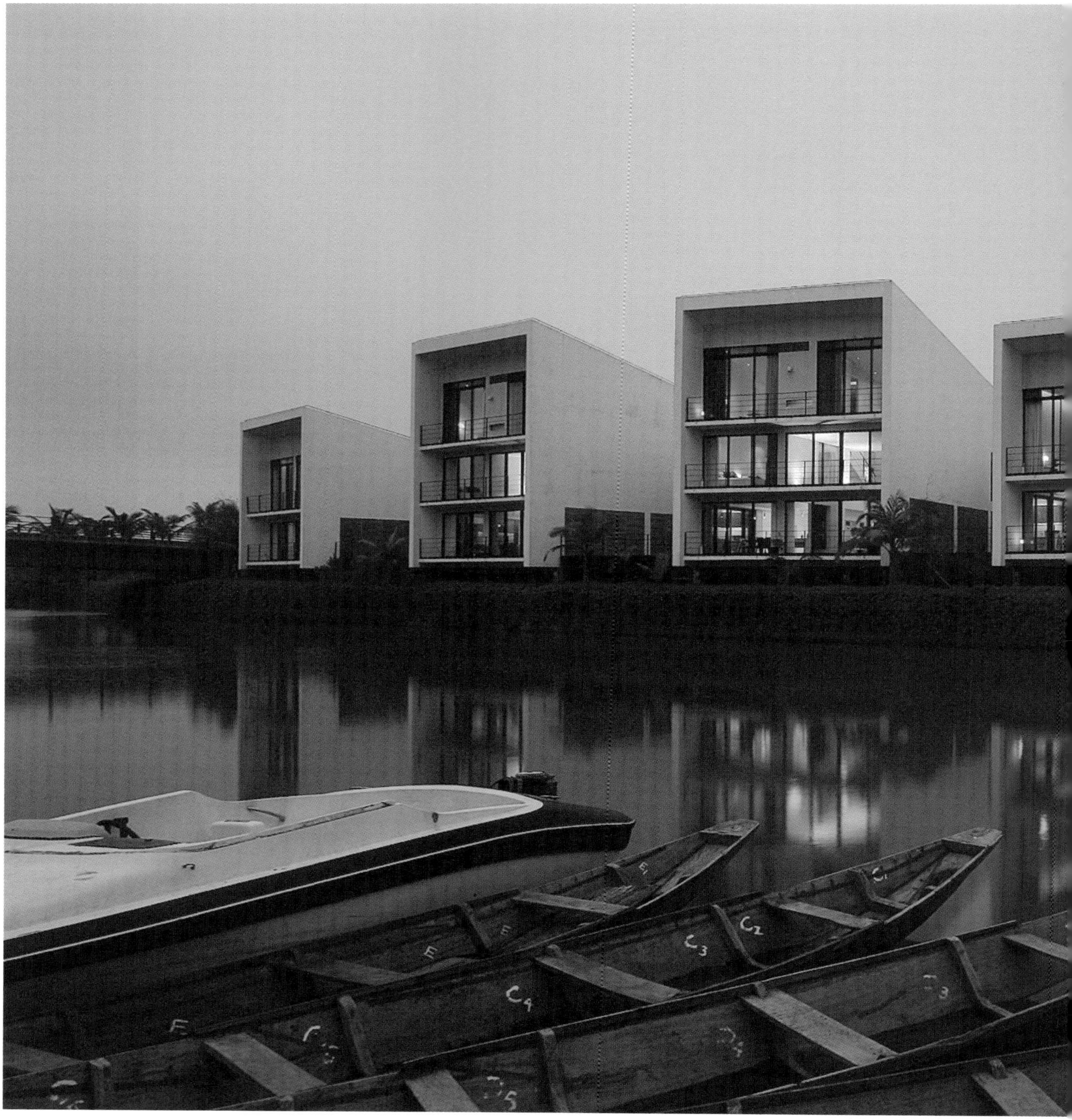

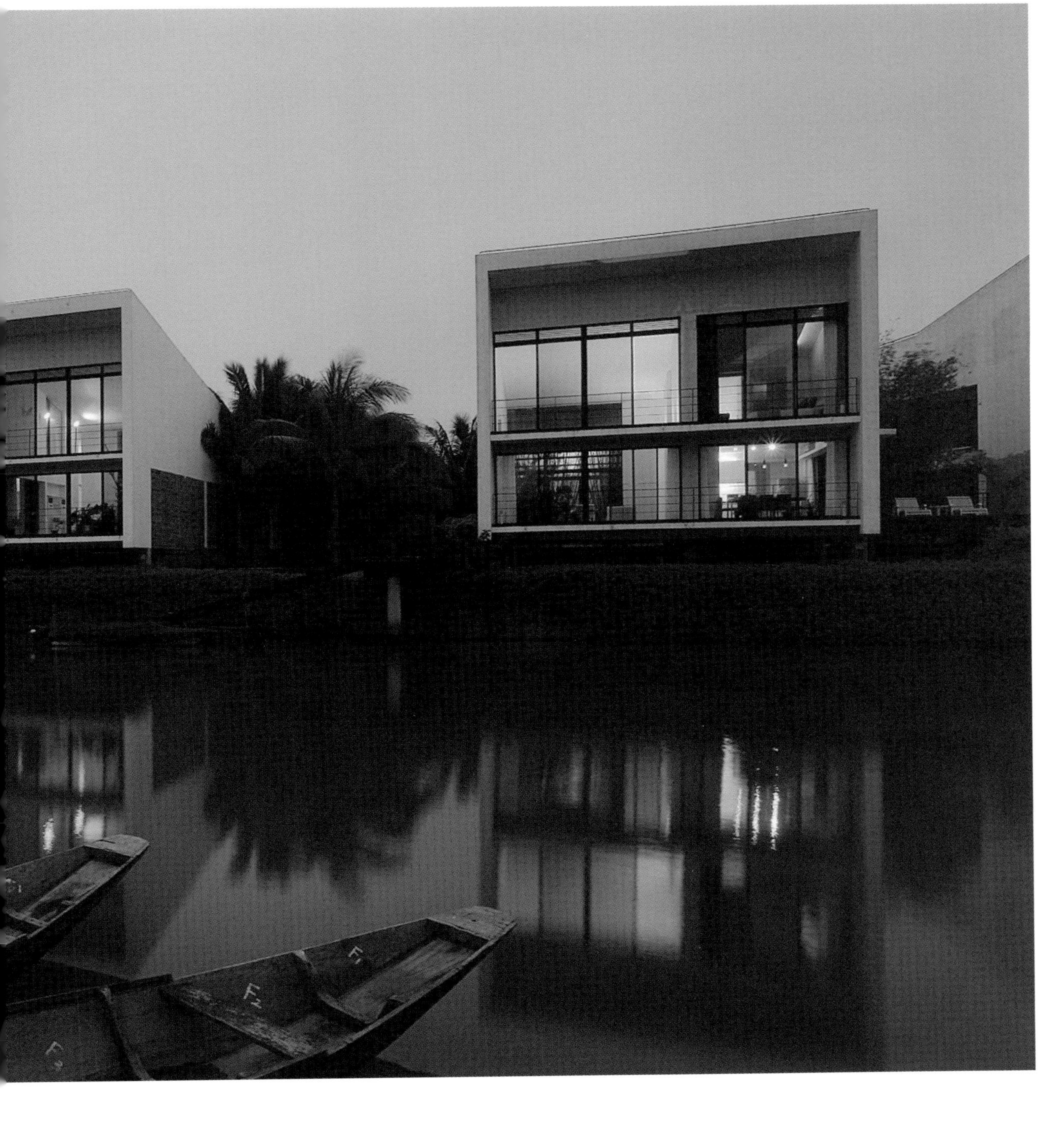

Boao Canal Village

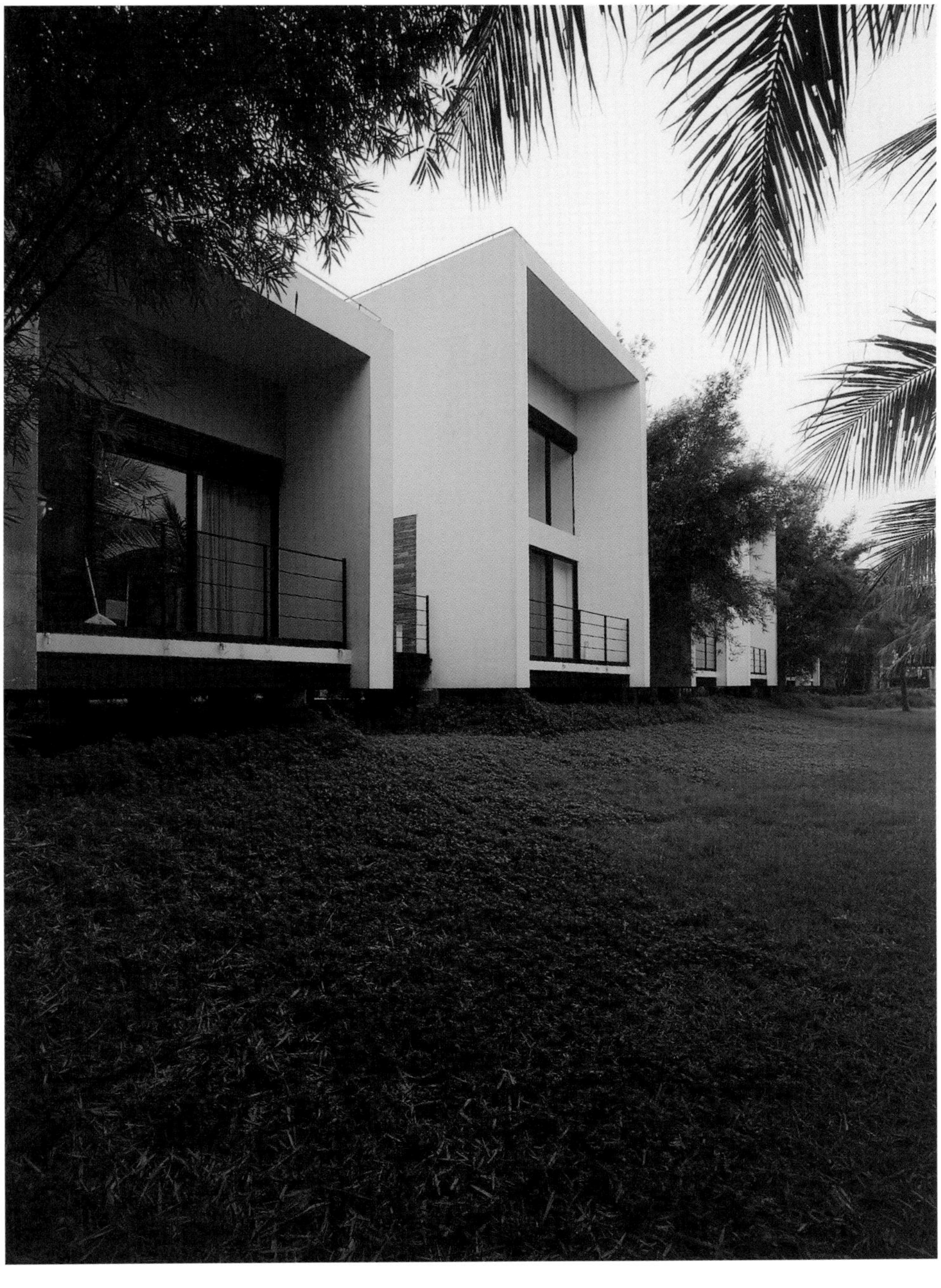

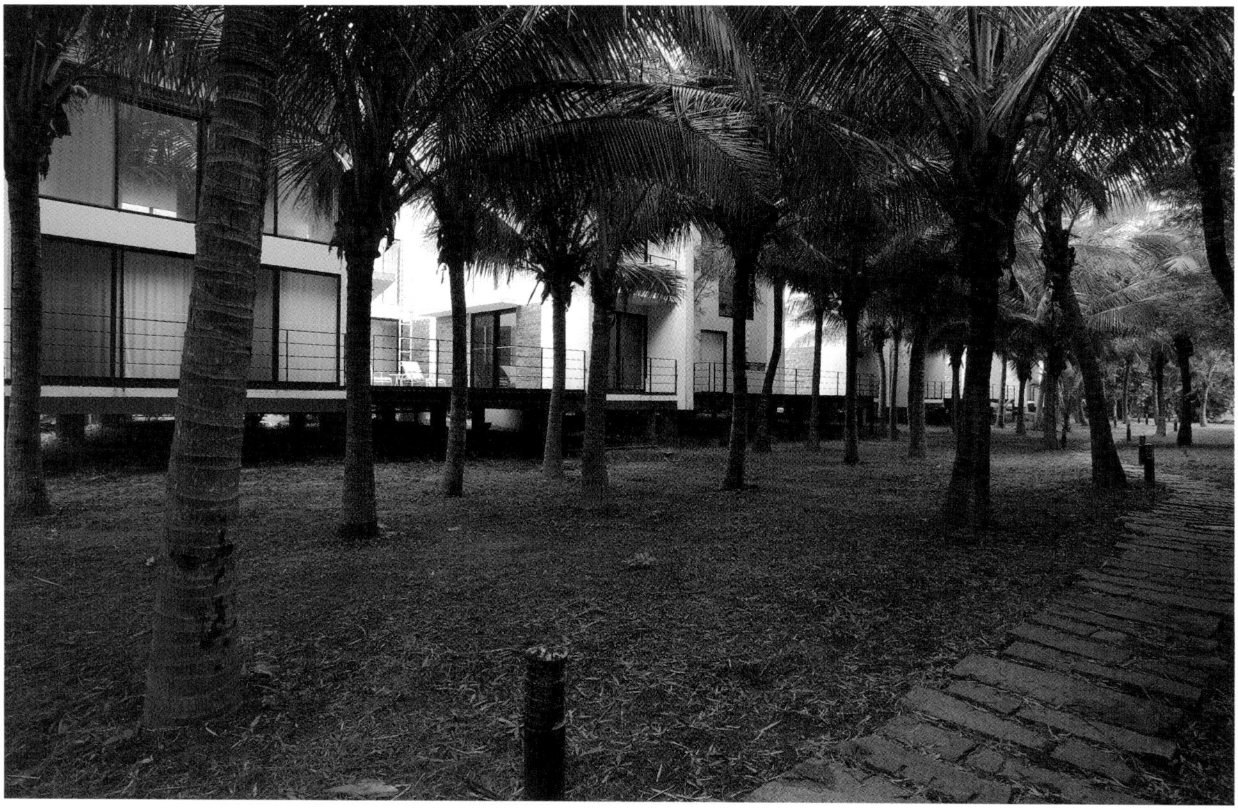

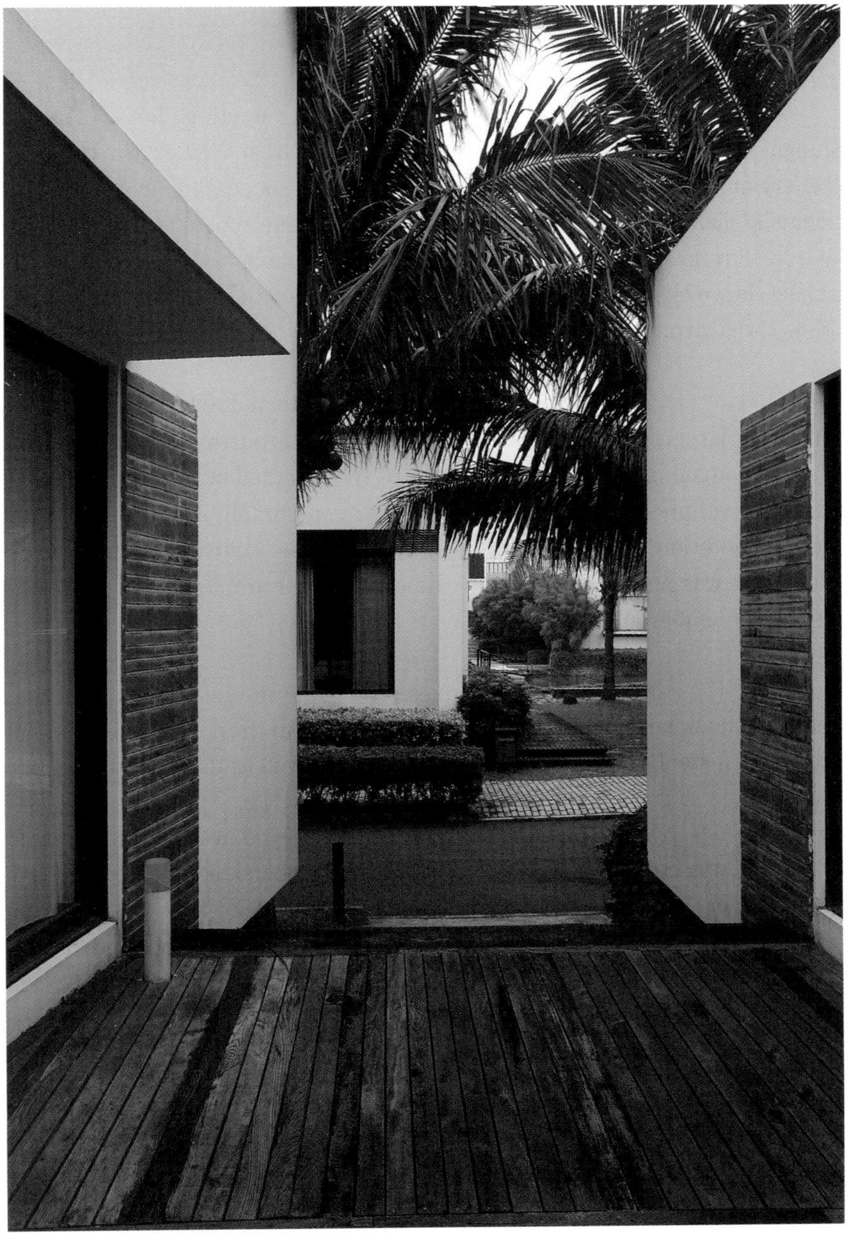

Commune by the Great Wall

The Commune by the Great Wall, a boutique hotel, is located in Shuiguan, 60km north of Beijing, bordered by the Great Wall. It has a very beautiful scenery of three valleys. The client SOHO China, a successful developer of China, originally planned to 50 lavish villas for the rich Chinese people. For this project, they invited 12 renowned Asian architects to design 11 model houses and a clubhouse. This project, however, was changed as to build a boutique hotel instead of villas after the project was given a special prize at the 2002 Venice Biennale of Architecture.

The size of the clubhouse, more than 3000m² in total floor area was somewhat larger, considering the mild terrain of the surrounding mountains. In order to avoid damaging the beautiful scenery, it was decided at the first field visit to divide the entire volume into smaller units and let the mountainous terrain flow down through them. In addition, there was a trace of time-honored cultivating paddy fields on the site, and it was necessary to make arrangements for architecture to make such a trace remain remembered.

Finally, five long boxes protrude from the mountains in the north. Between the boxes, nature flows to the mountains in the south. The clubhouse is finished with Corten steel that changes as time goes by as well as the surrounding scenery.

White poplar trees had already existed in the construction site. None of a single tree was cut as promised. Thus, some trees looked like they penetrated the wooden decks while some others piercing the building. As a place where lots of trees had grown became a courtyard. There seems be no division between outdoor and indoor, because a building was not designed but a landscape, meeting the requirements of the land.

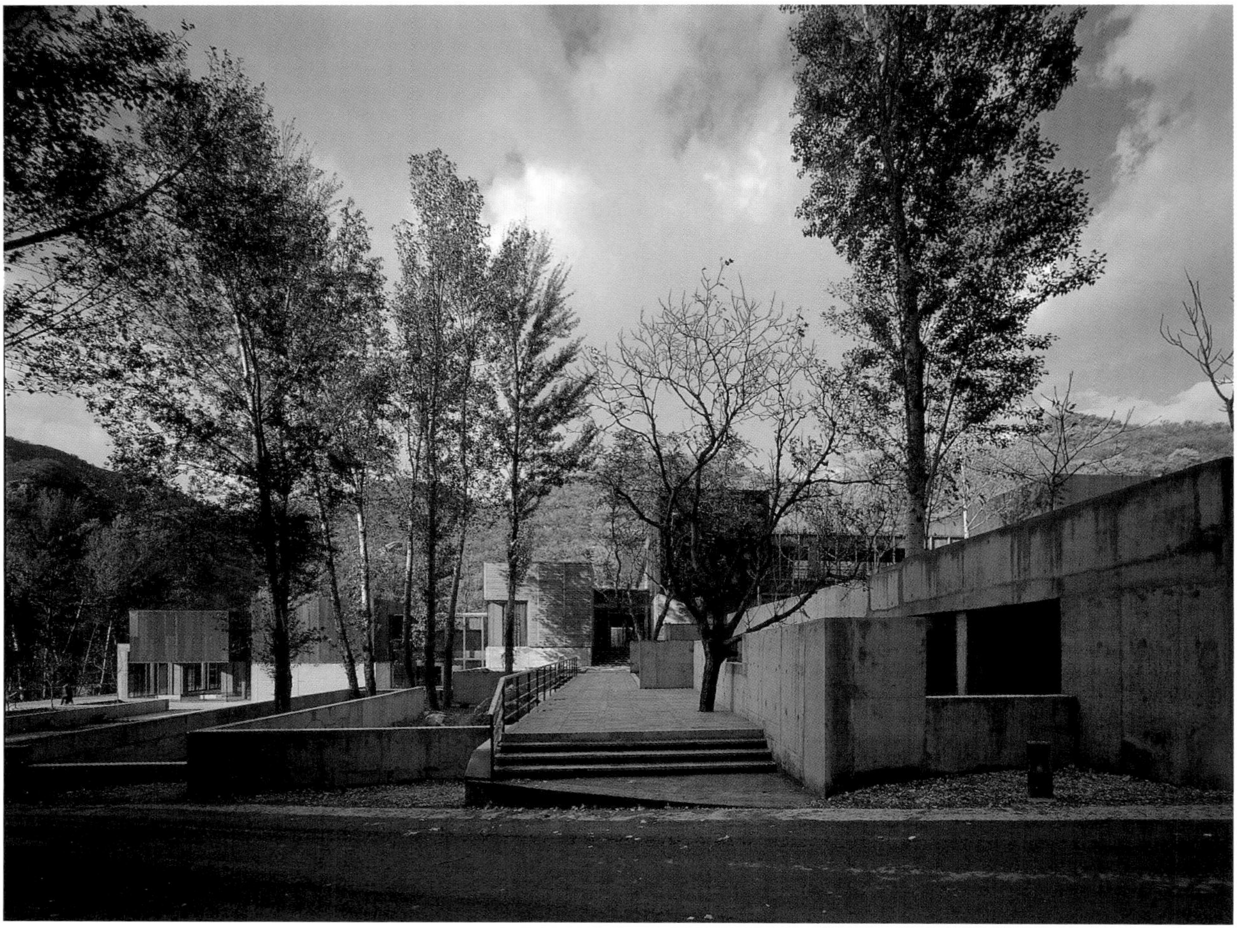

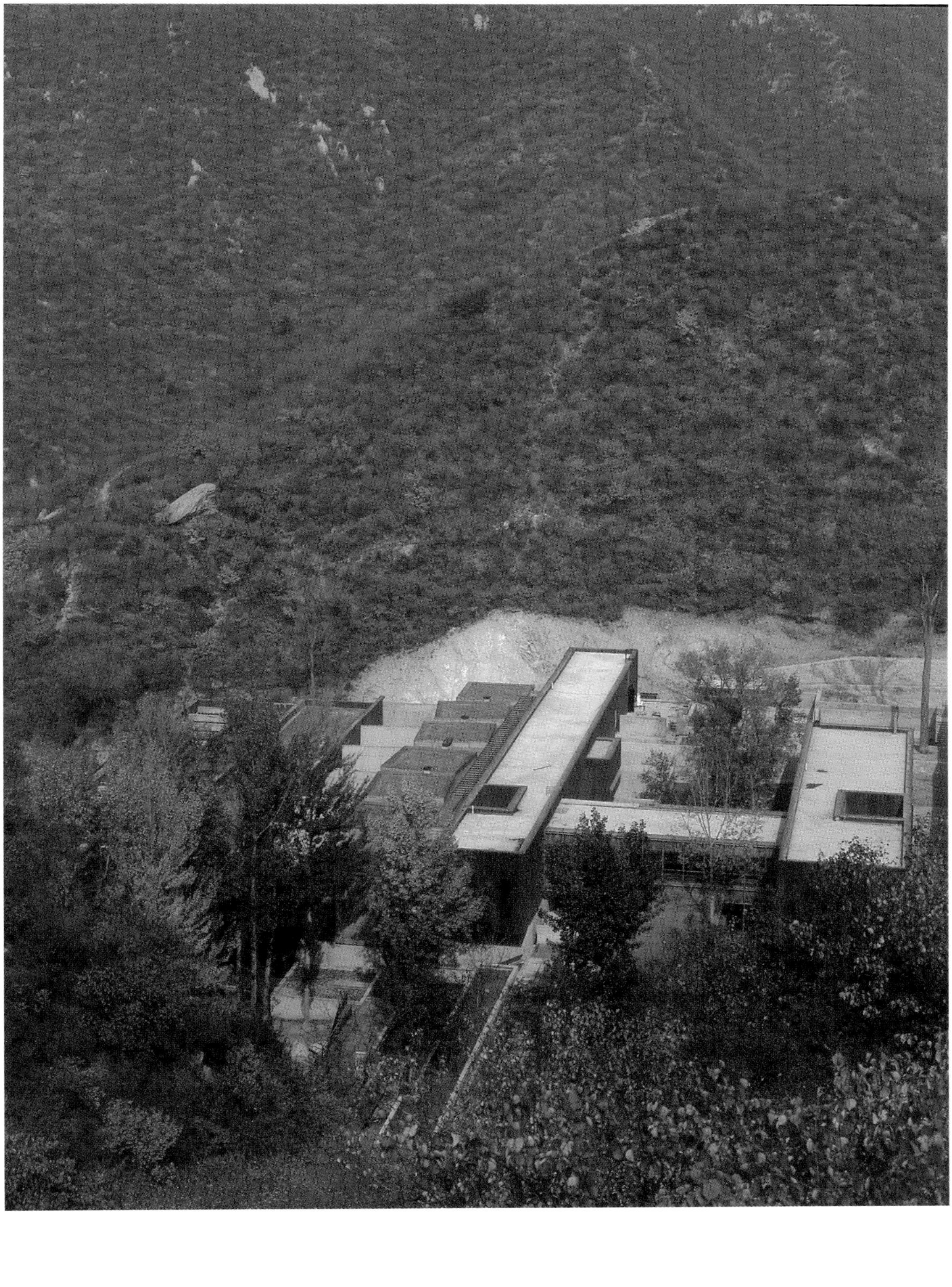

Commune by the Great Wall

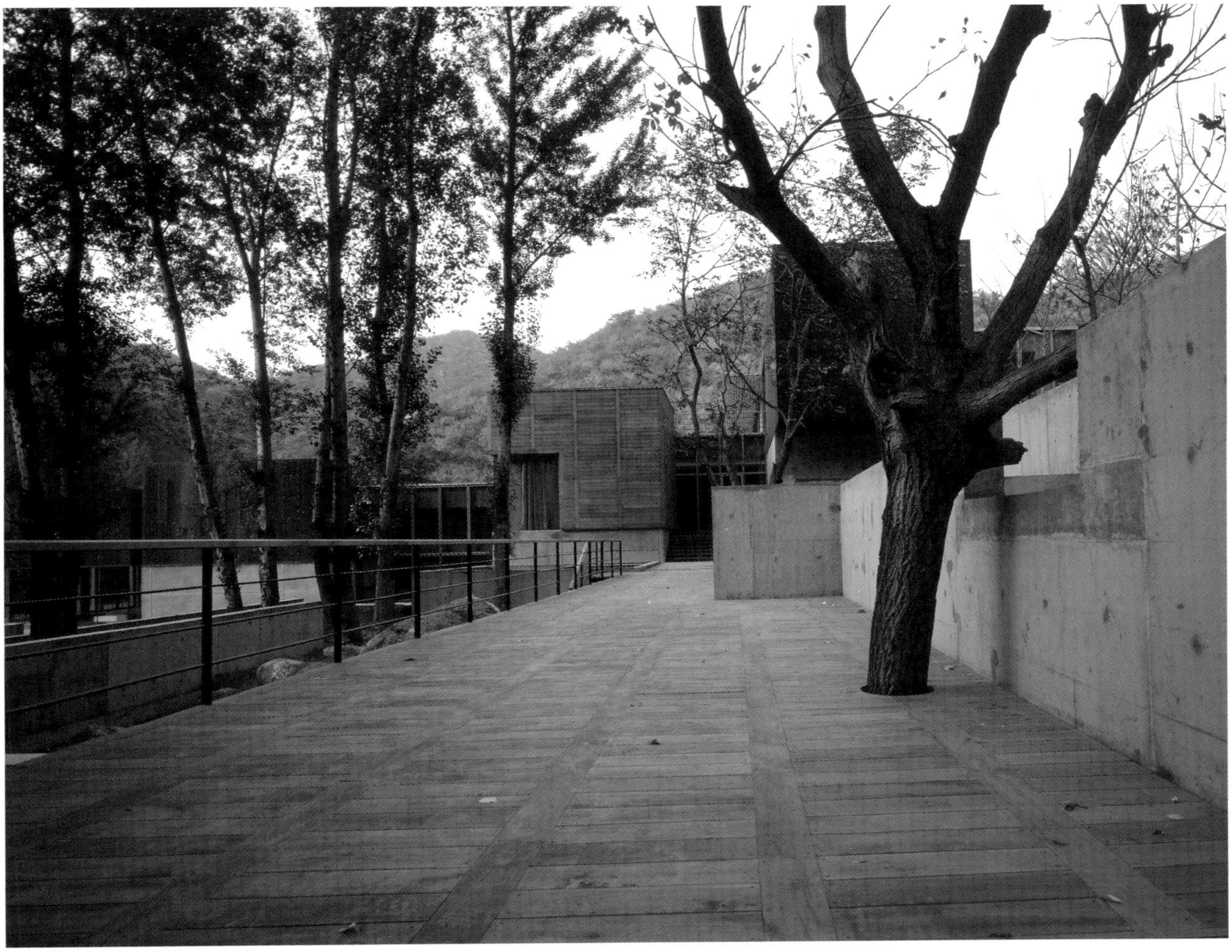

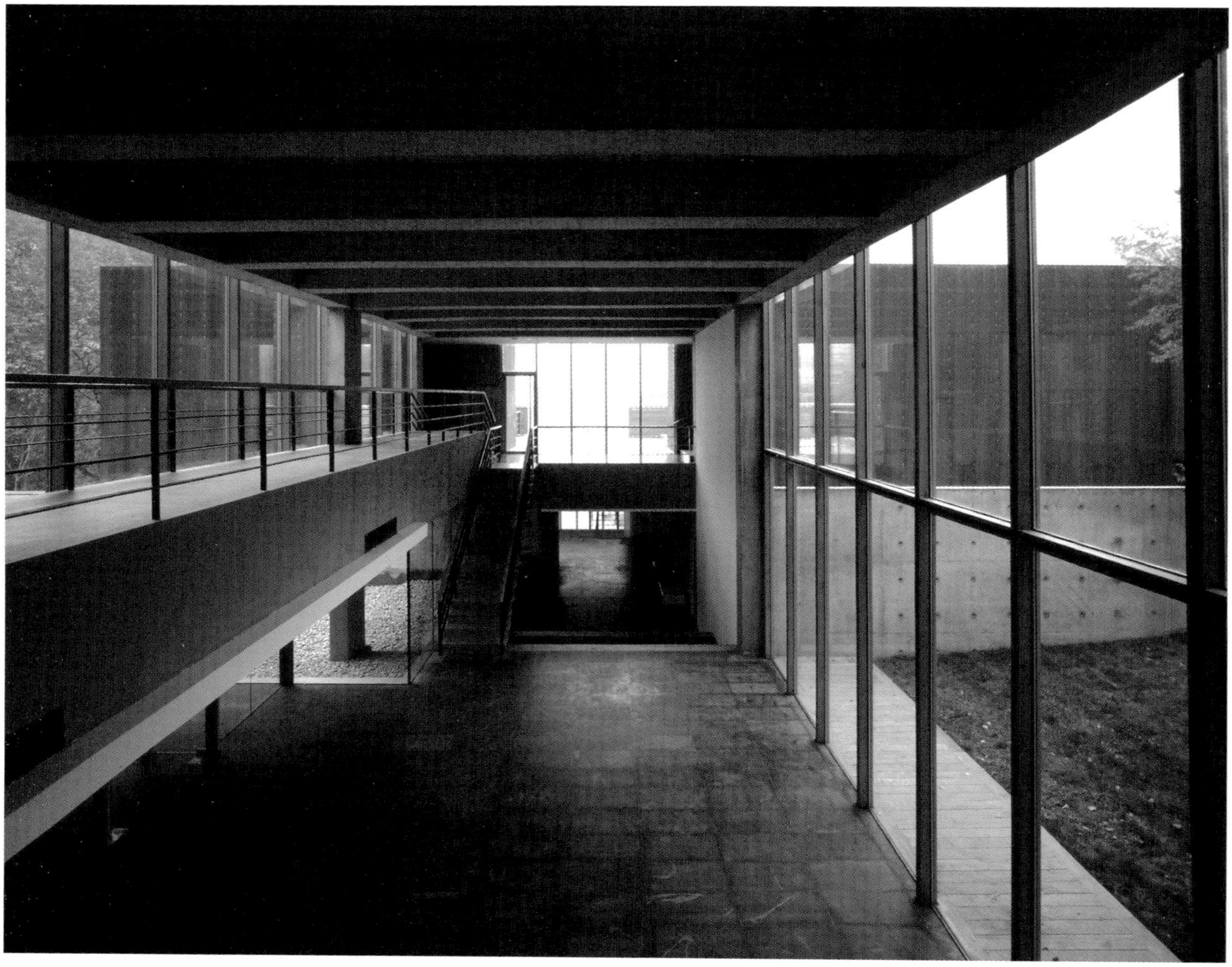

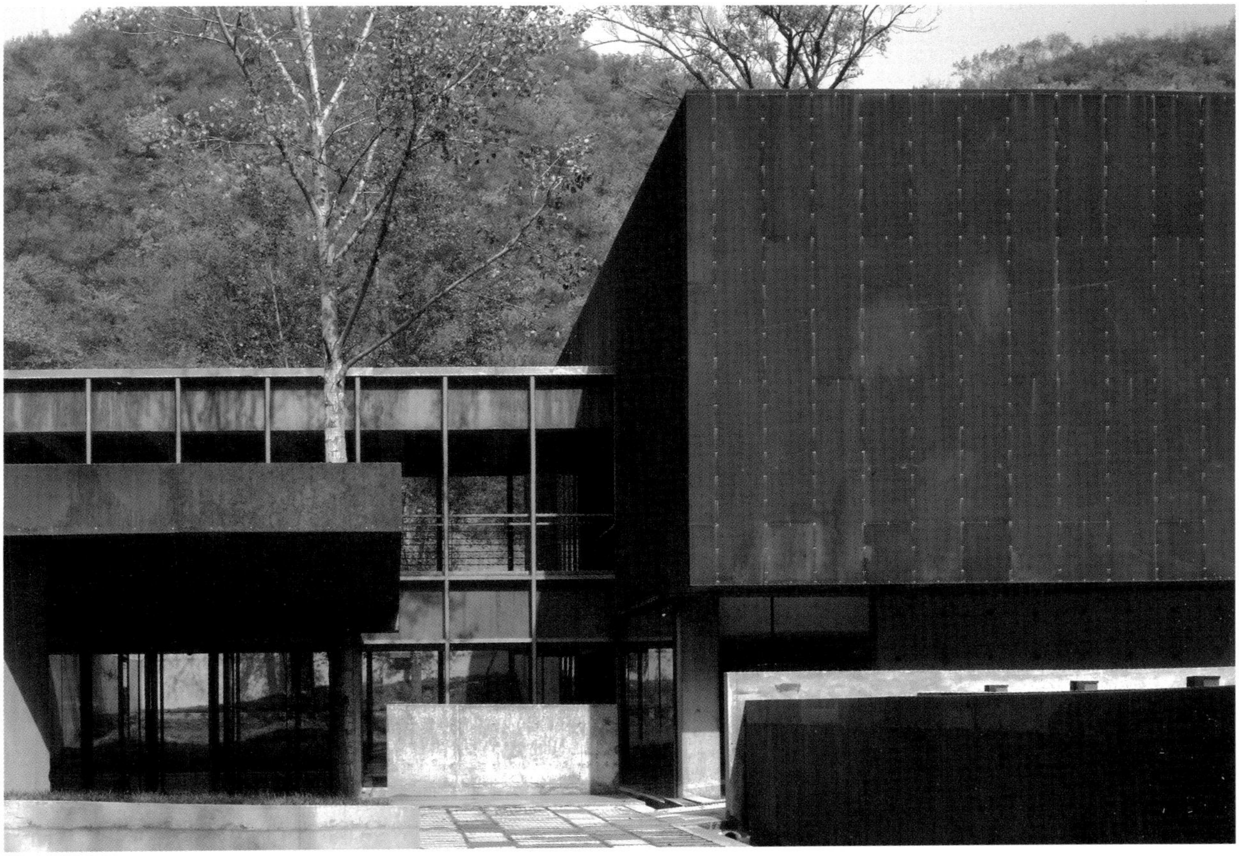

Daehakro, meaning university road, where this building belongs to, was the traditional habitation of the Joseon period, and, was also where numerous talented leaders of Korea were developed, as Seoul National University used is as its campus. After the university moved out in 1975, this area was sold to individuals in 330 square units, and had visions about a beautiful residential unit by attracting cultural facilities. However, the storm of economic development that soon followed put this area into a wild whirlpool. The price of the land, which increased tenfold every year, could not help to keep this area as a residential one, and being changed into entertainment and commercial facilities, the houses had their functions changed into shops. The galleries and bookstores had to leave, not being able to bear the pricey rent. The wholesome buildings turned in a day into a Mexican-styled one or Gaudi-styled structure or brought in the Magic Castle of Disney Land. The area became a place of congested, low, mercantile hegemony, finally leading to a loss of ethics for the city.

This building is located on the edge of the road. Because this land was originally outside the old campus of Seoul National University, it was only on the periphery of the so-called influential range of Daehakro. Also, the area behind this part of the land is still filled with inferior residential units and, therefore is definitely on the urban border. Just above it is the Naksan, a form of the traditional topography that shaped Seoul, where old and inferior apartments have been recently evacuated to develop a park.

The given area was small, and the program itself was to have a volume of twice the size of the area. The client is a modern master craftsman, who has been creating architectural hardware of a high standard for a long time; and he, suitably for his work, had collected an immense number of locks and keys, which he wished to form a lock museum with, to fill in this architecture. Apart from this museum, which will be the only one of its kind in Korea, a space for the client's habitation and events, and a restaurant and designing shop to provide for the maintenance of the building are included in this architectural program.

To introduce some weight was highly needed to this dense area where buildings of so many numbers of styles, the confusing signboards, the electric cables and telegraph poles overhead are not offering one bit of feeling of stability. The simpler it is, the more acutely the weight will be felt. No windows, no adornments, but only the weight of the metal will be there. It is a negative void to create tension in this brawling scenery. But inside it there is much brightness.

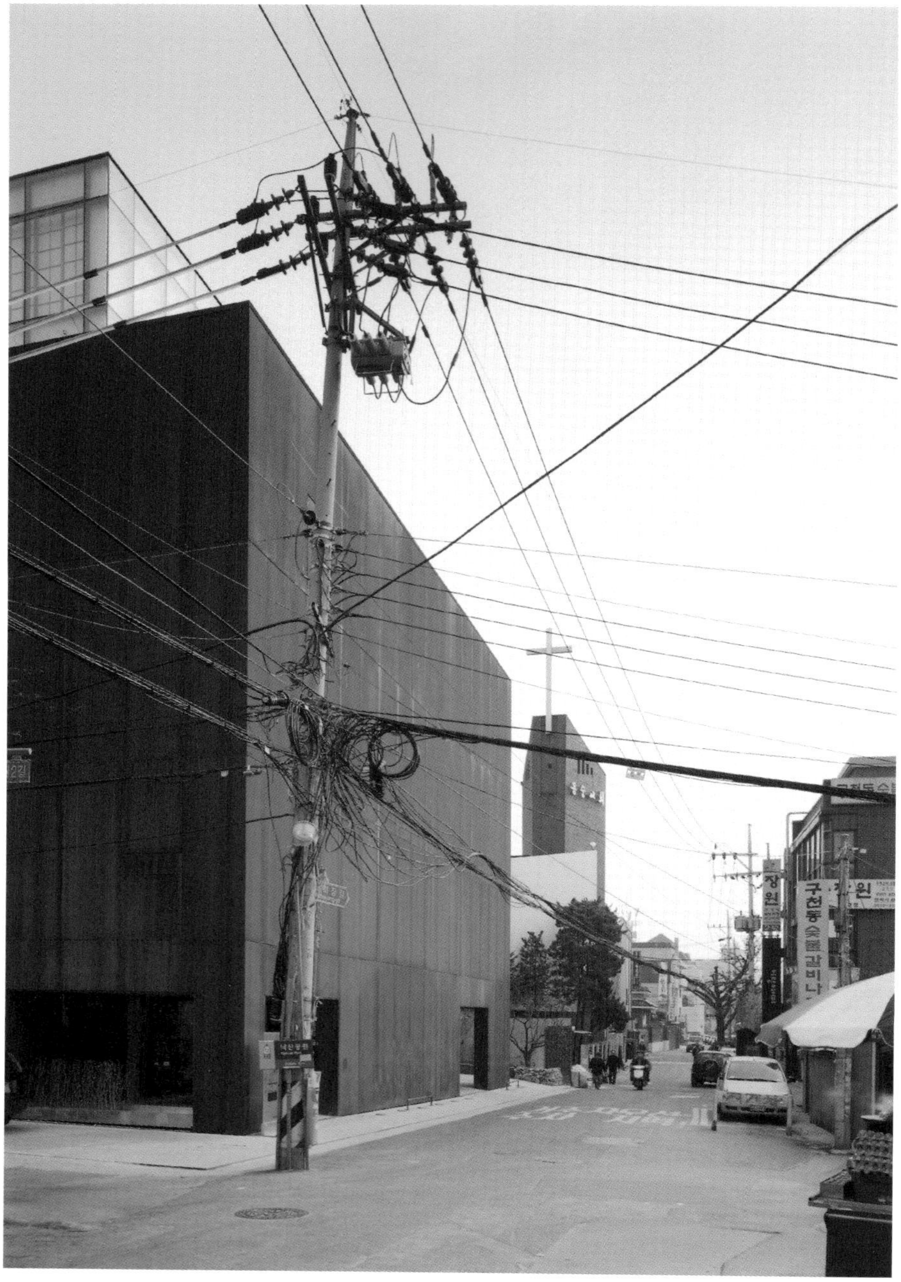

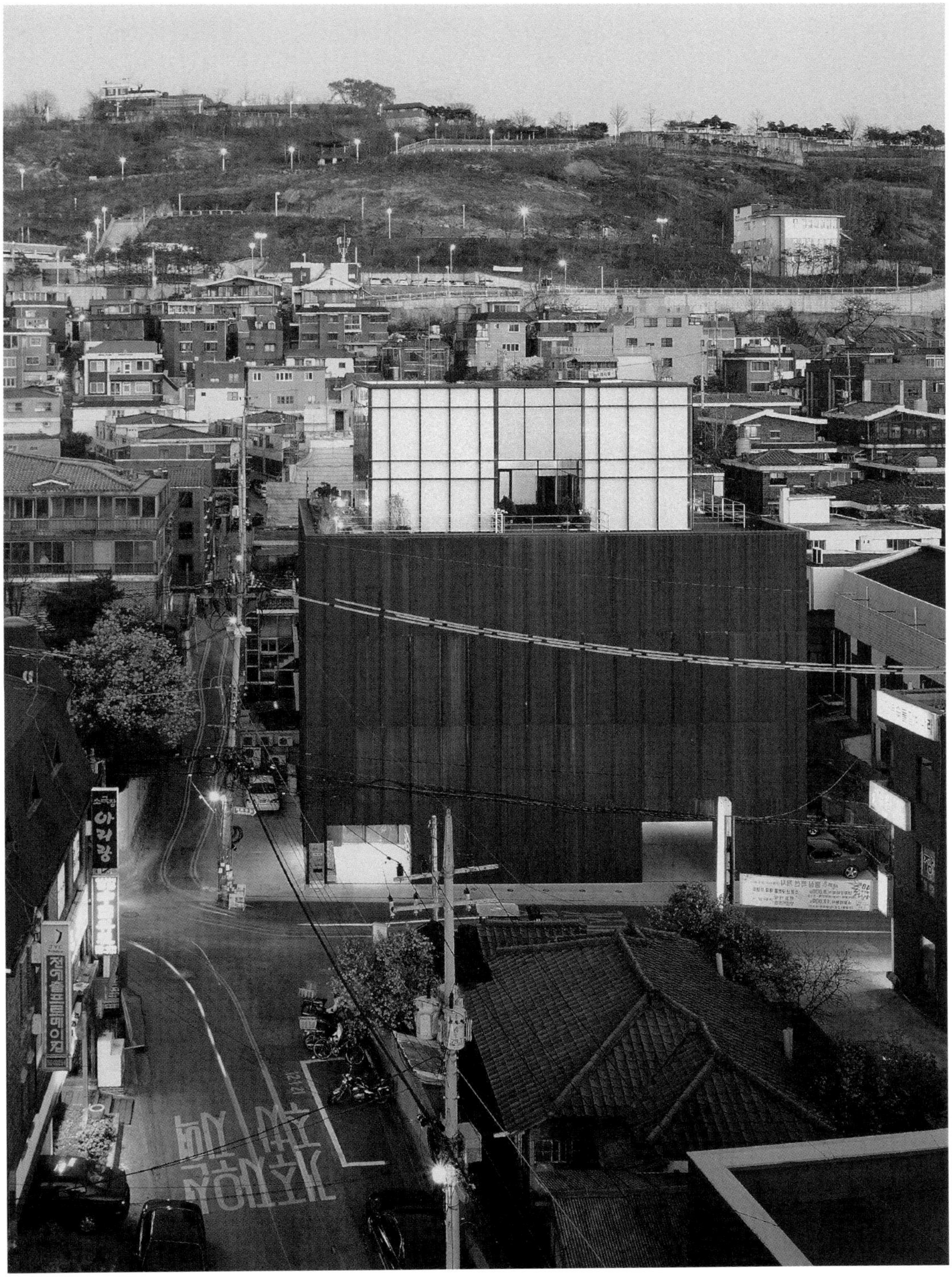
아리랑

Lock Museum

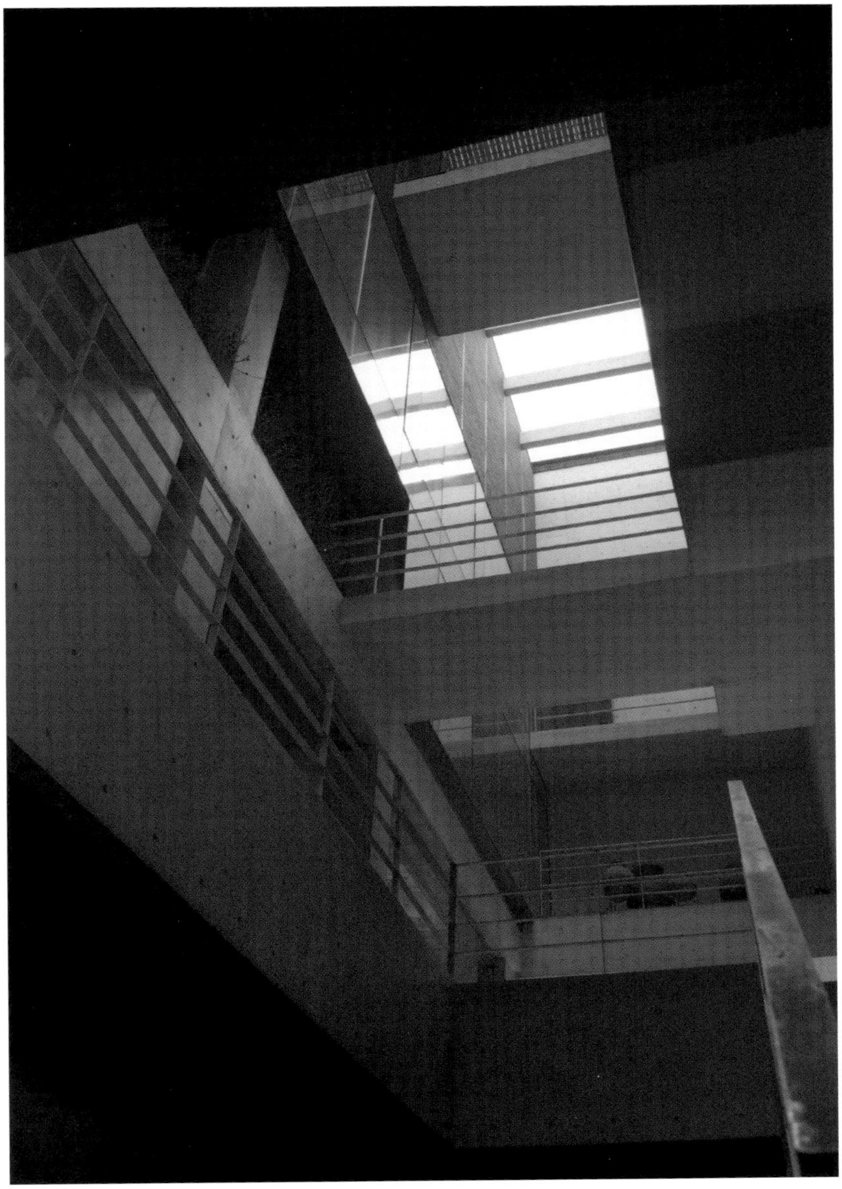

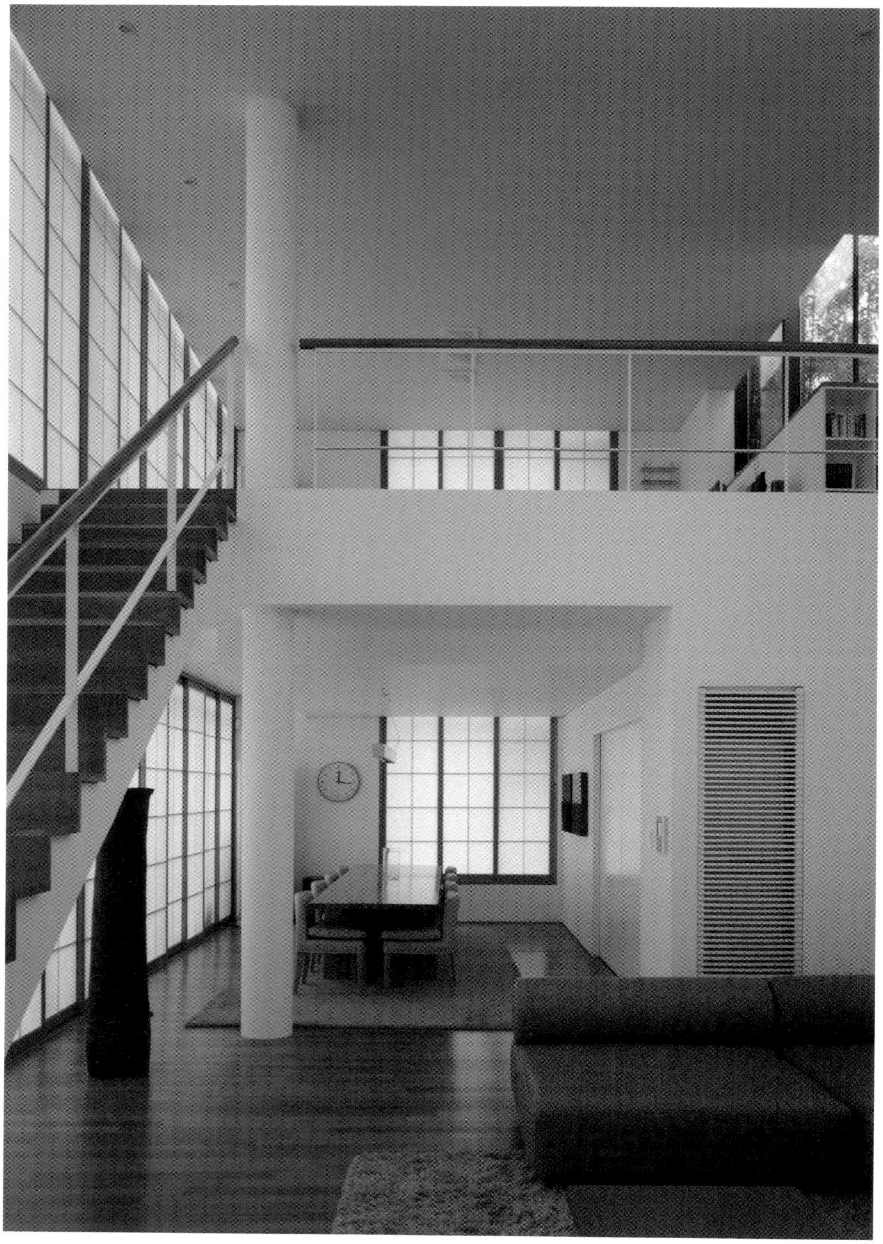

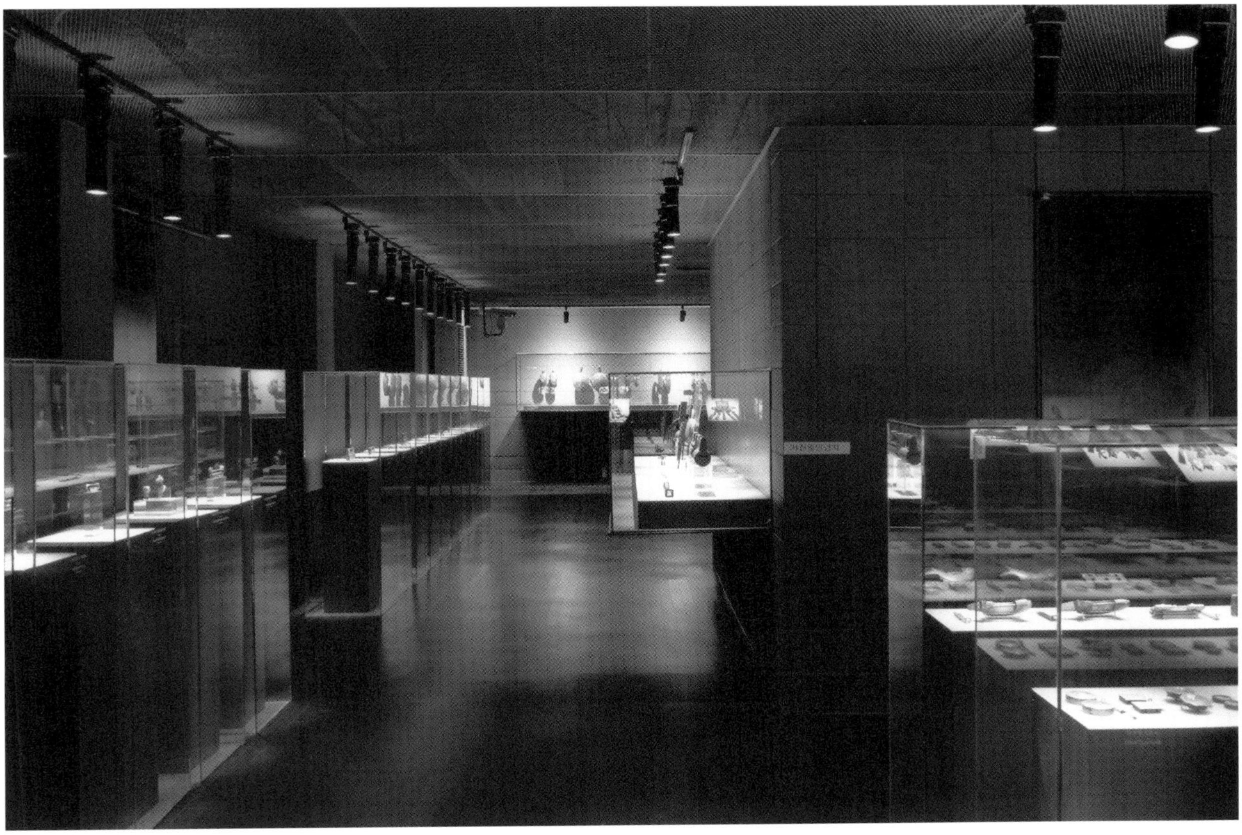

Welcomm City

Welcomm, which stands for Well-Communications, is an advertising and public relations company. In the summer of 1998, with the economic crisis of Korea, leading to the IMF bailout program, the structure for the basements of this building had been already completed. The construction contractor, however, went bankrupt, and the client was also in a difficult situation. Accordingly, the construction work had been suspended indefinitely. Fortunately, it took several months for the client turned the tide and succeeded in diversified management. He was even able to buy three houses adjacent to the project site of this project. As the three plots were incorporated into the site, a major re-design was inevitable.

At that time, I stayed in London as a visiting professor at the University of North London(Now changes as London Met). I invited the late professor Florian Beigel to join to re-design this project. The basic scheme soon began to take shape through our vigorous discussions. He and I easily agreed to make one podium in the project site, including the already completed underground structure and the newly purchased plots. However, as for the ground part of the podium, he insisted that three boxes surround a courtyard, and I proposed a parallel structure of four boxes as is now the case. I believed that this architectural structure should not be seen as an object, but a medium to connect the surrounding environment. Eventually, the client adopted my proposal though he seemed to prefer Florian's.

The inside space of the podium is used for shared space such as a reception hall and a dining room. The four separate boxes upon the podium are reserved for business and office work. Though four boxes covered with weathering steel are separate upon the podium made of heavy concrete mass, they are actually one box within the outline of the podium. I created three void spaces between the separate boxes as if I rubbed out three sections of the inside of the one imaginary box with an eraser. The row houses in the back of the building are open to sunlight, wind and view thanks to the spaces. When viewed from the road facing the Corten boxes, the landscape that the void between the Corten boxes contains changes with different viewing angles: The void hugs houses in the back, contains the skies, or sometimes fills itself with cloud and fog. Even if you do not have a chance to see such a landscape, some people of Welcomm, who make small talks sitting on benches, will fill the void to make other landscapes.

In terms of seriousness in choosing building materials, nothing is as reliable as exposed concrete. While exposed concrete is now found widely enough to be called a generally-accepted material, Corten steel used for the boxes may be somewhat unfamiliar. But this material contains memory during rusting in time. It is the first case to use for building in Korea.

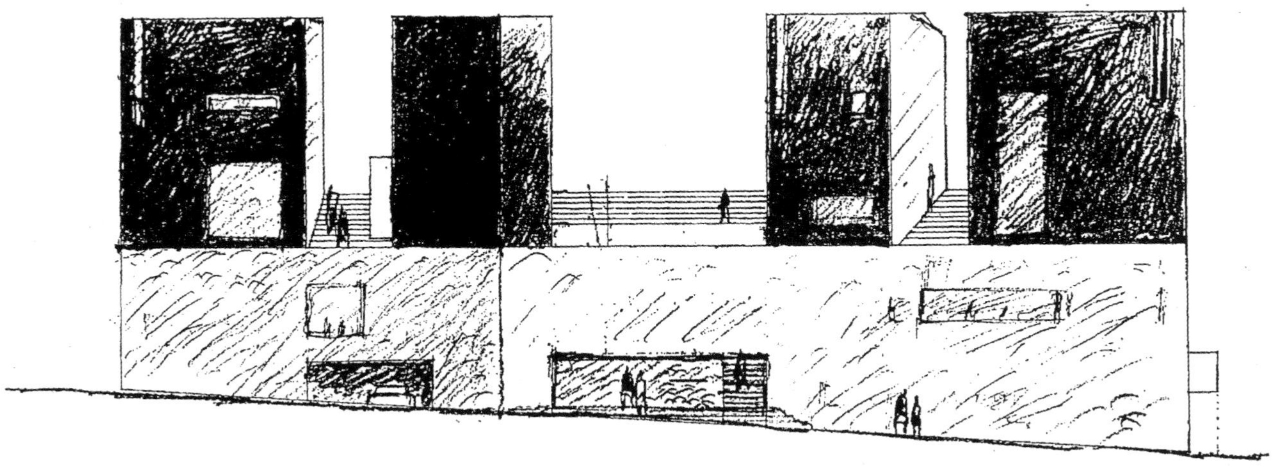

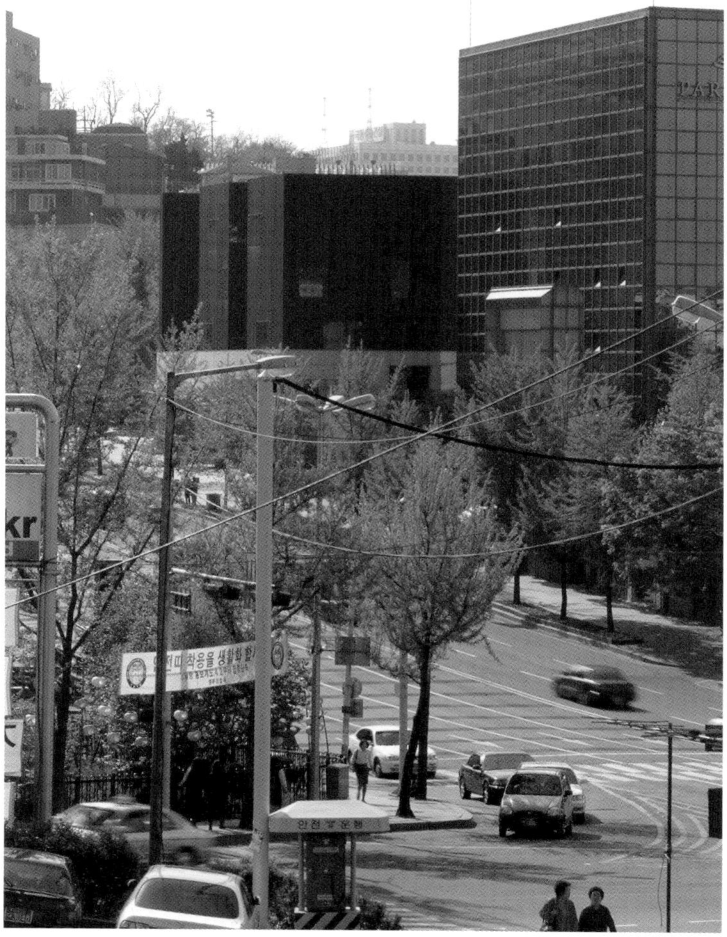
kr

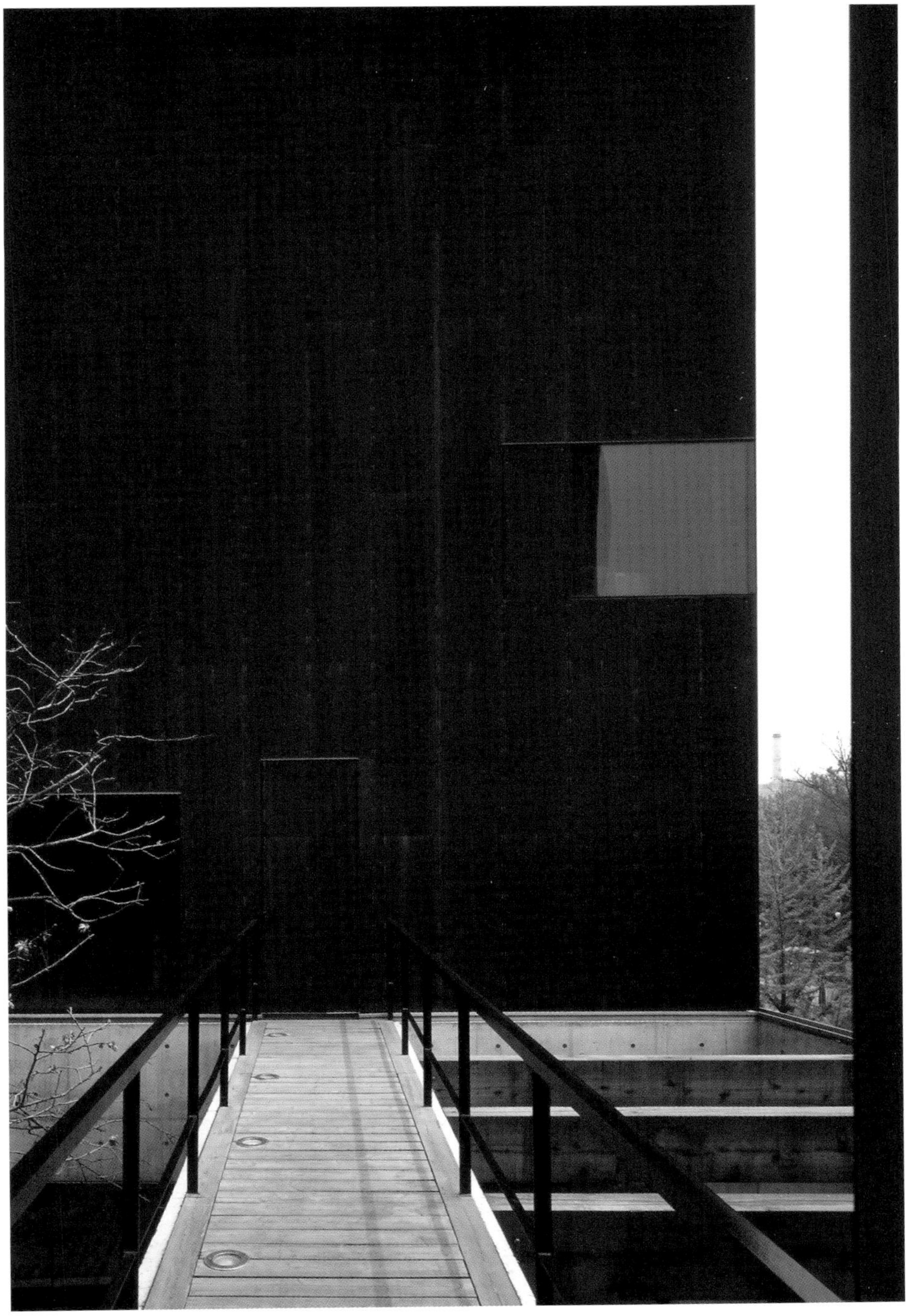

Welcomm City

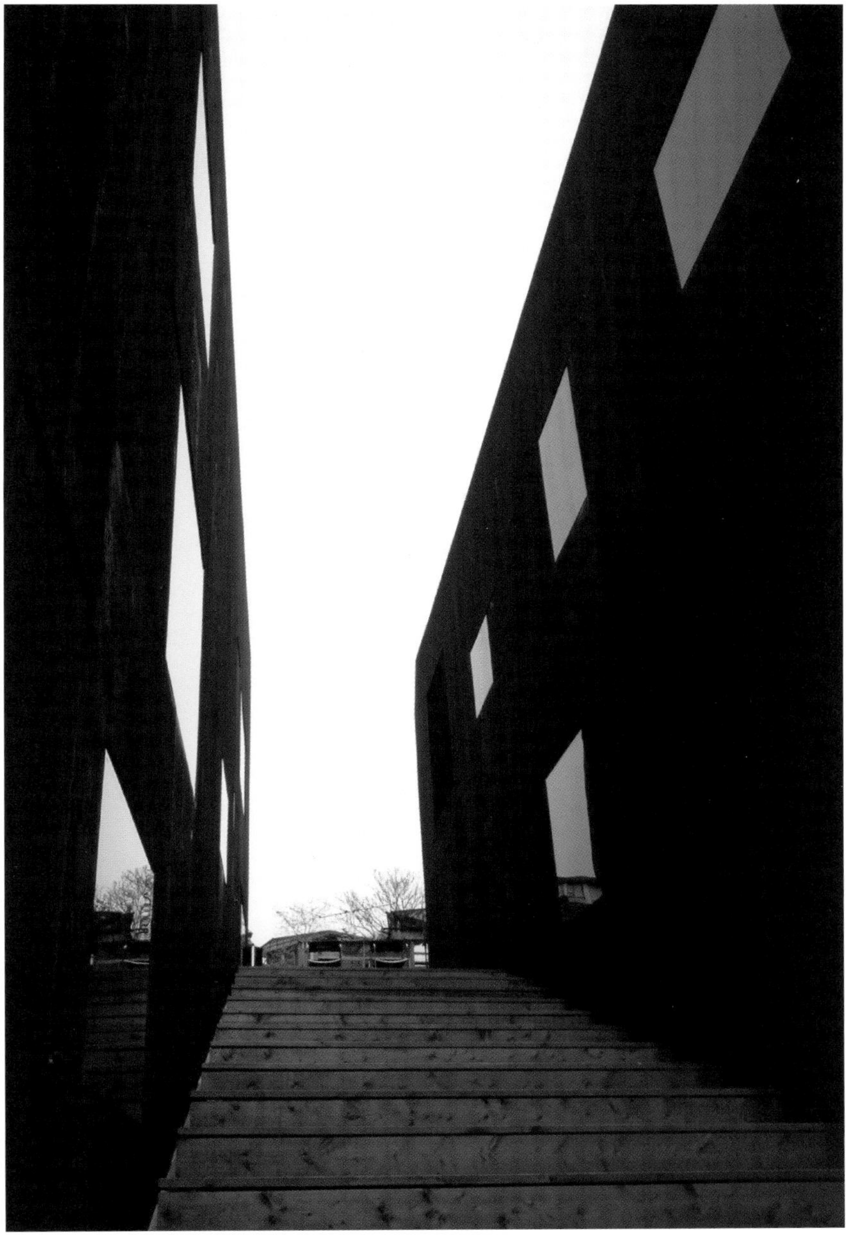

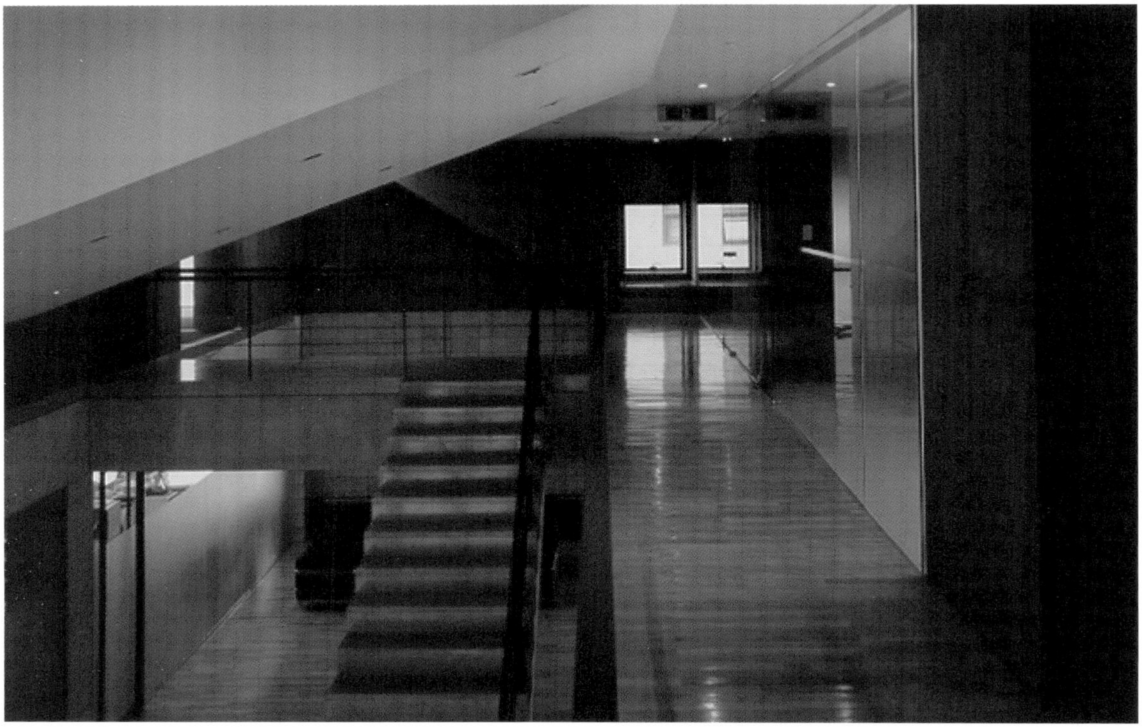

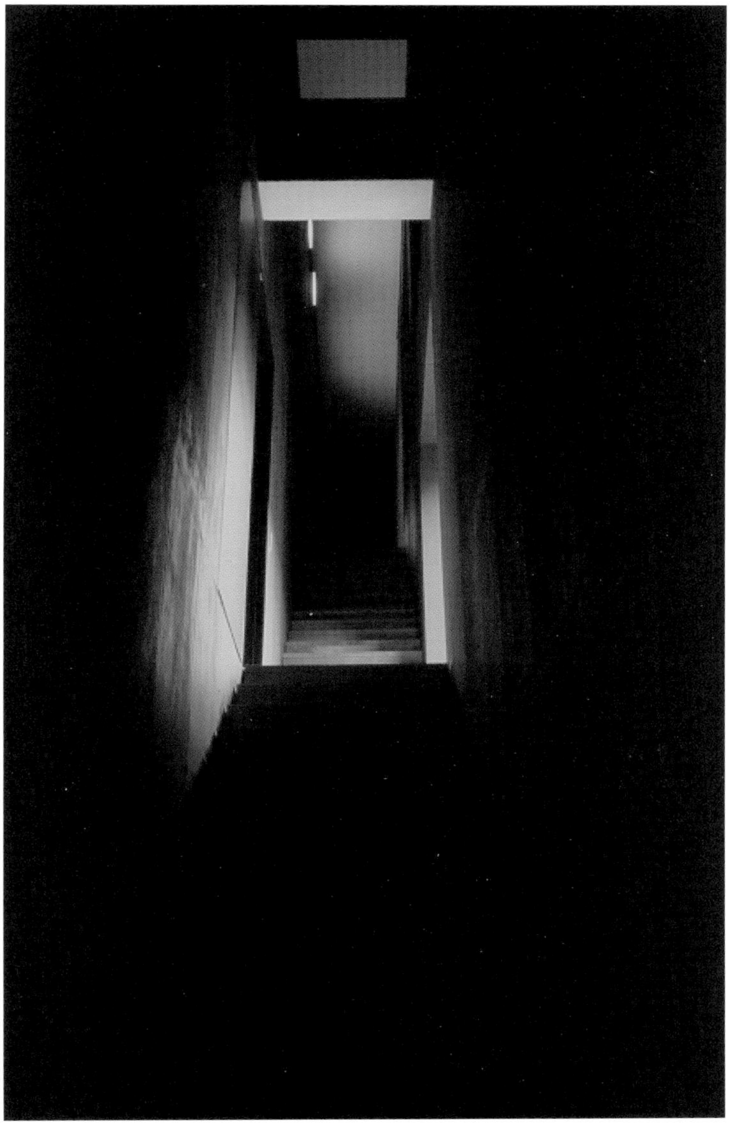

The main motive of this project is to create a new type of cultural community composed of various programs related to the media and publishing industry. Stretched in the land of 100 ha, the city consists of approximately 160 buildings of diverse publishing company office facilities, printing factories, and residential complex as well.

Paju Book City's site is located along the Jayu-ro, meaning freeway of freedom, which connects the city of Seoul to the Demilitarized Zone. As a politically important location sharing the 4.5km long edges of the Jayu freeway, the site also contains significance ecologically. Originally wet land with wild reeds adjoining the eastern delta area of Han River, it is also a home for rare migrating birds. But, the street plan already has been under construction before a new masterplan was provided by the design guideline team.

The prime issue was on creating 'emptiness' for this new landscape. Various 'emptiness' was set prior to filling the land with buildings, that could be found in the various places as like voids in green corridors, interstices between buildings or indeterminate spaces spreading over the site. All of them contribute to connect the Han River with Simhak Mountain. The places created by those 'emptiness' could determine special characters of several building types to be bound particularly. For example, one of building types, 'Highway Shadow' is for printing factories whose height will not exceed the freeway level providing green space in the roof area. Another type, ' Bookshelf Units' is for publishing company office facilities lined up in such a way to share views to the river and Simhak Mountain. 'Stone' type is massive and low buildings set on reeds like big stone, and 'Canal Loft' type is canal wharf building with sloped roofs allocated along the stream. 'Urban Hill' type is designed as a part of landscape form for the Distribution Centre, the biggest structure within the site, and there are 2 other types, 'Spine' and 'Urban Island'. All the kinds of architecture here are understood as landscape or infrastructure, even generator for urban life. And numbers of architects, domestic and foreign architects participated in designing individual buildings based on the design guideline.

A HIGHWAY SHADOW

Paju Book City

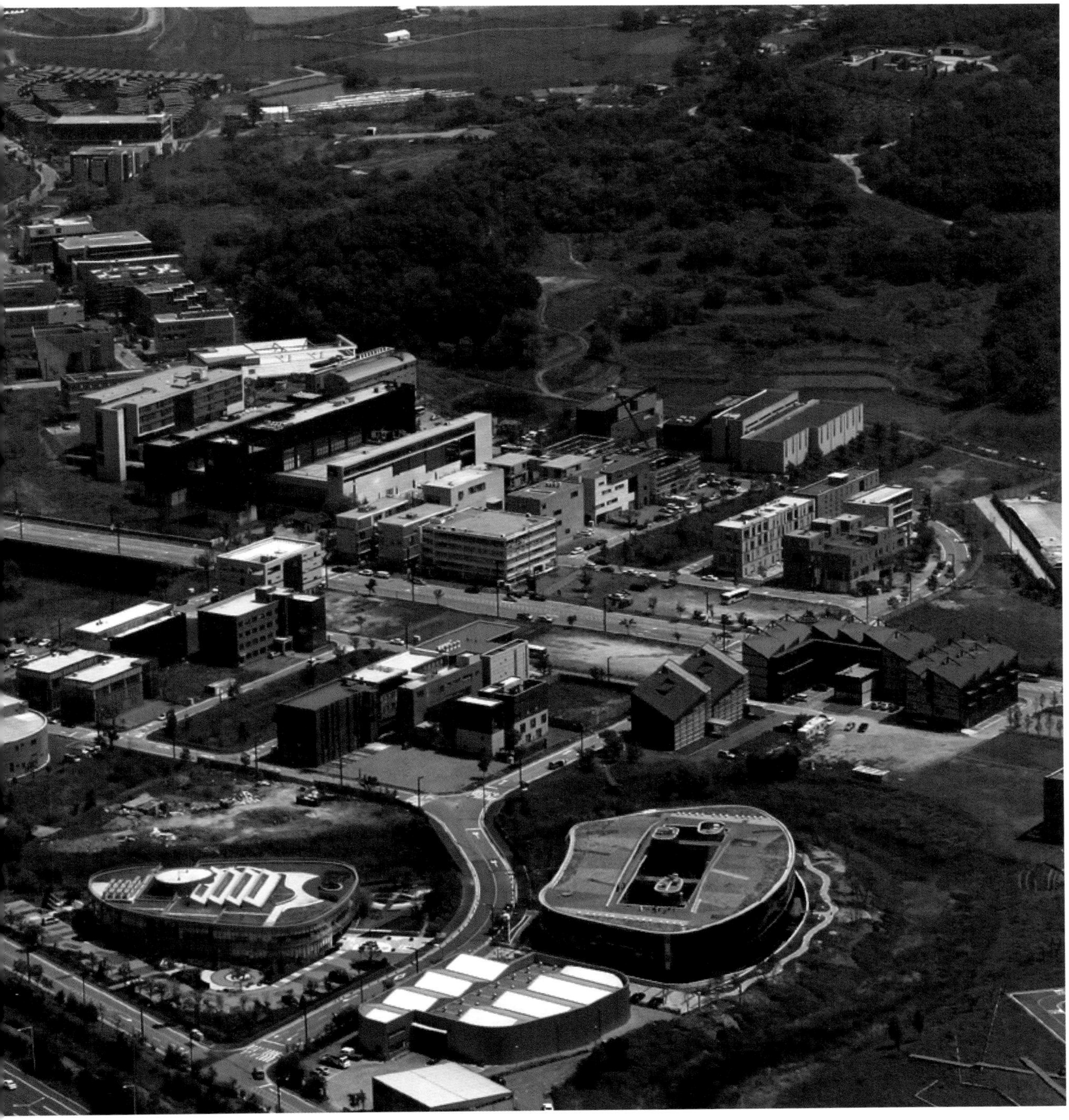

Paju Book City

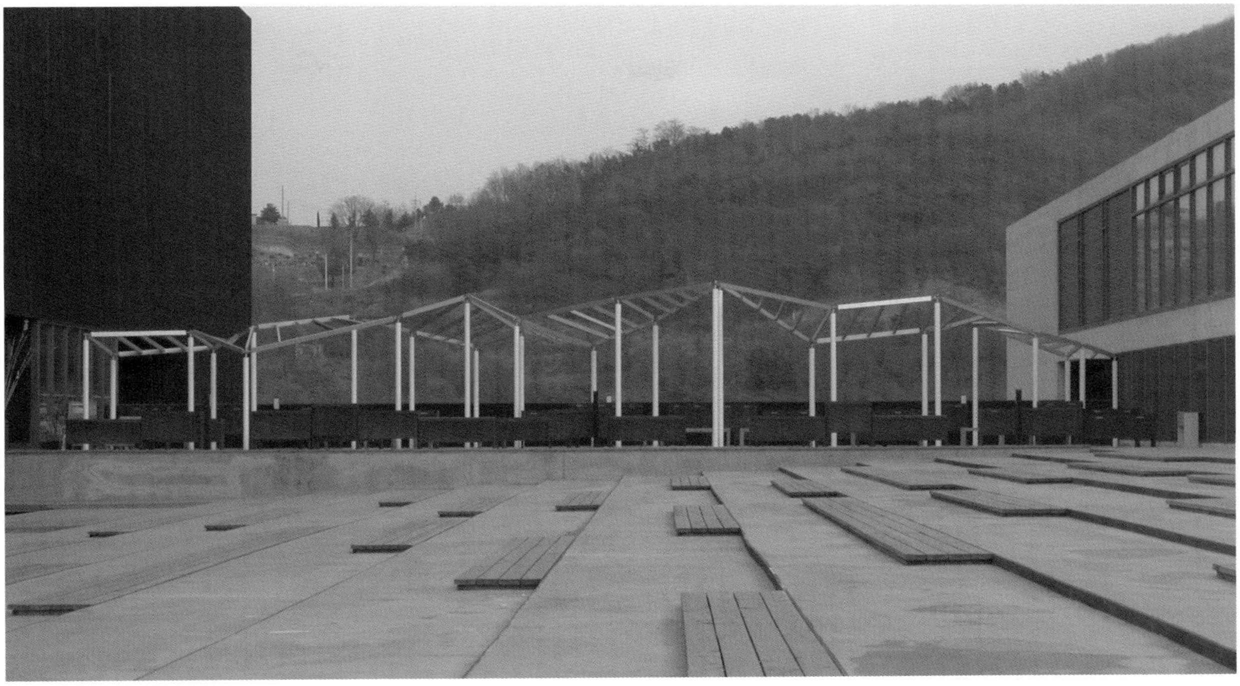

Paju Book City

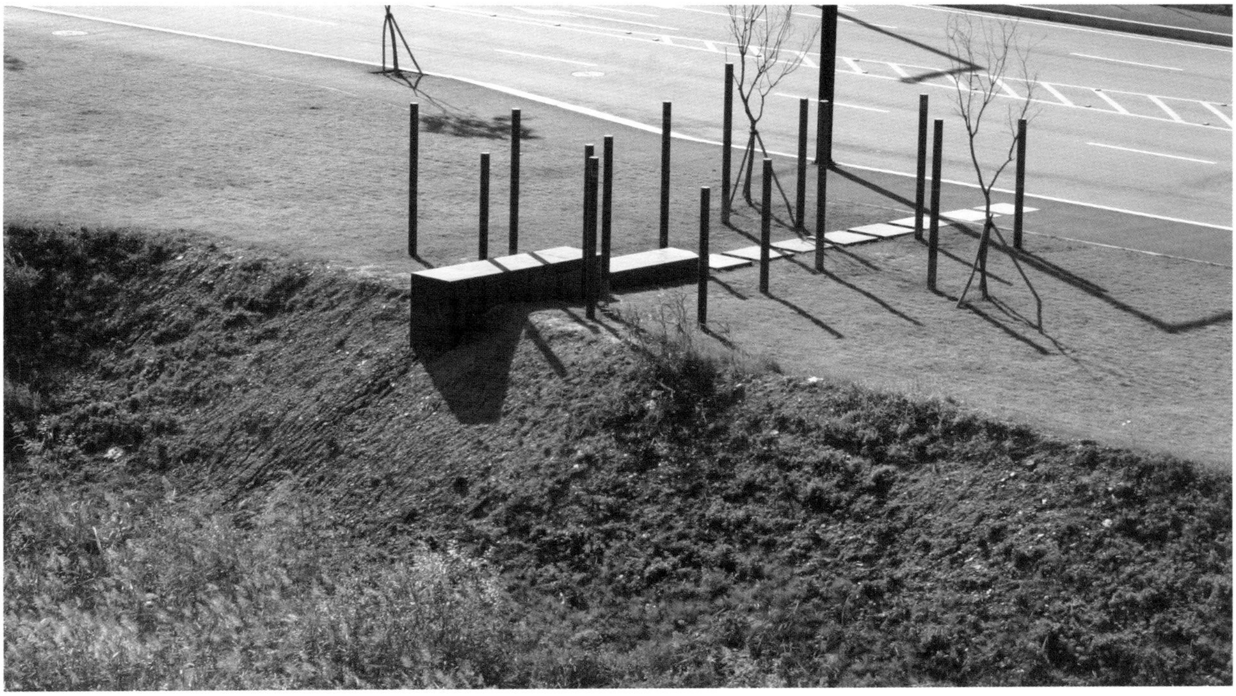

Kyobo Book City

Kyobo Book Center Building was designed completely along the Design Guidelines of Paju Book City. According to the Guideline, the city was divided into several districts, and each of which had its own urban pattern. The sector where Kyobo Book Center is located in had a pattern of 'Bookshelf Units', not to make a continuous mass of buildings that might block the view to the adjacent river and mountain. As a result, even though it occupied a long rectangular site, Kyobo Book Center was broken into small pieces, each piece facing the same direction of the confronting building masses from the opposite side of the road. Mass faces mass; void faces void. This arrangement was intended to create a collaborative scene so that every building can show its relationship with the others.

The facade of the lower body as podium is finished with light transparent glass so that the upper split body with basalt skin appears to be floating. Adequate twist was given to smaller masses to control the rhythm of the building mass. Once more, creating a void became an inevitable element of the design.

Bookshelf unit Type 표양식매층

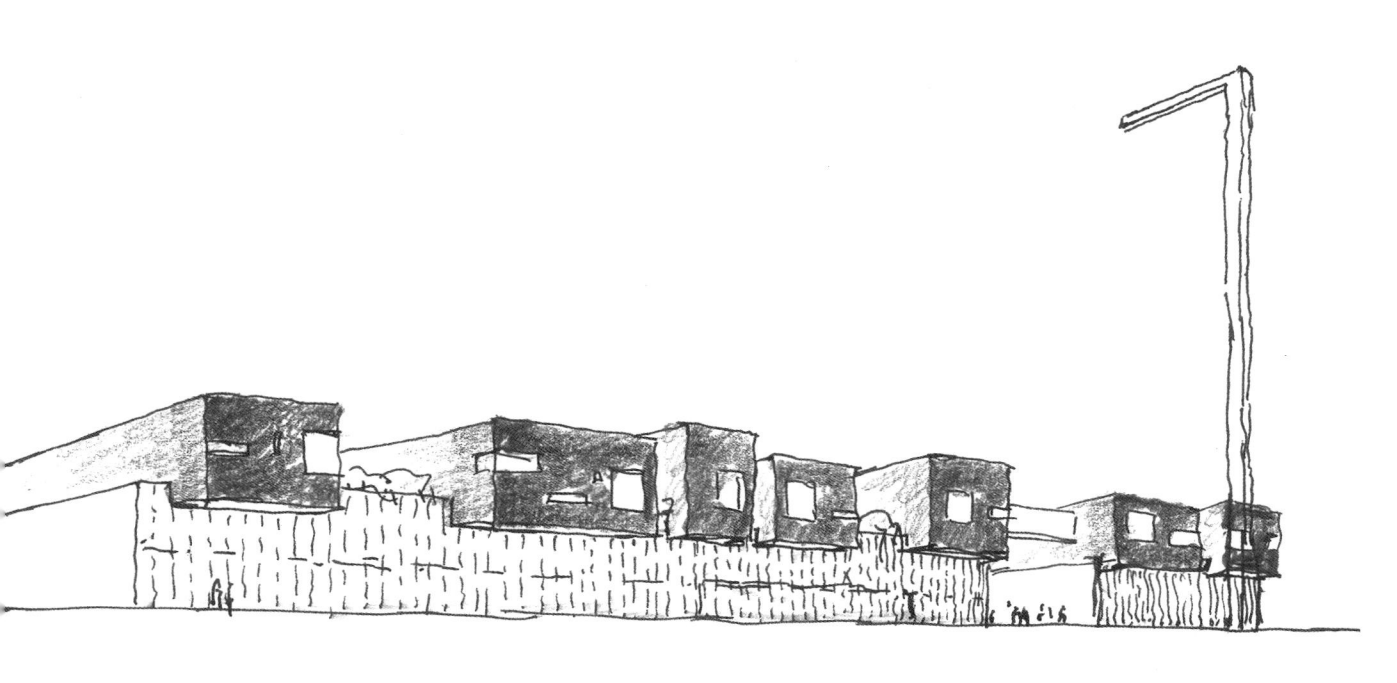

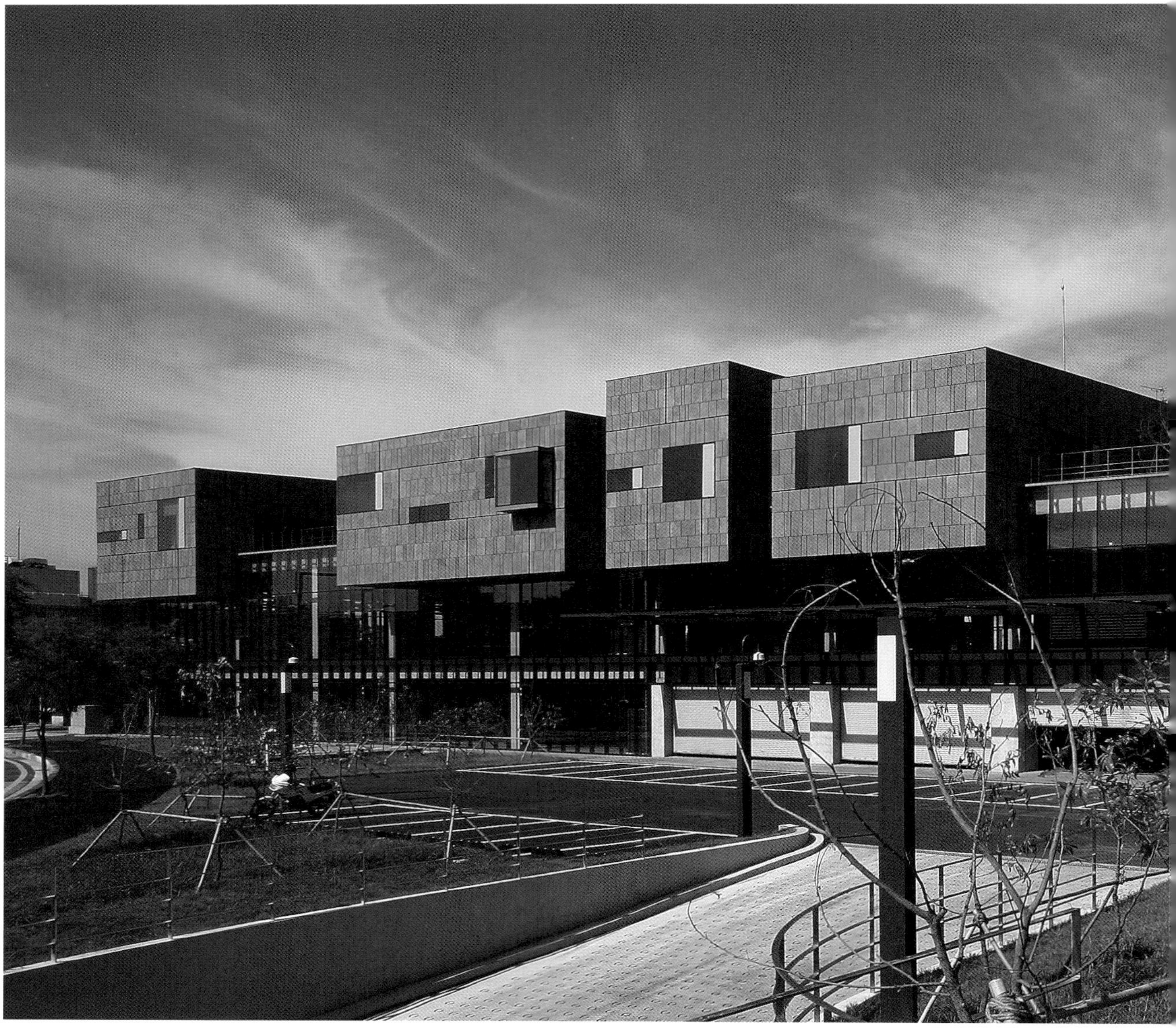

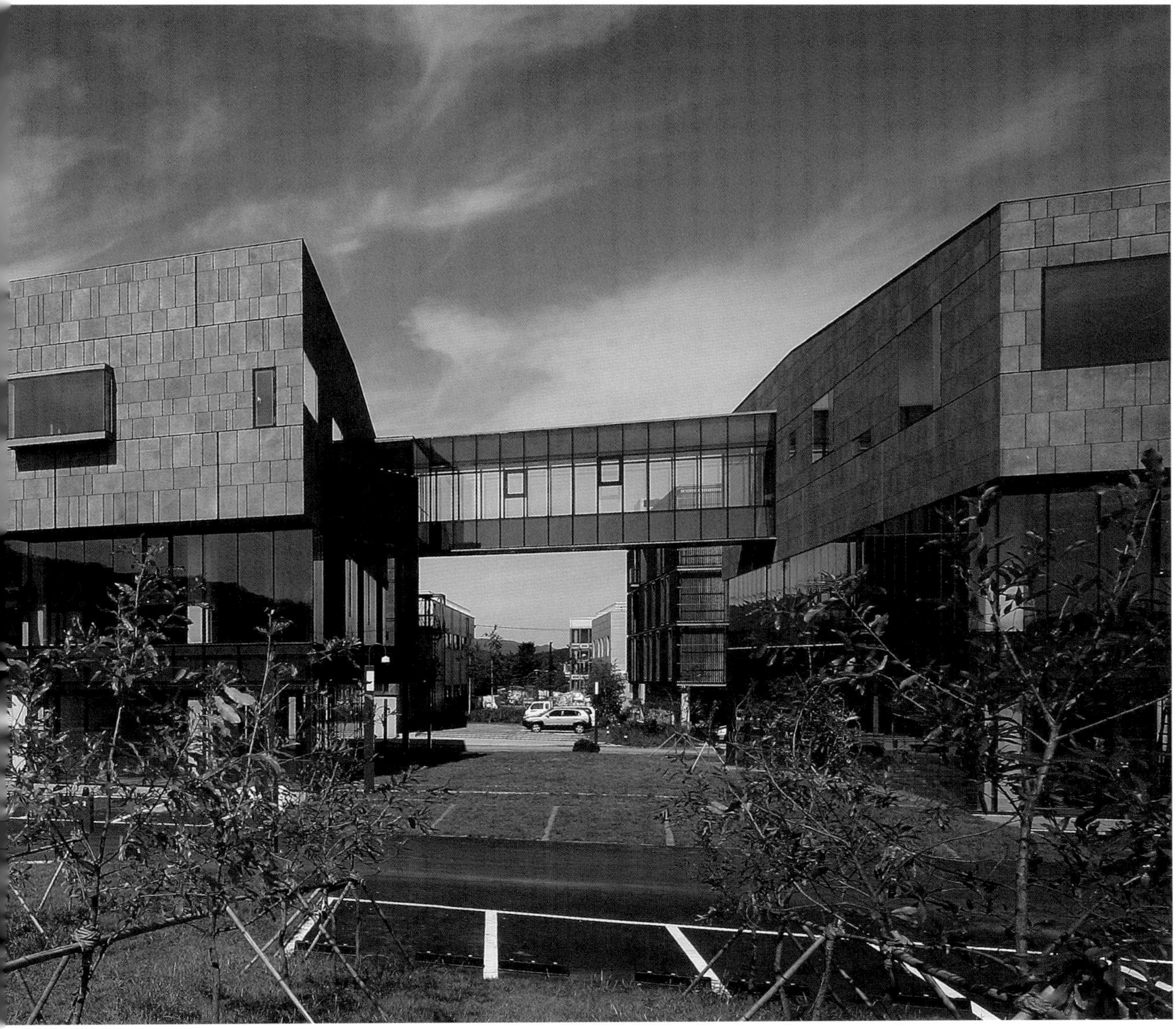

Kyobo Book City

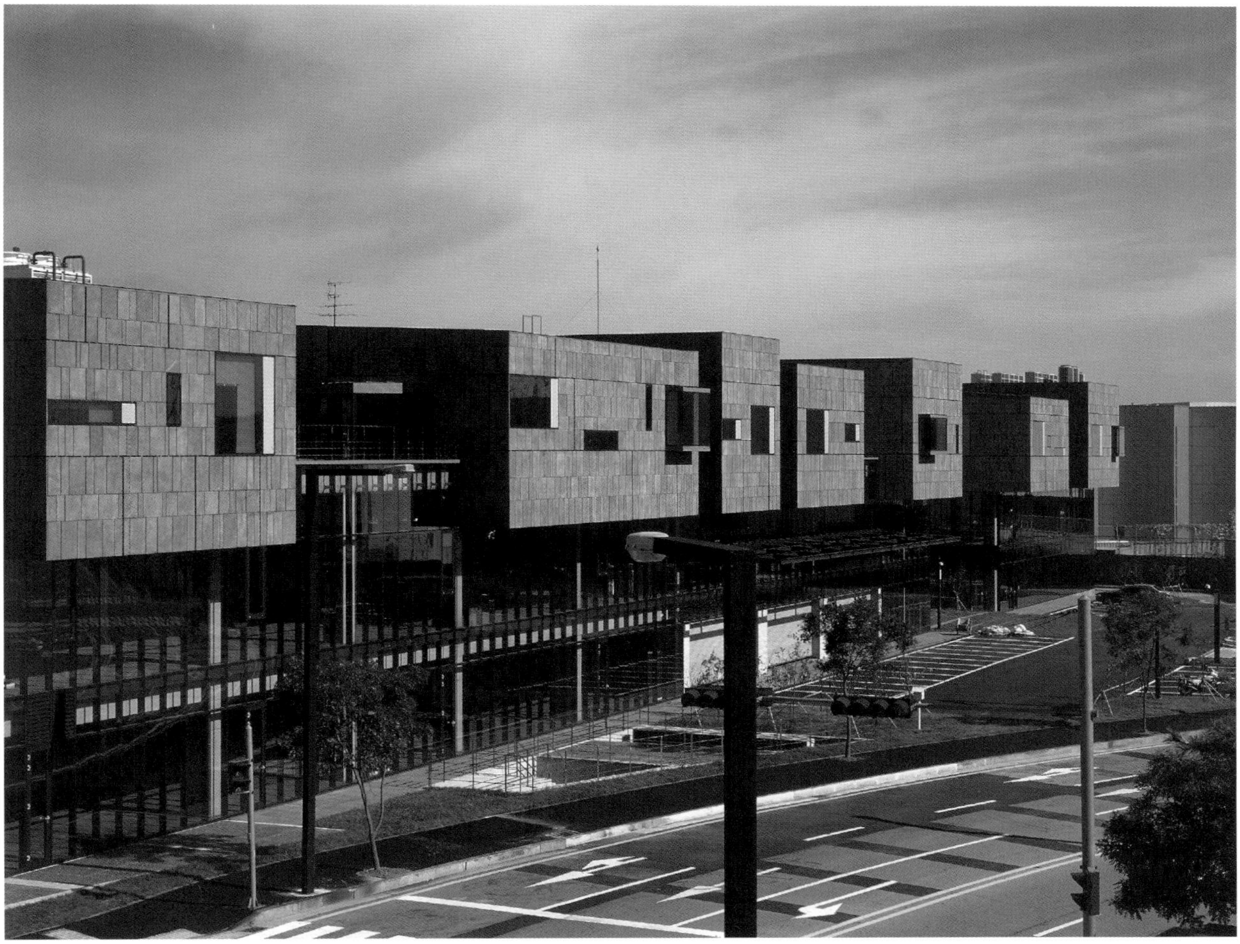

Kyobo Book City

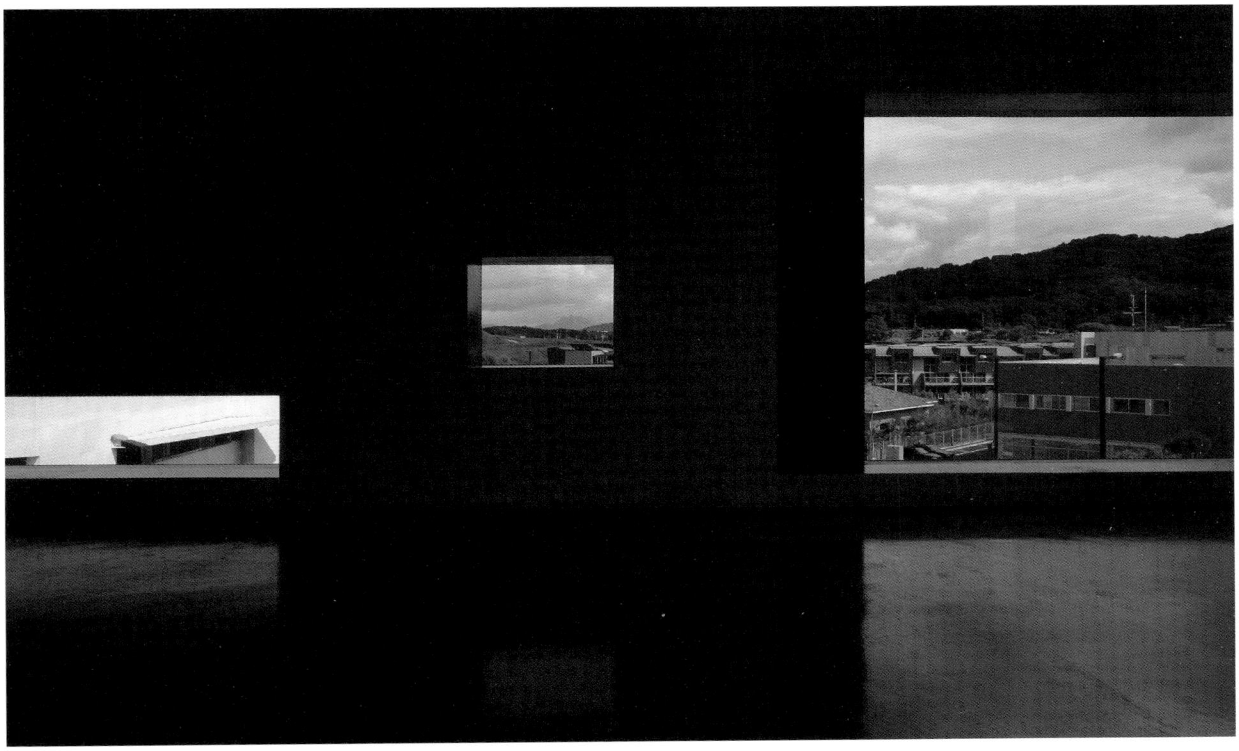

Residence "Soowoojae"

The village near Seoul where this house resides is an old town with about 600 houses. The village has been called Yeomgokdong, as it is surrounded by low mountains to resemble Yeomtong meaning heart in Korean. There is a plane ground on a gentle slope that is on the northern edge of the village and 600 years old zelkova tree rooted itself on the boundary of the site. As this tree was designated as a protected tree for its magnificent branches overarching the surrounding area, the new house design had to have the utmost priority to be well matched to the tree.

An aged couple who had lived in a house that had been built in 1970s for 10 years wanted to build their own new house that fits their lifestyle. The couple was devoted Christians who was working as amateur photographers.

Due to 4m height difference between a road in front of the site a green field on the back, the main floor of the house was built 3m above the road surface, which was higher than the existing houses in the area. With a passage that goes across the entry ground and main floor ground, a spatial composition of the house became vary while people can see different views from the spaces. The house has basic spaces for physiological needs such as dining room, bedroom and bathroom along with a living room as well as recreation room for the family. Also, the house has reception room, study and pavilion. These are additional spaces that were available in all traditional houses of Korea where the purpose was to make you enjoy the moment and uplift your mental health.

All four sides of the ground have different conditions. The southern part to the road has no wall but spaces out three masses to make a scenery. The western part places a long mass that harmonizes with a large mass on the next door to stabilize the scene. Although it is in the property of other people, the northern part where the house meets nature opens up to the space to let natural changes to come inside of the house. The most difficult side to face was the eastern side with the 600 years old zelkova tree. With its look of a sacred tree at the center of the yard, the scene changes every season following the changes of the tree. Furthermore, a separate room is located under the tree to make sure the tree and room become important objects that exist together. This small room that resembles a pavilion was named Hyeonwa, a dark house, in order to use it sometimes as a sanctum and other times as a shelter to be left alone.

The name of this whole house was decided as Soowooje meaning a housed of keeping foolishness. According to the Analects of Confucius, foolishness is better than too wiseness.

A HOUSE AT EDGE

Residence "Soowoojae"

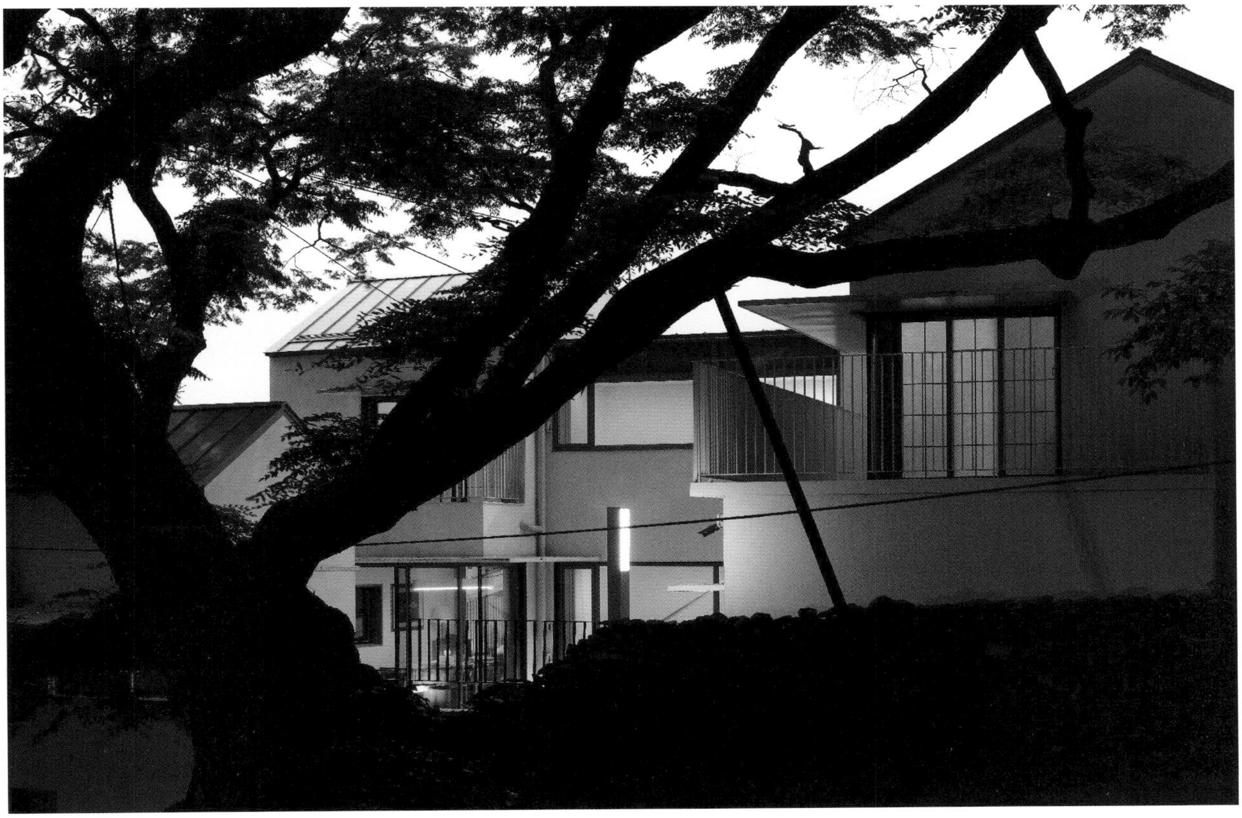

Residence "Soowoojae"

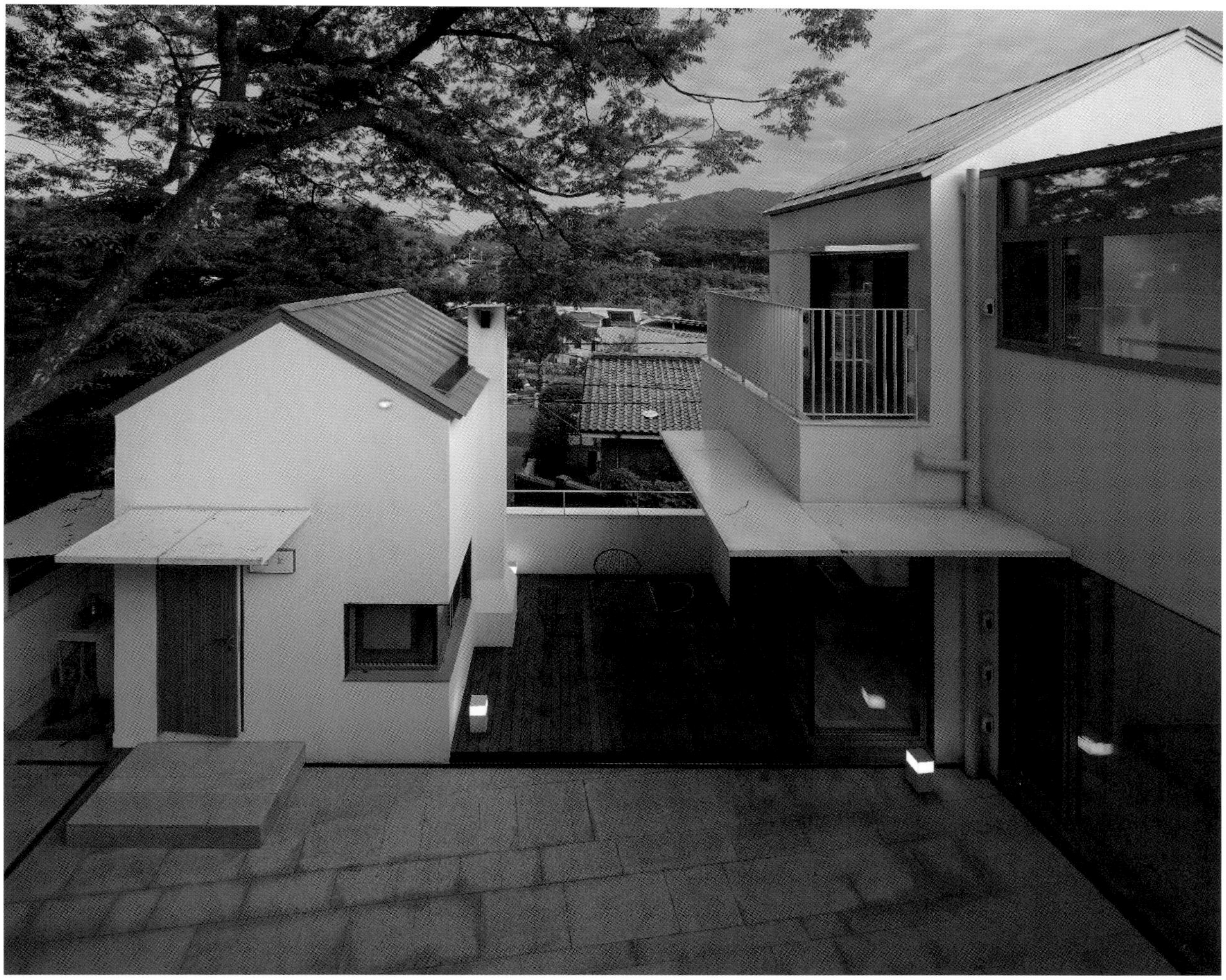

Residence "Soowoojae"

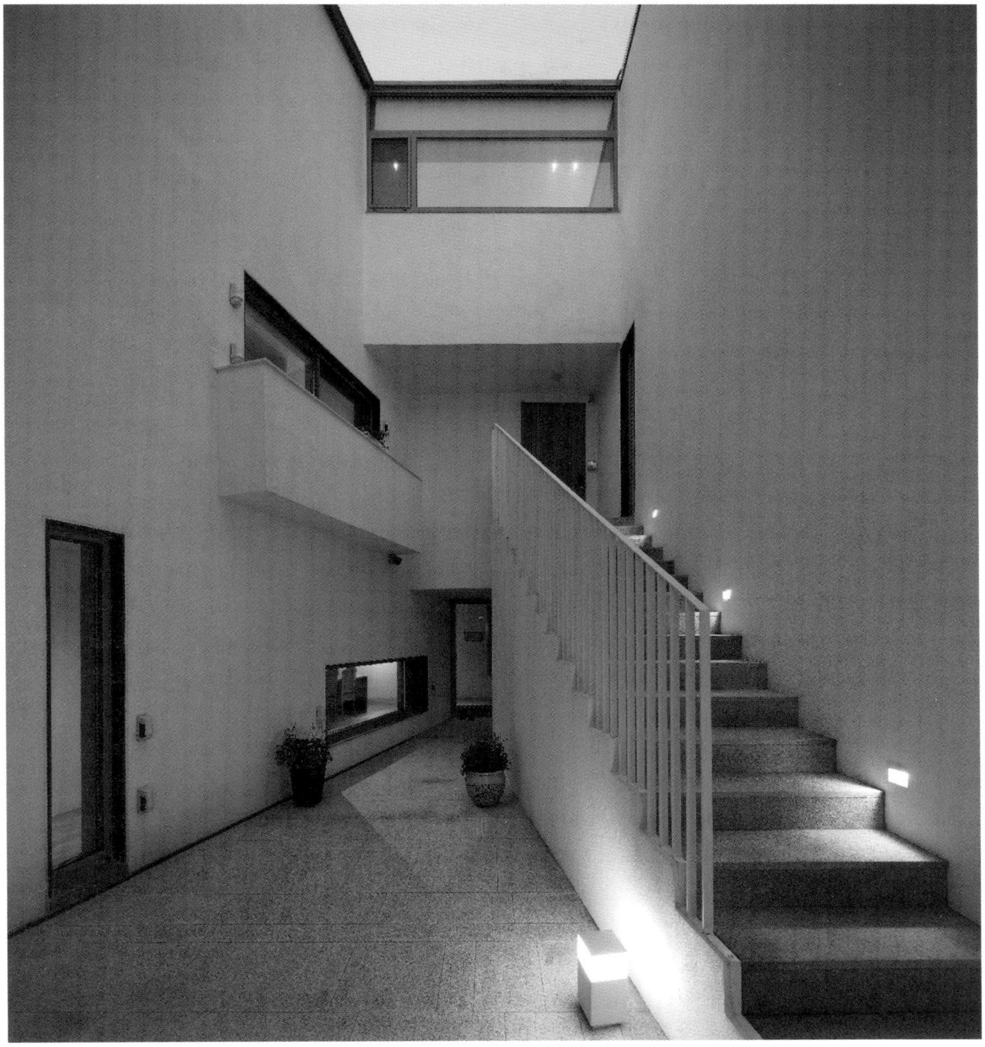

Reed House

The client of this house is same one with Welcomm City. He had purchased and remodeled an existing house in riverside area near Seoul when the Welcomm City were under construction. As the area in the boom of development was expected to be recklessly filled with buildings, he was worried about the horrible scene they would produce and finally purchased the land parcels around his house. And a new house was asked.

The client agreed to plant 10 thousand birch trees on the site as well as numerous reeds along the river. So this new house located in the middle of birch forest should be named *Reed House*.

Taking into account the 200-meter long road, and both sides of which to be lined with wild silver reed and birch trees, a concept came up: a wooden box 4.8 meters wide and 36 meters long. In more detail, considering the fact that the river would flood over two meters above the normal ground surface in times of flood, the main floor of the house was to be the second floor, and a work room, a warehouse, and others were assigned to the first floor. The main reason for a small annex cottage in front of the house was promote adequate tension between the house and the cottage, but such a placement of the small house was expected to make the view from inside the house look far better.

The frame was made of concrete, in preparation against deluge, but the exterior of the upper story, or the main floor, was finished with wooden materials. Unlike cases in general, protruding timber beams were placed here and there among the planks to increasing the waterproof function of the timber planks, and, at the same time, to have strong parallel shadow cast beautifully. The frame of the roof was made of timber, reinforced with steel, and covered with titanium. As the result, when viewed from across the river, a long shaped house among the birch trees, with an inclining roof shining in the sun, would look like a floating house.

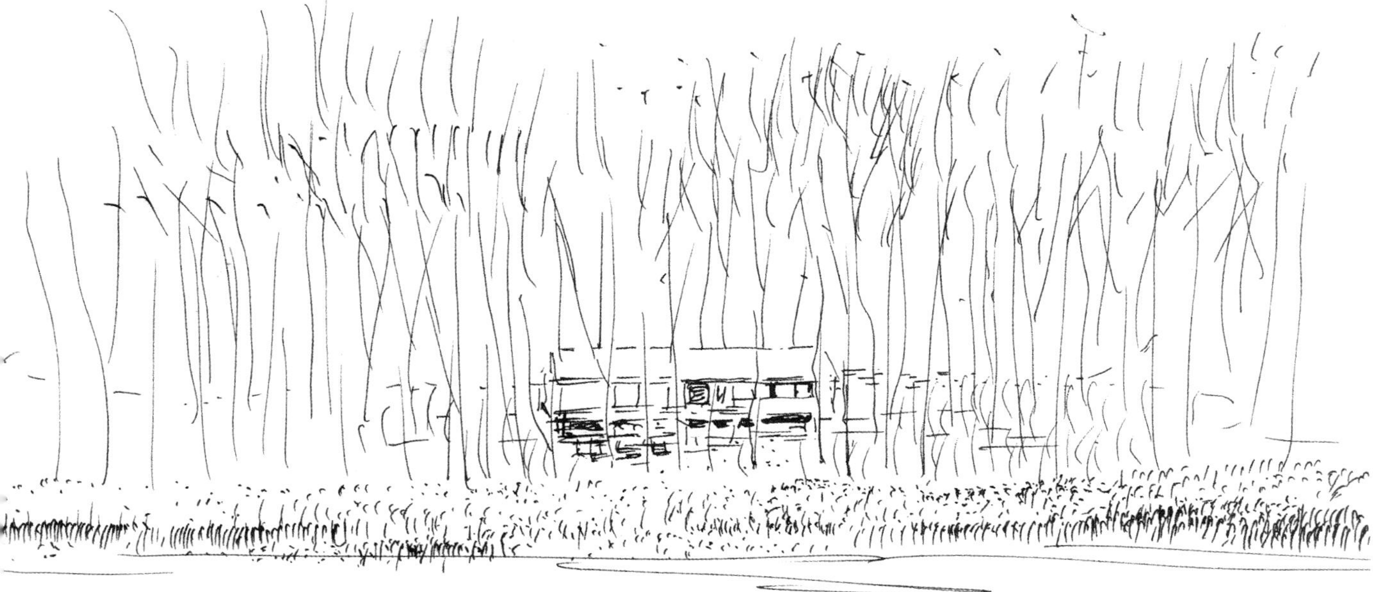

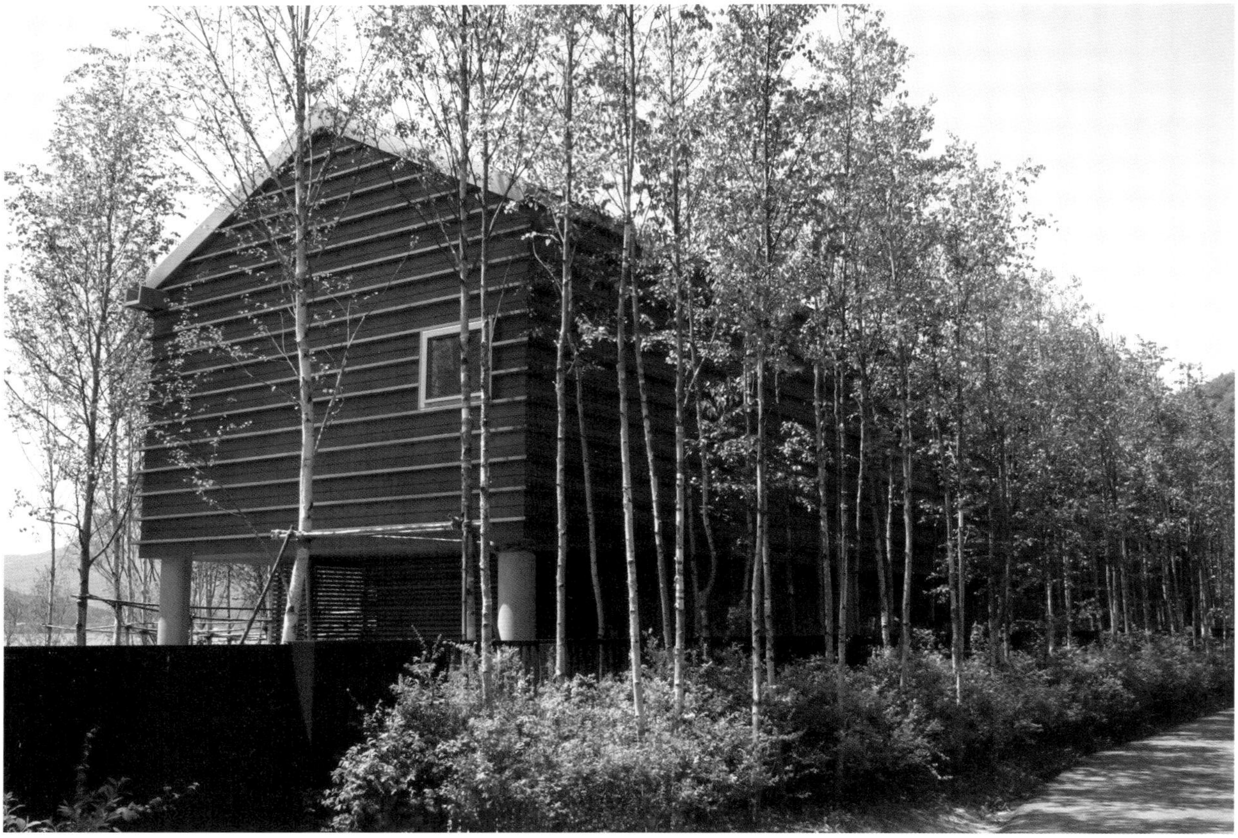

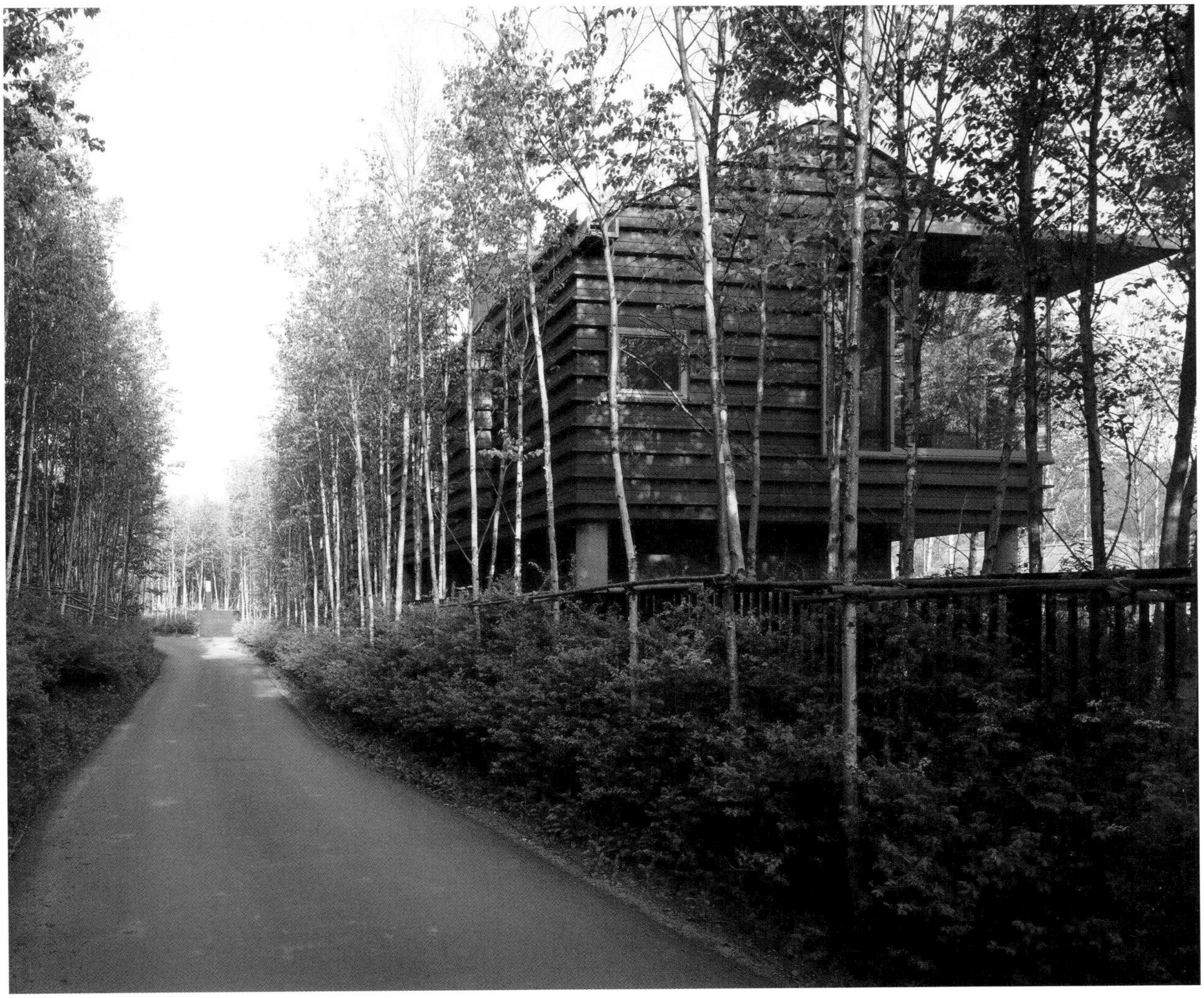

Reed House

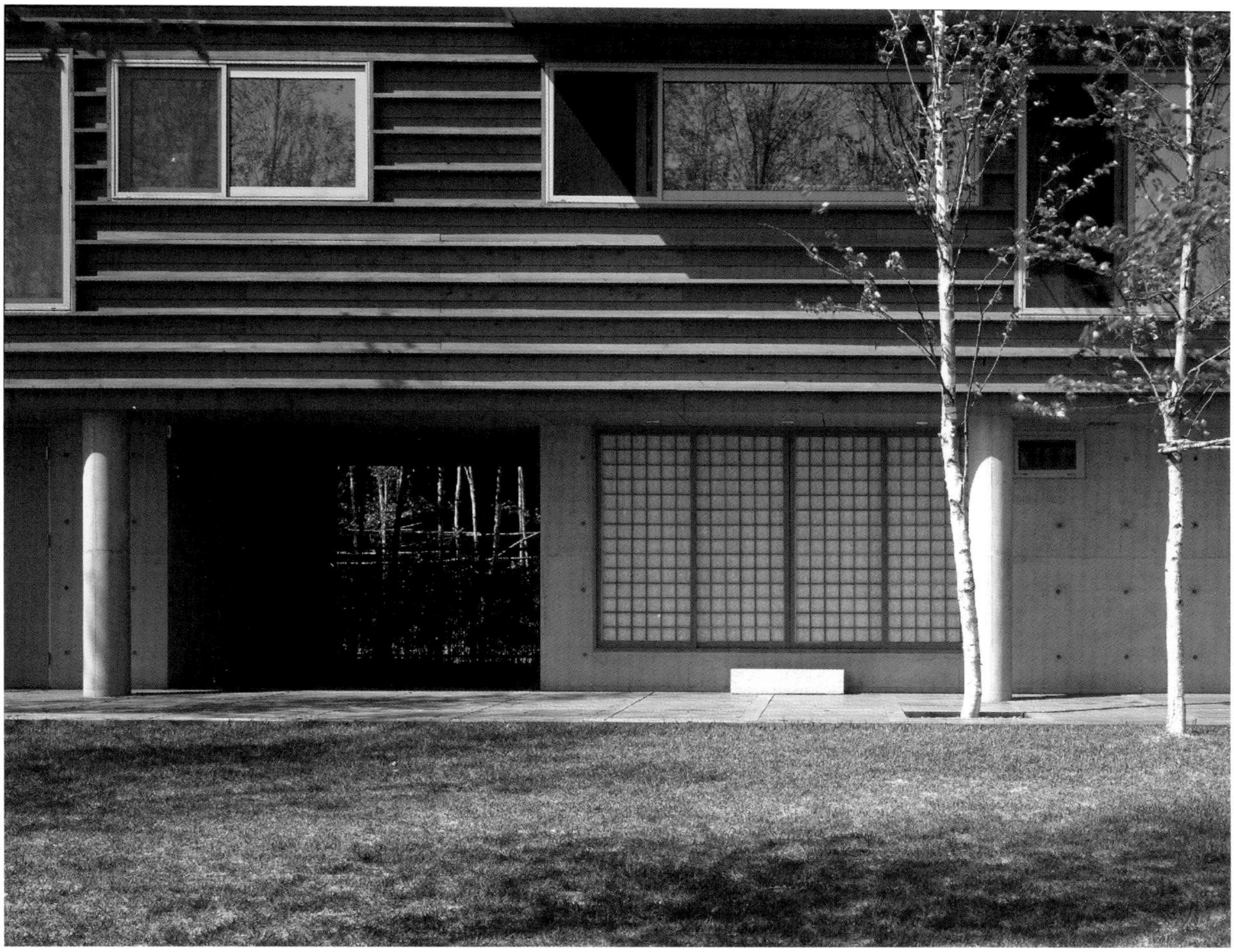

Reed House

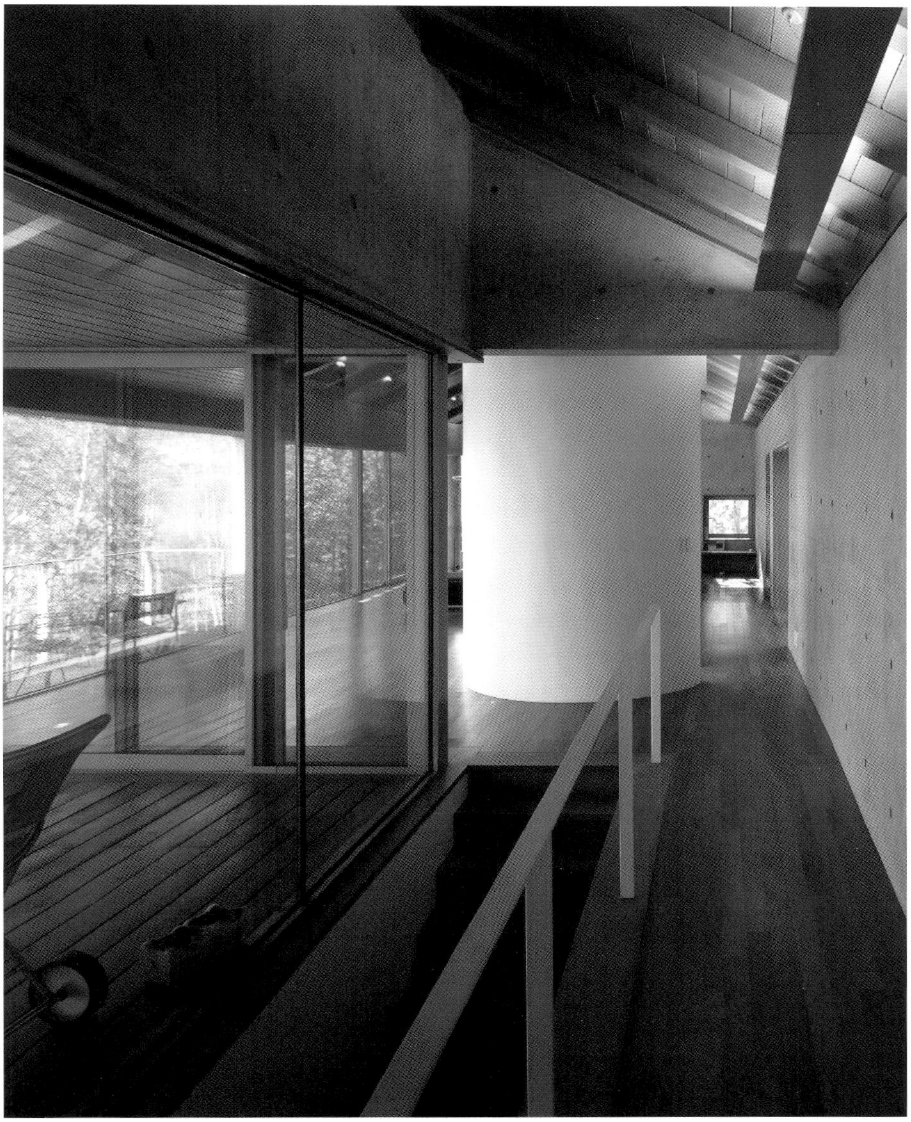

Toechon House

This house was for a professor couple with a progressive disposition, who wished to live with his son, a jazz pianist, in a place near the house of the professor's mother who lived in Toechon. Each of the couple scholars would need an independent room, in addition to another independent room for their son. As such, the way each of the family members lived became a crucial precondition for the design of the house. In other words, separate structures, which are independent of each other, should form a house for the family. Also, because this house is a farm house in accordance with the relevant building law, the applicable provisions stipulate that the main building and the extension building shall not exceed 100m and 65m^2 respectively. One of the reasons for making a house of detached rooms was partly due to the legal requirements.

The fundamental concept for this house, however, was based on the traditional notion of the house for a home. Our traditional house had long been a collection of several rooms. When our ancestors said a house of one kan(a unit for 3.3m^2) and a house of 100 kans, they referred to a total floor area of the rooms of a house. Each of the rooms were called not as a living room, a bedroom, a study, or a bathroom according to the functions used in the western world, but as an inner room, an opposite room, a gate-side room, a back room (for a lavatory, which was in the backyard of the house) according to the location of rooms. Our traditional house was, like this, a set of rooms without specific purposes. What was meant by this was that a room was independent of other room, and each room was versatile. When people spread out the bedding, the room becomes a bedroom; when a table, the room becomes a dining room; when a desk, it became a study; and when people spread out a mattress, it becomes a playroom. In other words, the room was an undefined room in emptiness. Like this, Korean ancestors had already translated one of the new keywords of the contemporary architecture into their practical life.

The traditional room with the afore-said characteristics is in direct contact with nature by making ventilation and lighting unrestricted, among others. It is, therefore, extremely healthful to human life. It must be very inconvenient for those who are accustomed to the enclosed living conditions of artificial environment surrounded by modern home appliances. Nonetheless, a house like the traditional one is well suited in Toechon, a beautiful rural area. Once people get accustomed to the inconveniences of living in this house, they will irrevocably become pleasures of life. "Inconvenient pleasures" – no doubt it is lost memory in Korea. So, this house is one recalled from the memory though it has been newly built, and it seems to belong to our long-cherished future for the contemporary people living in the times of fragmentary memory.

최욱집 / 8 BOXES DWELLING
箱居

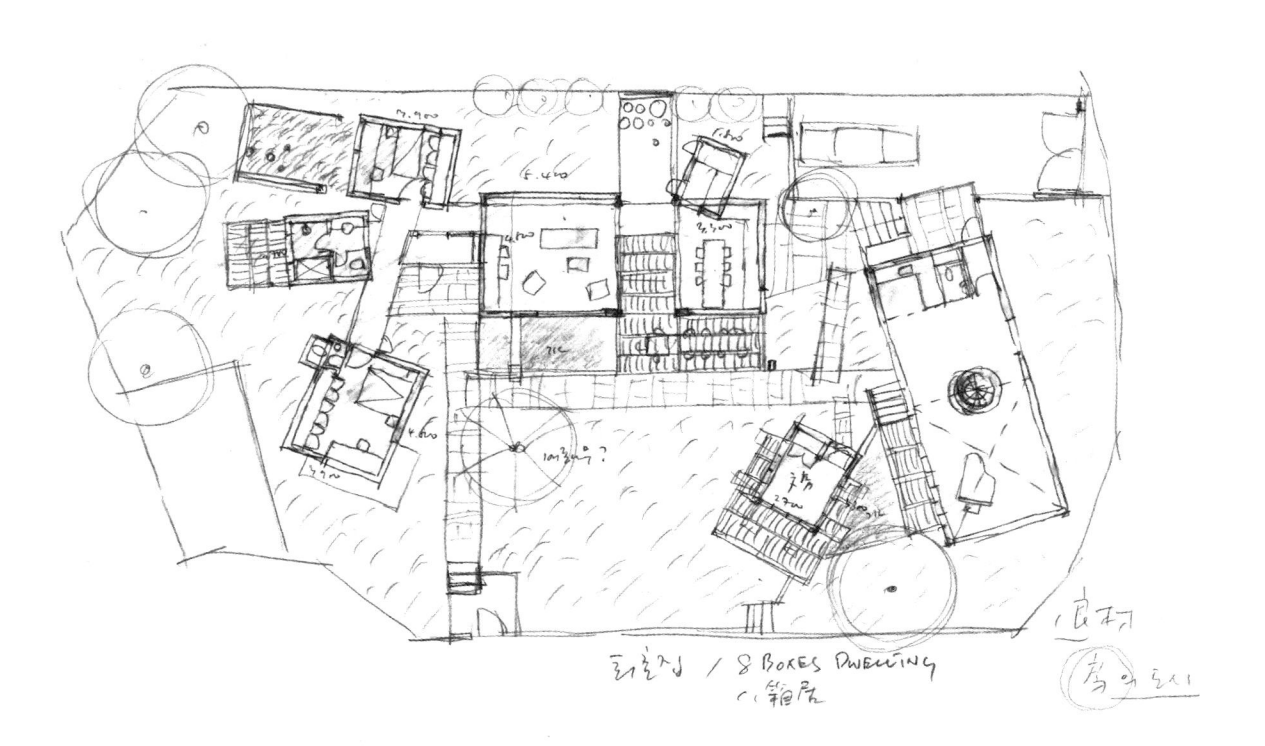

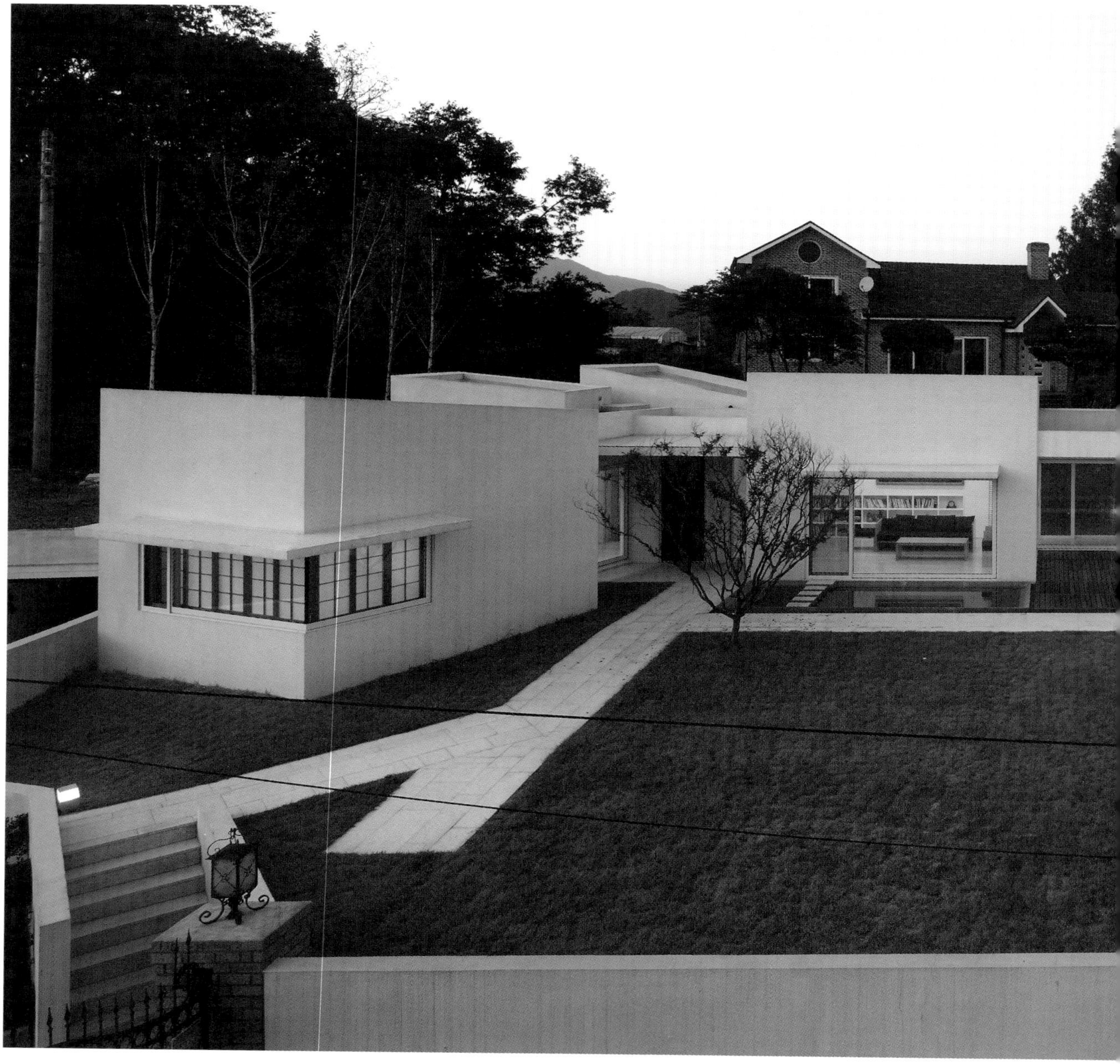

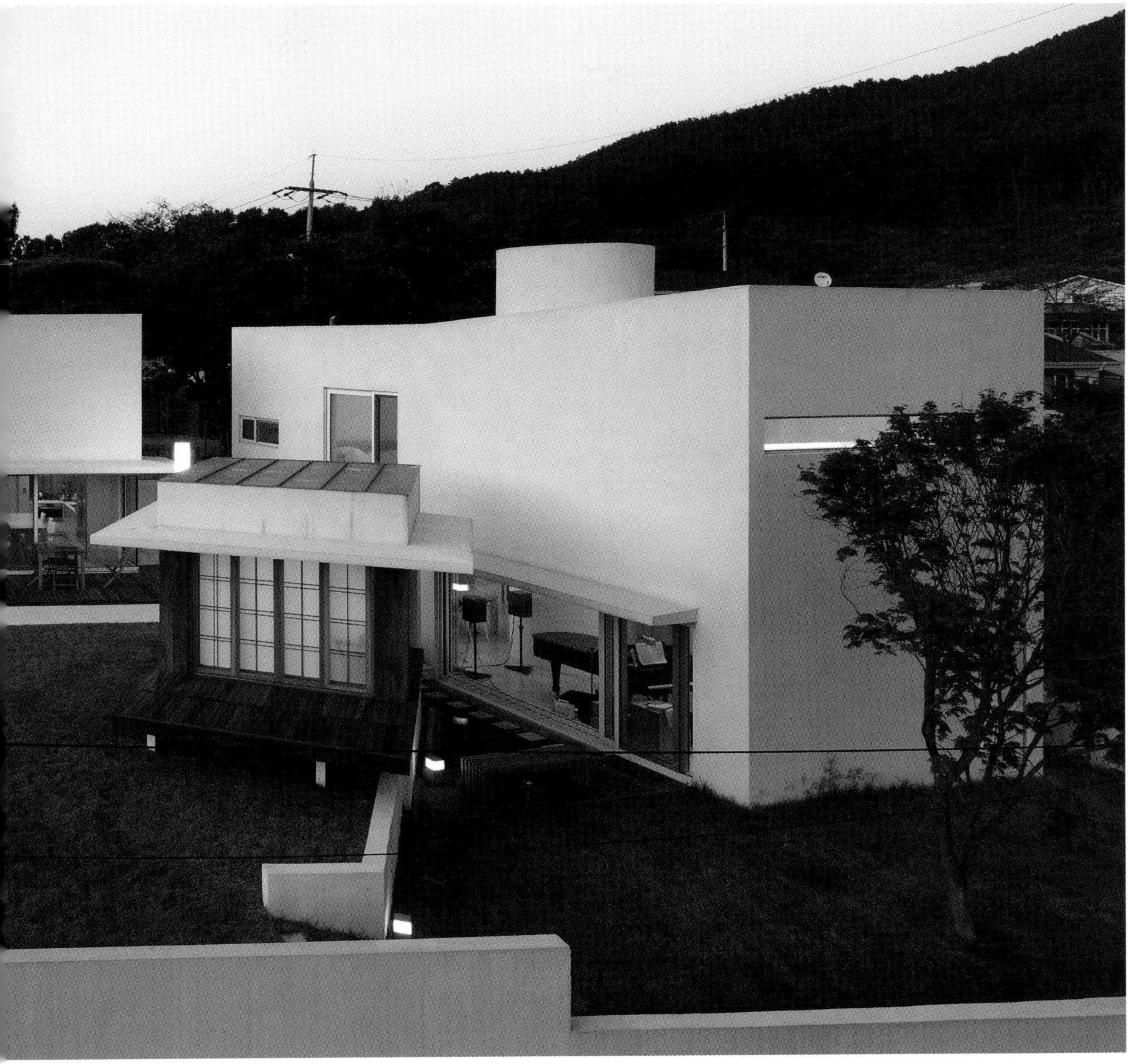

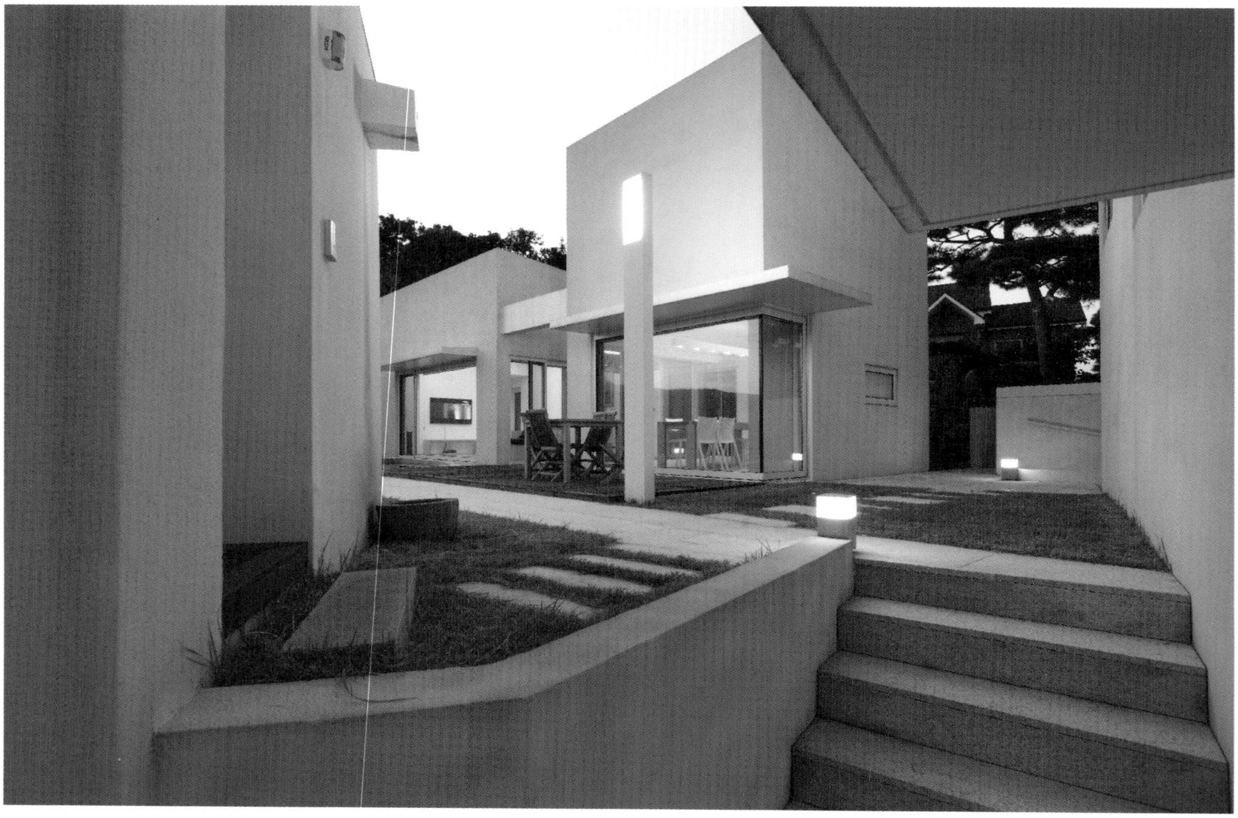

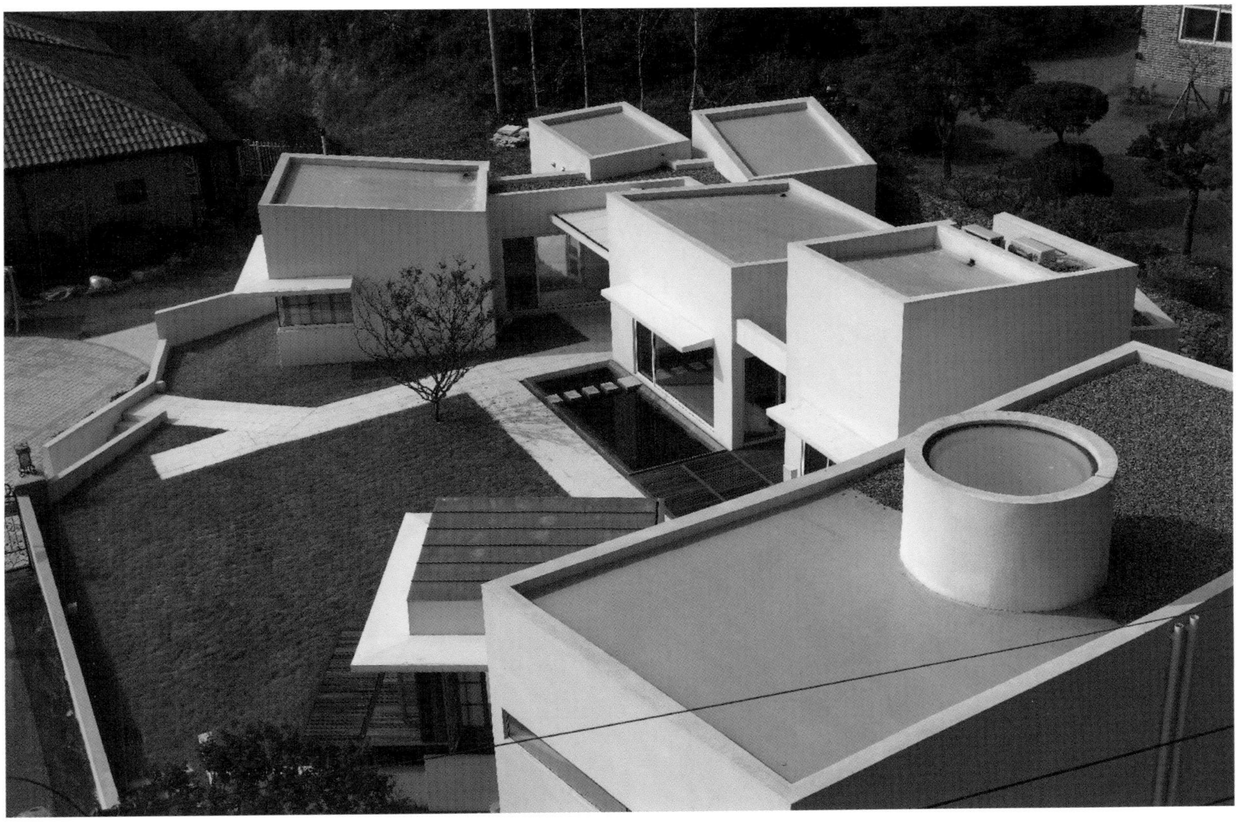

Toechon House

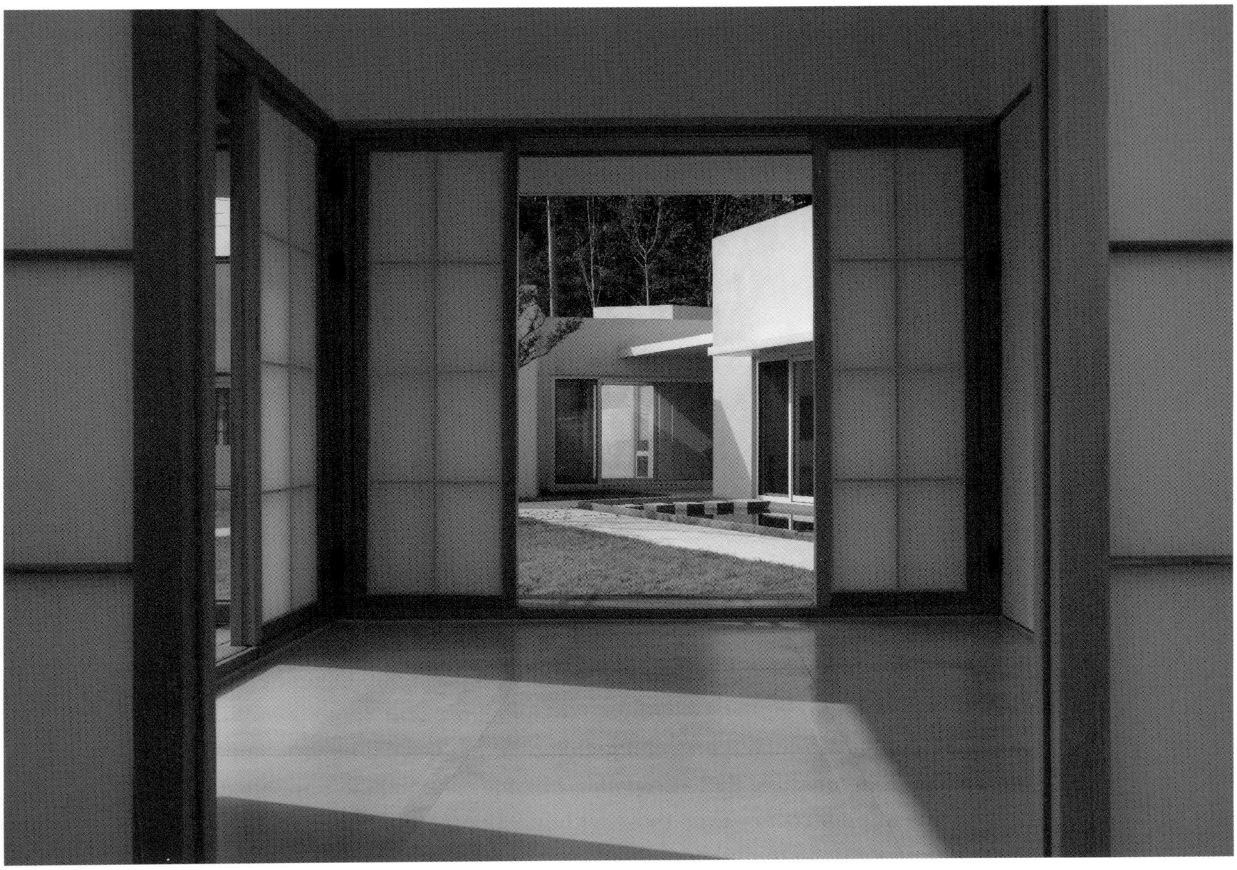

Residence "Subaekdang"

30km away from Seoul, the site is located deep in the woods quite disconnected from the outside world. As a place facing the outside world, boundary expresses the habitant's stance toward the neighborhood, the society and nature. The unfortunate construction of a retaining wall to even the slanted land necessitated the construction of a linear fence, and it became a primary task to incorporate this component into the overall design.

The dimension of 30m of the retaining wall became the frame of the house with 15 m depth. Of course the property of the client was much bigger, but, as stated above, the boundary of estate in the countryside is never as a determinant to architectural design as the territory formed by the natural conditions of the land.

The house, 200m2 in area is composed of twelve rooms: five interior rooms with roofs, and seven outdoor rooms opening up to the sky. Whether interior or exterior, every room is independent - each a world of its own. Although some rooms could be related to each other to form another territory, one, as a principle, is never subordinate to another.

The rooms open to the sky are basically without apparent function. Whether they store water, or be covered with wooden floor, earth, and pebbles, in essence these spaces are void. It is my hope that this void will not be called madang, nor garden, court, or anything that already has previous notion of use attached to it. Likewise, the interior rooms, even those with functional facility (e.g. bathroom, kitchen) that carries definite purpose, should not be understood solely by their use. The decision to distribute spaces along the 30m x 15m frame was to preclude the injection of functional aspects into each room, and their naming - the very act of specification - was only for practical reasons.

The house is made of white materials. The color would provide more room for time and life to leave their marks and traces. There was another reason also: this house was named Subaekdang originated from name of an old traditional house in southern Korea, actually meaning a house keeping white. It used to symbolize a life in purity. MoMA NY collected the model and drawing of this house as a permanent collection.

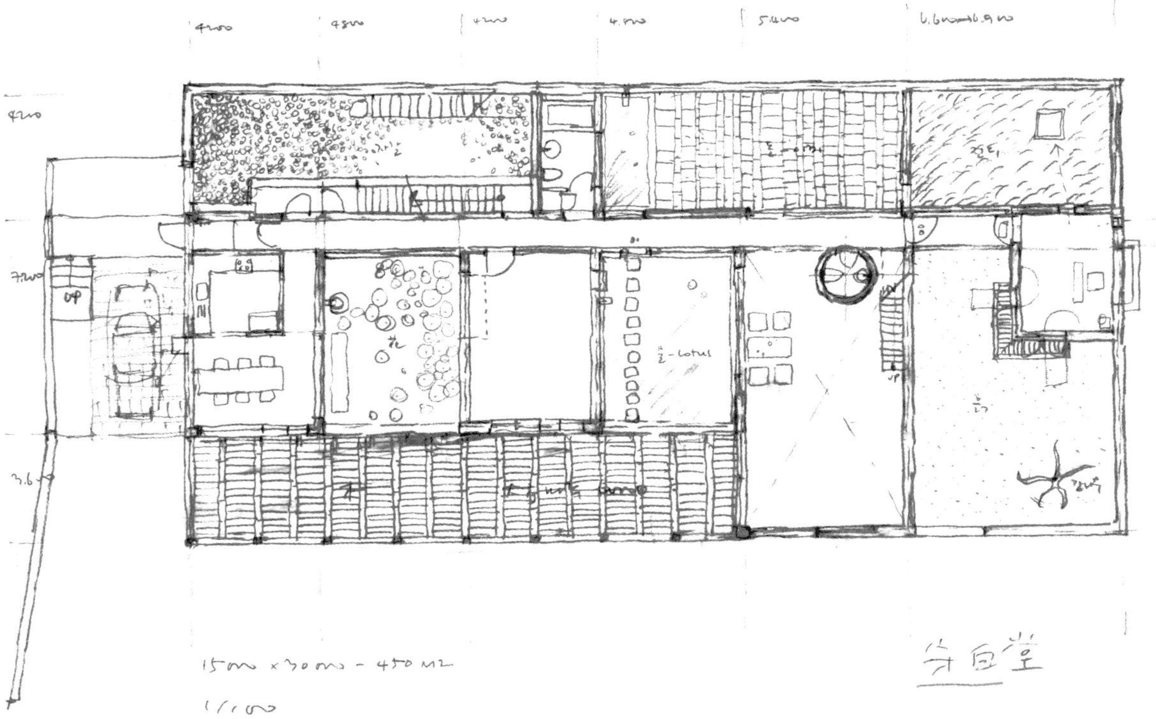
4200
4800
4200
4800
5400
7200
UP
Lotus
15000 x 30000 - 450 M2
1/100

Residence "Subaekdang"

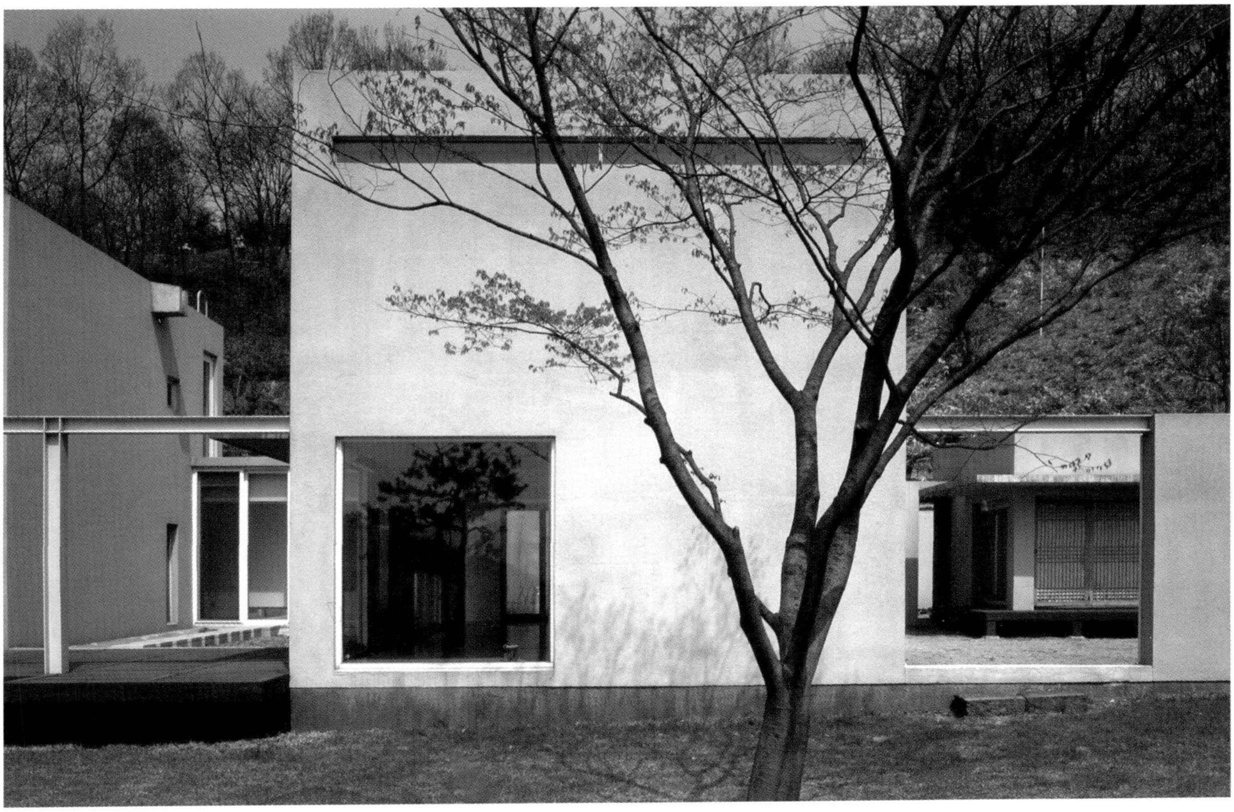

Residence "Subaekdang"

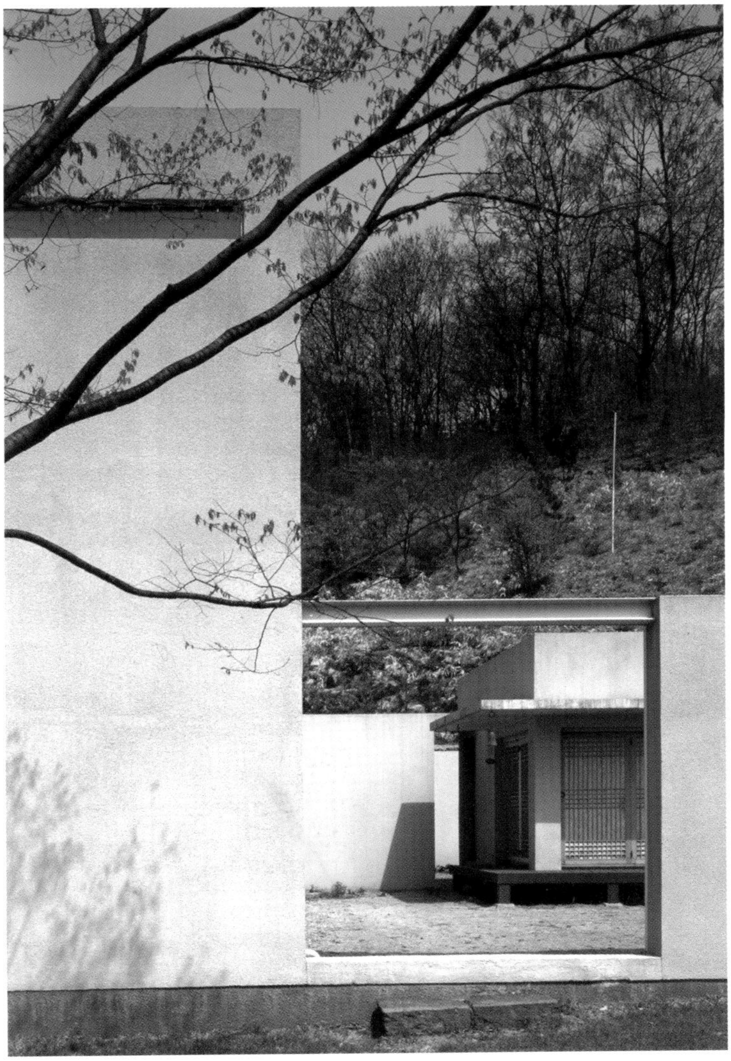

Residence "Subaekdang"

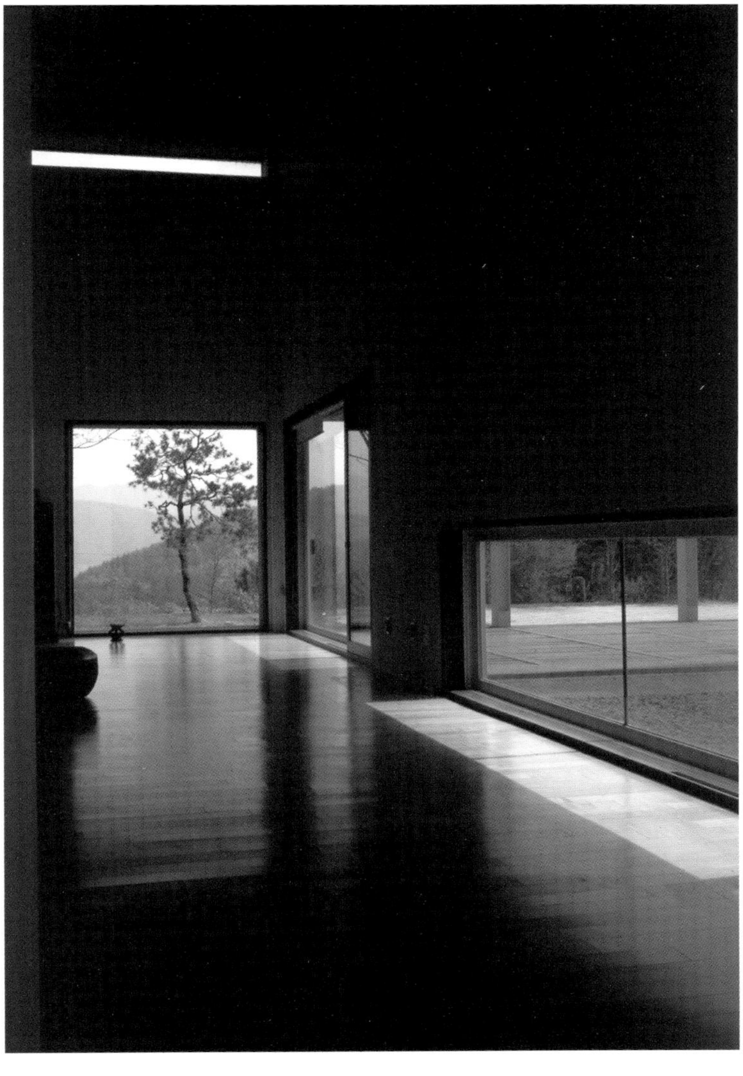

−379	Muhakro Methodist Church
−380	Bugye Arboretum "Sayuwon"— Hyeonam
−381	— Sadam
−383	— Myeongjeong
−386	— Wasa
−387	— Cheomdan
−388	Myungrye Sacred Hill
−390	Graveyard of President Roh Muhyun
−392	Public Cemetery Park "A Thousand Winds"
−395	Korea DMZ Peace and Life Valley
−398	Residence "Moheon"
−400	Korean Medicine Hospital of Daejeon University in Seoul
−404	Myung Films Complex
−407	Design Vita Office Building
−411	Chusa Memorial Museum
−412	Country Club House "360° Earth, Water, Flowers, and Wind"
−414	Traditional Buddhism Center of Jogye Order
−416	Shin Dongyeop Literary Museum
−419	Vanke Residential Culture Center
−421	Humax Main Office Bldg. "Humax Village"
−424	Hyehwa Residential College of Daejeon University
−429	30th Anniversary Memorial Building of Daejeon University
−431	Hyehwa Culture Center of Daejeon University
−432	Gudeok Presbyterian Church
−435	Chaowai SOHO
−438	Boao Canal Village
−440	Commune by the Great Wall
−442	Lock Museum
−447	Welcomm City
−450	Paju Book City
−451	Kyobo Book City
−452	Residence "Soowoojae"
−454	Reed House
−457	Teochon House
−459	Residence "Subaekdang"
−462	Technical Descriptions
−466	IROJE people
−468	IROJE partners

→ 90 Muhakro Methodist Church

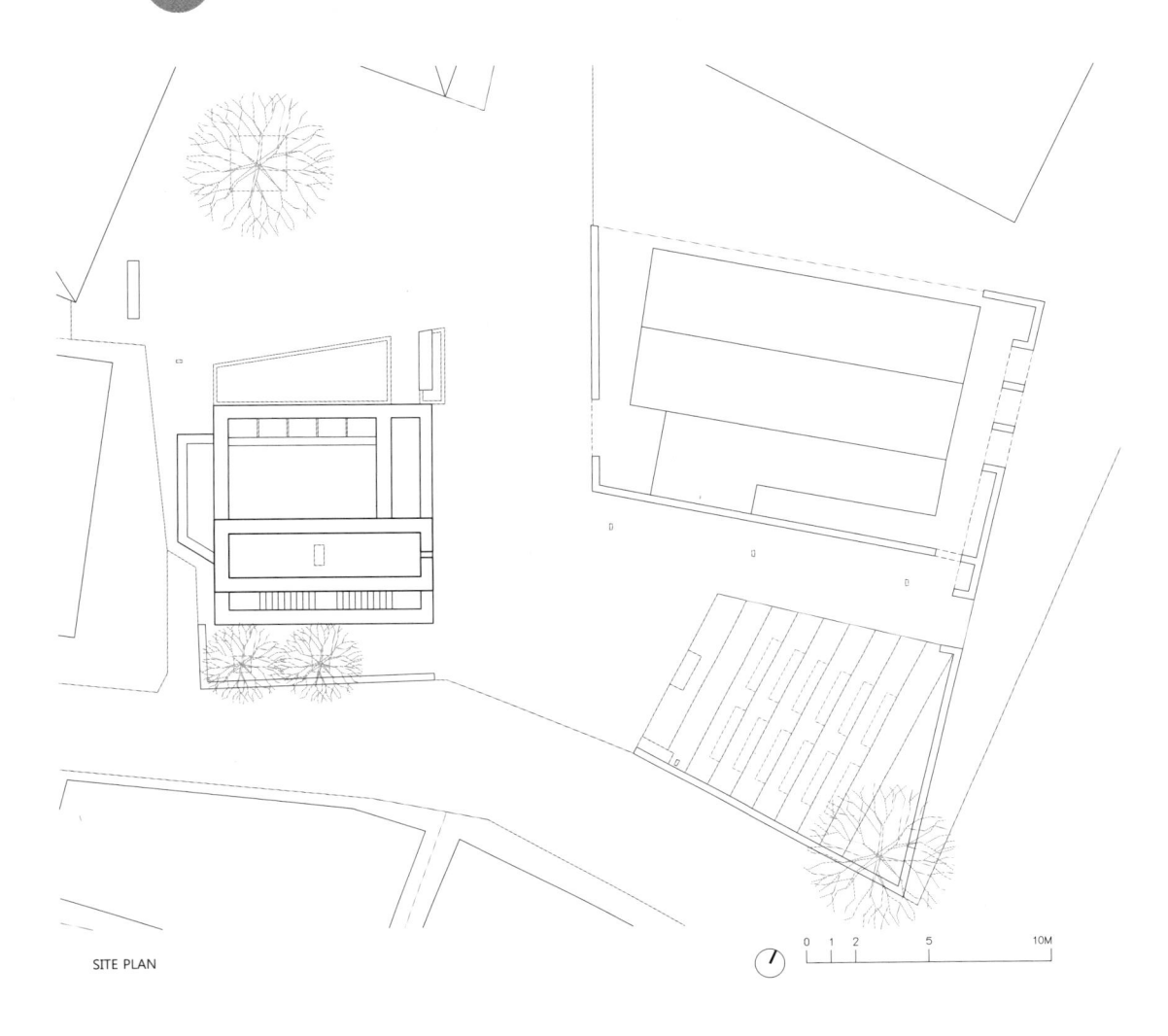

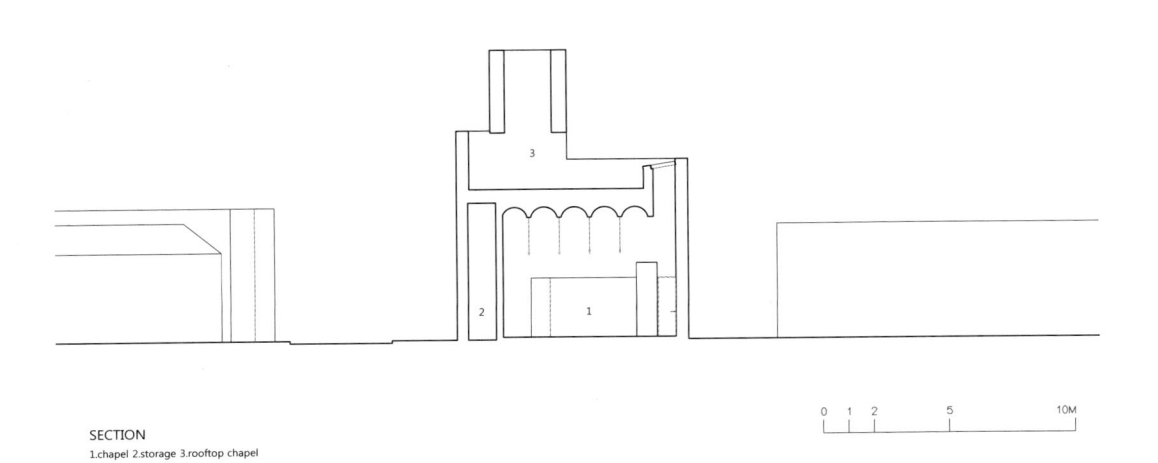

SITE PLAN

SECTION
1.chapel 2.storage 3.rooftop chapel

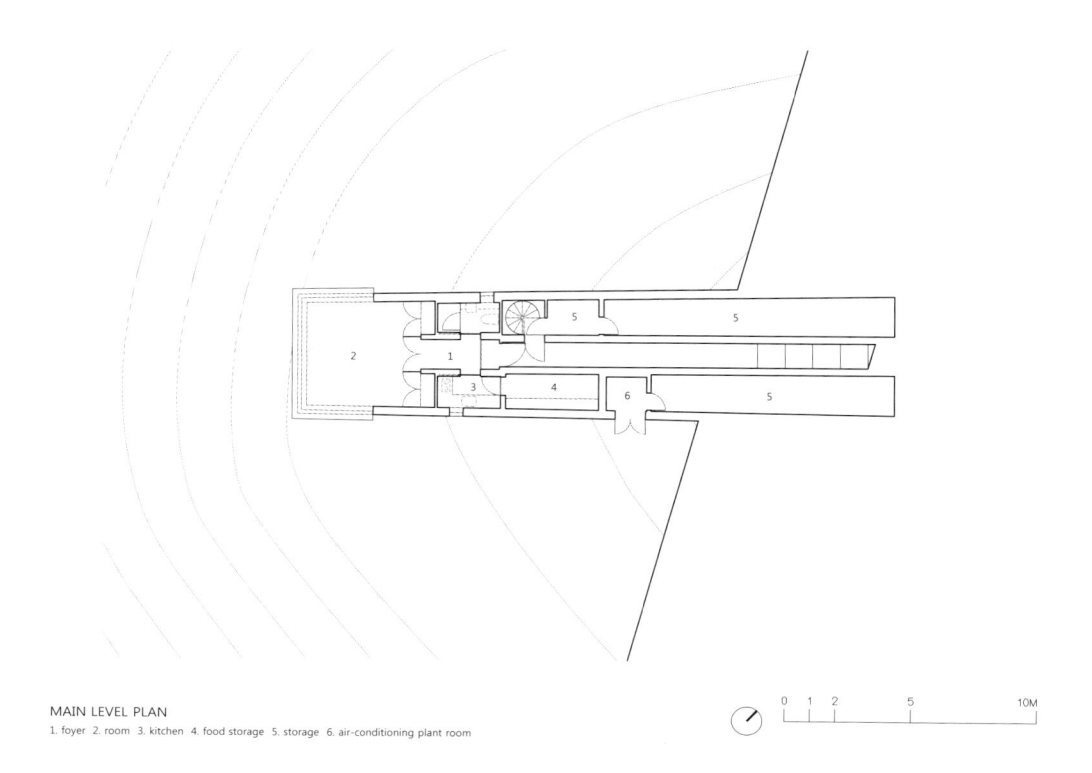

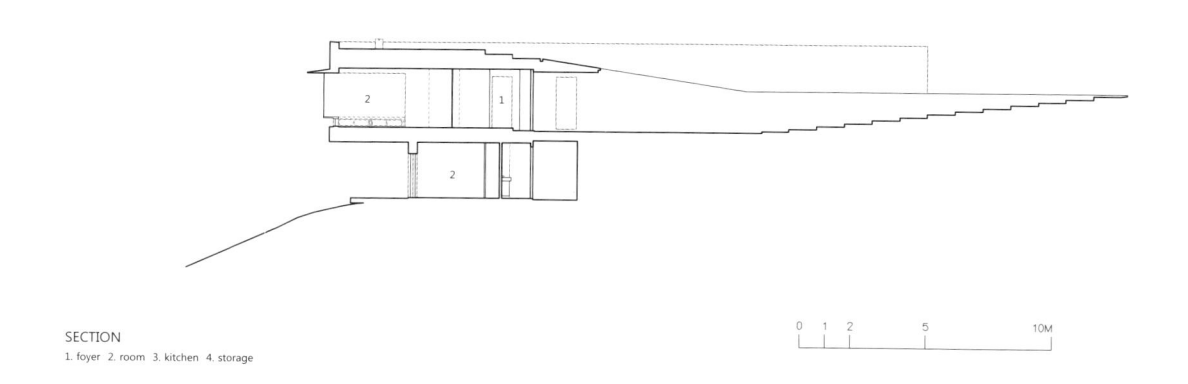

98 Bugye Arboretum "Sayuwon"— Hyeonam

MAIN LEVEL PLAN
1. foyer 2. room 3. kitchen 4. food storage 5. storage 6. air-conditioning plant room

SECTION
1. foyer 2. room 3. kitchen 4. storage

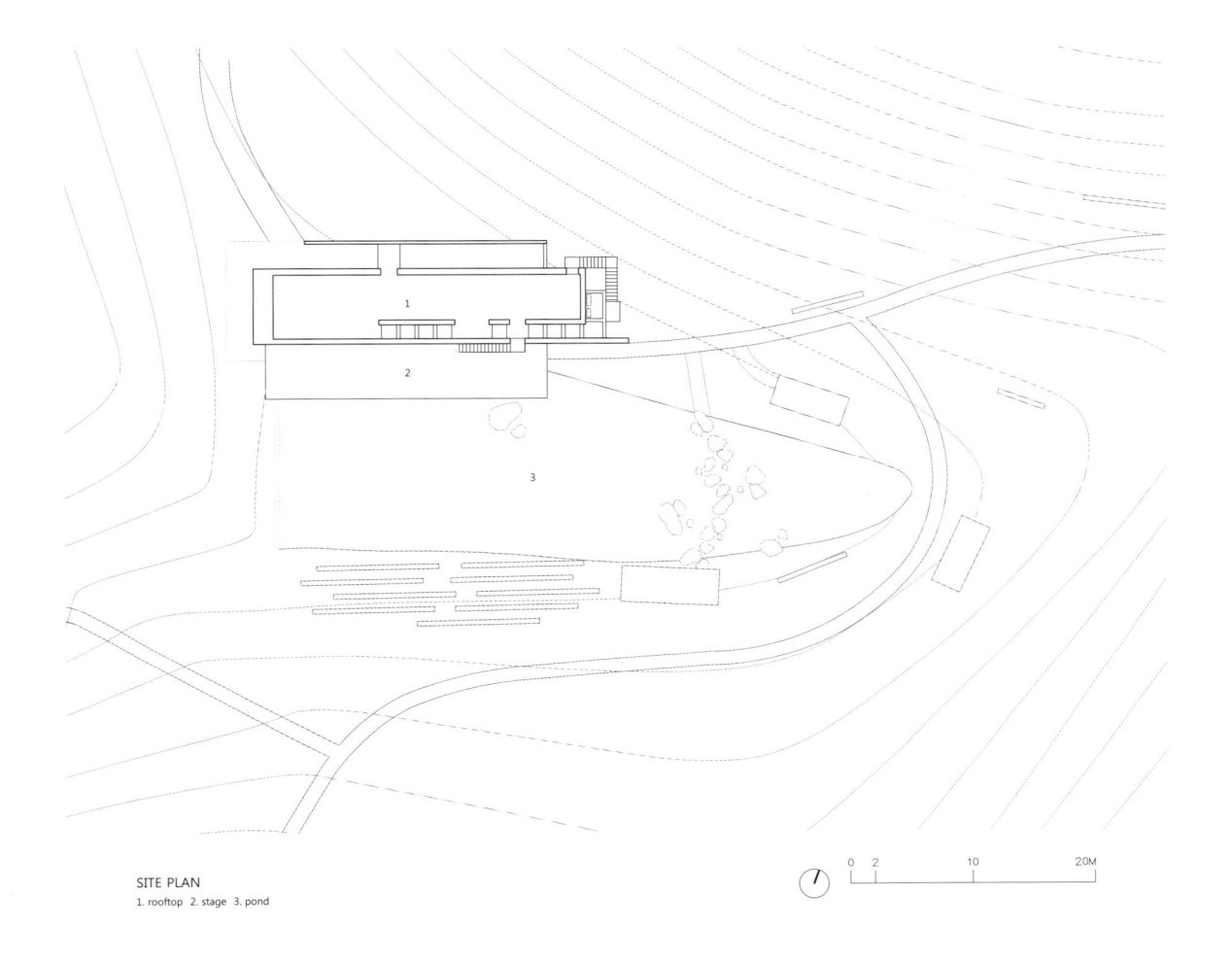

→ 106   Bugye Arboretum "Sayuwon"— Sadam

SITE PLAN
1. rooftop 2. stage 3. pond

0 2   10   20M

→ 112   Bugye Arboretum "Sayuwon"— Myungjeong

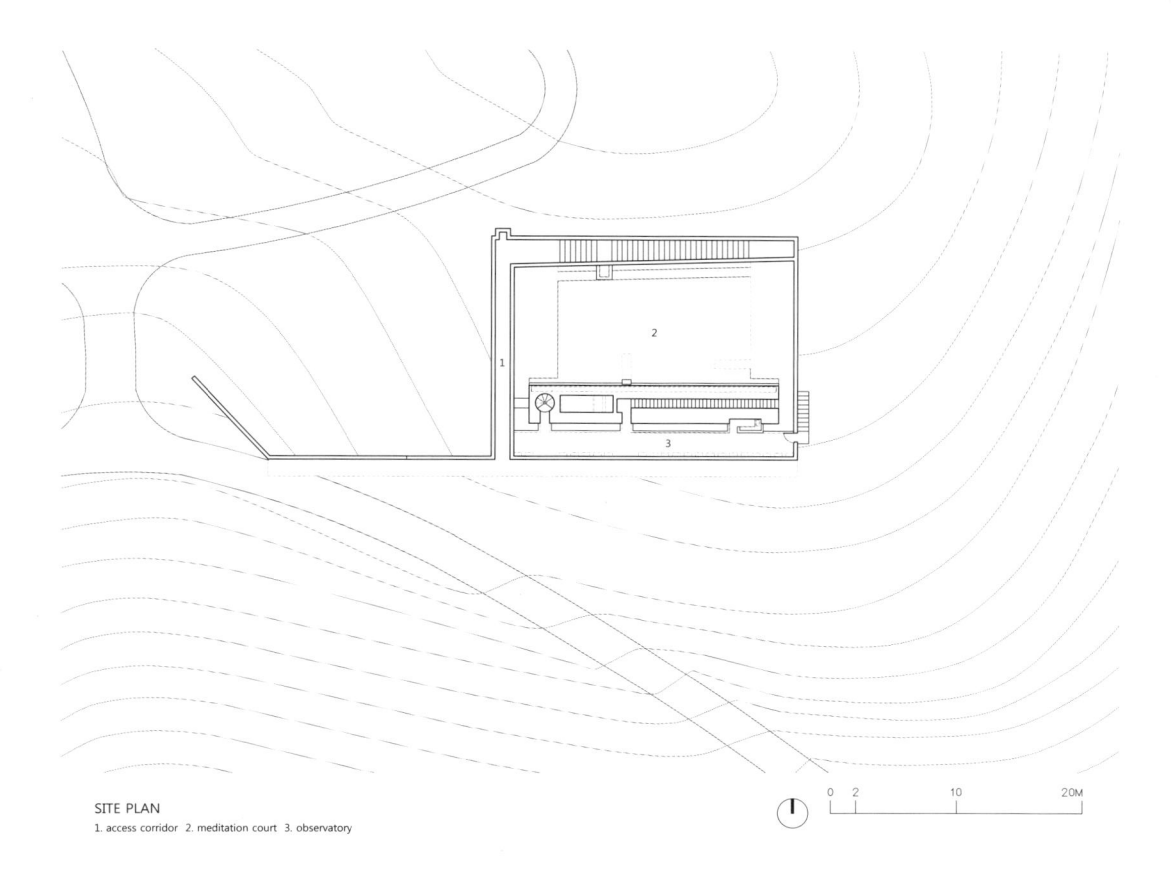

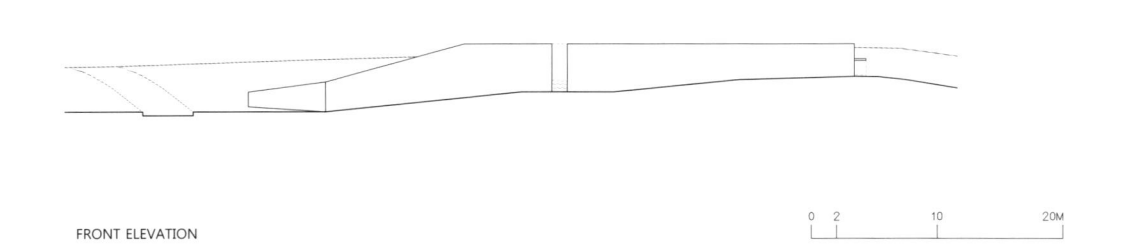

SITE PLAN
1. access corridor 2. meditation court 3. observatory

FRONT ELEVATION

Bugye Arboretum "Sayuwon" — Myungjeong

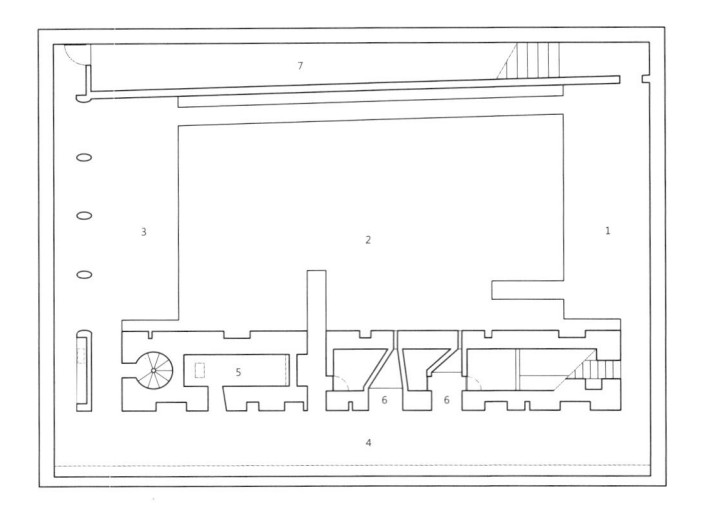

LOWER LEVEL PLAN
1. platform 2. water court 3. stage 4. meditation corridor 5. meditation room 6. sacristy 7. thinker's room

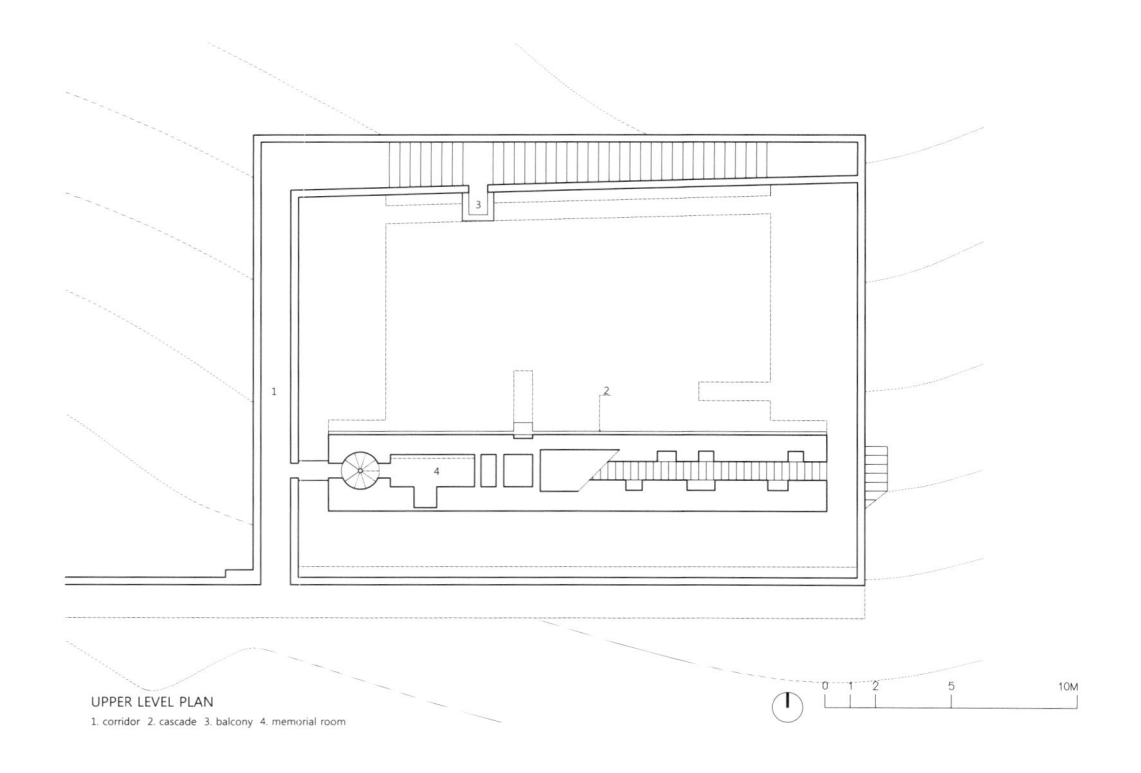

UPPER LEVEL PLAN
1. corridor 2. cascade 3. balcony 4. memorial room

Bugye Arboretum "Sayuwon" — Myungjeong

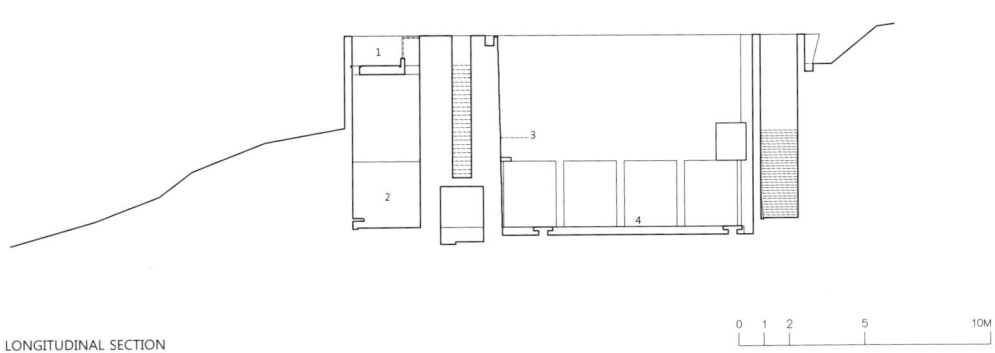

LONGITUDINAL SECTION
1. observatory 2. meditation corridor 3. cascade 4. water court

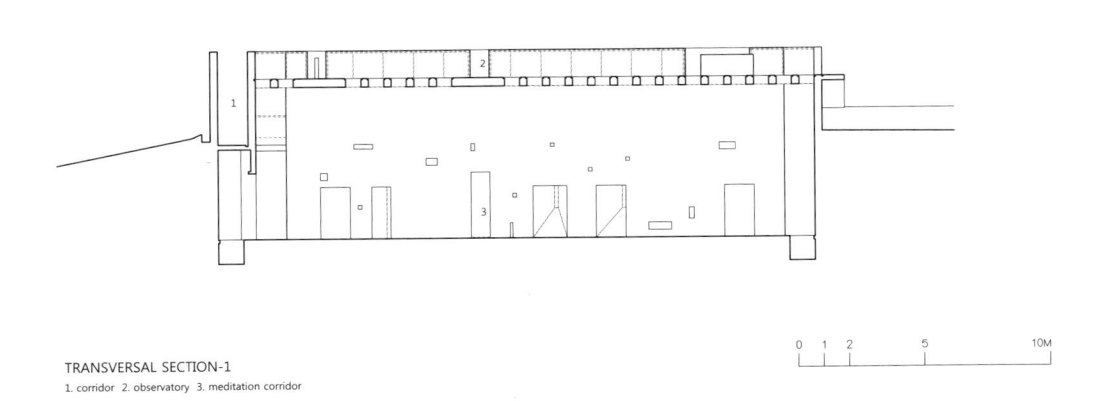

TRANSVERSAL SECTION-1
1. corridor 2. observatory 3. meditation corridor

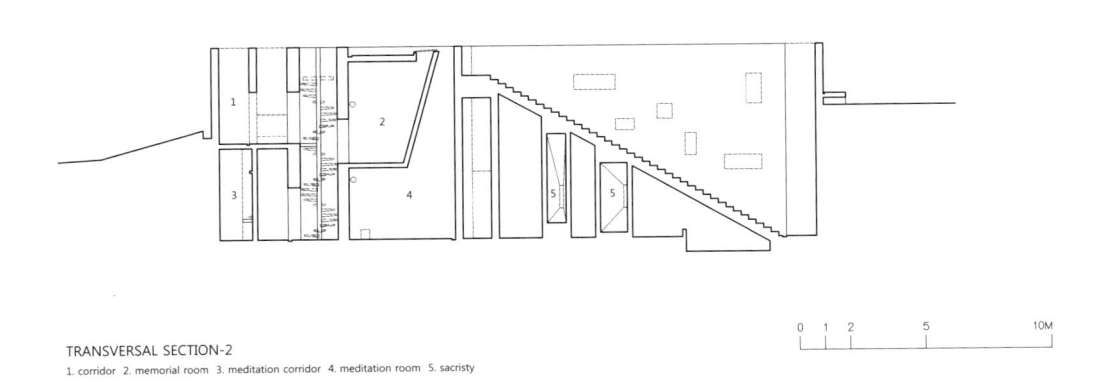

TRANSVERSAL SECTION-2
1. corridor 2. memorial room 3. meditation corridor 4. meditation room 5. sacristy

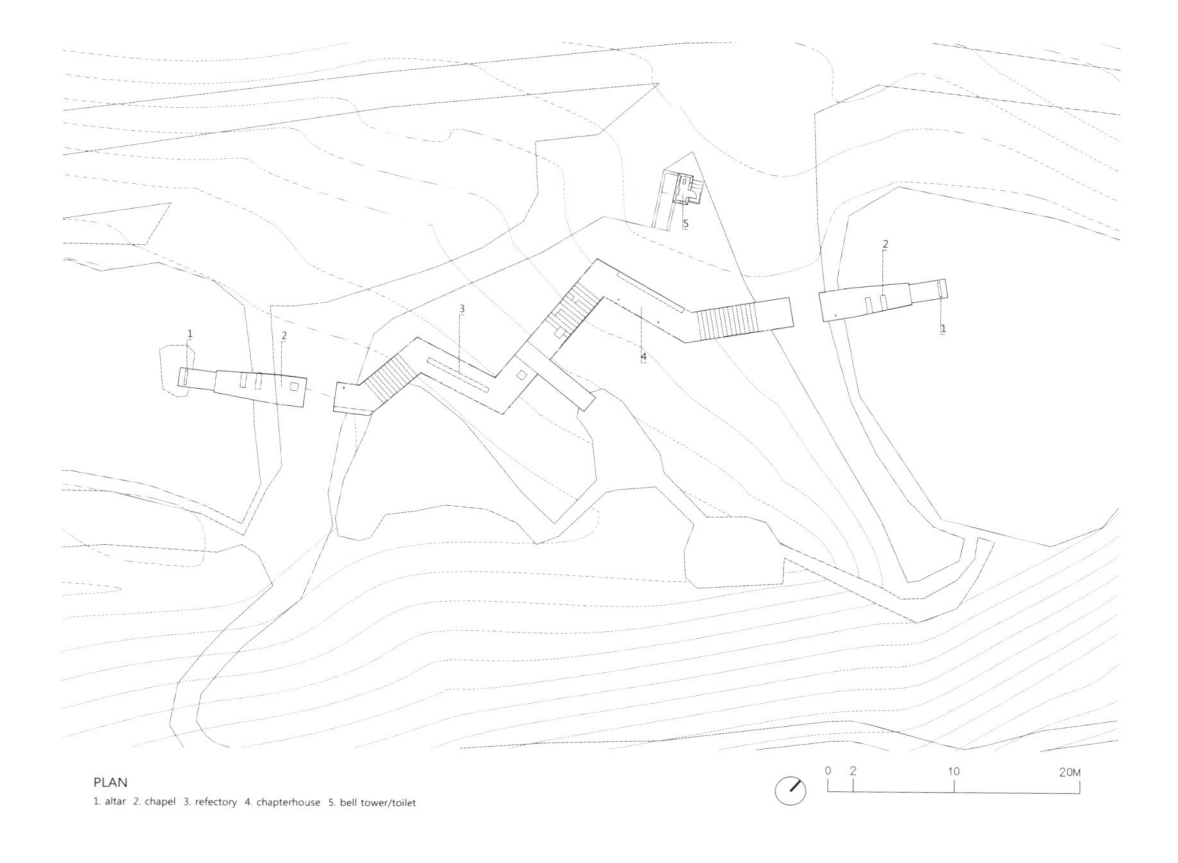

Bugye Arboretum "Sayuwon" — Wasa

PLAN
1. altar 2. chapel 3. refectory 4. chapterhouse 5. bell tower/toilet

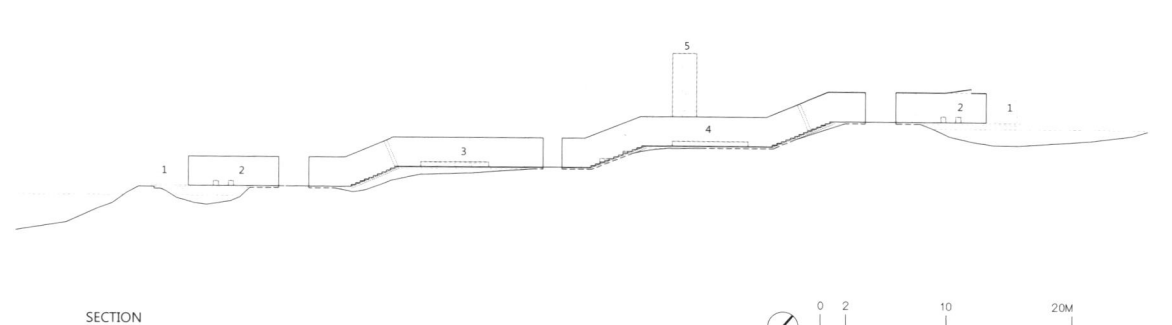

SECTION
1. altar 2. chapel 3. refectory 4. chapterhouse 5. bell tower/toilet

→ 128　Bugye Arboretum "Sayuwon"— Cheomdan

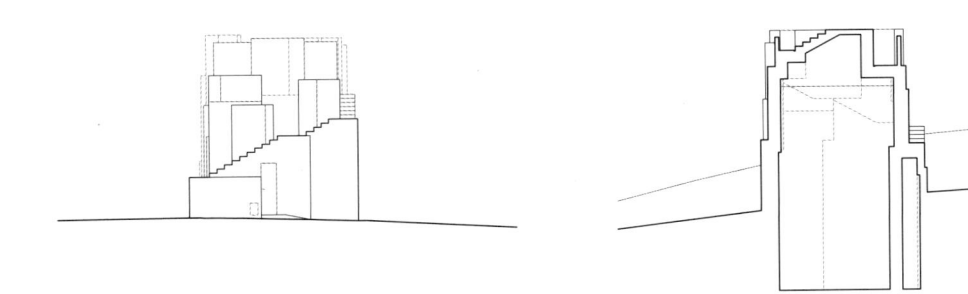

SITE PLAN

WEST ELEVATION

SECTION

Myungrye Sacred Hill

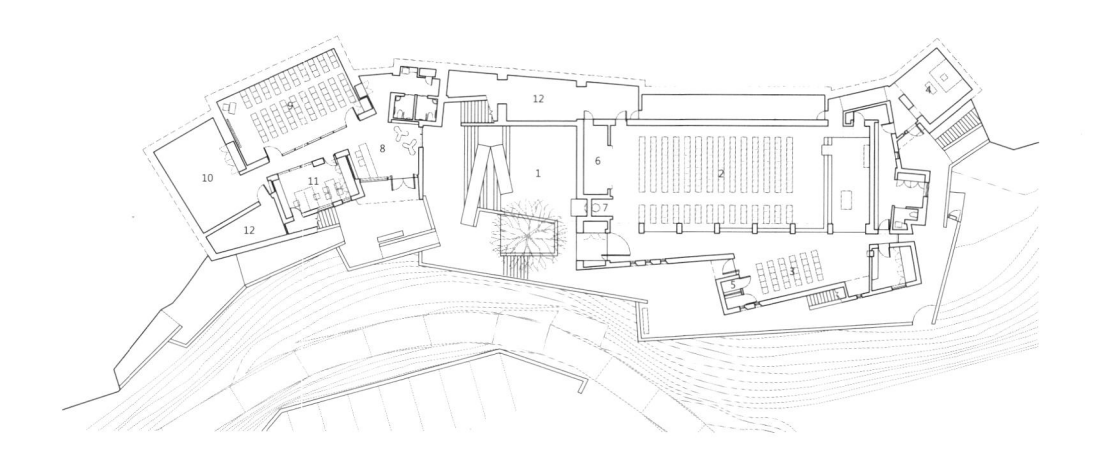

PLAN
1. entrance plaza 2. nave 3. colonnade 4. oratory of the martyr 5. confession room 6. organ room 7. stoup
8. info desk 9. seminar room 10. gallery 11. office 12. storage

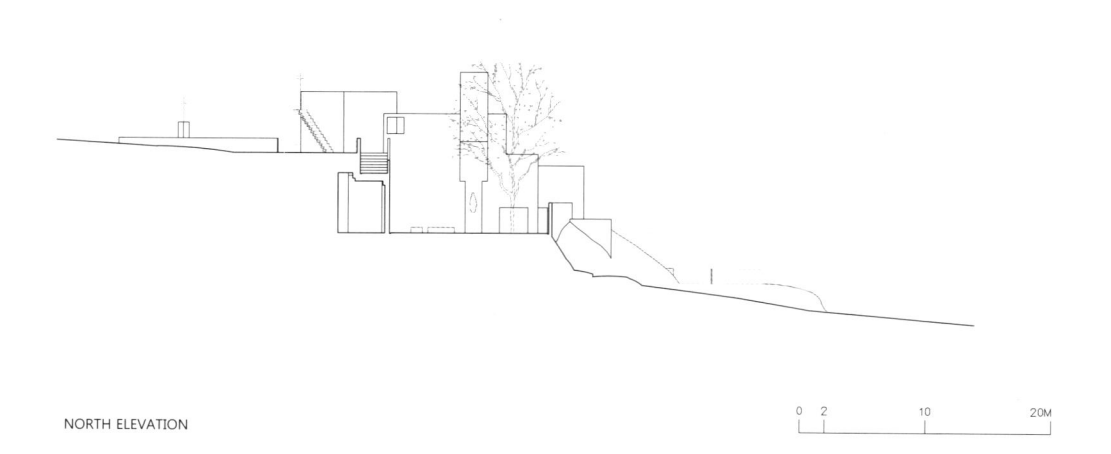

NORTH ELEVATION

Myungrye Sacred Hill

SECTION-1
1. entrance plaza 2. nave 3. gallery 4. office 5. info

0 2   10   20M

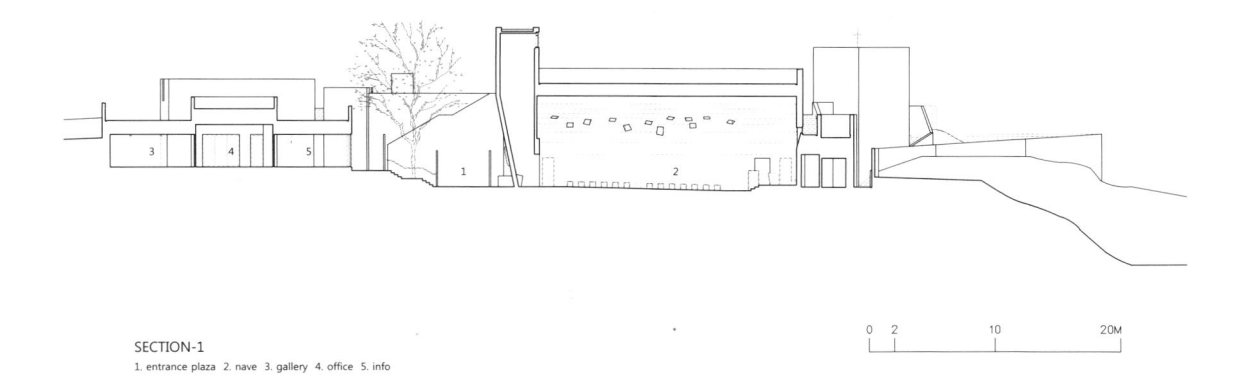

SECTION-2
1. altar 2. altar for open-air mass

0 2   10   20M

Graveyard of President Roh Muhyun

SITE PLAN
1. graveyard 2. rest area 3. private residence 4. birthplace 5. memorial library & museum (under construction)
6. glass house 7. eco-park 8. parking

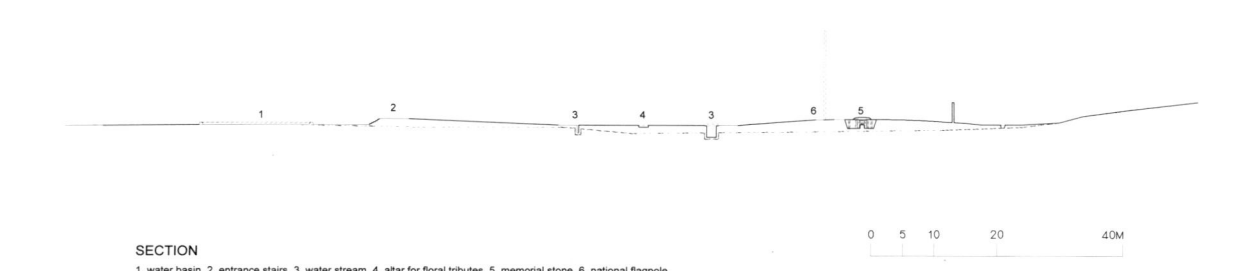

Graveyard of President Roh Muhyun

PLAN

0 5 10   20   40M

SECTION
1. water basin 2. entrance stairs 3. water stream 4. altar for floral tributes 5. memorial stone 6. national flagpole

0 5 10   20   40M

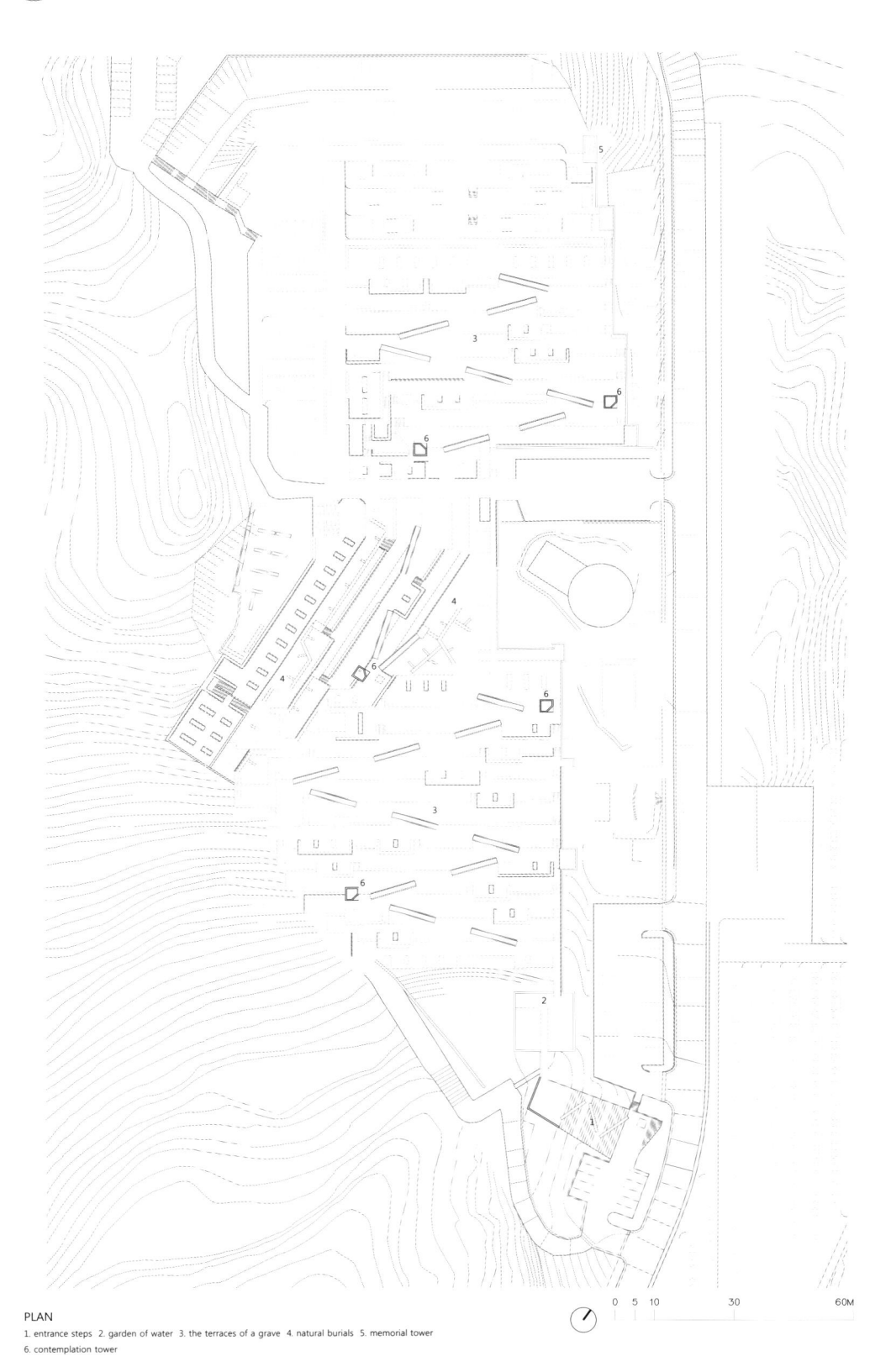

Public Cemetery Park "A Thousand Winds"

PLAN
1. entrance steps 2. garden of water 3. the terraces of a grave 4. natural burials 5. memorial tower
6. contemplation tower

Public Cemetery Park "A Thousand Winds"

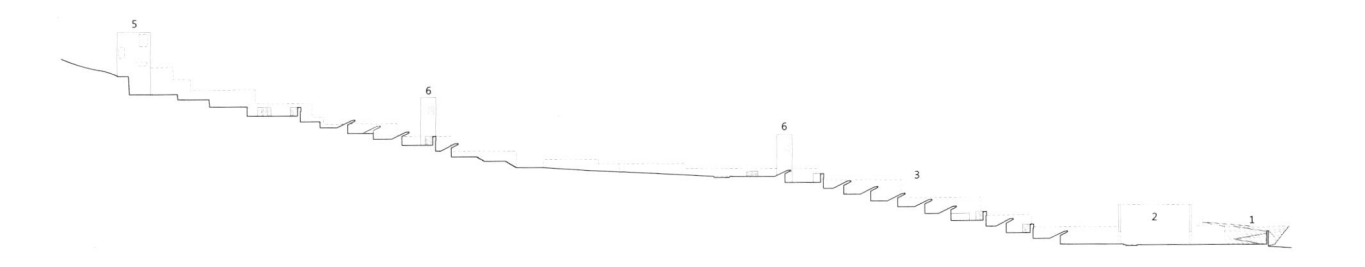

SECTION
1. entrance steps 2. garden of water 3. the terraces of a grave 4. natural burials 5. memorial tower 6. contemplation tower

→ 166 Korea DMZ Peace and Life Valley

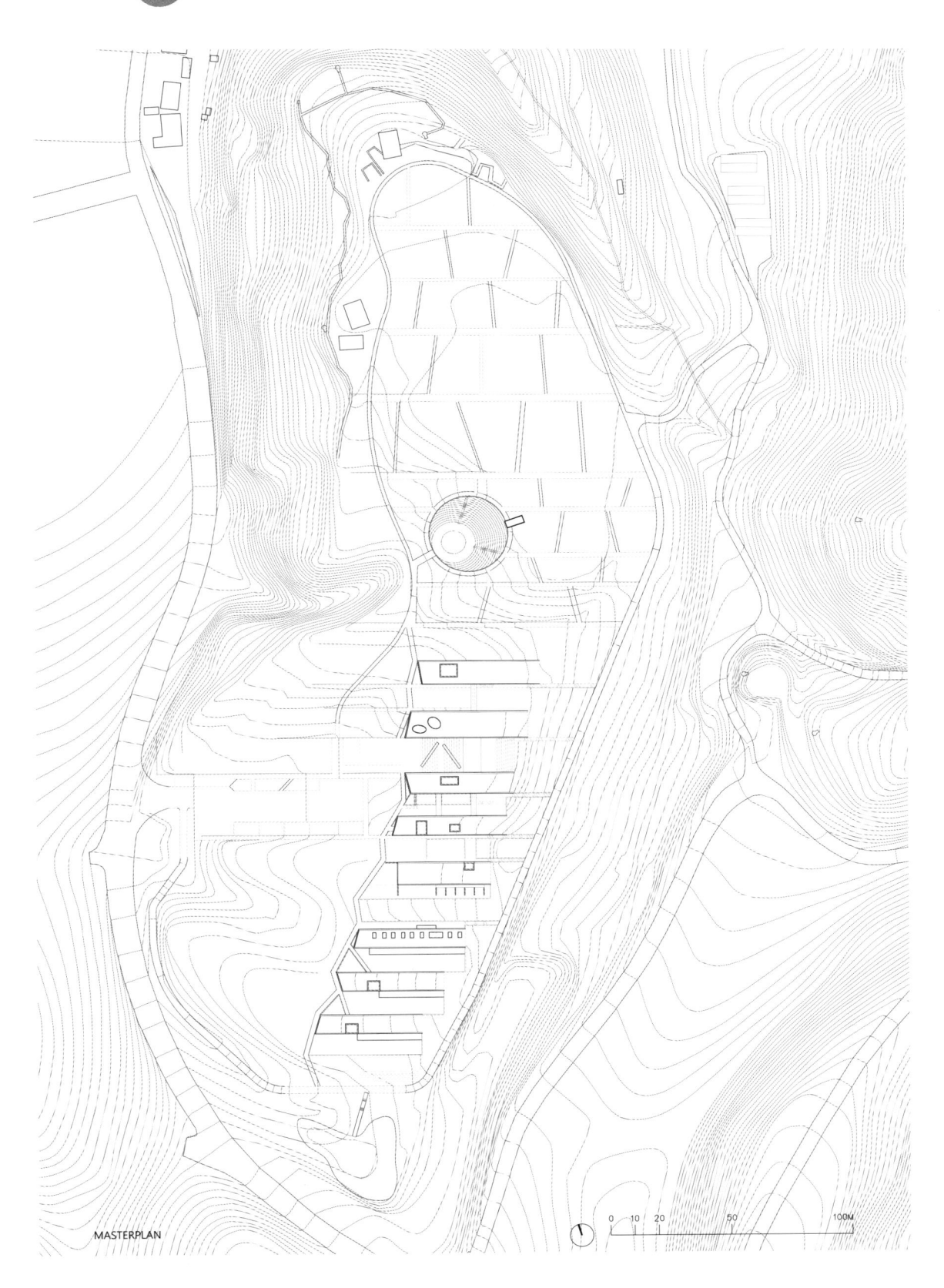

MASTERPLAN

Korea DMZ Peace and Life Valley

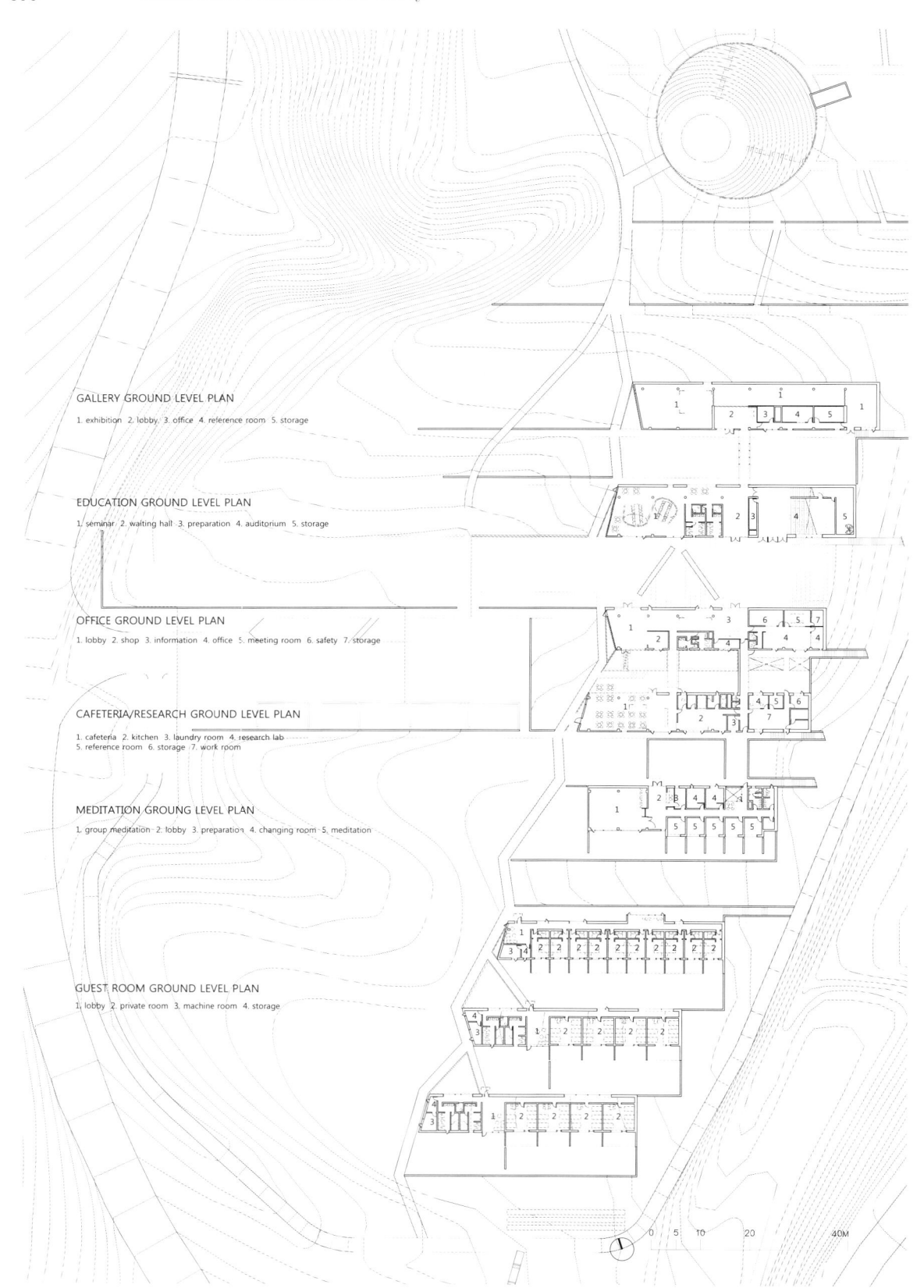

GALLERY GROUND LEVEL PLAN
1. exhibition 2. lobby 3. office 4. reference room 5. storage

EDUCATION GROUND LEVEL PLAN
1. seminar 2. waiting hall 3. preparation 4. auditorium 5. storage

OFFICE GROUND LEVEL PLAN
1. lobby 2. shop 3. information 4. office 5. meeting room 6. safety 7. storage

CAFETERIA/RESEARCH GROUND LEVEL PLAN
1. cafeteria 2. kitchen 3. laundry room 4. research lab
5. reference room 6. storage 7. work room

MEDITATION GROUNG LEVEL PLAN
1. group meditation 2. lobby 3. preparation 4. changing room 5. meditation

GUEST ROOM GROUND LEVEL PLAN
1. lobby 2. private room 3. machine room 4. storage

0 5 10 20 40M

Korea DMZ Peace and Life Valley

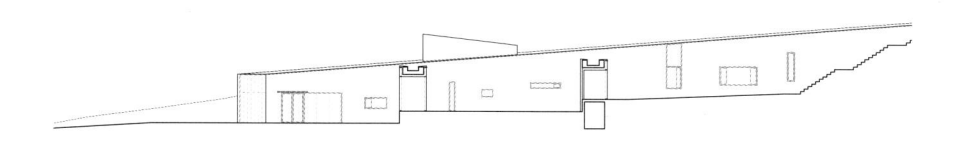

OFFICE SOUTH ELEVATION

0 2   10   20M

174 Residence "Moheon"

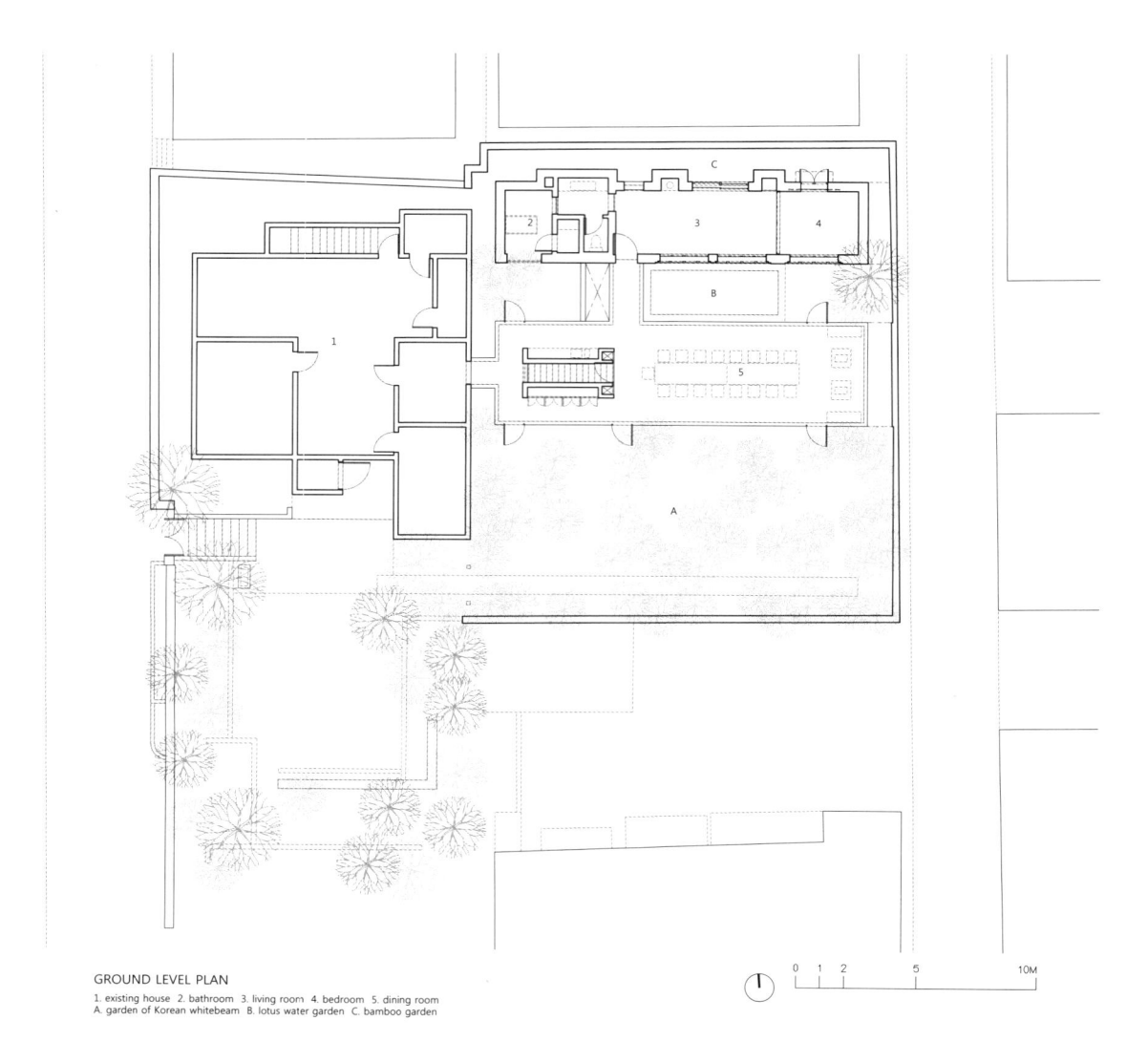

GROUND LEVEL PLAN
1. existing house 2. bathroom 3. living room 4. bedroom 5. dining room
A. garden of Korean whitebeam B. lotus water garden C. bamboo garden

Residence "Moheon"

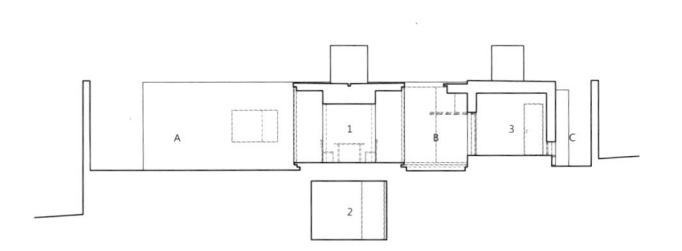

LONGITUDINAL SECTION
1. dining room 2. wine cellar 3. living room
A. garden of Korean whitebeam B. lotus water garden C. bamboo garden

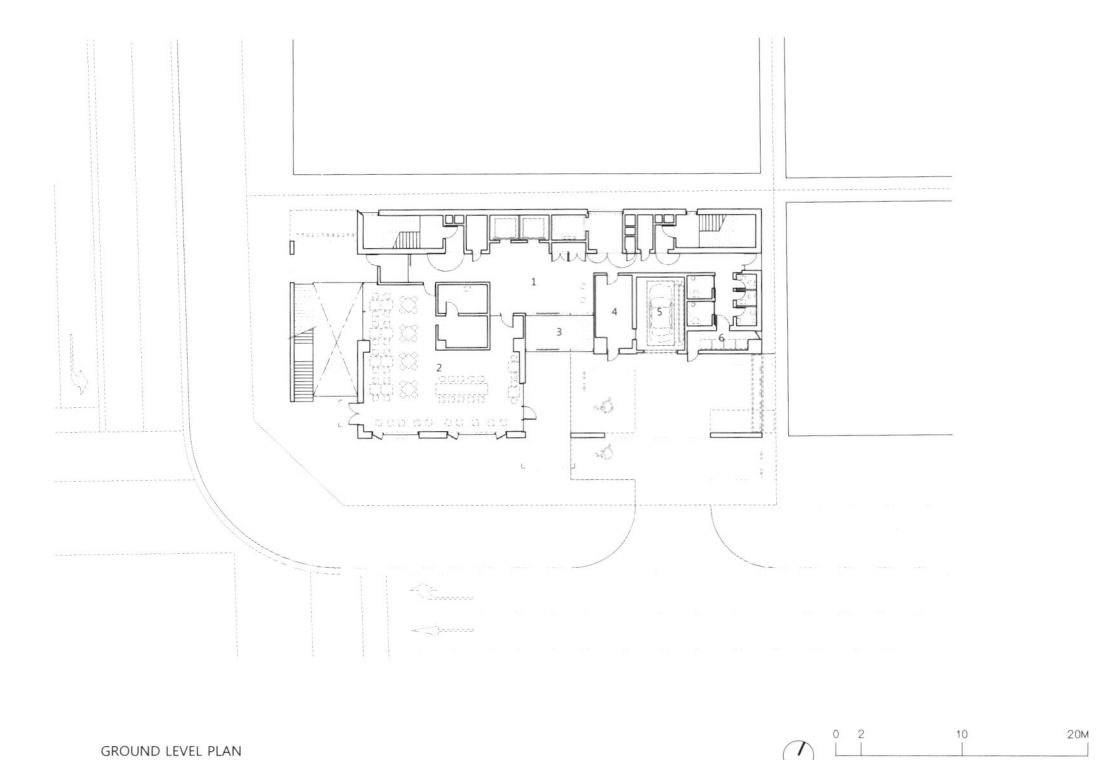

Korean Medicine Hospital of Daejeon University in Seoul

GROUND LEVEL PLAN
1. reception 2. restaurant 3. entrance 4. maintenance room 5. car lift 6. recycling room

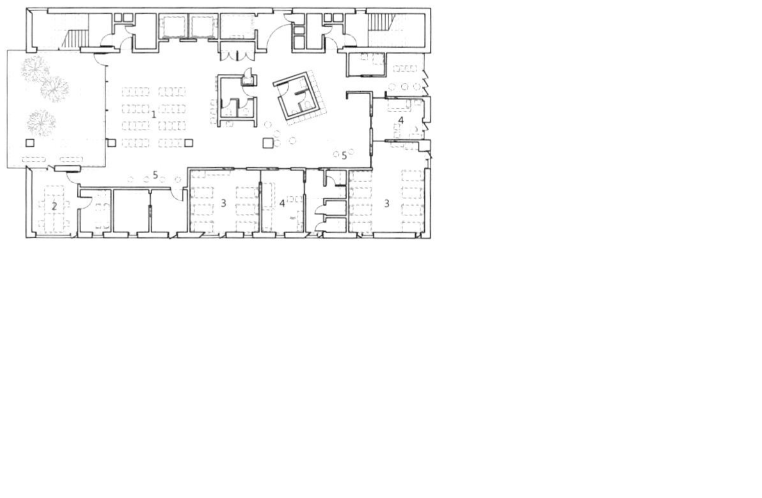

6th FLOOR PLAN
1. waiting room 2. meeing room 3. treatment room 4. doctor's office 5. nurse station

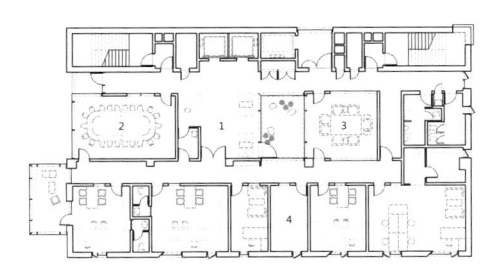

Korean Medicine Hospital of Daejeon University in Seoul

12th FLOOR PLAN
1. waiting room 2. conference room 3. reception room 4. the management

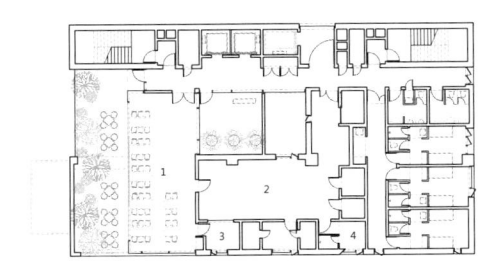

13th FLOOR PLAN
1. cafeteria 2. kitchen 3. the dietitian 4. staff room

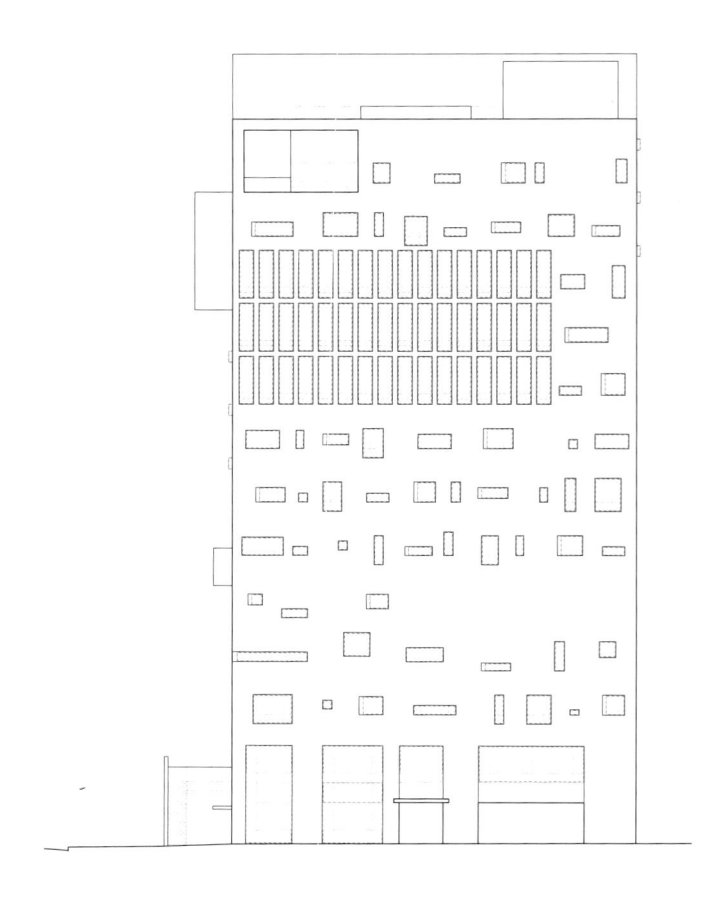

Korean Medicine Hospital of Daejeon University in Seoul

ELEVATION-1

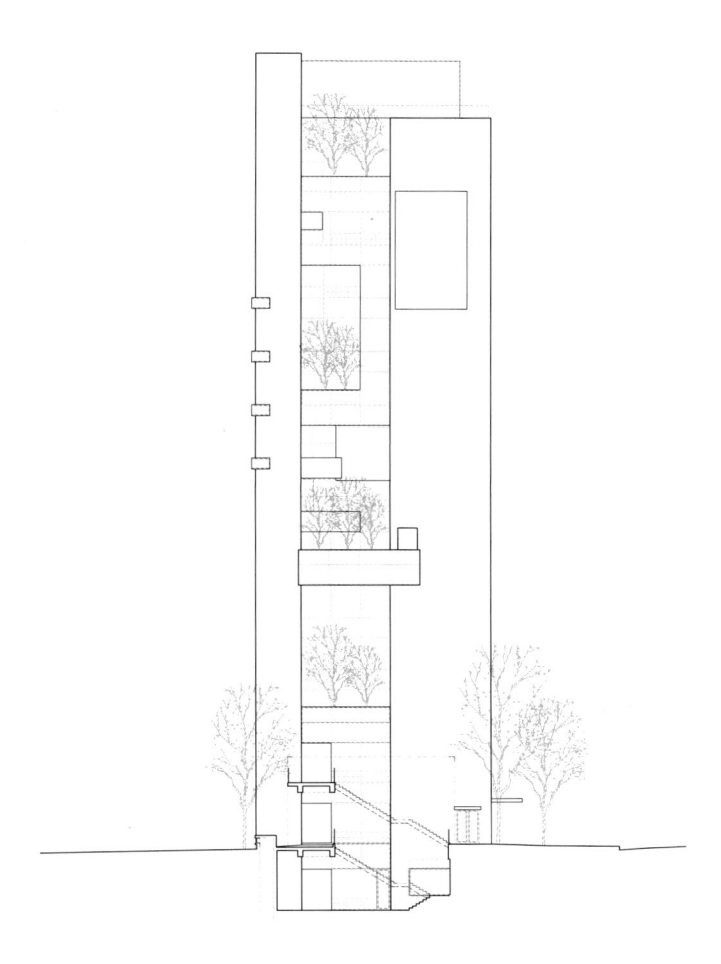

Korean Medicine Hospital of Daejeon University in Seoul

ELEVATION-2

→ 190　Myung Films Complex

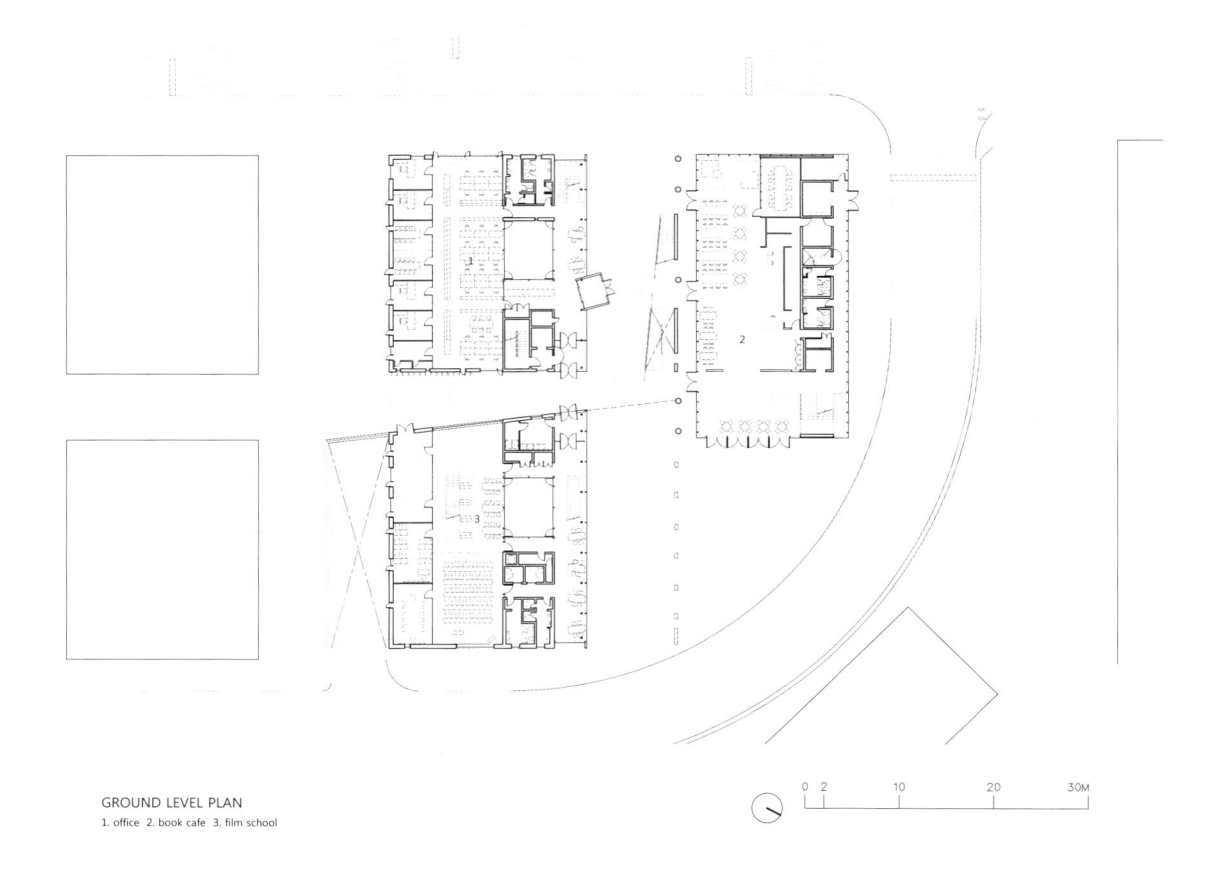

GROUND LEVEL PLAN
1. office 2. book cafe 3. film school

Myung Films Complex

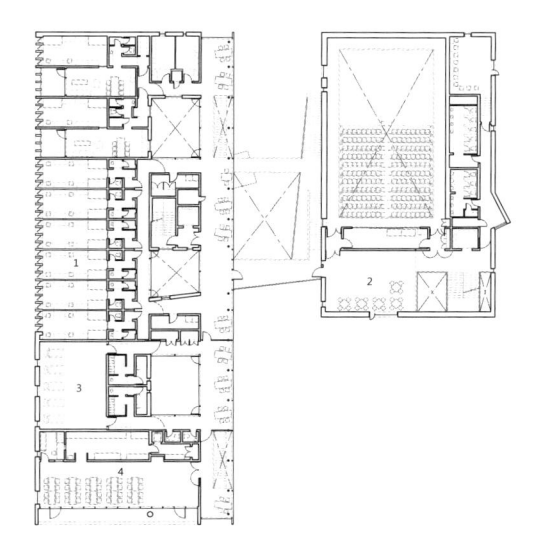

3rd FLOOR PLAN
1. dormitory 2. hall 3. fitness 4. cafeteria

198 Design Vita Office Building

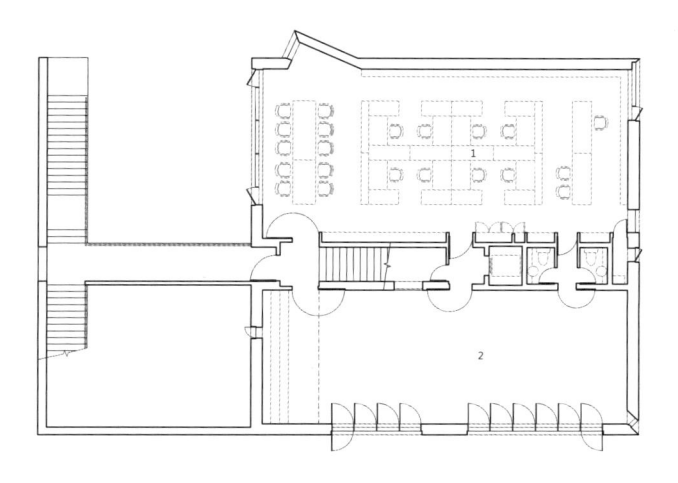

2F PLAN
1. office 2. multi-purpose hall

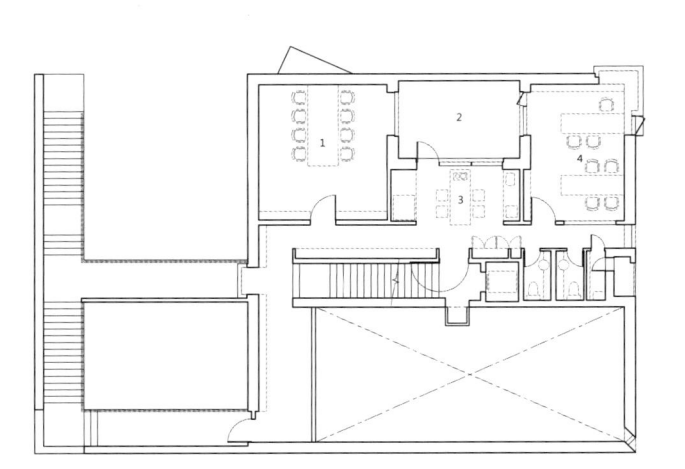

3F PLAN
1. meeting room 2. courtyard 3. lounge 4. head's room

Design Vita Office Building

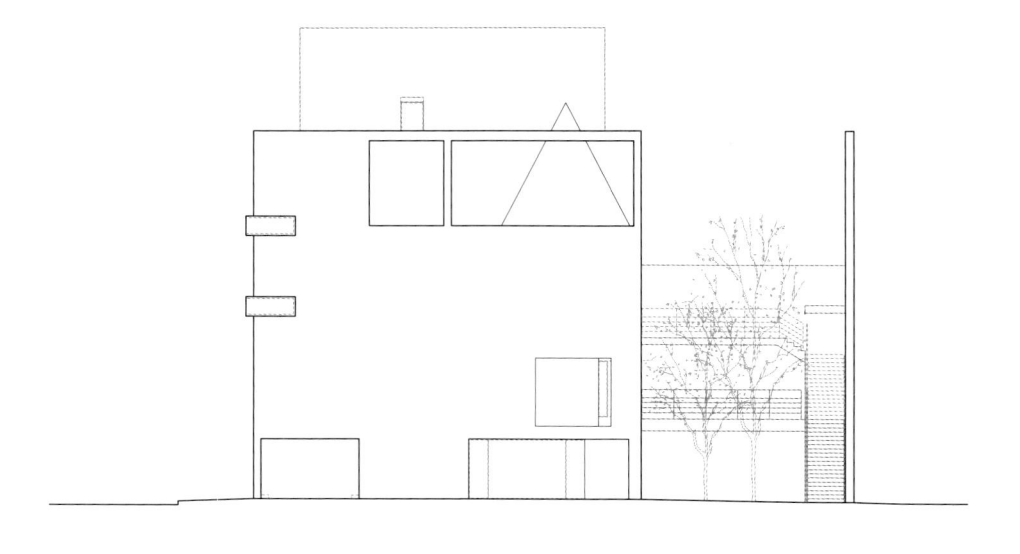

WEST ELEVATION

0 1 2   5   10M

Design Vita Office Building

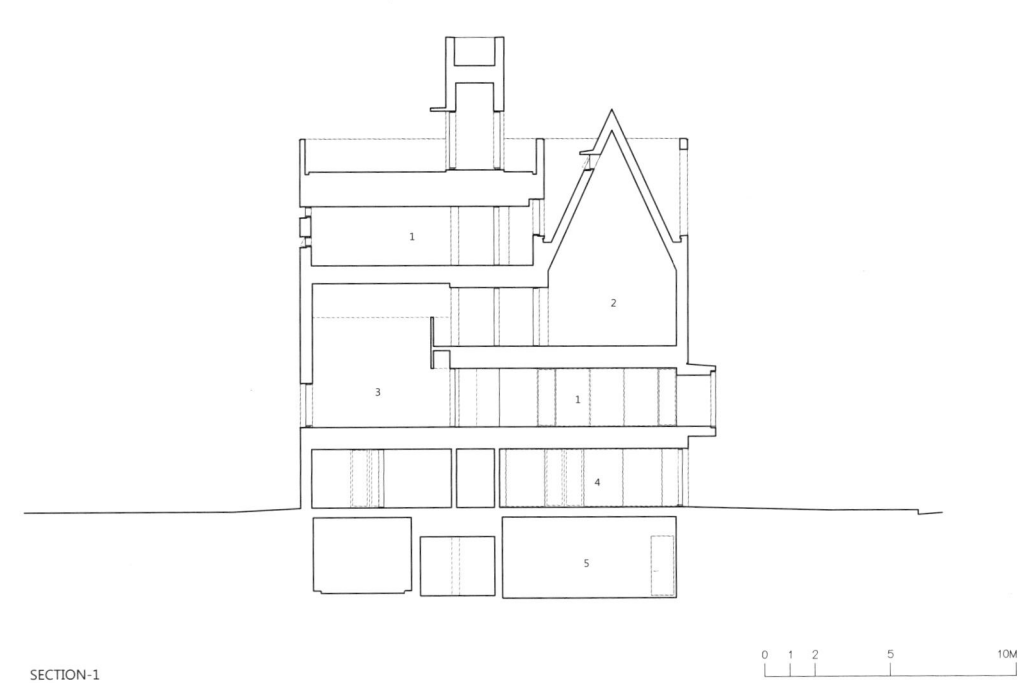

SECTION-1
1. office 2. meeting room 3. exhibition hall 5. lounge 6. parking

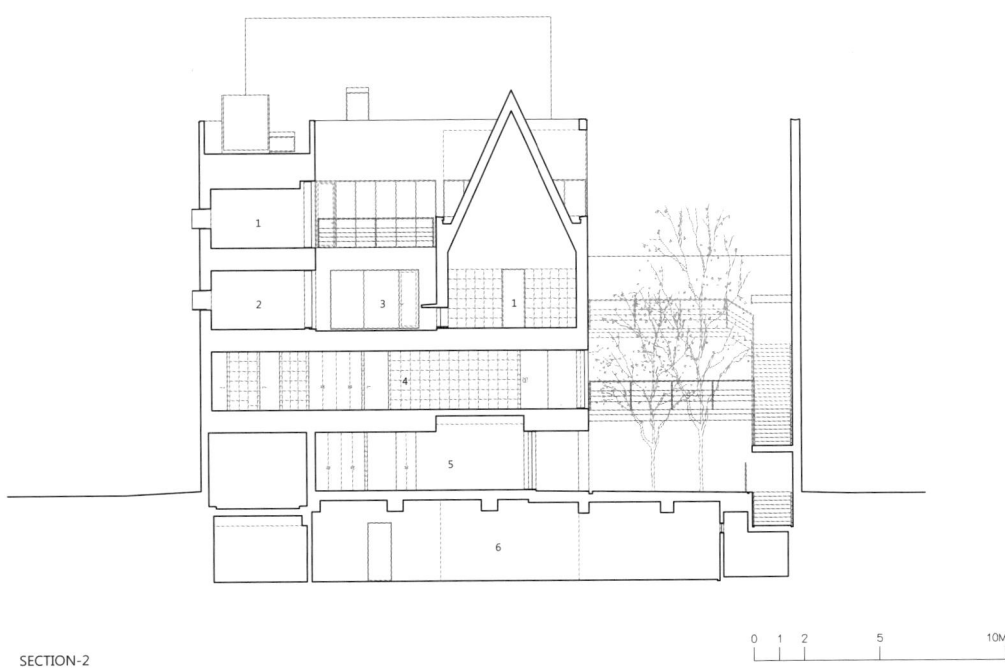

SECTION-2
1. meeting room 2. head's room 3. courtyard 4. office 5. shop 6. parking

Chusa Memorial Museum

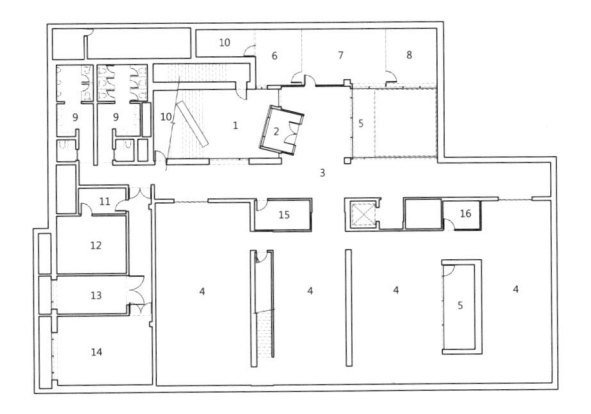

B1 PLAN
1. entrance 2. vestibule 3. hall 4. exhibition 5. courtyard 6. meeting room 7. management team 8. head of management
9. restroom 10. storage 11. preparation room 12. museum storage 13. generator room 14. electric room 15. gas fire extinguishing agent 16. server room

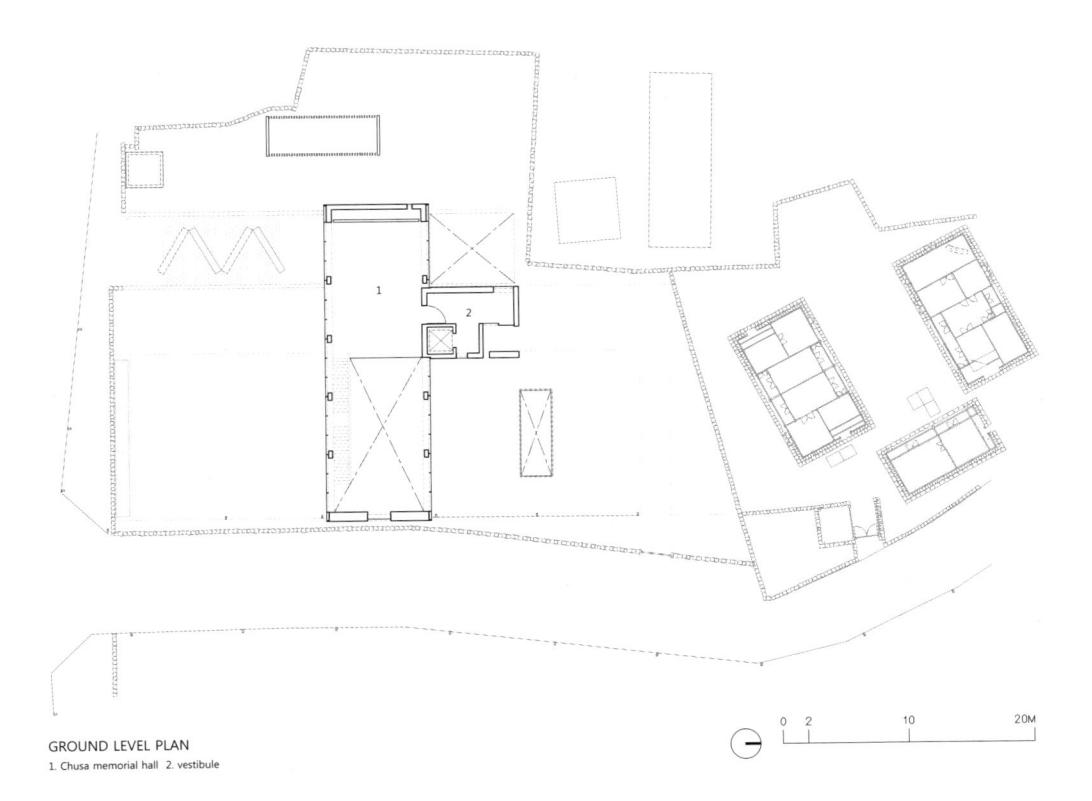

GROUND LEVEL PLAN
1. Chusa memorial hall 2. vestibule

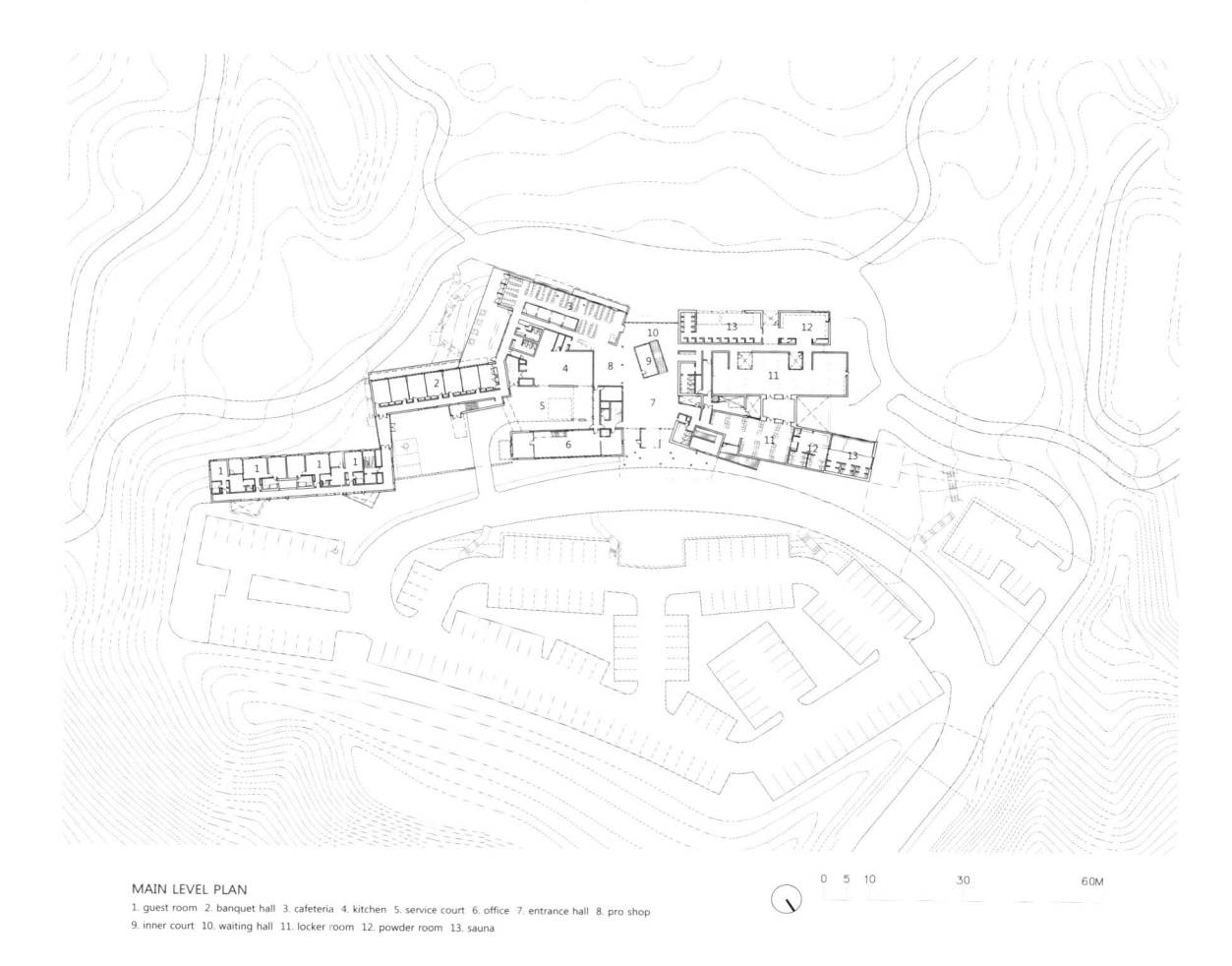

Country Club House "360° Earth, Water, Flowers, and Wind"

MAIN LEVEL PLAN
1. guest room 2. banquet hall 3. cafeteria 4. kitchen 5. service court 6. office 7. entrance hall 8. pro shop
9. inner court 10. waiting hall 11. locker room 12. powder room 13. sauna

0 5 10   30   60M

Country Club House "360° Earth, Water, Flowers, and Wind"

ELEVATION

ELEVATION 0 2 10 20 30M

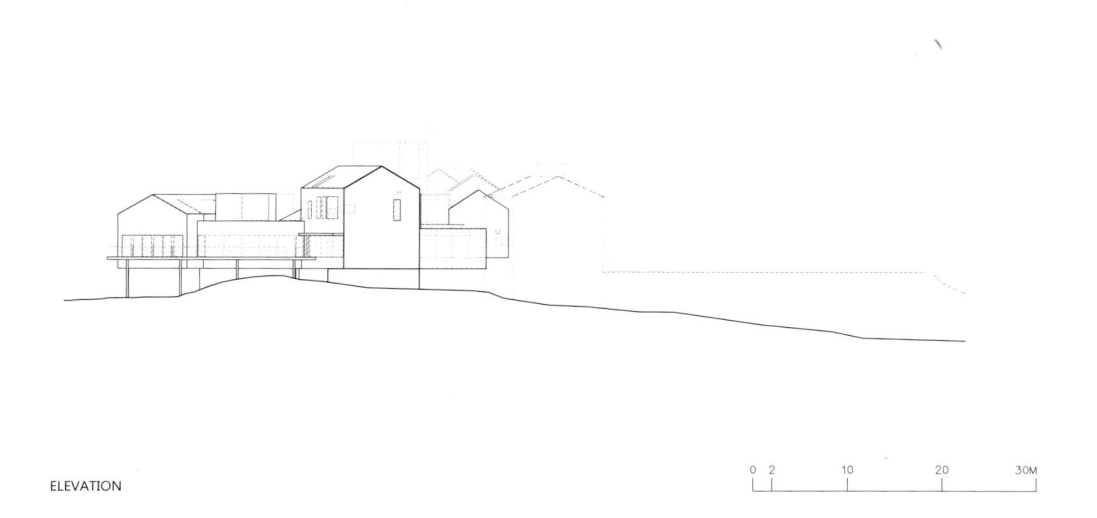

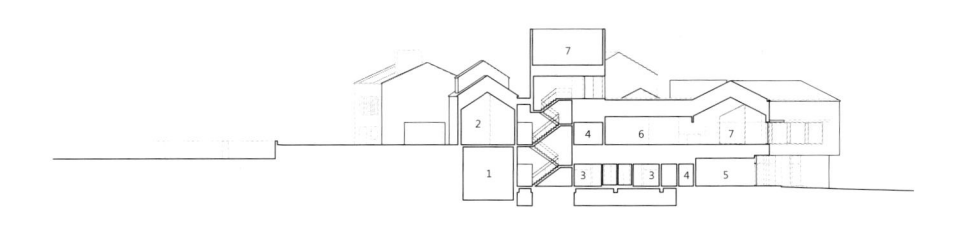

LONGITUDINAL SECTION
1. machine room 2. meeting room 3. toilet 4. storage 5. lounge 6. pro shop 7. cafeteria

Traditional Buddhism Center of Jogye Order

SITE PLAN
1. accommodation building 2. education center 3. guest house 4. field / parking

Traditional Buddhism Center of Jogye Order

ACCOMODATION BUILDING GROUND LEVEL PLAN
1. accommodation 2. inner garden 3. outdoor courtyard

EDUCATION CENTER GROUND LEVEL PLAN
1. lecture hall 2. conference room 3. multi-purpose hall 4. control room 5. reception 6. office

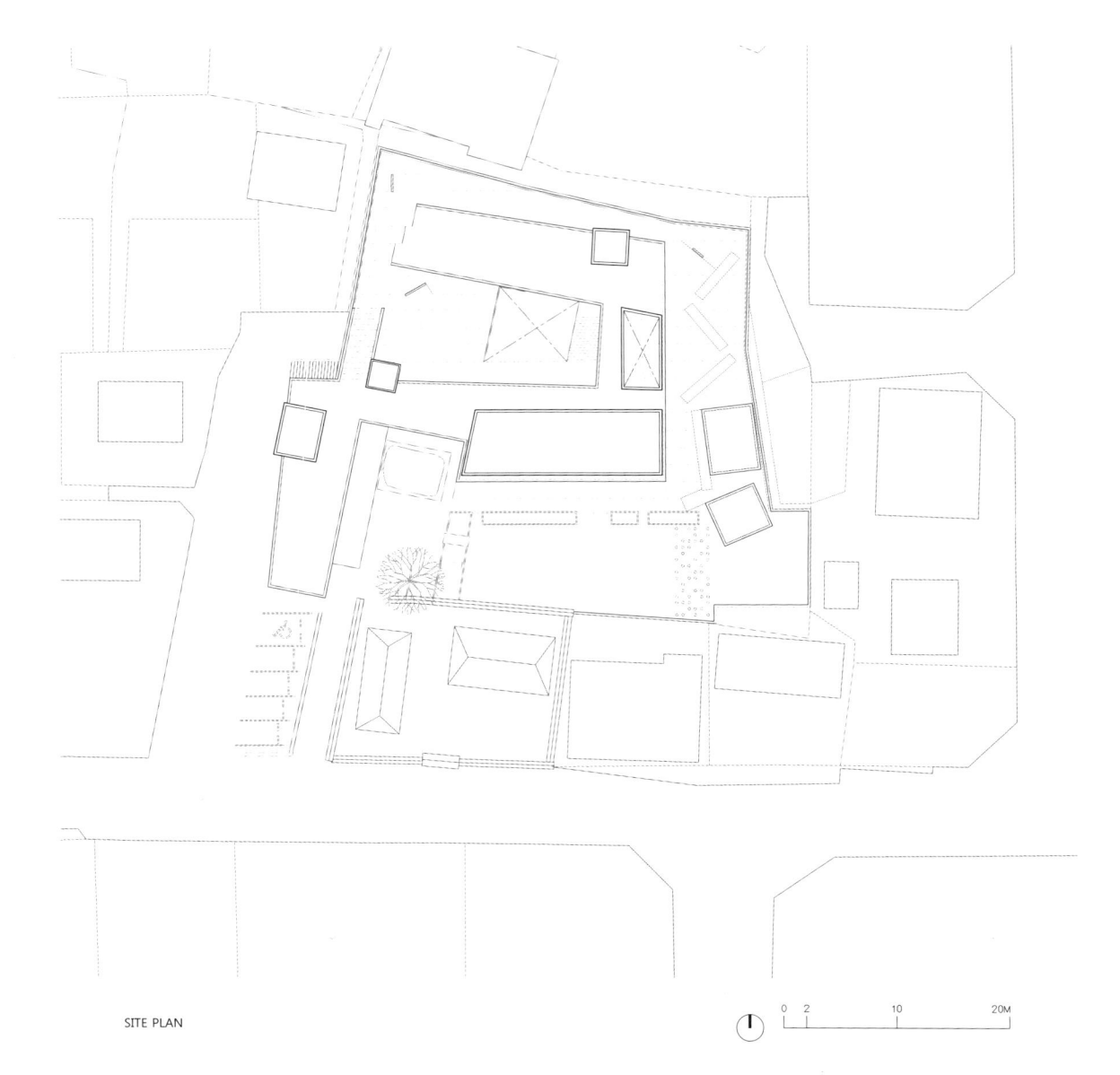

Shin Dongyeop Literary Museum

SITE PLAN

Shin Dongyeop Literary Museum

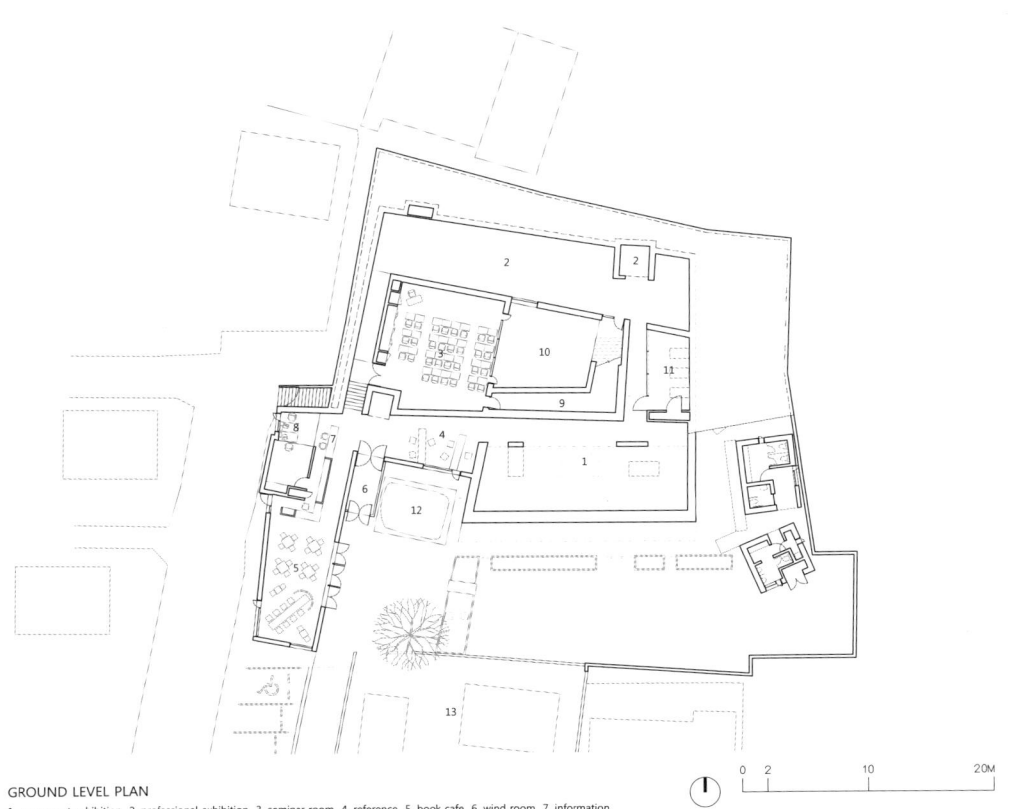

GROUND LEVEL PLAN
1. permanent exhibition 2. professional exhibition 3. seminar room 4. reference 5. book cafe 6. wind room 7. information
8. laboratory 9. storage 10. courtyard 11. supply room 12. BaekJe pit dwelling ruin 13. Shin Dong Yeop's birthplace

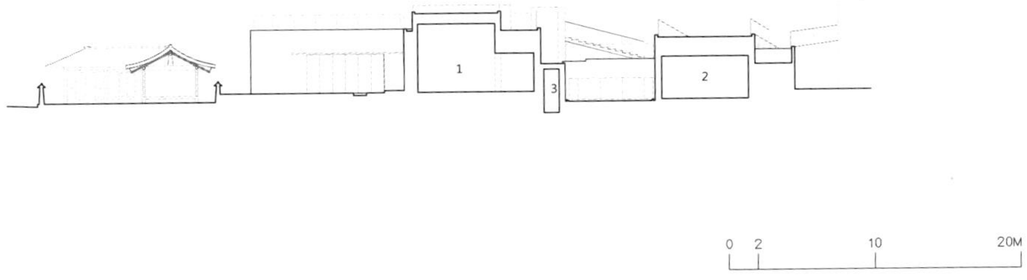

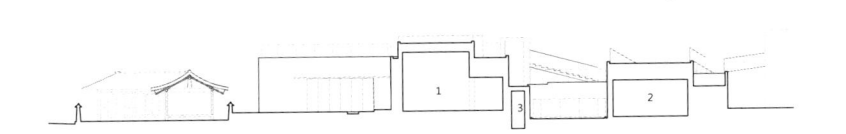

SECTION
1. permanent exhibition 2. professional exhibition 3. storage

240 Vanke Residential Culture Center

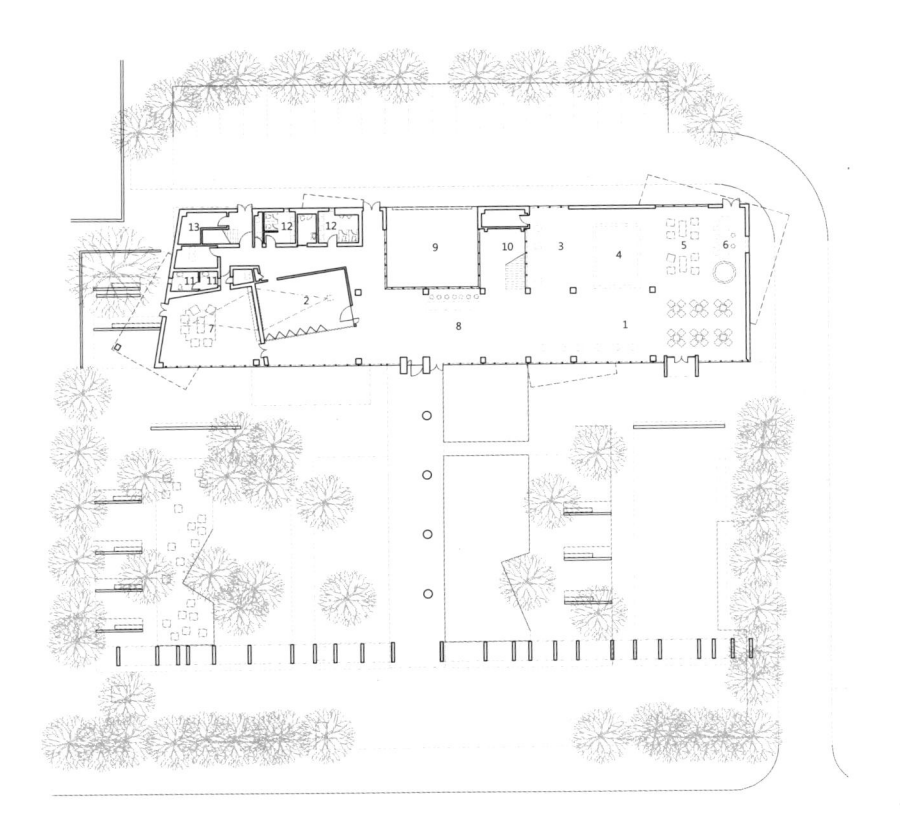

GROUND LEVEL PLAN
1. Vanke introduction & project exhibition 2. Pindu masterplan exhibition 3. unit model 4. masterplan model
5. consultation area 6. bar 7. VIP room 8. information 9. courtyard 10. staircase 11. VIP restroom 12. restroom 13. storage

248 Humax Main Office Building "Humax Village"

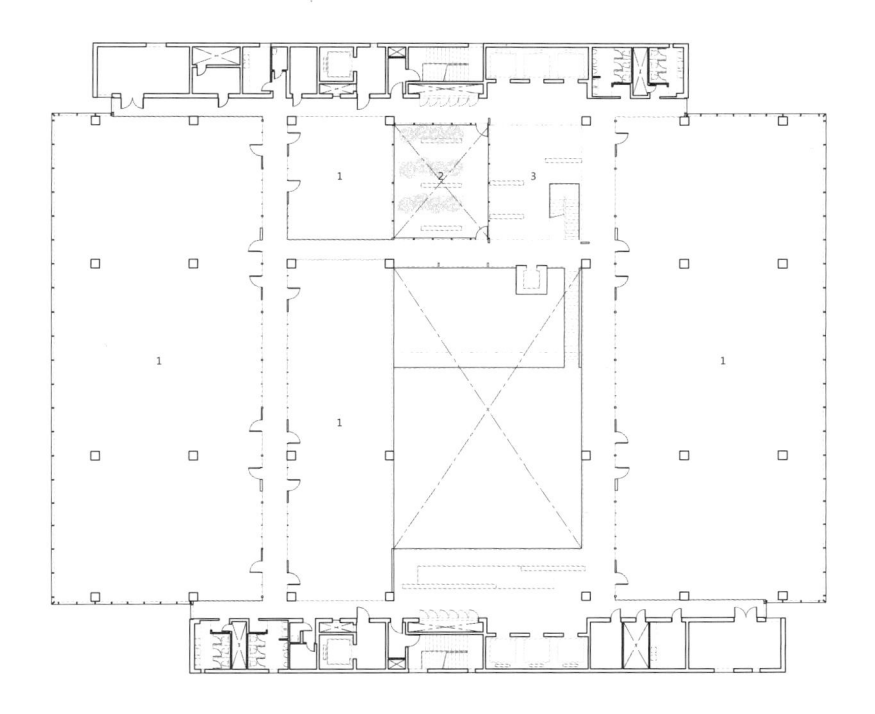

6th FLOOR PLAN
1. office 2. inner court 3. lounge

−422   Humax Main Office Building "Humax Village"

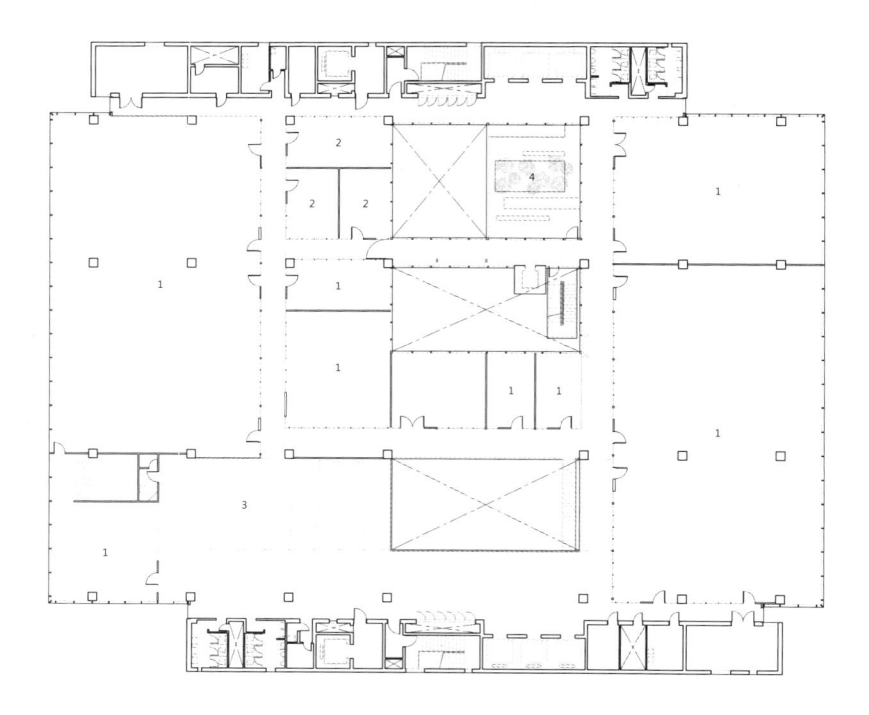

12th FLOOR PLAN
1. office 2. meeting room 3. lounge 4. inner court

Humax Main Office Building "Humax Village"

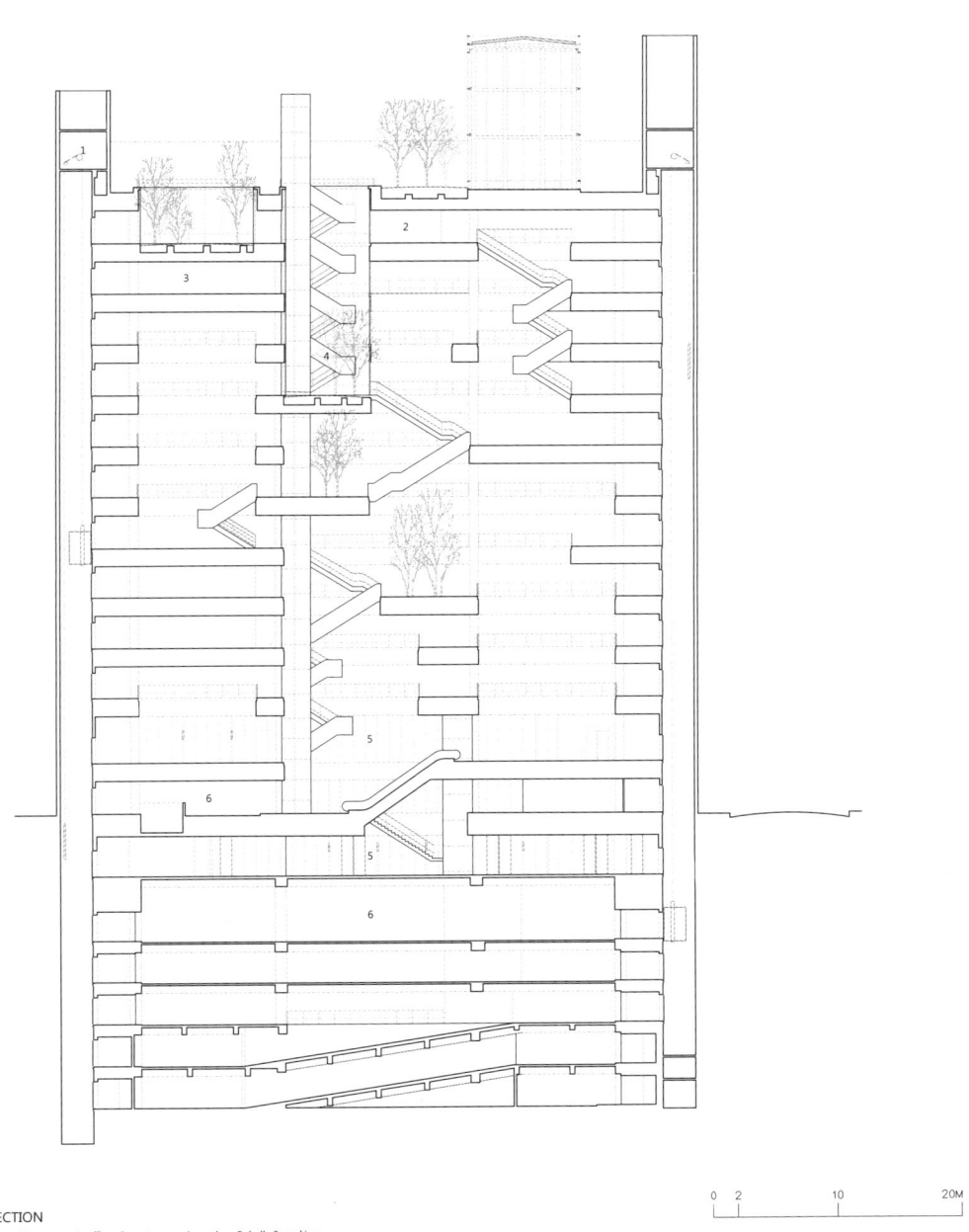

SECTION
1. machine room 2. office 3. rest room 4. garden 5. hall 6. parking

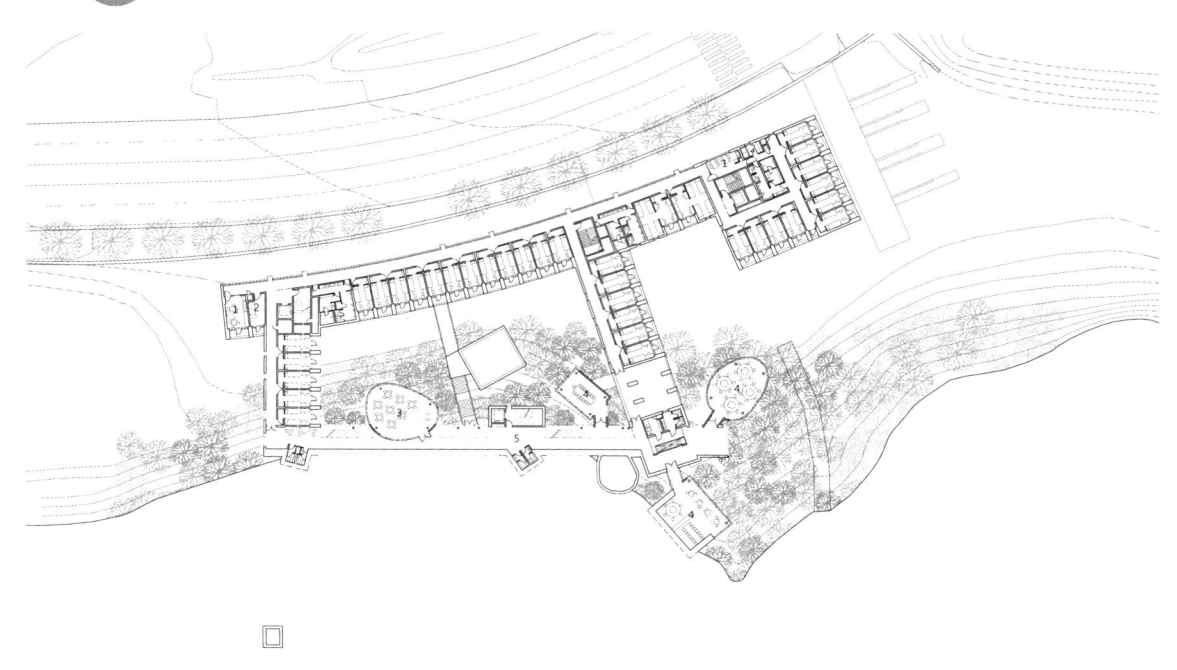

Hyehwa Residential College of Daejeon University

3rd FLOOR PLAN
1. common room 2. laundry room 3. study lounge 4. seminar room 5. hub lounge

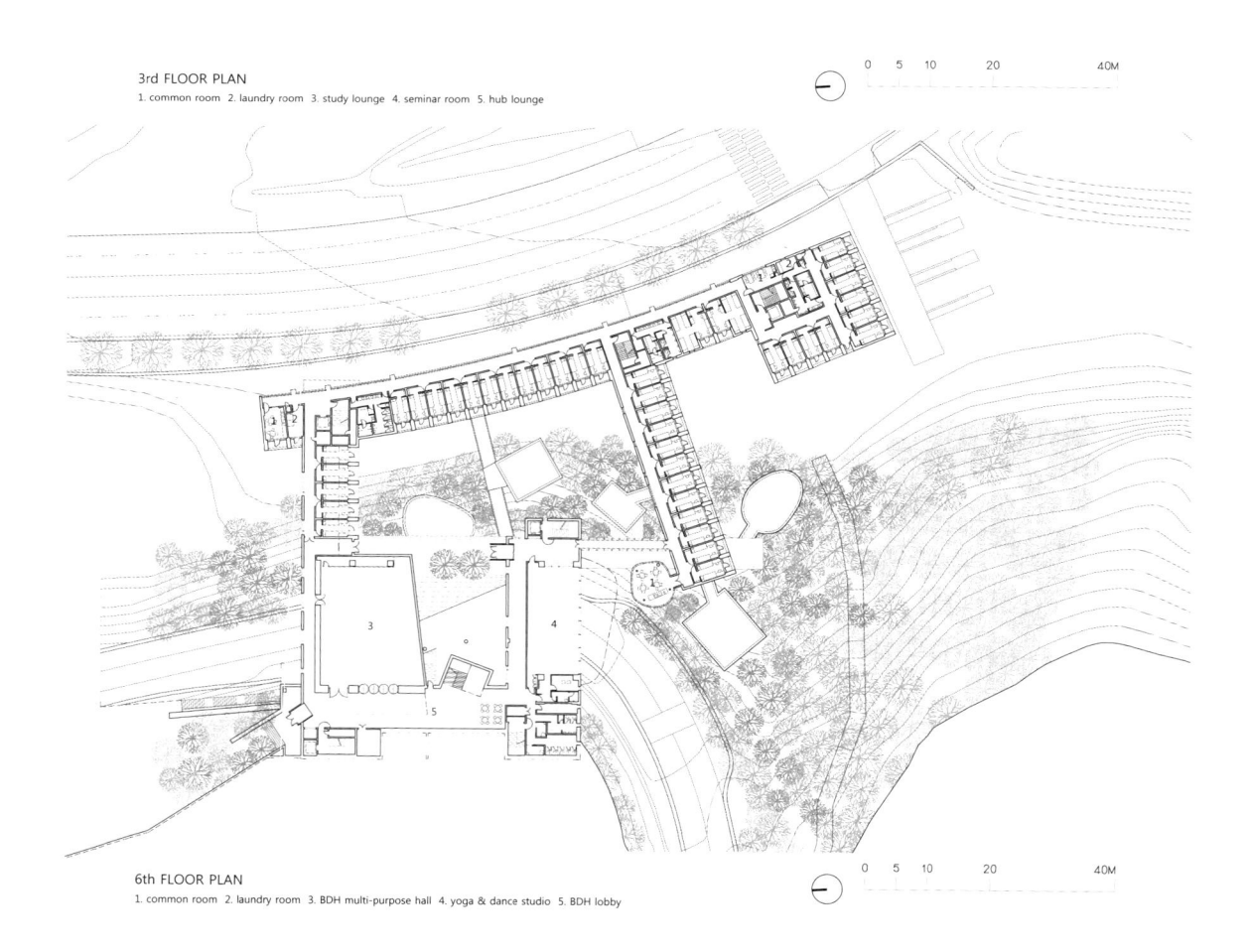

0 5 10 20 40M

6th FLOOR PLAN
1. common room 2. laundry room 3. BDH multi-purpose hall 4. yoga & dance studio 5. BDH lobby

0 5 10 20 40M

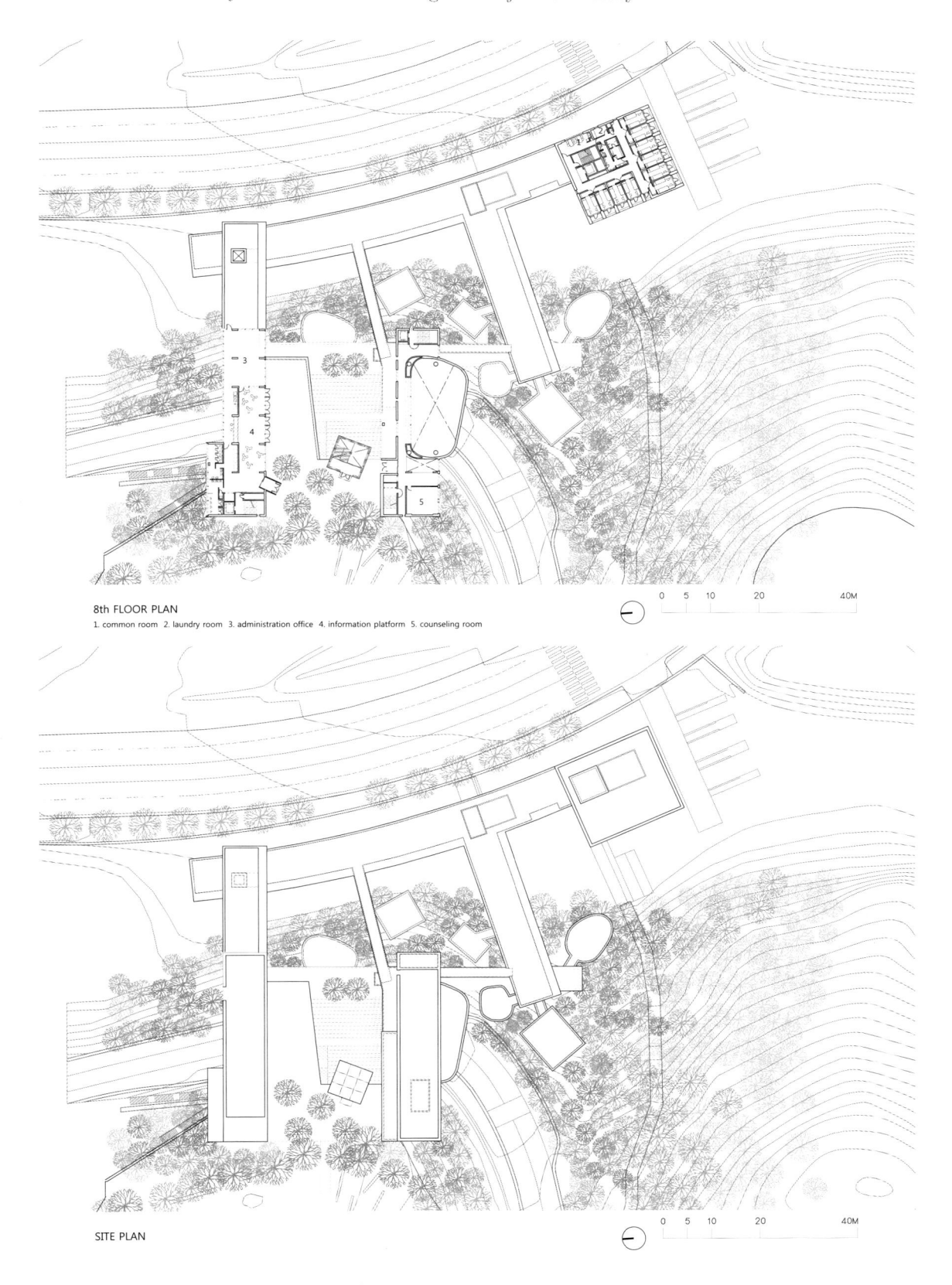

Hyehwa Residential College of Daejeon University

8th FLOOR PLAN
1. common room 2. laundry room 3. administration office 4. information platform 5. counseling room

SITE PLAN

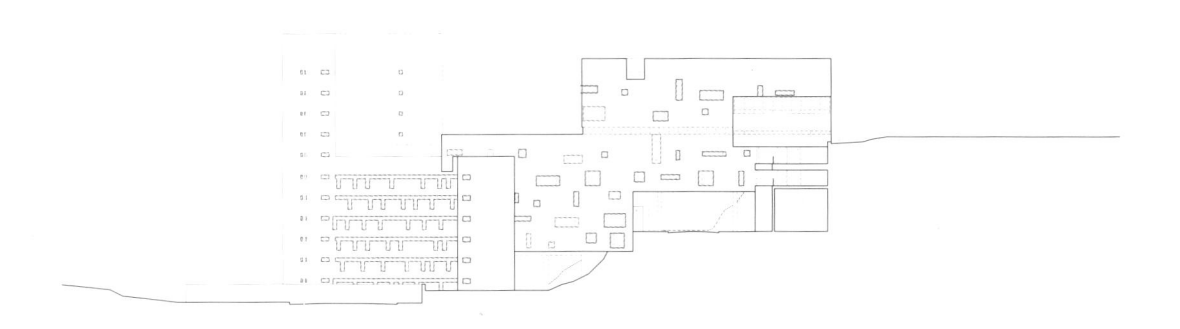

Hyehwa Residential College of Daejeon University

NORTH SIDE ELEVATION

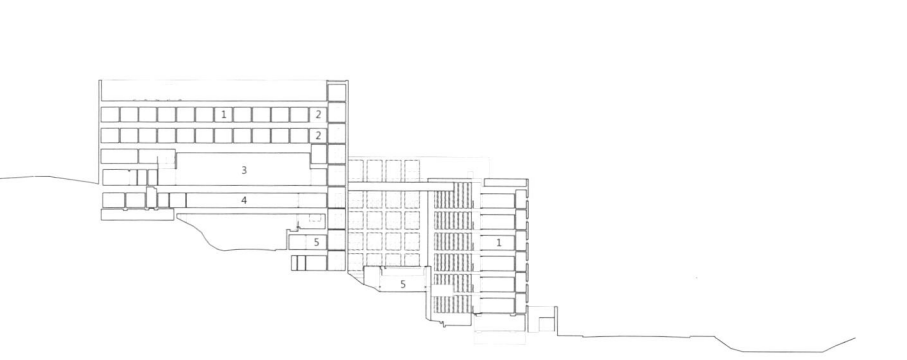

SECTION-1
1. dormitory 2. common room 3. fitness center 4. yoga & dance studio 5. seminar room

Hyehwa Residential College of Daejeon University

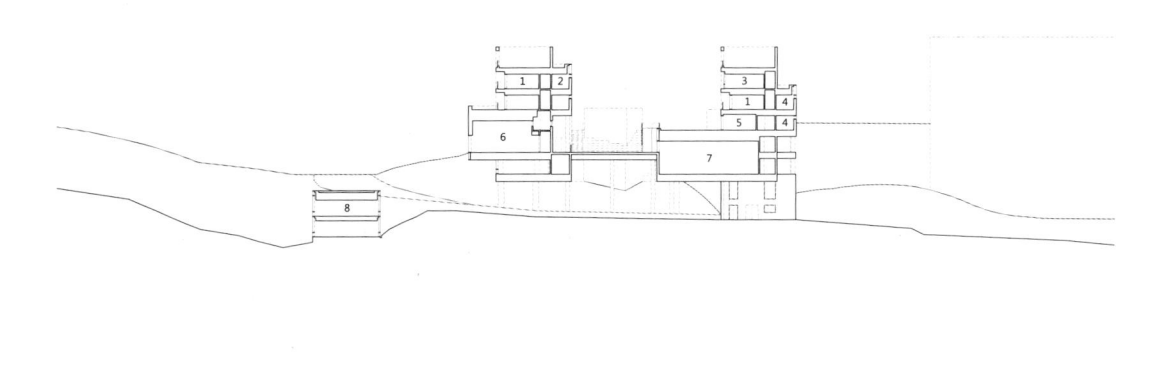

SECTION-2
1. dorm 2. shower 3. guest room 4. restroom 5. information platform 6. fitness center 7. BDH multi-purpose hall 8. seminar room

30th Anniversary Memorial Building of Daejeon University

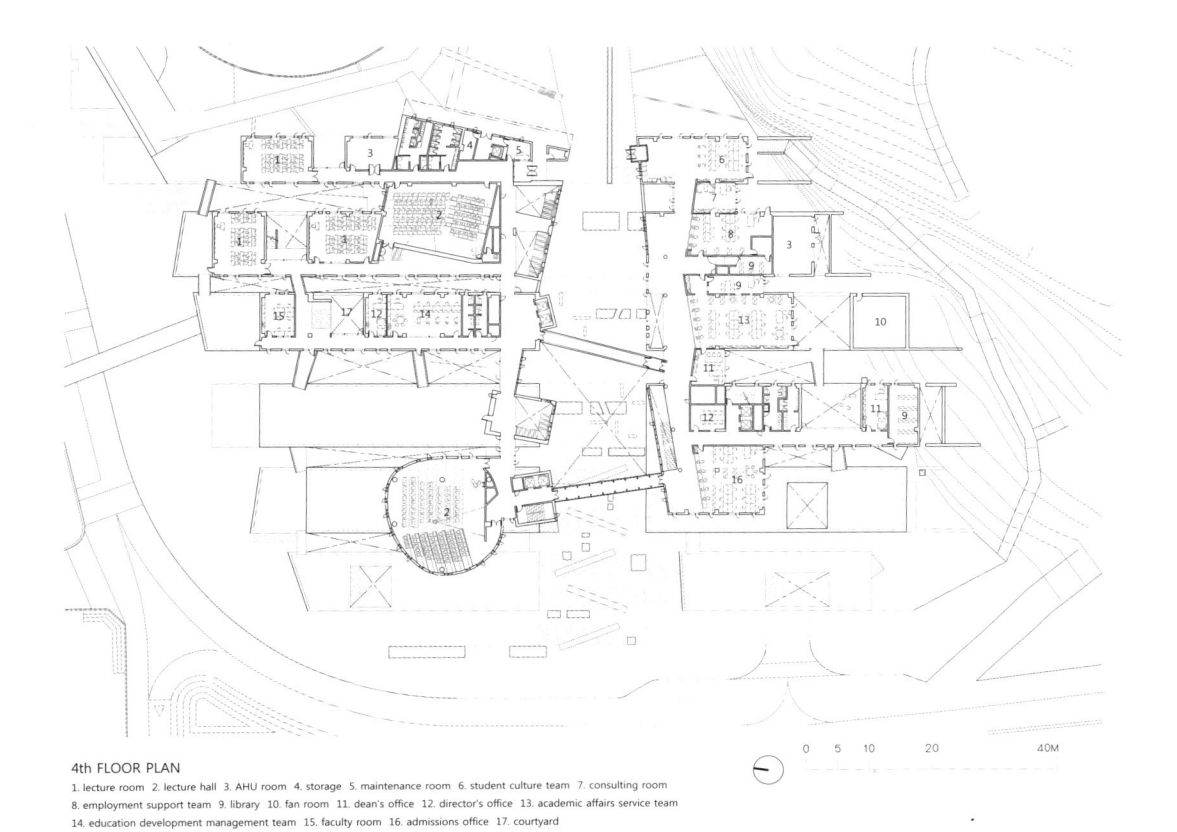

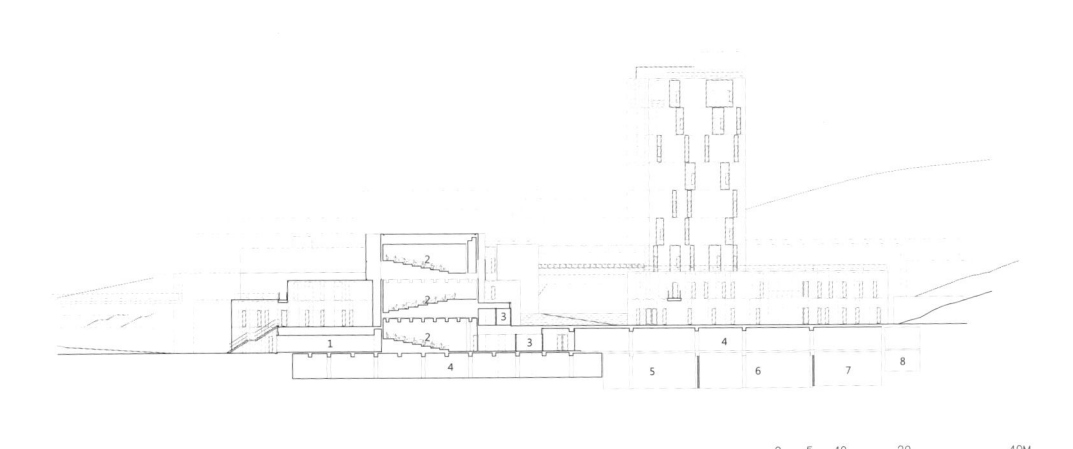

4th FLOOR PLAN
1. lecture room 2. lecture hall 3. AHU room 4. storage 5. maintenance room 6. student culture team 7. consulting room 8. employment support team 9. library 10. fan room 11. dean's office 12. director's office 13. academic affairs service team 14. education development management team 15. faculty room 16. admissions office 17. courtyard

SECTION
1. corridor 2. lecture hall 3. vestibule 4. parking 5. AHU room 6. machine room 7. transformer room 8. septic tank

Hyehwa Culture Center of Daejeon University

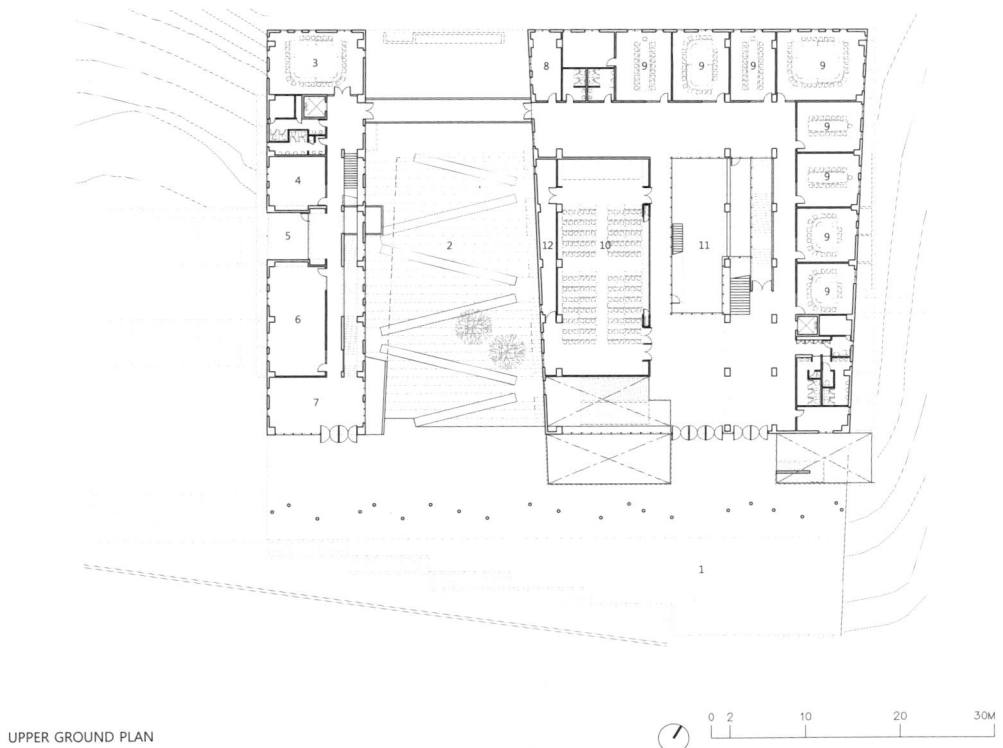

UPPER GROUND PLAN
1. entrance deck 2. open theater 3. meeting room 4. consulting room 5. terrace 6. office 7. entrance hall
8. waiting room 9. seminar room 10. conference & exhibition room 11. courtyard 12. storage

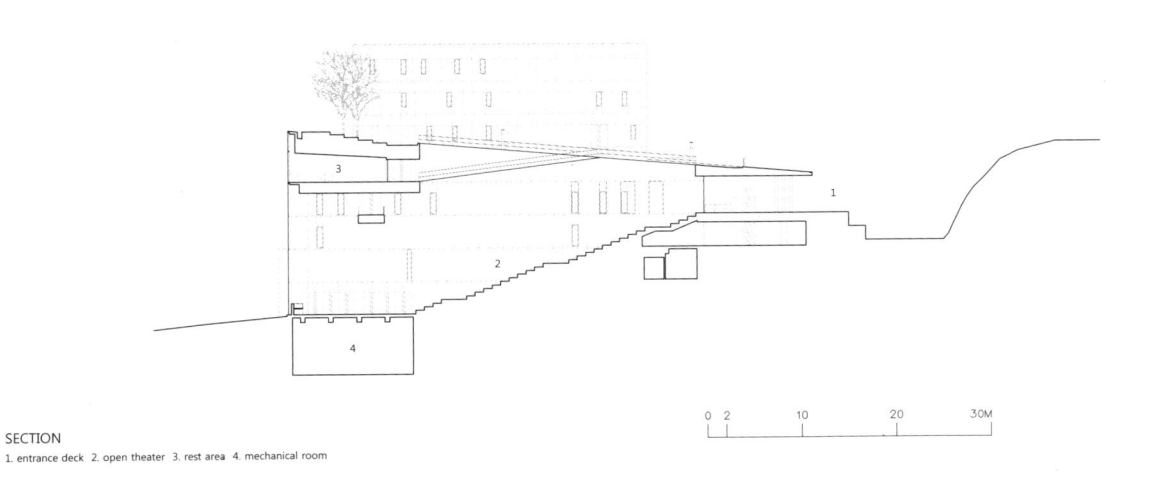

SECTION
1. entrance deck 2. open theater 3. rest area 4. mechanical room

Gudeok Presbyterian Church

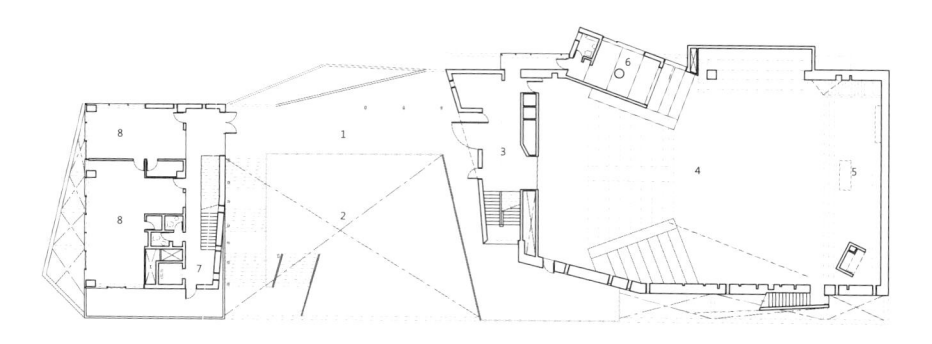

2F PLAN
1. entrance deck 2. entrance plaza 3. foyer 4. church 5. altar 6. children church 7. corridor 8. office

Gudeok Presbyterian Church

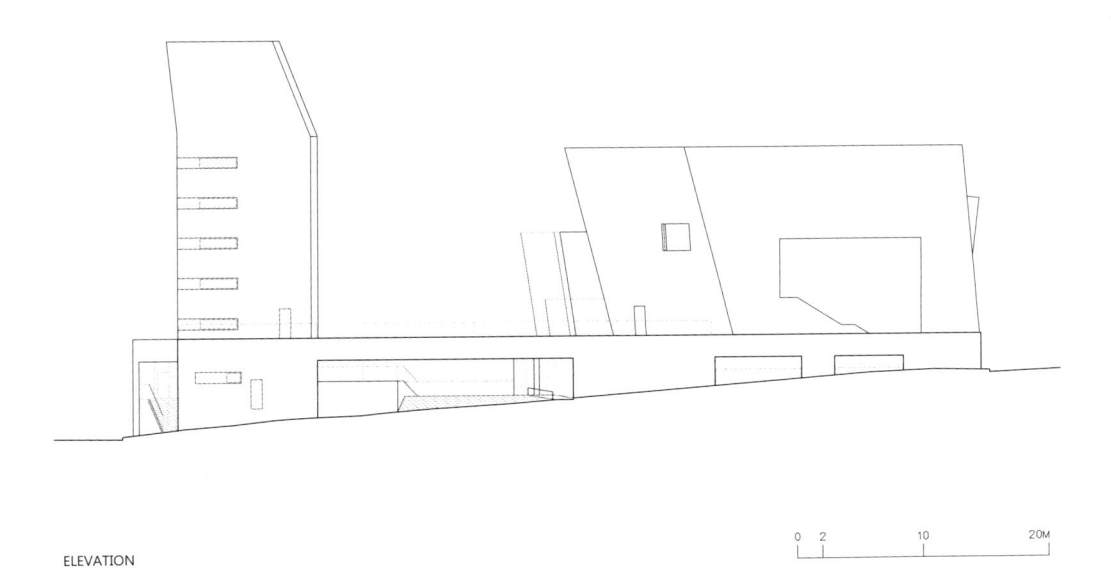

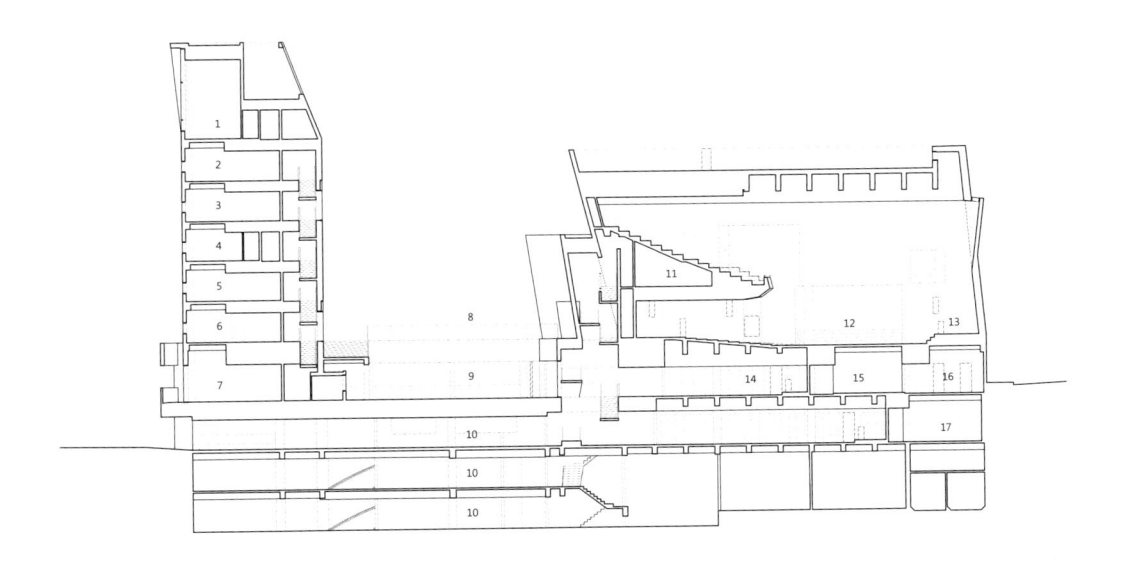

ELEVATION

SECTION
1. learning room 2. seminar room 3. office 4. seminar room 5. seminar room 6. office 7. book cafe 8. deck madang 9. entrance madang
10. parking lot 11. storage 12. church nave 13. altar 14. dining hall 15. chapel 16. lecture room 17. meeting room

288 Chaowai SOHO

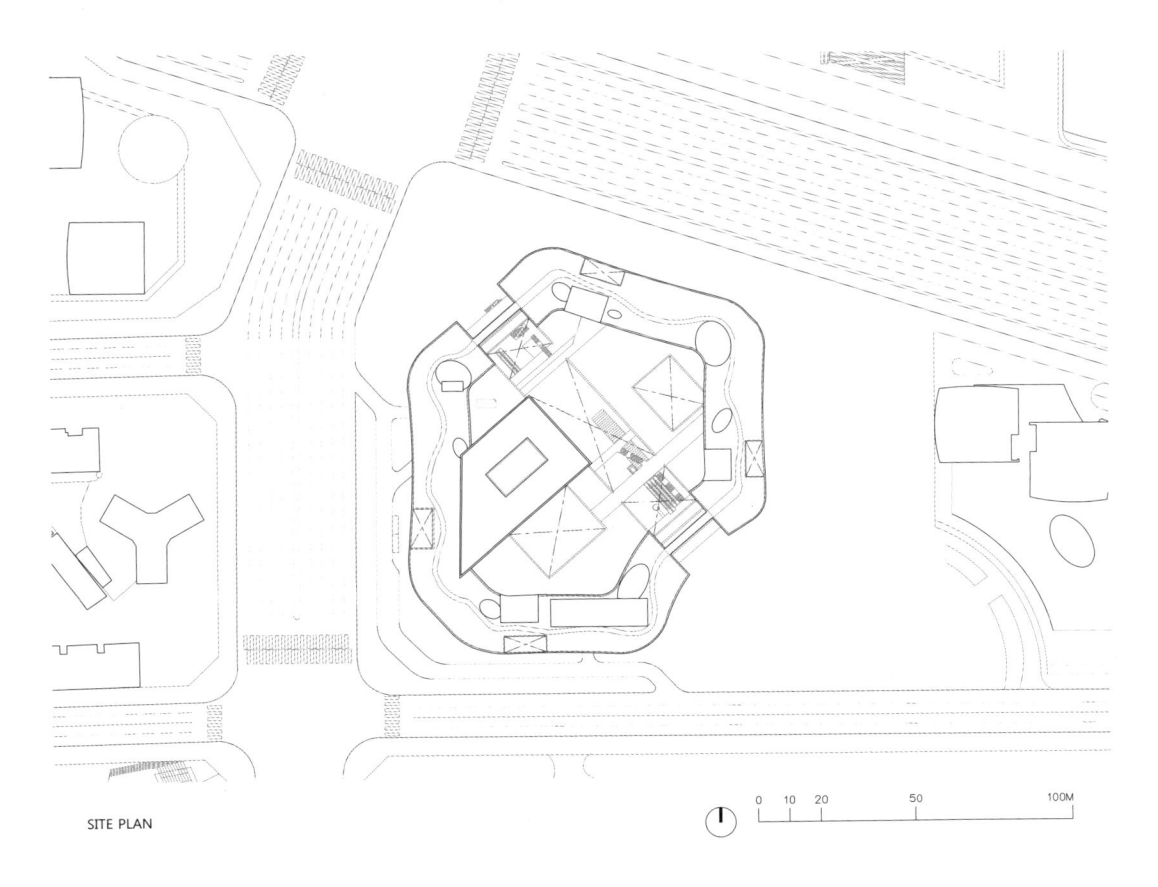

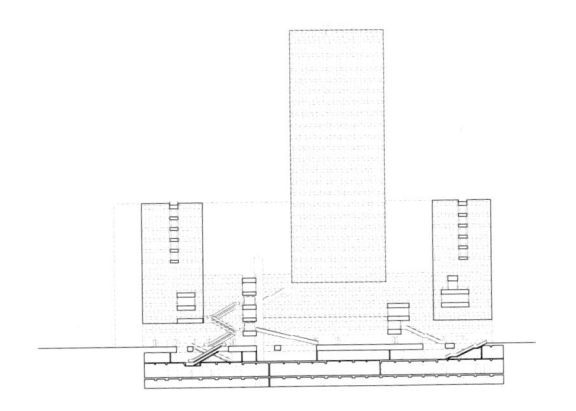

SITE PLAN

SECTION

Chaowai SOHO

GROUND FLOOR PLAN
commercial zone

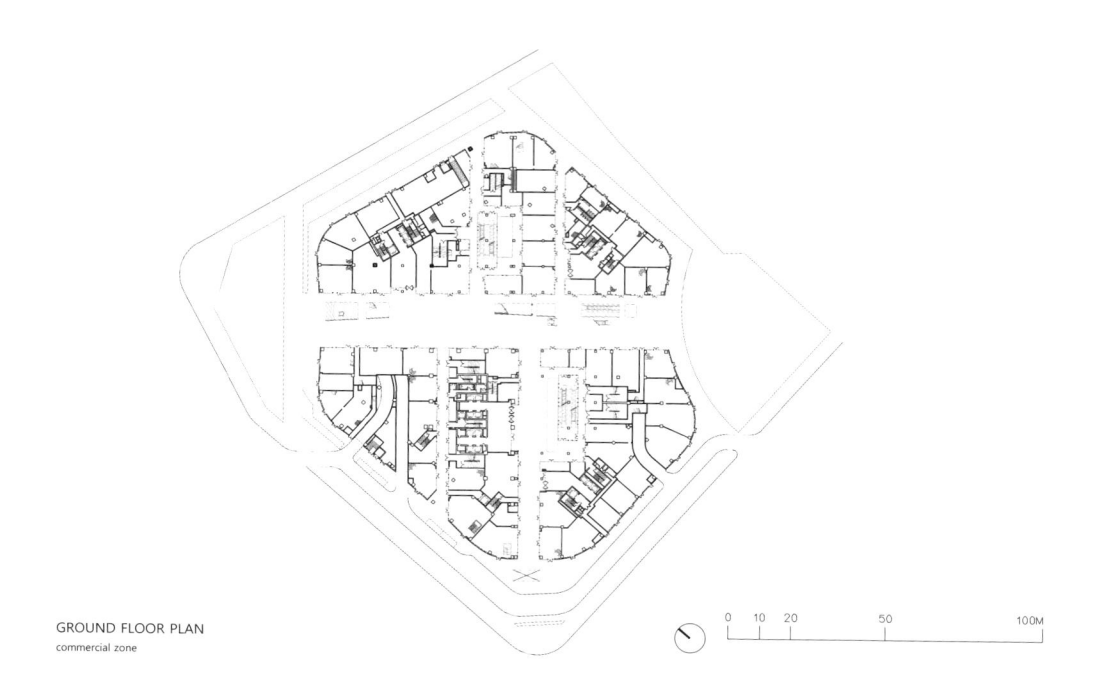

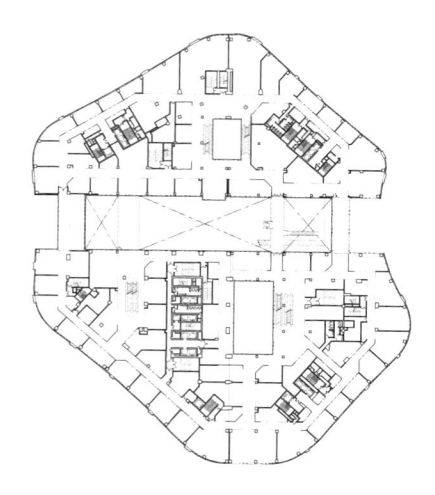

4th FLOOR PLAN
commercial zone

Chaowai SOHO

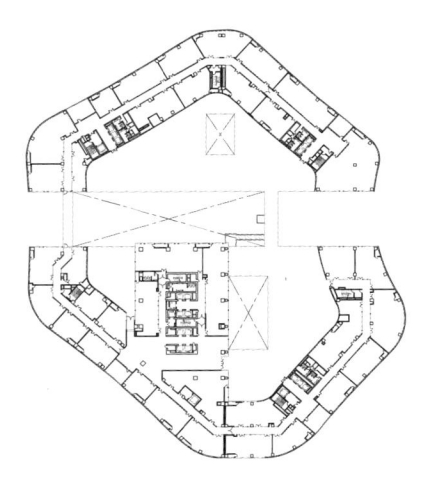

6th FLOOR PLAN
commercial zone

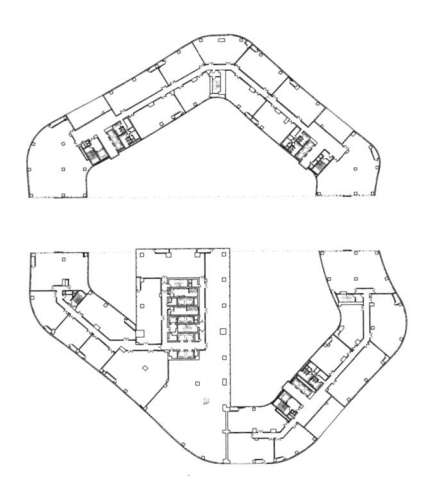

10th FLOOR PLAN
office zone

Boao Canal Village

DECK LEVEL PLAN

UPPER LEVER PLAN

ATTIC LEVEL PLAN

WATER FRONT TYPE-B PLAN

UPPER LEVEL PLAN

DECK LEVEL PLAN

FOREST FRONT TYPE-D PLAN

Boao Canal Village

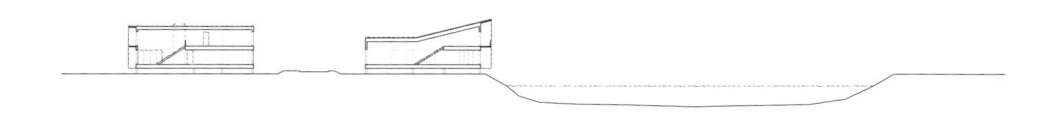

SECTION THROUGH HOUSES

0 5 10   20   40M

Commune by the Great Wall

MASTERPLAN of 1st phase Commune by the Great Wall
1. Seung H-sang 2. Gary Chang 3. Shigeru Ban 4. Cui Kai 5. Rocco Yim 6. Chien Hsueh-Yi 7. Antonio Ochoa 8. Kengo Kuma
9. Kanika R'Kul 10. Kai Ngee Tan 11. Nobuyaki Furuya 12. Yung Ho Chang

Commune by the Great Wall

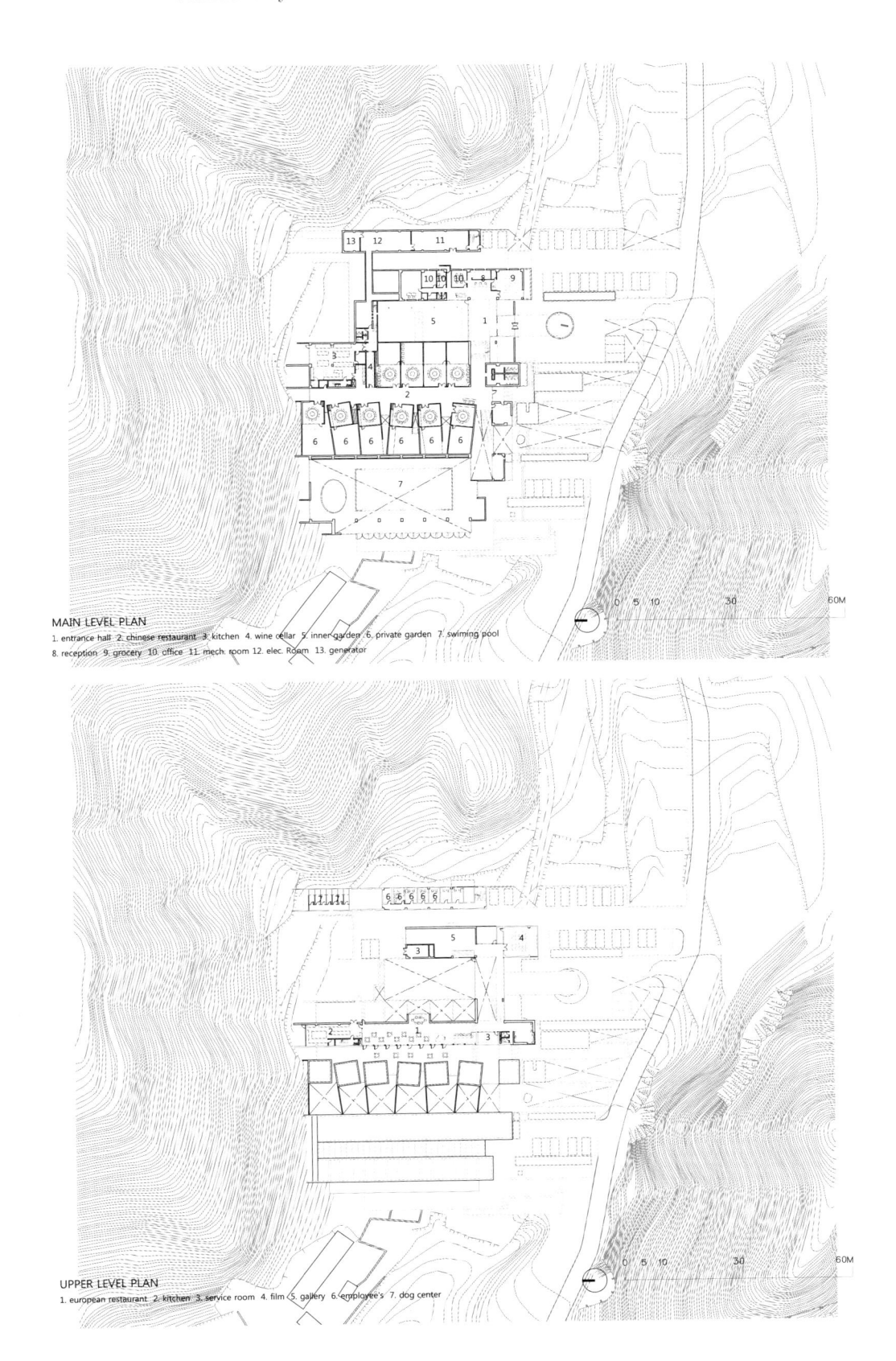

MAIN LEVEL PLAN
1. entrance hall 2. chinese restaurant 3. kitchen 4. wine cellar 5. inner garden 6. private garden 7. swimming pool
8. reception 9. grocery 10. office 11. mech. room 12. elec. Room 13. generator

UPPER LEVEL PLAN
1. european restaurant 2. kitchen 3. service room 4. film 5. gallery 6. employee's 7. dog center

—442 → 312 Lock Museum

SITE PLAN

0 5 10 20 40M

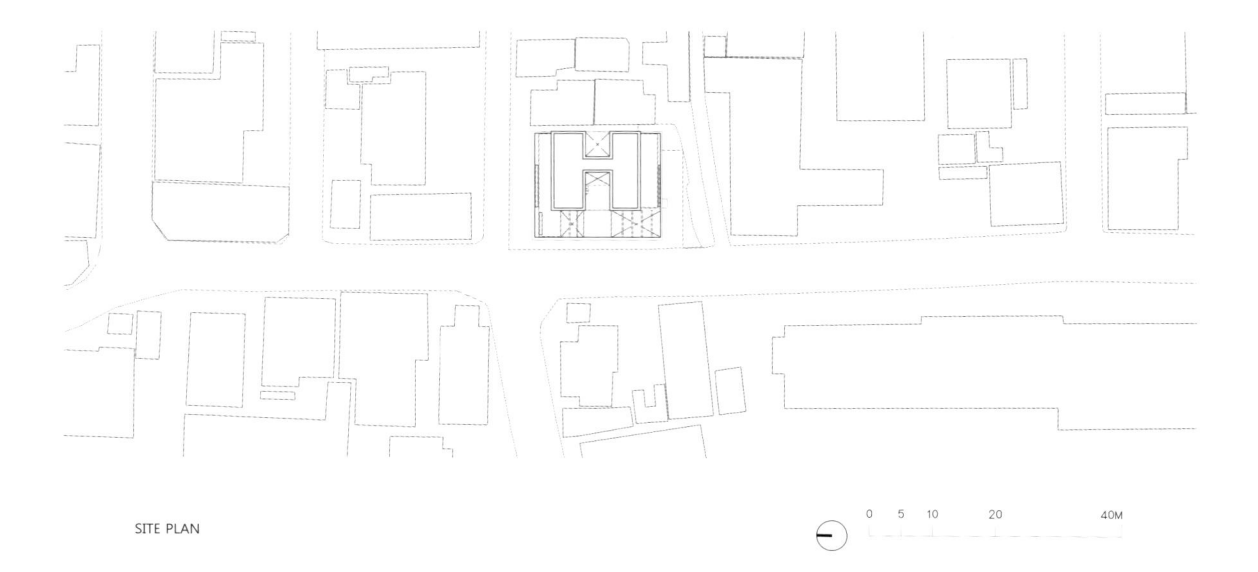

Lock Museum

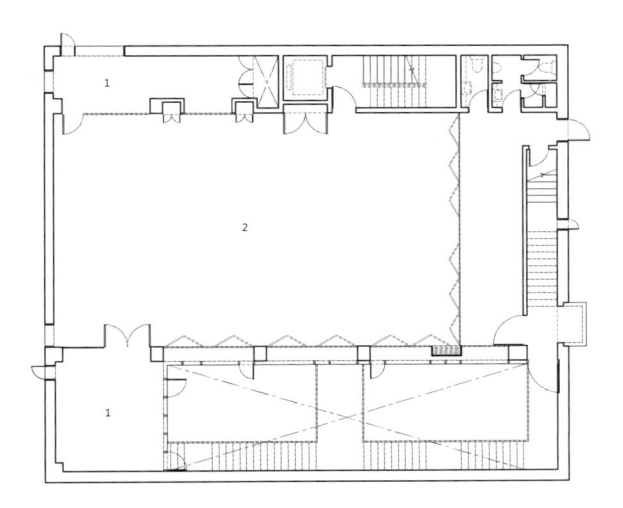

3F PLAN
1. preparation room 2. multi-purpose hall

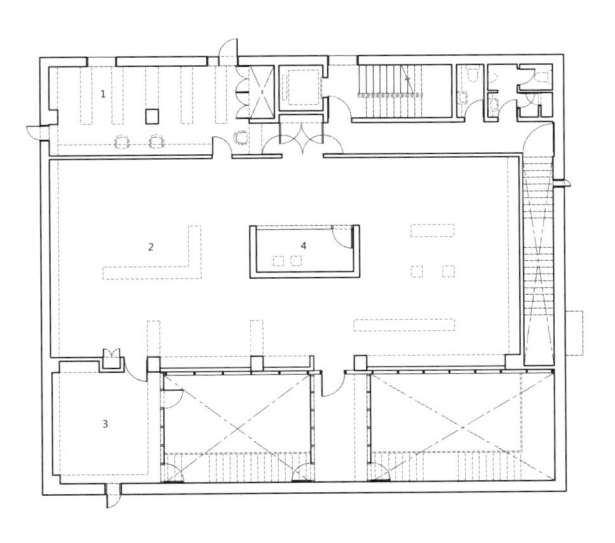

4F PLAN
1. archive room 2. museum 3. special exhibition room 4. inner court

Lock Museum

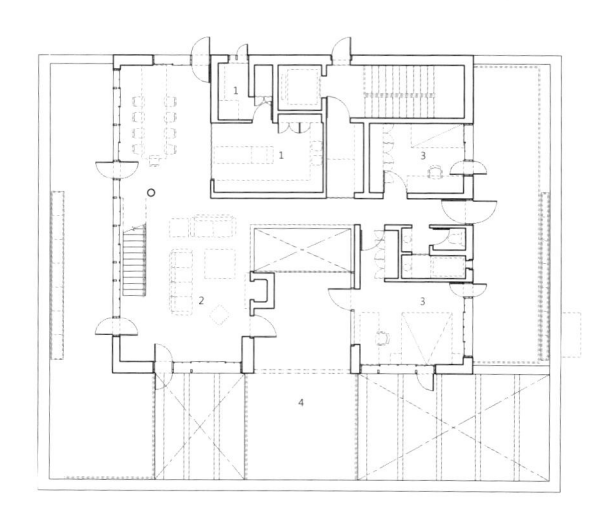

5F PLAN
1. kitchen 2. living room 3. room 4. outdoor garden

Lock Museum

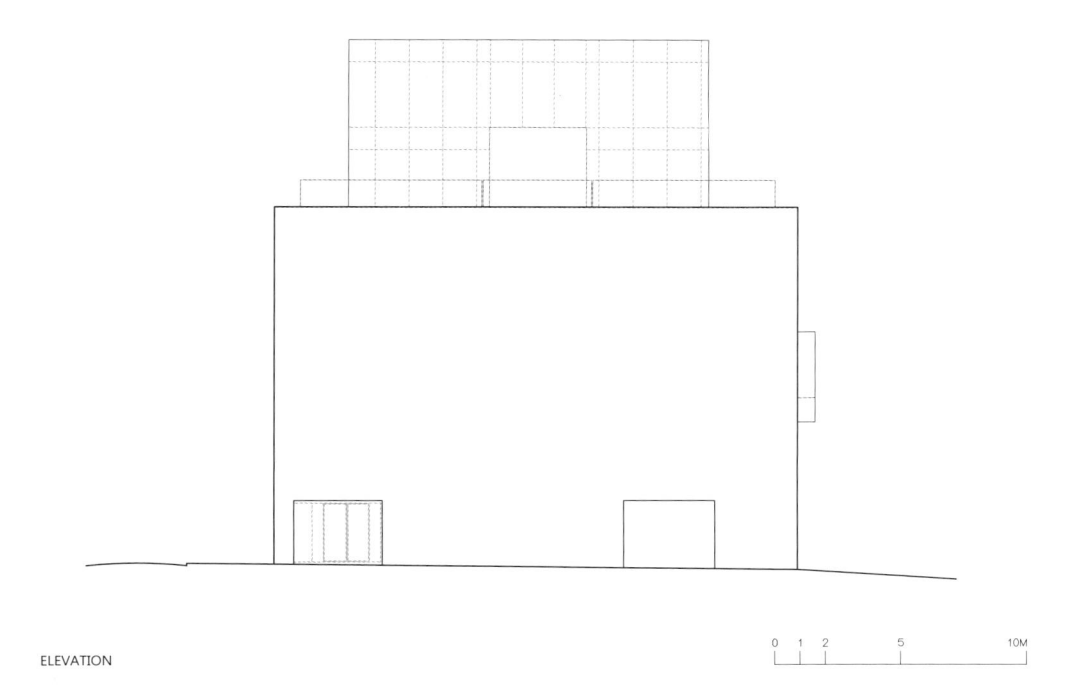

ELEVATION

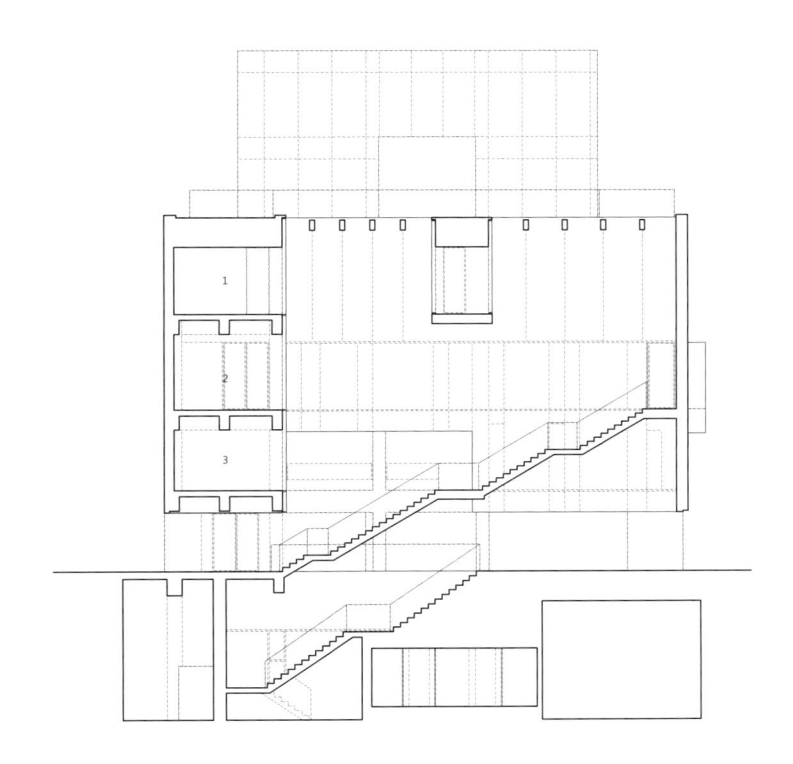

SECTION
1. special exhibition room 2. preparation room 3. shop

→ 320 Welcomm City

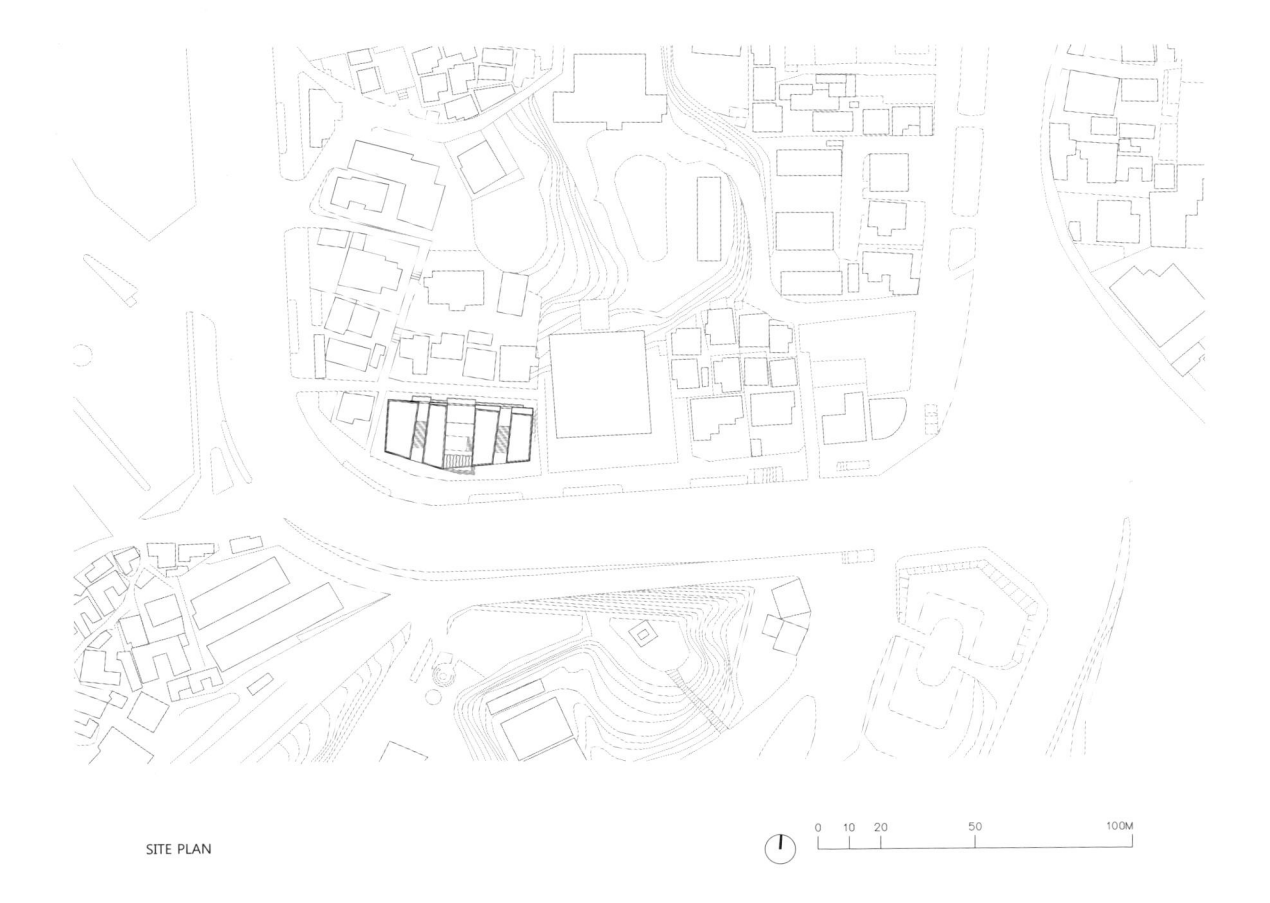

SITE PLAN

0 10 20   50   100M

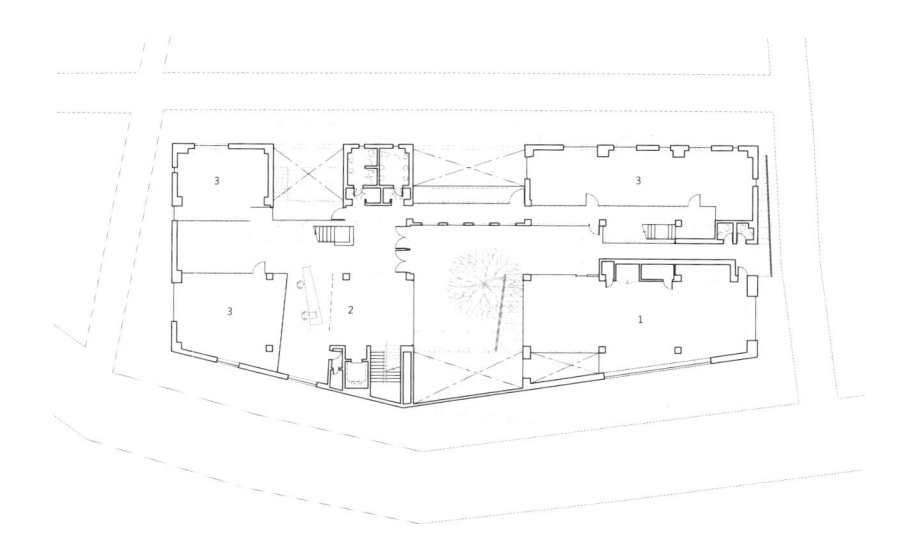

LOWER LEVEL PLAN
1. restaurant 2. reception 3. office

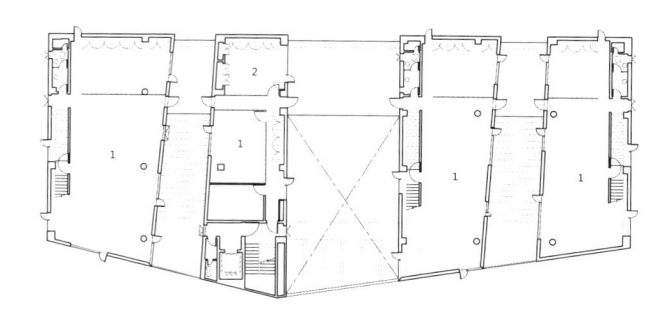

UPPER LEVEL PLAN
1. office 2. meeting room

Welcomm City

ELEVATION

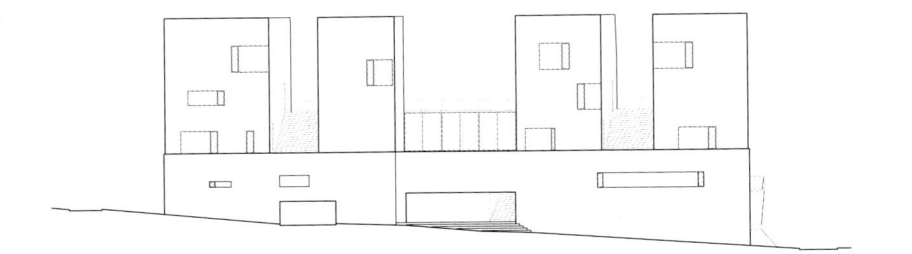

0 2 10 20M

Paju Book City

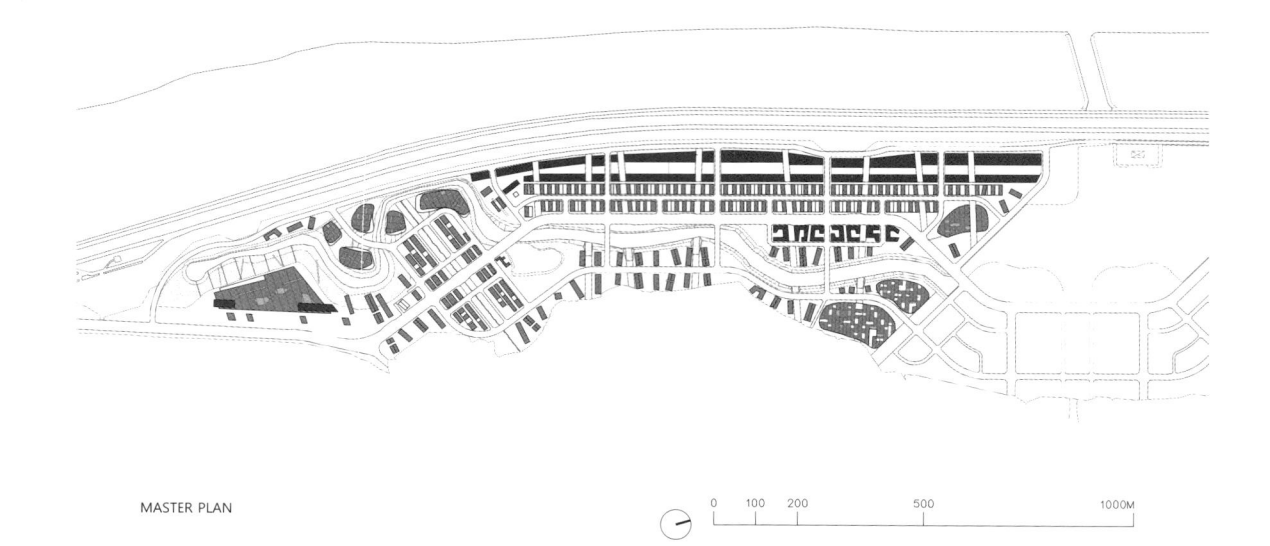

MASTER PLAN

→ 336 Kyobo Book City

SITE PLAN

0 5 10　30　60M

ELEVATION

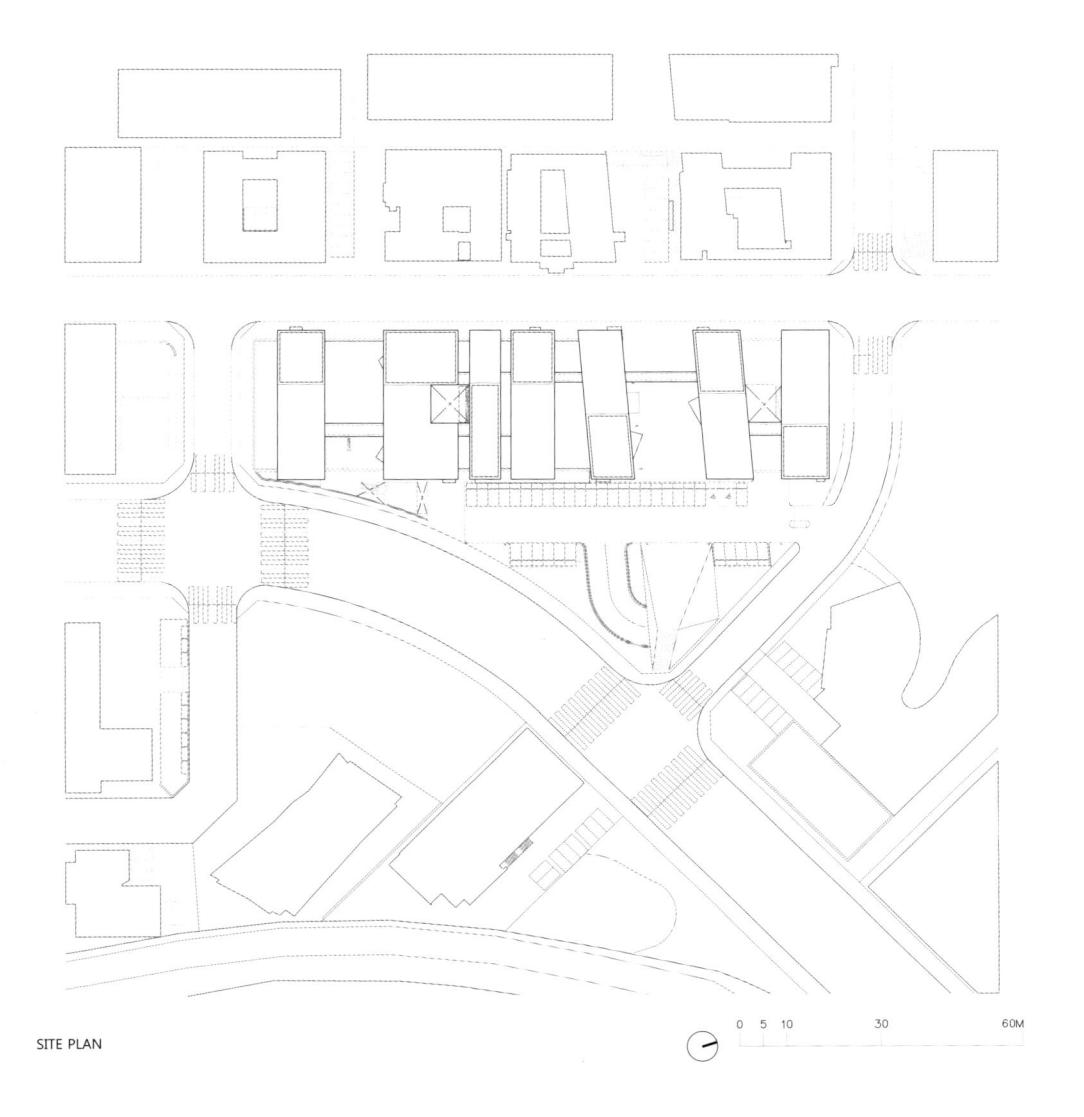

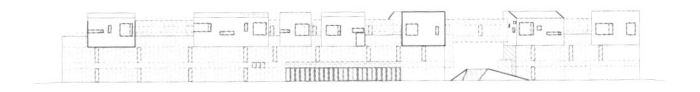

0 5 10　30　60M

Residence 'Soowoojae'

MAIN LEVEL PLAN
1. living Room 2. bedroom 3. toilet 4. courtyard 5. kitchen 6. dining 7. pavilion

UPPER LEVEL PLAN
1. bedroom 2. toilet 3. family room 4. dress room 5. study room 6. pavilion

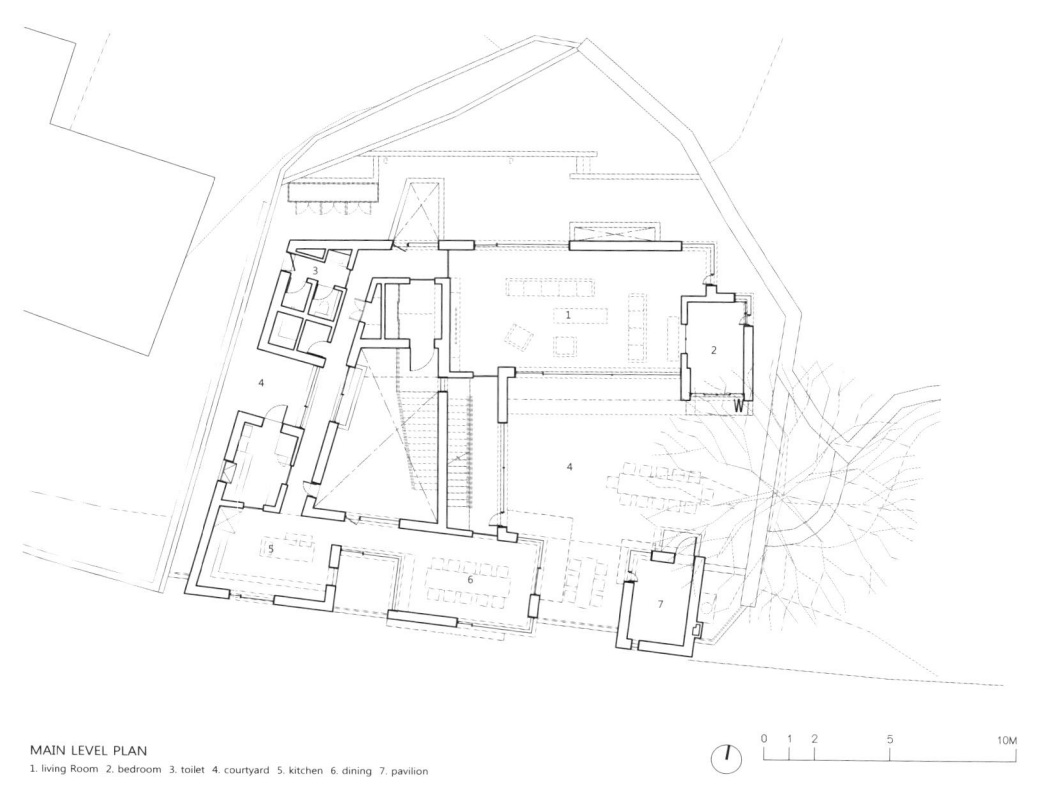

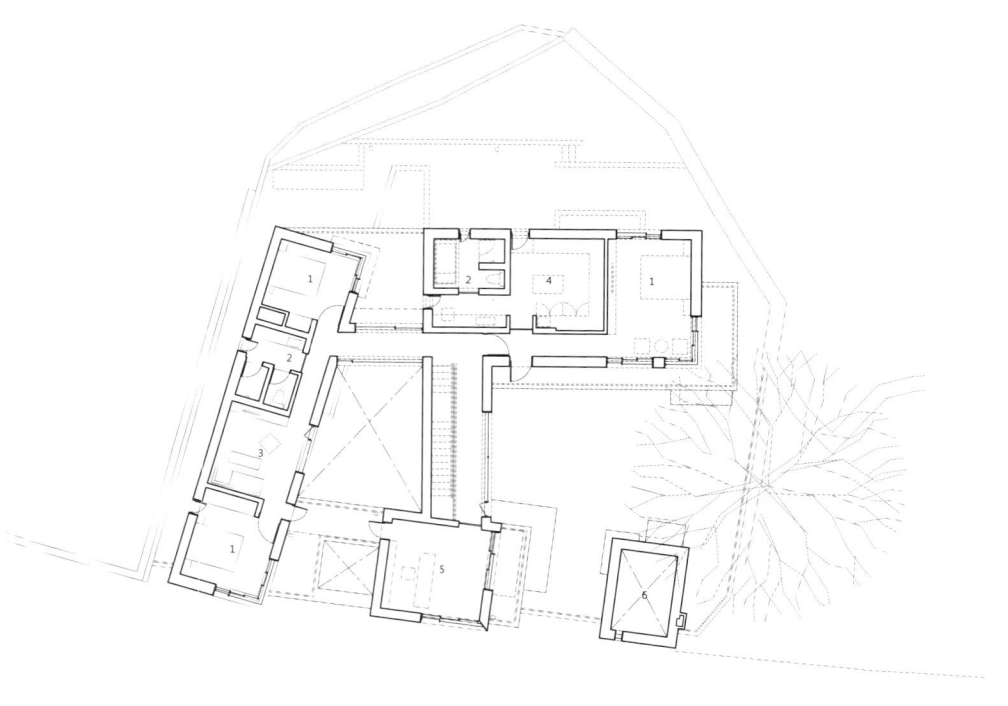

Residence 'Soowoojae'

ELEVATION

SECTION

— 454 → 352 Reed House

SITE PLAN

0 5 10   20   40M

Reed House

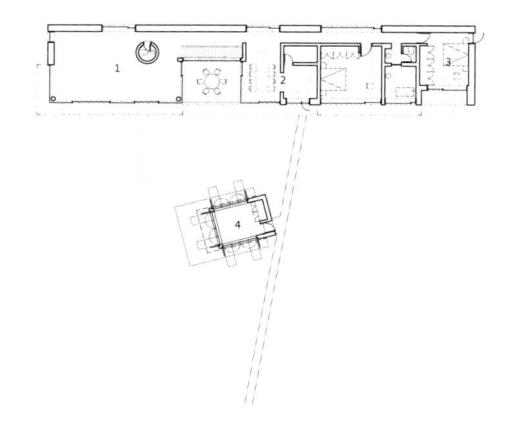

MAIN LEVEL PLAN
1. living room 2. dining room 3. bedroom 4. tea room

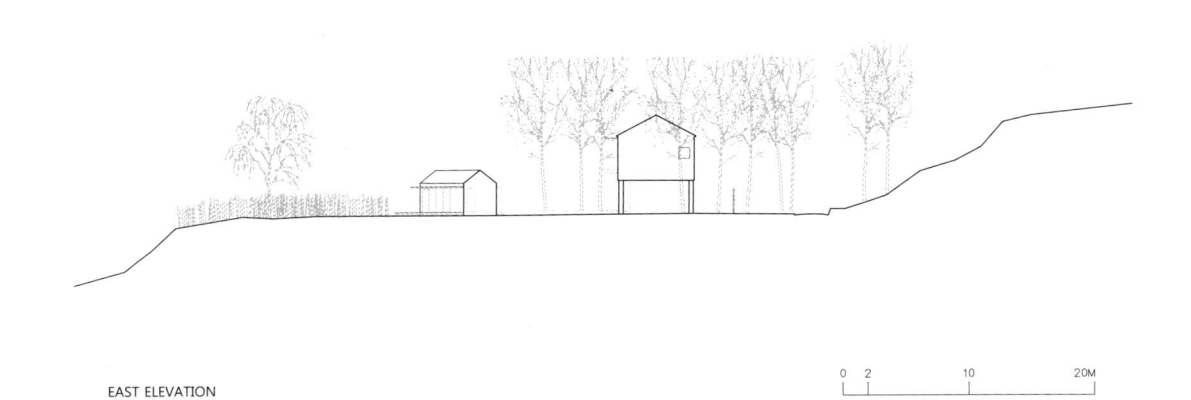

EAST ELEVATION

→ 360 Teochon House

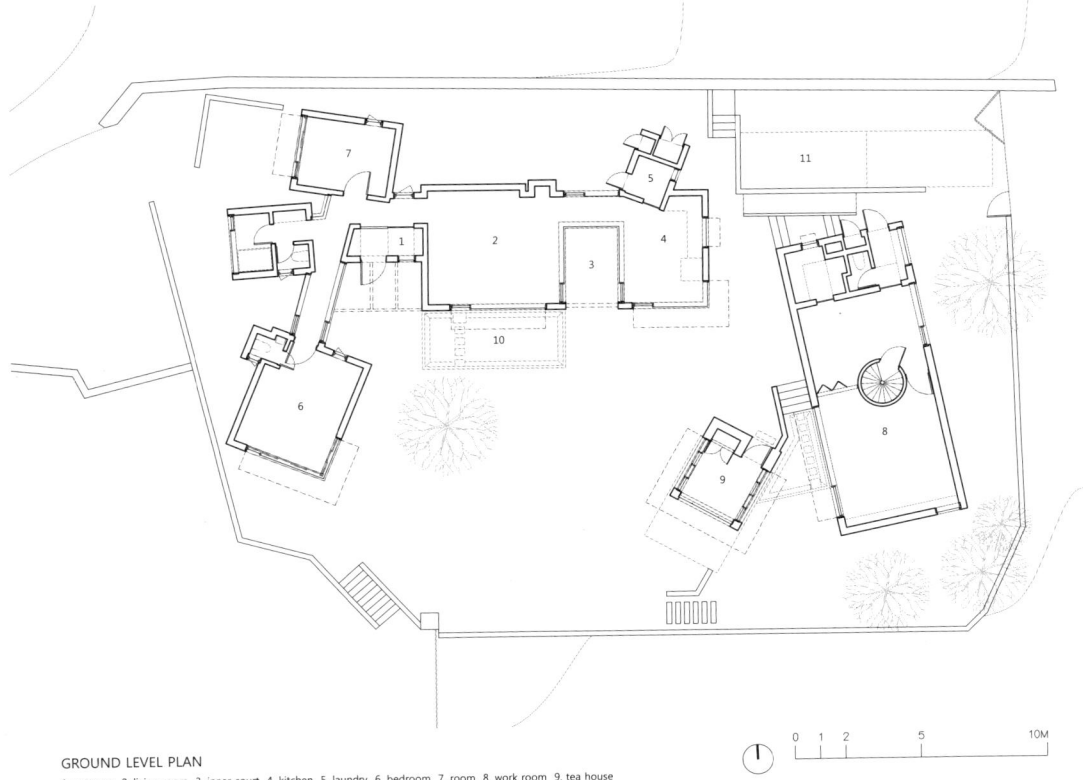

GROUND LEVEL PLAN
1. entrance 2. living room 3. inner court 4. kitchen 5. laundry 6. bedroom 7. room 8. work room 9. tea house
10. pond 11. parking

368 Residence 'Subaekdang'

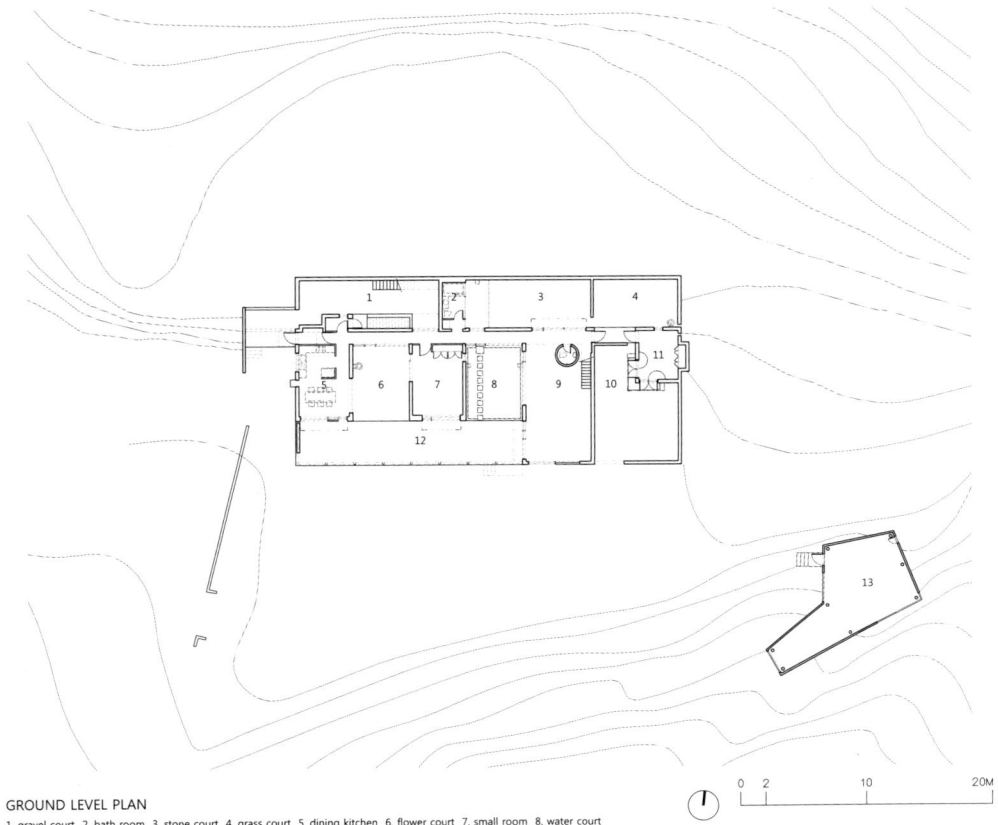

GROUND LEVEL PLAN
1. gravel court 2. bath room 3. stone court 4. grass court 5. dining kitchen 6. flower court 7. small room 8. water court 9. big room 10. soil court 11. special room 12. wood deck 13. workshop

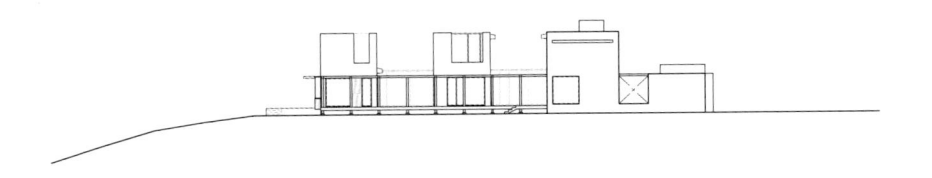

SOUTH ELEVATION

TECHNICAL DESCRIPTIONS

Muhakro Methodist Church

Completed in 2018
Location: Gyeongsan, Gyeongsangbuk-do, Korea
Site area: 178 m²
Bldg. area: 69 m²
Gross FL area: 69 m²
Lighting design: NEWLITE
Structural engineer: The Naeun Structural Eng.
Mechanical engineer: DE-Tech.
Electrical engineer: WooLim E&C
Contractor: Design M

Bugye Arboretum "Sayuwon"

2012~
Location: Gunwi, Gyeongsangbuk-do, Korea
Site area: 310,082m²
Landscape architect: Jung Young-sun(Seoahn Total Landscape), Kawagishi
Contractor: TC green, YoungJo, KUKDONG, EONE

Hyeonam

Completed in 2013
Bldg. area: 125m²
Gross FL area: 137m²
Landscape architect: Seoahn Total Landscape
Lighting design: bitzro
Structural engineer: I'ST Structure Solution
Mechanical engineer: SeAh Eng.
Electrical engineer: WooLim E&C
Contractor: KUKDONG

Sadam

Completed in 2016
Bldg. area: 137m²
Gross FL area: 128m²
Landscape architect: Seoahn Total Landscape
Lighting design: bitzro
Structural engineer: The Naeun Structural Eng.
Mechanical engineer: DE-Tech.
Electrical engineer: WooLim E&C
Contractor: EONE

Myeongjeong

Completed in 2019
Bldg. area: 150m²
Gross FL area: 150m²
Lighting design: NEWLITE
Structural engineer: The Naeun Structural Eng.
Mechanical engineer: DE-Tech.
Electrical engineer: WooLim E&C
Contractor: YoungJo Construction Co.

Wasa

Completed in 2019
Bldg. area: 130m^2
Gross FL area: 130m^2
Lighting design: NEWLITE
Structural engineer: The Naeun Structural Eng.
Contractor: YoungJo Construction Co.

Cheomdan

Completed in 2019
Bldg. area: 35m^2
Gross FL area: 35m^2
Lighting design: NEWLITE
Structural engineer: The Naeun Structural Eng.
Electrical engineer: WooLim E&C
Contractor: YoungJo Construction Co.

Myungrye Sacred Hill

Completed in 2018
Location: Miryang, Gyeongsangnam-do, Korea
Site area: 2404m^2
Bldg. area: 690m^2
Gross FL area: 695m^2
Landscape architect: Seoahn Total Landscape
Lighting design: NEWLITE
Structural engineer: The Naeun Structural Eng.
Mechanical engineer: DE-Tech.
Electrical engineer: WooLim E&C
Contractor: YoungJo Construction Co.

Graveyard of President Roh Muhyun

Completed in 2010
Location: Gimhae, Gyeongsangnam-do, Korea
Site area: 3,505m^2

Public Cemetery Park "A Thousand Winds"

Completed in 2016
Location: Gwangju, Gyeonggi-do, Korea
Site area: 18,860m^2
Landscape architect: Seoahn Total Landscape + Live Scape
Lighting design: NEWLITE
Structural engineer: The Naeun Structural Eng.
Mechanical engineer: Rainbow Scape
Electrical engineer: WooLim E&C
Contractor: HEESANG Construction

Korea DMZ Peace and Life Valley

Completed in 2009
Location: Inje, Gangwon-do, Korea
Site area: 124,210m^2
Bldg. area: 3,275m^2
Gross FL area: 3,304m^2
Mechanical engineer: HanIl MEC
Electrical engineer: WooLim E&C

Residence "Moheon"

Completed in 2010
Location: Daegu, Korea
Site area: 357m^2
Bldg. area: 120m^2
Gross FL area: 164m^2
Mechanical engineer: SeAh Eng.
Electrical engineer: WooLim E&C
Contractor: Samhyup Construction Co.

Korean Medicine Hospital of Daejeon University in Seoul

Completed in 2019
Location: Seoul, Korea
Site area: 1,038m^2
Bldg. area: 606m^2
Gross FL area: 8,156m^2
Lighting design: NEWLITE
Structural engineer: The Naeun Structural Eng.
Mechanical engineer: DE-Tech.
Electrical engineer: DaeKyong E&C
Contractor: BoMI Engineering & Construction

Myung Films Complex

Completed in 2015
Location: Paju, Gyeonggi-do, Korea
Site area: 3,294m^2
Bldg. area: 1,644m^2
Gross FL area: 7,929m^2
Landscape architect: Seoahn Total Landscape
Lighting design: bitzro
Structural engineer: Noori Structural Eng.
Mechanical engineer: SeAh Eng.
Electrical engineer: WooLim E&C
Contractor: Samhyup Construction Co.

Design Vita Office Building

Completed in 2016
Location: Paju, Gyeonggi-do, Korea
Site Area: 667m^2
Bldg. Area: 276m^2
Gross FL Area: 921m^2
Lighting design: NEWLITE
Structural engineer: The Naeun Structural Eng.
Mechanical engineer : DE-Tech.
Electrical engineer: WooLim E&C
Contractor: SI

Chusa Memorial Museum

Completed in 2010
Location: Seogwipo, Jeju-do, Korea
Site area: 5,245m^2
Bldg. area: 236m^2
Gross FL area: 1,191m^2
Landscape architect: Seoahn Total Landscape
Structural engineer: Seoul architects & Structural Eng.
Mechanical engineer: SeAh Eng.
Electrical engineer: WooLim E&C

Country Club House "360° Earth, Water, Flowers, and Wind"

Completed in 2013
Location: Yeoju, Gyeonggi-do, Korea
Site area: 818,806m^2
Bldg. area: 4,999m^2
Gross FL area: 9,566m^2
Landscape architect: Seoahn Total Landscape
Structural engineer: Seoul architects & Structural Eng.
Mechanical engineer: SeAh Eng.
Electrical engineer: WooLim E&C
Contractor: JT Construction

Traditional Buddhism Center of Jogye Order

Completed in 2008
Location: Gongju, Chungcheongnam-do, Korea
Site area: 14,867m^2
Bldg. area: 5,745m^2
Gross FL area: 9,600m^2
Structural engineer: Seoul architects & Structural Eng.
Mechanical engineer: SeAh Eng.
Electrical engineer: WooLim E&C
Contractor: SSANGYONG Engineering & Construction Co. Ltd.

Shin Dongyeop Literary Museum

Completed in 2012
Location: Buyeo, Chungchungnam-do, Korea
Site area: 2,026m^2
Bldg. area: 756m^2
Gross FL area: 863m^2
Landscape architect: Seoahn Total Landscape
Structural engineer: Seoul architects & Structural Eng.
Mechanical engineer: SeAh Eng.
Electrical engineer: WooLim E&C

Vanke Residential Culture Center

Completed in 2013
Location: Pingdu, Qingdao, China
Gross FL area: 2,340m^2
Structural/ Mechanical/ Electrical engineer: China Architecture Design & Research Group
Lighting design: IROJE
Landscape architect: Seoahn Total Landscape

Humax Main Office Building "Humax Village"

Completed in 2002
Location: Seongnam, Gyeonggi-do, Korea
Site area: 3,771m^2
Bldg. area: 2,995m^2
Gross FL area: 44,367m^2
Landscape architect: Seoahn Total Landscape
Lighting design: NEWLITE
Structural engineer: Seoul architects & Structural Eng.
Mechanical engineer: Samshin Eng.
Electrical engineer: Hyopin Co. Ltd.
Contractor: Samsung Corporation

Hyehwa Residential College of Daejeon University

Completed in 2017
Location: Daejeon University, Daejeon, Korea
Bldg. area: 3,913m^2
Gross FL area: 14,084m^2
Structural engineer: The Naeun Structural Engineering Co. Ltd.
Mechanical engineer: DE-Tech.
Electrical engineer: DaeKyong E&C
Contractor: Samyang Construction

30th Anniversary Memorial Building of Daejeon University

Completed in 2010
Location: Daejeon University, Daejeon, Korea
Bldg. area: 6,493m^2
Gross FL area: 20,325m^2
Landscape Design: Seoahn Total Landscape
Lighting Design: NEWLITE
Structural engineer: Seoul architects & Structural Eng.
Mechanical engineer: SeAh Eng.
Electrical engineer: DaeKyong E&C
Contractor: Samyang Construction

Hyehwa Culture Center of Daejeon University

Completed in 2003
Location: Daejeon University, Daejeon, Korea
Site area: 12,500m^2
Bldg. area: 2,915m^2
Gross FL area: 8,300m^2
Structural engineer: Seoul architects & Structural Eng.
Mechanical engineer: SeAh Eng.
Electrical engineer: Shinwon E&C
Contractor: GS E&C

Gudeok Presbyterian Church

Completed in 2008
Location: Busan, Korea
Site area: 1,678m^2
Bldg. area: 1,000m^2
Gross FL area: 5,412m^2
Structural engineer: Seoul architects & Structural Eng.

Mechanical engineer: SeAh Eng.
Electrical engineer: WooLim E&C
Contractor: YONGDONG Engineering & Construction Co. Ltd.

Chaowai SOHO

Completed in 2007
Location: Chaoyang, Beijing, China
Site area: 19,955m^2
Bldg. area: 12,950m^2
Gross FL area: 153,320m^2
Landscape architect: Seoahn Total Landscape
Lighting design: Consuline Lighting Design
Structural/ Mechanical/ Electrical engineer: China Academy of Building Research

Boao Canal Village

Completed in 2002 (First stage)
Location: Boao, Hainan, China
Site area: 495,000m^2
Gross FL area: 66,000m^2

Commune by the Great Wall

Completed in 2002
Location: Badaling, Beijing, China
Site area: 605,958 m^2
Bldg. area: 3,149 m^2
Gross FL area: 4,109 m^2

Lock Museum

Completed in 2003
Location: Seoul, Korea
Site Area: 582 m^2
Bldg. Area: 342 m^2
Gross FL Area: 1,588 m^2
Contractor: Jehyo Engineering & Construction

Welcomm City

Completed in 2000
Location: Seoul, Korea
Site area: 1,253m^2
Bldg. area: 745m^2
Gross FL area: 3,417m^2
Collaborator in Schematic Design: Florian Beigel
Contractor: Samhyup Construction Co.

Paju Book City

Location: Paju, Gyeonggi-do, Korea
Site area: 100ha
Coordinator: Seung H-Sang
Co-coordinator: Kim Young-joon
Initial master plan: Graduate School of Environmental Studies, Seoul National University
Urban landscape concept: ARU
Design guideline team: Florian Beigel, Min Hyun-sik, Seung H-sang, Kim Jong-kyu, Kim Young-joon

Kyobo Book City

Completed in 2008
Location: Paju, Gyeonggi-do, Korea
Site area: 6,696m^2
Bldg. area: 3,321m^2
Gross FL area: 15,260m^2
Structural engineer: Seoul architects & Structural Eng.
Mechanical engineer: Seah Eng.
Electrical engineer: WooLim E&C

Residence "Soowoojae"

Completed in 2017
Location: Seoul, Korea
Site area: 380m^2
Bldg. area: 188m^2
Gross FL area: 564m^2
Structural engineer:
Mechanical engineer: Seah Eng.
Electrical engineer: WooLim E&C
Contractor: YoungJo Construction Co.

Reed House

Completed in 2003
Location: Yangpyung, Kyoungi-do, Korea
Site area: 1,480m^2
Bldg. Area: 224m^2
Gross FL area: 416m^2
Contractor: Samhyup Construction Co.

Teochon House

Completed in 2010
Location: Teochon, Gyeonggi-do, Korea
Site Area: 817m^2
Bldg. Area: 164m^2
Gross FL Area: 164m^2
Mechanical engineer: Seah Eng.
Electrical engineer: WooLim E&C
Contractor: Junghee Construction

Residence "Subaekdang"

Completed in 1999
Location: Namyangju, Kyonggi-do, Korea
Site Area-1,162m^2
Bldg. Area-165m^2
Gross FL. Area-199m^2
Structural engineer: ALT Structural Eng.
Mechanical engineer: Saejong MEC
Electrical engineer: Myeongjin E&C
Contractor: Samhyup Construction Co.

IROJE PEOPLE

1989
Seung H-Sang
Choi Wonyoung
Kim Hyungtae
Kim Kyojung

1990
Chung Boyoung
Lee Myungjin
Kim Seung
Lee Sangjun
An Yongdae
Park Byungsoon
An Youngkyu

1991
Hwang Jun

1992
Lee Dongwoo
Kim Youngjun
Lee Dongsoo
Baek Eunjoo
Chang Yookyung
Kang Daesuk

1993
Park Jongyoul
Lee Taemin
Lee Jinhee

1994
You Jaewoo
Choi Sangki
Lee Kisuk
Lee Hyungwook

1995
Kim Mihee
Nam Soohyun
Kim Kihwan
Kim Sungho
Ryu Jaehyuk
Kim Sunghee

1996
An Woosung
Park Changyul

1997
Chun Younghoon
Ko Daesuk
Yim Jaeeun
Chang Youngchul
Kang Youngpil
Kim Jongbok
Chung Daejin

1998
Yun Jongtae
Chun Sookhee

1999
Kim Daiho

2000
Ham Euna
Kim Seungkook
Lee Kitae
Yang Hyojung
Yim Jinwook
Han Taeho
An Jaehyung
Kim Daesun
Choi Eunyoung

2001
Korn Stephan
Guillemoz Simon
Yim Youngmi
Park Wondong
Han Guihua

2002
Sung Sangwoo
Cho Sooyoung
Lee Jaejun
Jung Hyowon
Chung Kuho
Park Jonghoon
Won Jungmi
Cho Jinman
Lee Younju
Lee Chulhwan
Lee Jihyun

2003
Yum Juhyun
Sung Nayoung
Sim Hyungkeun
Oh Sewon
Chung Sueun

2004
Choi Wonjun
Cho Jangeun
You Youngsoo
Cho Younhee
Chung Sehoon
Lee Jongwon
Ham Kakyung
Kim Dongwook
Natalie Girth

2005
Kim Younji
Lee Jongchul
Chung Jongin

2006
Uh Hyeryung
Park Yangkeum
Chang Hyangmi
Hwang Sunwoo
Son Yongchan
Kwon Sookhee

2007
Kim Younggeun
An Jaeyoung
Cha Mijung
Chun Kayoung
Yang Hyunjun
Lee Changmin
Park Jooyeon
Kim Sujin
Kwon Ahjoo
Lee Jungmin
Han Junghan
Cha Seungyun

2008
Lee Kyoungjae
Mathias Dietsche
Kwon Sunwoo
Park Joohee
Lee Moonho
Oh Hyogyeong
Kang Hyemi
Min Kyungsik
Choi Hyeon
Yoon Kyungsup
Son Namyoung
Lee Donghee

2009
Kim Yehwon
Fu Xin
Cui Guangming
Jin Youngkwan
Kwak Donghyun
Yoon Bohyun
Yoon Gwangjae
Lee Haewon
Kim Inhan
Liang Fei
Joo Sungsuk
Lee Minjung

2010
Shin Joongsu
Kwon Misun
Yoon Duksang
Matthew Whittaker
Kim Taebum
Han Sinwook
Sun Zhijun

2011
Kim Taeyong
Kim Kihyun
Go Eunbi
Han Junbeom
Lee Wansun
Xu Lianhua
Choi Jungchul
Tian Hui
Min Sojung
Kim Bokyeon

2012
Kim Seonju
Chu Yoonjung
Strange Clayton
Lee Goeun
Filip Winiewicz
Kim Sehyun
Kim Zyiryong
Peng Kaining
Jung Solmin

2013
Pyo Harim
Kim Sanghyo
Kim Sunyeop
Wada Tsuyoshi
Shin Hyunkook
Lee Kyubin
Kim Soyeon
Hong Jonghwa
Kim Kiwon
Lee Joonghyun
Ahn Youjin
Jang Yujin
Xu Ying
Dolmans Frederik
Robert Hughes
Pei Yufei
Zheng Saisai
Yang Fei
Jia Mo

2014
Lee Kyehyeon
Ko Ilhwan
Ha Sangjoon
Jung Wooyeal
Oh Eunju
Jacob Kalmakoff
Shin Yeung
Hwang Hyosung
Pee Yejun
Zhao Taihao
Lee Seunghee
Lee Changheon
Yu Chen

2015
An Jinho
Yoon Soonhyuk
Lee Jaemin
Cha Hyerhan
Lee Sangjun
Choi Jiwoo
Zuo Jianing
Wu Tongyu
Yu Zhitao

2016
Esther Kim
Eom Kibeom
Choi Bora
Hyun Eunsoo
Lee Dasol
Kim Sujin
Lee Seungsoo

2017
Alice Chung
Kim Daehong
Kim Junyeong
Park Seulgi
Ahn Kihyun
Seo Jaegyo
Jo Eunji

2018
Yeo Jaewon
Jeong Hayoun
Lee Yeonho
Mok Eunyeong
Kim Sieun

2019
Lee Wonyoung
Koh Jongwook
Lee Jeonggeol
Lim Kyeongmin

Seung H-Sang

Born in 1952, he graduated from Seoul National University and studied at Technische Universitaet in Wien. Worked for Kim Swoo Geun from 1974 to 1989 and established his office "IROJE architects & planners' in 1989.

He was a core member of "4.3 Group" which strongly influenced Korean architectural society and participated in founding "Seoul School of Architecture" for a new educational system in architecture. He is an author of many essay books including 'Beauty of Poverty' (1996)', 'Landscript(2009)', 'All Oldies is Beautiful(2012)', 'Invisible Architecture, Inconstant Cities(2016)' and 'Meditation(2019)'.

He taught at Seoul National University and Korea National University of Arts, and was Visiting Professor of North London University and TU Wien. The America Institute of Architects invested him with Honorary Fellow in 2002, and Korea National Museum of Contemporary of Art selected him as 'the artist of the year 2002', the first time for an architect. In 2007, Korean government honored him with 'Korea Award for Art and Culture', and he was commissioned as director for Gwangju Design Biennale 2011 after for Korean Pavilion of Venice Biennale 2008.

He stepped down as the first City Architect of Seoul Metropolitan Government in 2016. Now he is Chair Professor at Dong-A University and visiting professor at CAFA in Beijing, and also is working as Chief Commissioner of Presidential Commission on Architecture Policy of Korea since 2018. Austrian government honored him in 2019 with the National Decoration, 'Cross of Honour for Science and Art 1st Class'.

IROJE

The origin of word IROJE (履露齋) comes from an old Chinese Literature. Its meaning, translating directly, is a house of stepping on dewdrops. According to Chinese Literature 'Yegi (禮記), there was a poor living scholar who served his old father. Every early morning he used to go to his father's quarter, wearing an overcoat, and wait for his father to wake up. When his father came out, the scholar handed over his warmed overcoat to his father. The way to his father's quarter was covered with dewdrops in the morning. Therefore, IROJE could be understood as a house for a scholar with voluntary poverty.

PARTNERS

SEOUL OFFICE
2-8 dongsung-dong, jongro-gu, seoul 110-809 korea

Lee, Dong Soo
Partner of Seoul office, KAIA

He studied at the Seoul National University and joined IROJE in 1991 and became the partner in 2002. Since 2003, he has been leading IROJE Seoul office and all the projects in Korea. He taught at Korea National University of Arts, also member of KAIA.

Kim, Sung Hee
Partner of Seoul office, KAIA

She studied at the Ulsan National University and joined IROJE in 1995. She became the partner in 2012 and has been leading IROJE Seoul office and all the projects in Korea. She taught at University of Ulsan, Myeongji University and Daejeon University, also member of KAIA.

BEIJING OFFICE
6/f, Building 1 No.53 Shunren Road, Shunyi District, Beijing, China

Min, Kyung Sik
Partner of Beijing office, AIA

He studied at the Seoul National University. Worked for Space Group New York office as general manager, and from S.O.M (Skidmore, Owings & Merrill), ISD (Interior Space Design) in New York and principle of FM Design Group in Seoul. Since 2007, he has been leading IROJE Beijing office. He taught at Seoul national university, Hanyang university and Kyunggi university, also member of AIA, KAIA, KOSID and the National Museum Society.

Natured
IROJE
Seung H-Sang

Published by
Actar Publishers, New York, Barcelona
www.actar.com

Text by
Hyungmin Pai

Editorial coordination
Ahn Kihyun, IROJE

Graphic Design
Ramon Prat Homs

Distribution
Actar D, Inc. New York, Barcelona

New York
440 Park Avenue South, 17th Floor
New York, NY 10016, USA
T +1 2129662207
salesnewyork@actar-d.com

Barcelona
Roca i Batlle 2-4
08023 Barcelona, Spain
T +34 933 282 183
eurosales@actar-d.com

Indexing
English ISBN: 9-781948-765497

Publication date: 2020
Printed in Europe by
Graficas Campas, Barcelona

All the photographs were made by
Kim JongOh, except:

Humax Village
250 Han Taeho

Hyehwa Cultural Center of Daejeon University
part1: Osamu Murai
274-276, 278-279: Osamu Murai

Commune by the Great Wall
part1: Seung H-Sang
306: Moon Jungsik
307-311: Asakawa Satoshi

Lock Museum
part1: Osamu Murai
314, 316-319: Osamu Murai

Welcomm City
all: Osamu Murai

Paju Book City
part1: Seo Heun Kang
330-331: Seo Heun Kang
332-333: Jung Hyowon
334-335: Seung H-Sang

Reed House
part1: Cho Yoonhee
354: Cho Yoonhee

Subaekdang
all: Osamu Murai

All rights reserved
© edition: IROJE, Seung H-Sang,
and Actar Publishers,
© texts: Their authors
© drawings, illustrations,
and photographs: Their authors

This work is subject to copyright. All rights are reserved, on all or part of the material, specifically translation rights, reprinting, re-use of illustrations, recitation, broadcasting, reproduction on microfilm or other media, and storage in databases. For use of any kind, permission of the copyright owner must be obtained.